THE
GOLF
BOOK

THE GOLF BOOK

THE **PLAYERS** THE **GEAR** THE **STROKES** THE **COURSES** THE **CHAMPIONSHIPS**

INTRODUCTION BY **NICK BRADLEY**

Penguin Random House

Senior Art Editor Michael Duffy
Senior Editor David Summers
Project Editors Chris Stone, Pip Morgan, Tarda Davison-Aitkins
Project Art Editors Adam Walker, Philip Fitzgerald, Brian Flynn, Phil Gamble, Dave Ball
Jacket design Lee Ellwood
Artwork Mike Garland
Production Editor Jonathan Ward
Senior Production Editor Vania Cunha
Senior Production Controller Shane Higgins
Managing Editor Stephanie Farrow
Managing Art Editor Lee Griffiths
Publishing Director Jonathan Metcalf
Art Director Bryn Walls

This American Edition, 2021
First American Edition, 2008
Published in the United States by DK Publishing
1450 Broadway, Suite 801, New York, NY 10018

The authorized representative in the EEA is
Dorling Kindersley Verlag GmbH. Arnulfstr. 124, 80636
Munich, Germany

Copyright © 2008, 2021 Dorling Kindersley Limited
DK, a Division of Penguin Random House LLC
21 22 23 24 25 10 9 8 7 6 5 4 3 2 1
001–323549–Sep/2021

A catalog record for this book
is available from the Library of Congress.
ISBN 978-0-7440-3669-5

Printed and bound in China

For the curious
www.dk.com

MIX
Paper from
responsible sources
FSC™ C018179

This book was made with Forest Stewardship
Council™ certified paper—one small step
in DK's commitment to a sustainable future.
For more information go to
www.dk.com/our-green-pledge

Contents

Introduction

Golf books have been a fundamental part of my development as a golf coach and mentor to a number of the top players in the world. Taking up the game at the relatively late age of 16, I knew very quickly that the game of golf—specifically the teaching of it—would be my life's work. I needed to make up ground quickly, learn as much as I could, and digest the intricacies of the sport in order to bring me up to speed with my peers. I did this largely through golf books; with five books on the golf swing, three books on course design, and a number of autobiographies of the best players, I started to compile quite a library.

However, what I actually needed was a golf book such as the one you presently have in your hands. *The Golf Book* is just that, a celebration of everything that is commendable, exciting, and worthwhile knowing in the sport of golf. This book distills a collective global knowledge of golf and binds it into one comprehensive document; it cuts to the chase with its information and presents essential text and images. This book would have saved me a considerable amount of time and much shelf space in my bedroom.

Like any new activity that one may take up, there is always that fragile gap between learning the basics and developing enough competency to then enjoy the activity itself. This is where golf is unique—there are so many aspects to the sport that a "trial and error" process may be timely. *The Golf Book* cuts through that trial and error, giving the reader the essential, important, and usable information associated with every department of this great game. With "state of the art" presentation, the information is easily absorbed and remembered, making the process of reading this book light but extremely informative.

PLAYING THE GAME

Steve Newell, with whom I have worked on numerous occasions, expertly delivers the section on the golf swing, short game, and strategy. The photography and the art direction during this chapter leave nothing to the imagination, as its content gives the reader a concise and common-sense assessment of golf technique. In addition to the fundamental motion of the golf swing, there is also detailed advice on the short game and sloping lies—something we all face whenever we play. There are subtle yet important adjustments to be made when changing from club to club through the bag, and this subject, along with fairway woods and the art of putting, is an integral part of this chapter. This section sums up great golf instruction; it informs you with drills, bullet pointed tips, and notable positions and feelings. It is a perfect way to receive great advice.

One of the beautiful aspects of golf is that we can play the same golf courses that great championships have been played on and top golfers have graced. I could not play soccer at Wembley or pitch a baseball at Shea Stadium, for example. The section "The Greatest Courses" provides the reader with some amazing insights into some of the great links around the world.

What I ... needed was a golf book such as the one you presently have in your hands.... It distills a collective global knowledge of golf and binds it into one comprehensive document.

Each course you read about has made its own unique mark on the game. Waterville Golf Club in Ireland (my favorite course in the world), for example, played host to one of the first transatlantic communication points between Europe and the United States. It was during the construction of this station that the workers unwittingly carved out the great links of Waterville as a form of recreation during their rest days. Blind luck or the luck of the Irish? Either way, it is a great links! The book also details the organic growth of a course like Augusta National. How did the course that we see every April in such magnificent condition evolve and become a benchmark in course design? Why do the players on the PGA Tour liken the 17th hole at Pete Dye's Sawgrass Stadium Course to enduring root canal tooth surgery? All of these courses are written about and complemented with some fantastic photographs and insights into their rich history.

In the 18 years that I have been a golf performance consultant, the biggest change I have seen in the game is in respect of the equipment we all use nowadays. Suffice to say that to a large extent, the equipment revolution has been responsible for the evolution of the golf swing over the years. In the early days, the club makers could only forge and mold new designs with the materials that they had at their disposal—wood and steel.

So while clubheads and indeed the shafts often took on different guises, the actual difference in performance from club to club was marginal. Then manufacturers started to apply different composites to the shafts and the heads; titanium, graphite, beryllium, copper, and rubber inserts are just some of those examples. Instantaneously, we started to "feel" different strikes from the clubface, and the behavior of the ball took on another dimension. Dovetailing this composite evolution was the advancement in computer software and analysis; instant feedback on the ballistics of a strike can now be displayed on a screen in seconds—we do not even need to look up at the ball to see where it is going. We are at the point now where launch angles and spin rates are factors that we can genuinely "dial in" before the ball is even struck.

I will enjoy studying and piecing together the information provided in *The Golf Book*.

The ball has come full circle, too; no pun intended! We now have the ability to produce a hard-covered golf ball (for distance) that has a soft bounce (for control around the greens) and spin characteristics for a perfect combination. In what can be a minefield of technological jargon, this book strips this information down for you on a "need to know" basis.

Since its conception, golf has always delivered dynamic, colorful, and absorbing characters. Why is this? The answer can be found when you understand that golf at any level is fairly emotive and will always draw out the true character in most of us at some point. This book profiles the golfers who have played significant roles in the development of the game. It covers not only the champions but the larger-than-life personalities, too. To my mind, Bobby Jones, Ben Hogan, Jack Nicklaus, Seve Ballesteros, Annika

Sorenstam, and Tiger Woods have been the key instigators in the introduction and reintroduction of the sport to the masses. Their achievements, skills, records, and flamboyant play have captured the public imagination and driven people to their local driving ranges and golf courses all over the world. Contained in this chapter are rare facts and insights into the careers of these golfers and many, many more. This chapter in the book is a personal favorite of mine. It is essential when working with a top tour star to understand their character as much, if not more, than their golf swing technique. Introverts, extroverts, perfectionists, and showman alike make up a small portion of the tour's golfing fraternity. They seek one common goal, however—to get the best out of themselves and their games throughout their careers. So when you read about the extroverted Lee Trevino or the deeply introverted Ben Hogan, understand that, although they walked the same path, they did so in completely different ways. That is the beauty of this game—a diversity of characters linked together by the common thread of hitting that little white sphere the least amount of times.

SOMETHING FOR EVERYONE

I see this book appealing to every genre of golfer. For the established player, the chapters that relive the history of the great golfers, golf courses, and championships will serve to reinspire and jog the memory pleasantly. The beginner will find that they have everything in the instruction section to save time and gain knowledge that will ultimately add to their enjoyment of this great game. The golfer or fan who currently plays on a regular basis has the chance to add further value to their experience as they read about the "where," "why," and "how" of the game that they pursue.

For me, I will continue to look for the "x" factors that make up the DNA of a great golfer. You have never fully learned golf; you are continually learning it. So I will enjoy studying and piecing together the information *The Golf Book* gives me, ever expectant of a new clue that assists my own personal quest as a golf coach.

Nick Bradley

NICK BRADLEY, GOLF PERFORMANCE CONSULTANT

1 PLANET GOLF

Golf's Origins

Winston Churchill once said, "golf is a game in which you try to put a small ball in a small hole with implements singularly unsuited to the purpose." Golf always has been a difficult game, but that has never dented its appeal. The game taps into that strangely compulsive human desire to want to swing a stick in order to strike an object at rest on the ground.

Where it all started, nobody really knows. But it certainly began in the most primitive and basic form imaginable. Some visual and historical references bear little resemblance to the game of golf as we know it today but, rather, are more closely related to hockey. By the 16th and 17th centuries, however, what might be described as "real" golf was being played all along the east coast of Scotland. At that time, it was genuinely a classless game, played with considerable enthusiasm by the poor, the good, and the great. The Royals weren't always keen to encourage such frivolity. King James II of Scotland did his best to stamp out the game, the suggestion being that it prevented youngsters from doing more constructive things with their time—such as archery practice. The Scots were, after all, at war.

GOLFING PIONEERS

However, it is comforting to know that golfers then were just like golfers today—once bitten by the golf bug, forever smitten. Not even the beheading of Mary Queen of Scots—among the charges laid against her was that she was playing golf the day after her husband was murdered—could deter these golfing pioneers.

By the mid-18th century, the first golf clubs were being established. Also key was the introduction of the first official Rules of Golf. There were only 13 rules, but they marked a vast improvement on the chaotic game that was typical of the era. Also at that time, the Society of St. Andrews Golfers determined that a round of golf should consist of 18 holes. Golf was on the map.

▶ **THE ROYAL AND ANCIENT GOLF CLUB** of St. Andrews had, by the start of the 20th century, taken command of the rules of the game. This match was captured there in 1905.

▲ **A GROUP OF GOLF ENTHUSIASTS** enjoy an evening's game at the seaside links at Musselburgh, near Edinburgh, in 1859. By this time, golf clubs were being established around the coastal areas of Scotland.

Golf Ball Revolution

It is believed that by the mid-18th century there were only 17 established golf clubs in the world; and of those, 14 were in Scotland. Incredibly, golf in Britain at this time was a game actually in decline. In some ways, the foundations were in place for the game to blossom, but in other key respects, the general public were faced with insurmountable obstacles that deprived them of the opportunity.

There was a shortage of places to play golf; but more crucially, golf equipment had become prohibitively expensive for the average person in the street. The manufacture of golf balls—a highly labor-intensive and skilled process that involved stuffing wet feathers into a leather pouch and then sewing it up—pushed unit prices way beyond the budget of ordinary people.

For a while, then, golf became very much a game for the wealthy and the privileged classes. It was a perception, and, indeed, in many respects a reality, that existed for decades and which prevented and put off many people from taking up the game.

THE GUTTA-PERCHA ARRIVES

The arrival of the "gutta-percha" golf ball changed everything. This rubbery substance was easy to fashion into golf balls, so they were cheap to produce. Whereas a skilled ball maker could make four "featheries" a day, they could make 100 from gutta-percha. The balls were also far more robust and lasted longer, provided you did not lose them.

The ball was rolling, and with some considerable momentum. By the end of the 19th century, there were almost 2,000 golf clubs in Britain, and the game had begun to spread into the far reaches of the British Empire. Golf exploded among the masses, and the game never looked back.

Today, there is almost nowhere in the developed world where golf is not a multibillion-dollar industry. The technology used to make today's golf clubs and balls is unrecognizable from that used a century ago, but the essential appeal of the game of golf remains unaltered.

◄ **THE INVENTION OF THE GUTTA-PERCHA BALL** was a turning point in the history of golf. Golf balls made of gutta-percha were cheap and durable, helping dispel golf's image as a rich man's pastime.

▲ **MASS PRODUCTION OF GOLF BALLS** was a key factor in making the sport more accessible. Today, more than a billion golf balls are produced every year (see pp.44–45).

Golf's Great Triumvirates

The establishment of golf's early tournaments, in particular the Open Championship in the mid to late 19th century, brought with it the emergence of the game's earliest superstars and legends. And when superstars collide, rivalries are born. The history of golf is punctuated with great triumvirates—chapters in time where three outstanding players of a generation compete against and inspire each other throughout their playing careers.

Harry Vardon, JH Taylor, and James Braid were golf's first Great Triumvirate (see pp.106–107). All were from relatively poor backgrounds and born within 12 months of each other. For a 20-year period, they dominated the Open, winning 16 titles between them. Vardon won six times— a record that still stood at the turn of the 21st century.

They each left an indelible mark on the game, a legacy that went way beyond mere numbers and entries in the record books. Taylor was largely responsible for establishing the Professional Golfers Association; Vardon lent his name to the trophy awarded to the golfer with the lowest stroke average on the PGA Tour, and to the grip adopted by most of

the game's top players; Braid became a successful golf course architect.

Next to take the baton were Walter Hagen (see p.108), Gene Sarazen (see p.109), and Bobby Jones (see pp.110–113). Between them they won 25 career Major titles and splashed the game of golf with color, character, and a sense of "joie de vivre" that has never since been surpassed.

Byron Nelson (see pp.116–117), Sam Snead (see pp.118–119), and Ben Hogan (see pp.120–121) followed in their footsteps. They were born within four months of each other, but were three very different men with a distinct style and temperament. Nelson's career was spectacular but, through his own choosing, relatively brief. He retired at the age of 34. Hogan had a career of two halves—both brilliant, with a life-threatening car crash in between (see pp.220–221). No one played great golf for longer than Sam Snead. His talent was sublime, and his swing was blessed with the greatest rhythm of any golfer.

THE GREATEST RIVALRY

However, the greatest rivalry of them all was that between Arnold Palmer (see pp.128–131), Gary Player (see pp.132–135), and Jack Nicklaus (see pp.136–139). Between them they won an impressive 34 Major titles and dominated the game in the 1960s and 1970s (see pp.224–225). Nicklaus and Player, in particular, managed hugely impressive longevity at the absolute top of their games, with Big Jack's Major wins spanning 24 years.

In the 21st century, perhaps for the first time in the history of golf, the game has been defined by the domination of one golfer alone. Peerless in the modern game, Tiger Woods may well go down as the greatest golfer of them all (see pp.32–33).

▲ **GENE SARAZEN INTERVIEWS** two-thirds of a celebrated triumvirate—Sam Snead (left) and Ben Hogan (right). Sarazen himself formed an illustrious threesome with Bobby Jones and Walter Hagen.

▶ **PICTURED HERE PLAYING TOGETHER** in the World Series of Golf, in 1962, Gary Player, Arnold Palmer, and Jack Nicklaus were great friends, as well as rivals. Their combined success led to them being known as "The Big Three" (see pp.224–225).

The Majors

Golf's most important championships are the four Majors—the Masters, the US Open, the Open, and the USPGA. These are the tournaments that every golfer dreams of winning, the ones that matter the most. It is no coincidence, then, that the person considered by most people to be the greatest golfer who ever lived is the one who has the most victories in Major championships—Jack Nicklaus with 18. The number of Major victories is ultimately what determines a player's claim to greatness.

THE OPEN

It is not clear when the term "Major" was first used, but there is no doubt that the original Major was the Open Championship, first played in 1860 at Prestwick and won by Willie Park from an entry of just eight players (see pp.210–211). The Open remained at Prestwick for the next 12 years, but soon it began to visit other courses. Today, the Open rota consists of 10 of Britain's finest links courses—St. Andrews, Turnberry, Royal St. George's, Royal Troon, Hoylake, Carnoustie, Royal Birkdale, Muirfield, Royal Portrush, and Royal Lytham & St. Annes (see pp.248–279).

THE US OPEN

The first US Open was won by an English golfer, Horace Rawlins, who on October 4, 1895, shot 173 for four rounds at Newport, Rhode Island's 9-hole golf course. At that time, the US Open was considered a sideshow to the more prestigious US Amateur Championship, and it was even tagged on to the end of that tournament, allocated just one day's play as opposed to the three days it took to find an Amateur champion. The next year, the US Open moved to the 18-hole course at Shinnecock Hills, New York (see pp.278–279), and it did not stay the second-class citizen for long.

THE USPGA

The USPGA Championship began its life as a match-play tournament in 1916 and remained so until 1957. At least during its early years, the USPGA suffered in the same way as the US Open had, in the sense that professional golf tournaments were perceived as inferior to those of their amateur counterparts.

It wasn't long before Walter Hagen, the undisputed king of match play, began his reign. He dominated the event, reaching the final in six out of seven years and winning the title five times in the 1920s (see pp.218–219). He was an extraordinary man, a larger-than-life character.

THE MASTERS

The Masters was the last of the four Majors to arrive on the golfing calendar, although it was not immediately accorded Major status. It is the only one of the four tournaments to be played at the same venue every year— the sensational Augusta National in Georgia (see pp.296–299).

This tournament was originally merely an invitational event organized by Bobby Jones and was played for the first time in 1934. It was the following year's event that truly put the Masters on the map, however, thanks to Gene Sarazen's stroke of genius—holing a 4-wood from 220 yards for an albatross-two on the 15th in the final round.

The Masters gathered momentum as one of the game's premier tournaments, although it was not until 1949, when Sam Snead won the first of his three titles, that the organizers started handing out the now iconic green jacket to the winner.

The order of the Major championships runs as follows: the Masters in April, the US Open in June, the Open in July, and the USPGA in August.

◄◄ **THE FIRST OPEN CHAMPION** to receive the Golf Champion Trophy, commonly referred to as the Claret Jug, was the 1873 winner, Tom Kidd.

▲▲ ◄ **BEN HOGAN** holds the US Open trophy in 1948. Today, as then, the winner receives a replica of the Championship Cup for one year.

▲ ◄ **GARY PLAYER** kisses the trophy, after winning the USPGA on July 22, 1962. Wealthy businessman Rodman Wanamaker first donated the trophy in 1916.

◄ **PATTY BERG AND BABE ZAHARIAS** collected 25 Majors between them, with Zaharias winning the US Women's Open three times in the 1940s and '50s.

Arnie's Army

In the early 1950s, it is thought that fewer than 10 percent of households in the US owned a television set. Less than a decade later, that figure was approaching 80 percent. Despite this, golf did not convert particularly well to the small screen—that is, until Arnold Palmer came along (see pp.128–131).

Golf can consider itself fortunate that when the television era dawned, its No. 1 player—the undisputed star attraction—was Arnold Palmer. He had the kind of appeal that transcended his sport; Lee Trevino described him as "the greatest role model that any sport ever had."

Palmer was, by far, the most exciting personality in golf. He was good-looking, with a physique more like that of a boxer than a golfer. He was photogenic and possessed a charisma that jumped out of the television screen and into people's living rooms. At the same time, he had that man-of-the-people appeal that made the public feel like he was one of them.

Not only was he a winner, but the manner of his winning was extraordinary to watch—an absolute roller coaster of heroic shots, powerhouse drives, sublime chips and putts, and the occasional disaster. Palmer always appeared to be walking the thin line between triumph and failure. The crowds adored him, and soon "Arnie's Army" was on the march. Golf had seen nothing like it. Television and Arnold Palmer were made for one another, and both parties benefited from this happy marriage. "It was a classic case of the right man being in the right place at the right time," said Palmer's great rival Jack Nicklaus.

Palmer's popularity grew beyond that of any other golfer in history, and he was the first sportsperson to establish the link between success on the field of play and lucrative product endorsements off it. He whipped up a frenzy of media and commercial interest, flooding the game with cash. He completely transformed the economics of professional sport, and television had a star who could be guaranteed to bring in the ratings.

▶ **PALMER WAS GOLF'S FIRST SUPERSTAR**
His presence and his visionary manager Mark McCormack are partly responsible for the global popularity of golf (see pp.224–225).

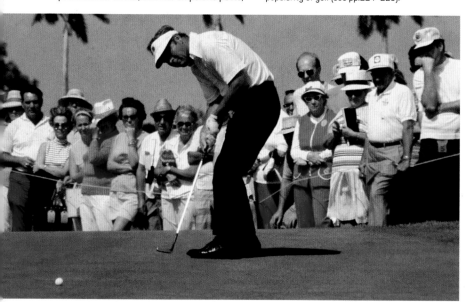

▲ **ARNIE'S ARMY FOLLOWED HIM** wherever he played and was most vocal in its support for him. They also bought the products he endorsed and boosted the television ratings. When Palmer eventually retired, they turned out in the thousands to say farewell.

The Golf Business

It is a fact of modern professional sports that many leading players make far more money off the field of play than on it. Certainly, this is the case with the world's top golfers.

For this select band, golf is their passion, but it is also their business—a business as diverse as it is lucrative. Arnold Palmer was the first golfer to connect with the public in such a way that companies were willing to pay him not-so-small fortunes to use and endorse their products (see pp.24–25).

Product endorsement is easy money for today's top golfers, although there is such a spotlight on the game these days that you would not catch a player endorsing a product he or she does not either use or at least strongly believes in.

ENDLESS OPPORTUNITIES

By featuring a logo on a shirt or golf bag, and perhaps a few personal appearances, players now endorse anything from cars, technology, and watches to global fashion brands, luxury resorts, and even health products. It is great exposure for the company and nice business for the player.

Personal appearances and product endorsements are, however, just a small part of a player's commercial activity. Golfers are lucky in having a long shelf life, but they know all too well that their prime is relatively short-lived. Understandably, they want a life after golf but one that keeps them in touch with the game.

Almost all the top players are, to some extent, involved in golf course design (see pp.244–245). Ernie Els, one of the game's global players, designs golf courses all over the world. "I love the whole process. I mean, to be able to create something special and unique, something to be enjoyed by generations of golfers for decades to come, that's any golfer's dream. I take it very seriously. That's why I want to do it right," says Els. Players often start at the peak of their playing careers, so the business is established when their prime playing days are nearing an end.

Clothing is another area of opportunity. Tiger Woods has his own range within the Nike brand; Ernie Els has his own "Tour Collection" of golf clothing, as do former US Open champion Michael Campbell and the flamboyant Englishman Ian Poulter. All play an active role in the design of the clothes that they wear, which then find their way onto the shelves of pro shops.

For many golfers, the wine business has also proved attractive. Nick Faldo, Greg Norman, Ernie Els, and Luke Donald have all launched their own wines. It is reasonable to expect the same traits that make them great players—commitment, professionalism, and a perfectionist streak—to be evident in the production of their wines. So it is no surprise that many of the golfers' wines have won awards.

But do not for a minute think that they are neglecting their sport. Behind every successful golfer is a team of managers and advisors helping keep the wheels of their industry turning (see pp.40–41).

▲ **WINE PRODUCTION** has become a favored business opportunity for many of the leading golfers eager to develop interests outside of golf.

◄ **MANY TOP GOLFERS** now have some business interest in clothing, whether it is their own brand, as with Ian Poulter, or a range within the brand of a sports manufacturer, as in Tiger Woods's case. It has become a way for golfers to create an identity while increasing their earnings.

A Fine Line ...

In sports, one assumes that there is a precariously fine line between success and disappointment. In the case of professional golf tournaments, this is certainly true. Between winning a golf championship and merely finishing in the top five, we are talking about wafer-thin margins. However, comparing those at the top and bottom of the Tour money lists highlights a gaping chasm that all aspiring young players would do well to contemplate.

For the purposes of this comparison, we introduce to you former US Open champion Jim Furyk and former Open champion Todd Hamilton. Both, as is evident from their Major-winning credentials, are great golfers, although Furyk is the more prolific. In the 2006 season, their fortunes were mixed, to say the least.

BEST ON TOUR

Jim Furyk was, for the purposes of statistical validation (determined by a player competing in a minimum number of tournaments), the best player on the PGA Tour in that season. Never mind that Tiger Woods won more money, Furyk won the Stroke Average. For the 24 tournaments in which he competed, his average score was 68.86. That was good enough to win him well over $7 million in prize money.

CONTRASTING FORTUNES

Todd Hamilton competed in a total of 27 tournaments in 2006. His stroke average was 72.84—hardly shabby but, on average, four shots a round higher than Furyk. That is 16 shots over the duration of a four-round tournament (although Hamilton will have missed some cuts and therefore played only two rounds of golf). The vast gulf in prize money hits home more than any one of those 16 shots could. Hamilton won just $165,000 over the season—some way short of Furyk. And if anyone thinks that $165,000 for playing golf sounds like a pretty good living, think again. Hamilton's expenses traveling the tour will have eaten up as much as half of that amount, and then there is the taxman taking his chunk. It

is lucky for him that he had some money behind him from winning the Open in 2004. He may well have sponsors picking up the tabs some weeks, too.

STATISTICS TELL THE STORY

The comprehensive performance statistics prepared by the PGA Tour (www.pgatour.com) tell the whole story. The only category where Hamilton beat Furyk was the category that matters least in the pro game—distance off the tee. Hamilton averaged 283 yards, Furyk 281. In every other department of the game, Furyk had the better of Hamilton, and by some margin. Furyk was 8th on tour for driving accuracy with 74 percent of fairways hit; Hamilton was 184th, averaging just 56 percent. Furyk was 4th for greens in regulation, hitting 70 percent; Hamilton was 196th with 57 percent. Furyk was 8th for putting average; Hamilton was 132nd.

And if you add up these differences, four shots a round is the end result. Not so much a fine line, then, more a gaping chasm.

▶ **DURING HIS SUCCESSFUL 2006 SEASON,** Jim Furyk won three titles: (clockwise from top) the Nedbank Golf Challenge at the Gary Player Country Club, Sun City, South Africa; the Canadian Open at the Hamilton Golf and Country Club; and the Wachovia Championship at Quail Hollow Club, Charlotte, North Carolina.

▶ ▶ **HAVING WON THE OPEN IN 2004,** Todd Hamilton had a less successful season in 2006. Out of the 27 tournaments he played in, he missed the cut in 19, and his best result was a tie for 10th place.

The Women's Game

For centuries, women golfers have had to put up with restrictions of one form or another. Amazingly, until the end of the 19th century, it was even considered unladylike to swing the club above shoulder height. Although, looking at early images depicting the garments women golfers had to wear, you wonder if they had a choice.

Slowly the world changed, and golf changed with it. First, Joyce Wethered came along in the early part of the 20th century, winning championships with such style and panache that the great Bobby Jones proclaimed, "she is the finest golfer I have ever seen" (see p.114).

The women's game went from strength to strength, especially in the US. The LPGA Tour, established in 1950, is a phenomenal success story. As far back as 1976, the leading money winner, Judy Rankin, won more than $100,000 in a single season. At the start of the 21st century, the leading money winner on the LPGA Tour can expect to win $2 million-plus in prize money. This figure compares favorably with the men's equivalent on the European Tour.

ROSY FUTURE

At club level, the picture is equally rosy. For the most part, women golfers can boast a degree of equality, especially in the US. Indeed, there has been a world of difference between women's golf in the US and, for example, the UK.

Even though the UK has produced some of golf's best talent, at most golf clubs, women have been restricted in the times that they can play, and even excluded from certain parts of the clubhouse. Happily, times are changing, and many new golf clubs, and an increasing number of established clubs, are dispensing with such prehistoric values.

At the professional level, the women's game has never been stronger. Golfers such as Annika Sorenstam (see pp.176–177), Ko Jin-young, Nelly Korda, Park Sung-hyun, and Michelle Wie represent the biggest draw in the women's game (see pp.204–207). All are inspirational role models and a marketing agent's dream, and it is reasonable to expect that young girls will aspire to be like them and follow in their footsteps on the LPGA Tour.

This is the showcase for women's golf. Whether there is any additional benefit for women such as Annika Sorenstam or Michelle Wie playing in men's events is a subject that provokes debate. Would you rather watch them produce stunning performances to win the women's Majors or see them struggle to make the cut against the men? The answer to this question settles the matter for most people.

▲ **THERE HAS ALWAYS BEEN** scope to be daring with golf fashions, as demonstrated by Diana Fishwick, British Ladies Amateur Champion of 1930.

◄ **SOUTH KOREAN STAR INBEE PARK** won seven Majors between 2008 and 2019, making more than $16 million since her rookie year in 2007.

The Greatest?

Tiger Woods plays the game as it has never been played before. He hits career shots with every club in the bag. He has no weaknesses, only strengths, and none of those strengths is greater than his mind. It is what allows Tiger to do extraordinary things as a matter of routine. We have grown used to it, but we should never forget how remarkable it is.

He has broken numerous records along the way. Playing in his first Masters as a professional, he won by 12 shots (see pp.232–233). At Pebble Beach in 2000, he won the US Open by 15 shots, breaking a Major record that had stood for more than a century (see pp.238–239). He won his first Open Championship by eight shots.

His appetite for setting new standards in the game is insatiable. By the time he turned 30 years old, Tiger had played in 210 PGA Tour events, of which he had won 50—the youngest man by three years to reach that landmark. Just as remarkable is that he had finished second in another 20, and third in 17. That is a top-three finish in 41 percent of the events he had entered. Along the way, he had banked more than $60 million in prize money—nothing more than loose change compared to the money he has received in endorsements.

Tiger Woods has enough money to sustain himself and his family for the rest of their lives, yet it is clear that his motivation shows no signs of waning. Woods is addicted to the thrill of winning, and no record is safe. The leading PGA Tour winners are Arnold Palmer (62 wins), Ben Hogan (64 wins), Jack Nicklaus (73 wins), and Sam Snead (82 wins). In October 2019, Woods matched that record with victory at the Zoho Championship.

Of more significance to Tiger is Jack Nicklaus's tally of 18 victories in Major championships. There was a time when most people found it hard to believe that any golfer would ever win more Majors than Nicklaus. At the 2019 Masters, Tiger ended his 11-year wait for another Major, collecting title number 15 to take him closer to the all-time record.

▶ **TIGER WOODS HAS REWRITTEN** the record books since bursting on to the scene. He has demonstrated a mental strength and steely determination that has set him apart.

▲ **WOODS IS NOT THE LONGEST DRIVER** in professional golf, but a look at his official PGA Tour statistics over many years reveals that he was top, or ranked close to the top, in most areas.

Behind the Scenes

The Open is one of the greatest sporting shows on earth. It attracts the attention of the world's media, thousands of spectators, and millions of TV viewers, all of whom are focused on the very best golfers on the planet.

The Open is organized and administered by the R&A (Royal and Ancient), golf's world rules and development body. The R&A works in collaboration with the host club, of which there are nine on the Open rota. Each hosts the event once every 10 years, except St Andrews, which usually plays host once every five years.

Although the competition takes place over just four days, there are so many logistical considerations that it usually takes five or six years of planning to make sure that all the necessary arrangements are in place. What we see on TV gives only the briefest impression of what goes on behind the scenes.

▼ **THE MEDIA CENTER** is the hub for all the journalists and the many marketing and public relations specialists. During the Open, it is always open for business.

THE MEDIA CENTER

At any Open, the media center forever buzzes with activity—fingers tap-tapping on laptops, phones ringing, and voices from 101 different conversations filling the air. When a top player is ushered in through the door, a kind of black hole effect takes place—journalists are sucked into the interview room by the pull of a huge star.

Pretournament interviews with the leading players are prearranged, and, once the tournament starts, the same leading players are expected to make an appearance after each round. For some, there is no get-out clause; whether they shoot 65 or 75, they are obliged to sit and answer questions.

Running the media center is a huge task that falls to the R&A's press officer. "It's a 12-month planning process," said press officer Stewart McDougall in the past. "As soon as one championship finishes, we start work on the next one. We meet with the golf writers and photographers to give them a chance to voice their opinions on what they feel were the pluses and minuses. We always listen. There's always something that can be improved on."

◄ **BUNKER RAKERS ARE USUALLY VOLUNTEERS** who are employed to keep the bunkers manicured during the day. The bunkers are raked before and after the day's play and also after any of the players have found themselves playing out of one of them.

▶ **THE SCOREBOARDS IN THE MEDIA CENTER** are constantly updated, from the first shot to the last putt of the day. Match officials walking with each playing group maintain radio contact with the scorers to provide real-time updates.

ARMIES OF VOLUNTEERS

The newly crowned Open champion will, almost without exception, pay tribute in their winner's speech to the armies of volunteers who help make sure that the event runs smoothly. It is a gracious touch and one that reflects the extraordinary efforts of those who are happy to be involved and take part, not for money, but for the love of the game.

Steve Carr manned one of the scoreboards at the 1988 Open at Royal Lytham and loved every minute. "I remember in the final round when Seve [Ballesteros] and Nick Price were playing together," recalls Carr. "Seve was two shots ahead and we got the news that they'd both eagled the 7th. I updated Nick's score first, so it looked like he'd drawn level with Seve. Then I waited for a moment before I put up Seve's eagle. The crowd went bananas. It was brilliant. I was jumping up and down. I think the power went to my head! I realized I could control the crowd's reaction with a numbered magnetic strip."

Course marshals probably do not have quite so much fun, but they are very close to the action, which brings its own rewards. Tens of thousands of spectators sometimes need shepherding—although a line of rope is all it ever takes—and all the course marshals are given instructions at preround briefings about how to successfully carry out their jobs. Greenskeepers from other clubs, taking time off from their day jobs, carry out bunker-raking duties; one walks with every group on the course. It may be a busman's holiday, but walking inside the ropes alongside your heroes is about as good as it gets for any golf fan.

THE PRACTICE GROUND

There was a time when the practice ground at any tournament, even the Open, was populated almost solely by players and caddies. However, in recent years, this area has become so overcrowded that the authorities have put their collective feet down and restricted this area to only those working for the players (see pp.40–41).

That means caddies, obviously, and teaching gurus, too. You might recognize only the likes of David Leadbetter and Butch Harmon, but on the practice ground at the Open, there are probably another dozen or so coaches, each working with their pupils, trying to fine-tune techniques with the precision of a Swiss watchmaker.

Player's agents and managers can also be spotted, but they typically move in mysterious ways, recognizable to only the tour regulars. A nod here, a wink there; these are the deal-makers. Most of the serious business is done behind the scenes, but the practice ground is a place for them to "press the flesh."

For the Tour reps of all the major equipment manufacturers, the practice ground is their office. They set up camp in huge tour buses, resplendent in the company livery. A peek inside reveals every golfer's version of an Aladdin's Cave, filled wall-to-wall with clubs of every type. This is no place for the public, though. Each bus is effectively a mobile workshop where a team of skilled technicians is able to tweak any aspect of a club's setup.

RULES EXPERTS

The appointed referees and rules experts have regular meetings in the months and weeks leading up to a tournament. These obviously become more frequent as the big week approaches.

During tournament week, official referees are responsible for the setup of the golf course: the pin positions; the location of the teeing areas from one day to the next; the way the fairways and greens are cut; and the depth and texture of the sand. All these crucial elements are overseen in conjunction with the greens staff. They must also adjudicate on any rules-related queries that arise during play.

These are not volunteers, however, but paid professionals with serious responsibilities. To referee at any Major, they must first pass a series of exams set by the PGA and the R&A. For many, this is the culmination of years of hard work, starting at small events and progressing up the golfing ladder. To referee at a Major is the ultimate accolade.

▶ **TELEVISION PLAYS A LARGE ROLE** in the staging of the Open, and the broadcasting companies invest a huge amount of money in trying to improve their service.

Team Orders

Golf is perhaps the ultimate individual sport—the golfer alone hits the shots. There is no one to blame when things go wrong; equally, there is no one else to soak up the warm glow of victory. At the highest level, however, golf has also become something of a team game in the sense that every one of the leading golfers in the world has an entourage of various support staff. Each has a common purpose: to do everything in their specialist powers to bring out the best in their boss.

Some of these staff might be deemed surplus to requirements, but not the caddie. Players rely on their caddies to a large degree; they do much more than simply carry a heavy bag. The personal chemistry between a player and a caddie needs to be absolutely right; they need to know what to say, when to say it, and when not to say it. Basically, caddies require a deep knowledge of the game and of their player.

PERCENTAGE REWARDS

Good caddies are worth their weight in gold—often quite literally. During Tiger Woods's dominant phase at the start of the 21st century, his caddie Steve Williams was routinely the highest-earning New Zealander in sport, based on the percentage he received of Tiger's on-course earnings. Typically, with most players, this will be 10 percent for a win and a reduced figure on a sliding scale based on the player's finishing position.

A coach will also tend to receive a percentage of a player's on-course earnings. As with the caddies, this is a job that comes with a huge degree of responsibility. A coach literally has a player's livelihood in his hands. Some players like their coach to be on hand most weeks and will even meet up between tournaments. Others might get together with their coach only five to 10 times a year for their swing-health checkups. It is very much a personal thing.

The mind coach is a relatively new feature in the modern game. Not all players are convinced of the need for such help, but there are others who could not do without one. The nature of conversations between both parties tends to be very private, but much of it is

▶ **ERNIE ELS HAD BOTH** his mind coach and caddie to thank after his victory at the 2002 Open at Muirfield. Els triumphed in a four-man playoff that tested his mental strength.

▶ ▼ **CADDIE, COACH, AND MIND COACH** are each a key part of the Ernie Els team. Here, they come together to support their player on the practice range at the 2003 US Open.

based purely around the need to get the player into a positive and stable frame of mind for tournament play—one they are then able to maintain in moments of pressure.

Almost all top golfers have a personal trainer. The level of fitness in the professional game is extraordinary; there really are some fine physical specimens out there on tour these days. In terms of physical fitness, the game has changed beyond all recognition in the last 20 to 30 years. As former Ryder Cup star and BBC commentator Ken Brown says, "People just didn't go to the gym at tournaments in the '80s. I suppose I might have done a bit of jogging during the week, and some of the other players did too, but that was it really. To be honest, we felt like we needed to save our energy for playing golf!"

These days, it is quite common for a Tour player to pay a visit to the gym and have a workout before a round of golf, and possibly even afterward, too.

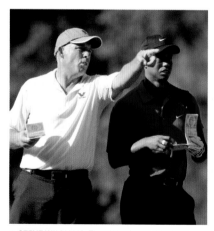

▲ **STEVE WILLIAMS**, Tiger Woods's caddie from 1999 to 2011, was an essential part of the Tiger team. Woods has remarked on the importance of Williams to his success.

2 PLAYING THE GAME

Golf Balls: The Design

Buying a sleeve of golf balls used to be a simple task; almost the only way to differentiate one ball from another was the manufacturer's stamp and the model number. With improvements in technology, however, it has come a bewildering choice. Should you play cheap or premium brand, low compression or high compression, soft or hard, control or distance, XL or V1, XTour or Tour? Let us start with the basics.

VARIATIONS IN CONSTRUCTION

The dimensions and weight of the modern-day golf ball are strictly monitored by the game's governing bodies, the United States Golf Association (USGA) and the Royal & Ancient (R&A). A golf ball must weigh no more than 1.62oz (46g), and it must have a diameter of at least 1.68in (4.6cm).

Companies use different materials for both the cover and the core. Many have a urethane cover, which is soft for improved feel, or ionomer, which is slightly harder. The core of a golf ball varies from one ball to another—a mixture of synthetic rubbers and special compounds. Golf balls are either one-piece, two-piece, three-piece, or even four-piece.

The USGA and R&A also put limits on the maximum initial velocity allowable under the current rules, a scientific measurement designed to prevent golf balls from becoming too "hot" and therefore to preserve the integrity of today's golf courses and the inherent shot values.

There are also so-called "overall distance standards." The reasoning is the same: it is not in the interests of the game for the ruling bodies to allow manufacturers free rein in terms of how far a golf ball flies. It would soon get out of hand; the golf ball would, in essence, go too far—perhaps not in the hands of amateurs but certainly in those of the leading pros.

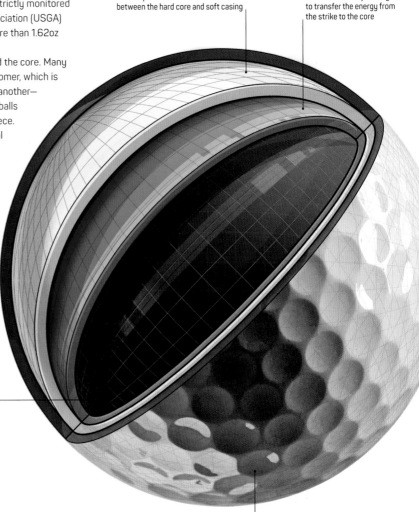

The middle cover is unique to four-piece balls. It strikes a balance between the hard core and soft casing

The inner cover (a thin layer of enhanced rubber) is designed to transfer the energy from the strike to the core

The inner core of two-, three-, and four-piece balls are made of solid rubber or liquid and are primarily intended to offer explosive distance

The outer casing is covered in aerodynamic dimples. For two-piece balls, this is made from a durable ionomer; for three- and four-piece balls it is made from softer urethane

▲ **THE FOUR-PIECE GOLF BALL,** as used by world No. 1 Tiger Woods, is the latest development in golf ball design. The four-piece golf ball offers superb feel, but the casing is susceptible to cuts. It differs from the three-piece ball by having an additional layer directly under the outer casing.

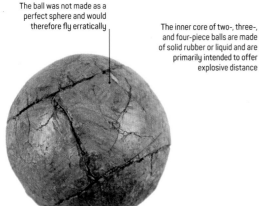

The ball was not made as a perfect sphere and would therefore fly erratically

▲ **EARLY GOLF BALLS** were simply hand-sewn cowhide bags stuffed with goose feathers. In wet weather, the stitching tended to rot, rendering the ball useless.

DESIGNING THE DIMPLES

The important thing to understand is that the dimple patterns on golf balls vary, albeit subtly, from one ball to the next. It is all about aerodynamics (see box, right). Those little dimples, in conjunction with the actual golf ball's construction, impact on the air flow around the ball and influence the trajectory of a ball's flight—how high or low it typically flies, how much it spins, how much it swerves in the air. A smooth golf ball would have reduced lift; basically dipping abruptly in flight.

The depth of the dimple indentation is usually standard, as is its spherical shape. However, in recent years, Callaway has led the way in a new hexagonal dimple design.

The arrangement of dimples varies between designs—from random patterns to formal rows

An even number of dimples is usual for almost all balls on the market, in the interests of symmetry

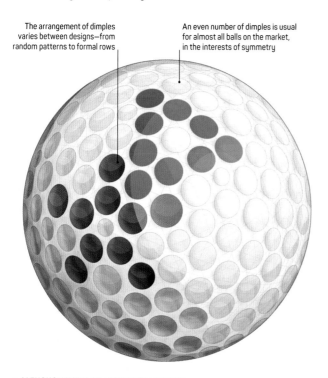

▲ **ALTHOUGH THERE ARE NO RULES** governing the number of dimples on a ball, most manufacturers use between 300 and 450.

MAKING HISTORY

It is natural to assume that until the late 20th century, one golf ball was much like another. In fact, between 1931 and 1988, the R&A sanctioned a ball that was, at 1.62in, slightly smaller than the now universal American/USGA ball of 1.68in. Although a subtle difference, it meant that the leading professionals from the PGA Tour and British circuit had to play with an unfamiliar golf ball when competing overseas.

◯ A golf ball factory in the 1950s

PHYSICS OF THE GOLF BALL

The physics of golf ball design is concerned with the flow of air around the object when it is in flight. In scientific terms, there are two types of drags behind a sphere when it is airborne—laminar and turbulent. Laminar flow occurs over a smooth ball; the air separates very early in front of the ball, resulting in less carry. Turbulent flow occurs with a dimpled ball; it hugs the surface of the ball and separates later. The net result for the golfer is this: a player hitting a driver would carry the ball approximately 150 yards (137m) less with a smooth ball compared with a dimpled one.

Air grips surface of ball reducing drag

Air separates on impact and slows ball flight

Limited air resistance equals unhindered ball flight

Air drag causes nondimpled ball to lose height

◯ Air flow and trajectory of dimpled ball   ◯ Air flow and trajectory of smooth ball

IT IS ALL JUST SPIN

The many different types of golf balls exist for a reason: to offer golfers of all standards, whatever their preference or personal requirements, a ball that suits the way they play their game. Understanding what you want, and then matching the golf ball to your needs, is the single major factor in the buying process. Broadly speaking, golf ball types can be divided into three categories—distance, compromise, and control balls—although there is some blurring in these lines of definition.

Distance golf balls tend to be used by less-experienced golfers and high-to-mid handicappers; they have a relatively low spin rate, which offers good distance. The drawback is lack of control; they have a relatively hard feel off the clubface and the low spin rate can be a drawback for short shots around the green.

However, the drawbacks are less marked than, say, 30 years ago. Through clever construction techniques (essentially the materials and methods used in the inner core and outer layer of the golf ball), the manufacturers can offer golfers a compromise golf ball—one with more rounded qualities, so to speak. It means that many golf balls designed for distance now also offer reasonably soft feel and high-performance control characteristics.

GOING FOR CONTROL

In the feel and control department, manufacturers cannot, however, compete with golf balls designed primarily for those purposes. This premium end of the market features golf balls designed for maximum feel and control, typically used by professional golfers and accomplished amateurs. The construction and dimple patterns are designed to generate a higher spin rate and, just as importantly, a soft feel off the clubface. This enables the player to hit a greater variety of "feel" shots from around the greens. The ball is more "workable" on long shots, too.

Drivers: The Design

The evolution of the driver has been an extraordinary success. Clubhead design, technology, and multi-material construction techniques are such that golfers today are more adept at hitting the driver than at any time in the history of the game. With so much choice, however, it is hard to know which club is best and, consequently, easier to make the wrong selection and buy a club that does not suit your game.

CLUBHEAD DESIGN

The use of light metals such as titanium and carbon composites has meant that driver clubheads have grown in size, although not in weight, and the effective sweet spot has consequently grown larger, too. It is one of the reasons drivers have become comparatively easy to hit. That and the lower center of gravity, which makes it easier to get the ball airborne, and the clever weight distribution, which means that off-center strikes are not punished as severely as was the case a generation ago.

The actual shape of the clubhead is dictated by more than aesthetics. The form is dictated largely by function. Square-headed drivers are a 21st-century innovation. It seems bizarre, but the reasoning can be summed up with one phrase—moment of inertia, or MOI.

In layman's terms, this means "resistance to twisting"; the significance for golf clubs being that the less a club twists when it strikes the ball, the straighter the shot flies. Square-headed drivers are found to possess high MOI.

MAKING HISTORY

The principles of modern-day golf club manufacture, with its emphasis on moment of inertia and shaft bend profiles, are far removed from the origins of the game. As recently as the mid-1990s, driver heads were made of wood, especially persimmon, into which a metal face was screwed, representing the sweet spot. This is the origin of the phrase "hit it out of the screws"—a phrase used to denote a sweetly struck drive.

● A club maker in 1950

▼ **THE PRINCIPLE OF MOVABLE WEIGHTS,** whereby players alter the characteristics of the club, is now commonplace. The rules state that these clubs can be set with a range of weight biases, provided this is not altered midround.

9.5°

Heavy weights at the rear of the club promote a high launch angle

Weights positioned near the heel and toe of the clubhead can preset a right-to-left or left-to-right ball flight

Extra-large clubhead provides maximum forgiveness for off-center strikes

MOMENT OF INERTIA

The characteristics of MOI are designed to promote stability of the clubface and maximum efficiency of energy transfer from club to ball. The advantages this brings may be acutely evident with off-center hits.

Every club designer has at least one eye on MOI, but if you lined up the 10 current top-selling drivers at any given time, no two would be identical in shape. Form follows function in other ways, too. Some drivers feature a clean, simple design and use movable weights in the sole of the club to encourage a particular shape of shot—be that a fade, a draw, or a higher or lower ball flight.

Other manufacturers rely on the actual shape of the club to determine its playing characteristics, manipulating the club's center of gravity, balance, or clubface angle so the club has a draw or fade bias, for instance.

The combination of MOI geometry and weight-saving results in maximum distance, forgiveness, and accuracy. Nike's square-headed drivers were popular in the early 21st century

The club's face and body are made of titanium

Graphite shaft is standard in drivers. The lighter weight translates into higher clubhead speeds and greater distances

▲ **THE SQUARE-HEADED DRIVER** used light composite metals, except in the face and body, where strength and durability are key.

COMPARING THE SWEET SPOT

On modern golf clubs, the sweet spot is much larger than on traditional clubs (even those from only 30 years ago), making solid hitting easier for all. On drivers, the sweet spot is positioned higher up the face. This is to encourage a higher launch angle, less spin, and extra distance.

Large sweet spot aids ball-striking

Smaller hitting area of the traditional "wood"

● A metal-headed driver   ● Traditional persimmon clubhead

▼ **THE LATEST DEVELOPMENT** in club design, the square-headed driver, has particularly high moment of inertia.

TaylorMade's M1 driver uses multi-materials to help personalize a golfer's swing

A 12-position variable loft sleeve will suit a golfer's preference of face angle, loft, and lie

This example of a long driver creates an efficient power transfer and therefore increased ball speed

The M1's T-Track system allows for a range of settings on the front and back track to help with neutral, draw, and fade preferences

MULTI-MATERIAL CONSTRUCTION

Many 21st-century drivers are of multi-material construction; typically, the body of the clubhead and the face-insert itself will be made of different metals. Titanium is among the most popular metals used because it is durable and much lighter than steel.

This dual construction approach is more than just a sales gimmick. It allows the club manufacturers greater creative license to manipulate the weight distribution and performance of a club, typically in the body. However, the thickness of the face-insert can even be tapered to promote a particular type of launch angle, maximize ball speed, or offer greater forgiveness for the player when struck.

HOW BIG?

The R&A and USGA have placed limitations on the size of clubheads, with particular reference to the technological advancement of drivers. The volume of the clubhead must not exceed 28.06 cu in (460 cu cm), and the distance from the heel to the toe (in the normal address position) cannot be more than 7 in (17.8 cm) and must not be greater than the distance from the face to back.

ANGLE OF LOFT

Most modern-day drivers come in a range of different lofts, typically from around 7.5 degrees to 14 degrees, although there is a slight variation from one manufacturer to another. A high loft produces a high launch angle; a low loft produces a low launch angle.

▼ **A DRIVER SHOULD BE CHOSEN** depending on your ball flight. If you have a low ball flight, a 10- or 11-degree driver is better.

The limited loft on a driver makes it difficult to hit solidly from the fairway

Weight distribution in the clubhead works with the loft to determine launch angle

SHAFT MATERIALS

The shaft of a golf club is a complex piece of equipment and requires much consideration. There are three key factors that contribute to a shaft's overall performance characteristics—the material, shaft flex, and bend profile.

Materials come in two forms, steel or graphite. These days, it is rare to see a driver fitted with a steel shaft. Graphite (essentially woven carbon fiber) is preferable, for expert and novice players alike. It is lighter and more flexible than steel and therefore helps a player generate more clubhead speed, which can be converted into distance.

▲ **STIFF SHAFTS** are used by accomplished players who generate great speed and clubhead power with their swings. Professional players typically use extra-stiff shafts.

A stiff shaft will maximize speed and power through the drive

▲ **REGULAR SHAFTS** have more flex than stiff shafts and are suited to the majority of amateur players who possess slower or medium swing speeds. Swinging too fast with this shaft may lead to a loss of accuracy.

This shaft weighs 2oz (50g). The letter "R" denotes regular

▲ **MANUFACTURERS PRODUCE** special shafts for ladies that are both lighter and more flexible than standard versions. These shafts are also suitable for junior golfers.

Made from graphite composite, this shaft is very light and flexible

OPTIMUM FLEXIBILITY

Shaft flex refers literally to the amount a shaft bends as a result of the forces generated in the golf swing. Powerful golfers and tour professionals require a stiffer-flex shaft. The less accomplished golfer requires a bit more "give," thus many amateurs will fare best with a regular-flex shaft. Matching the correct shaft flex to your swing and physique is essential so that you optimize the performance of the club. Too "soft" a shaft may result in too much whip and a closed clubface at impact; too stiff a shaft often results in an open face.

The bend profile, which used to be known as kickpoint, essentially describes the point at which the shaft is most prone to flexing. It is possible to make two shafts of the same flex but with different bend profiles. This in turn determines to some extent the trajectory of the golf ball.

Choosing the right shaft often requires more than just a personal feel. It needs proper performance-related data, which only a launch monitor can accurately measure. This is why custom fitting is such an attractive option, whatever standard you play to.

The flex of the shaft may determine the angle of the clubface as it approaches impact

Power stored in the shaft and clubhead is unleashed from the top of the backswing

Shafts that bend at a higher point contribute to lower ball flights; low bend profiles lead to higher ball flights

▲ **USING A DRIVER FITTED** with the correct shaft flex and bend profile will contribute to an improvement in your standard of play as surely as using an ill-suited shaft will hinder you.

A PERFECT FIT

There are a lot of different drivers and a dizzying number of options as regards loft, shaft, and head design. Hardly surprising, then, that a lot of golfers unwittingly use drivers that are not suited to either their swing or their physique, and that is sadly to the detriment of their golf game.

This is why custom fitting is so compelling. The process begins with a golfer hitting drives, while a computer known as a launch monitor captures all the data relating to the impact conditions of each shot—clubhead speed, ball speed, spin rate, launch angle, trajectory, ball flight, distance carried through the air, and the amount the ball runs on landing.

Through trial and error, it is then possible to use this information to pinpoint the perfect club for a golfer's swing characteristics, one that optimizes the performance characteristics of the club to produce the best, most consistent drives off the tee with the tightest dispersion pattern. No golfer is skilled enough to be able to afford to ignore the potential benefits of custom fitting.

▲ **CUSTOM FITTING CENTERS** measure data relating to your swing and translate it into a clubhead and shaft combination that best fits your game. Give custom fitting a try; it can only help your game.

DRIVING DISTANCES FROM PGA TOUR

The advancements in golf technology have resulted in players hitting ever-greater distances from the tee. Statistics from the PGA Tour demonstrate just how much impact this has had on the performance of the world's best players.

Graph denotes average driving distance of the longest hitter on tour

YARDS: 330, 320, 310, 300, 290, 280, 270
YEAR: 1972, 1980, 1988, 1996, 2004, 2012, 2020

TIMES CHANGE

If anyone was ever in any doubt about the massive effect golf club technology, and in particular driver technology, has had on the pro game, they need look no further (literally) than the PGA Tour's performance statistics. Bryson DeChambeau, the PGA Tour's biggest hitter, averaged a mighty 329 yards (301 m) off the tee in early 2021. In 1983, Bill Glasson was the PGA Tour's biggest hitter, and he averaged 276 yards (252 m) that year. That is an increase in distance of 19 percent.

▼ **THESE EXAMPLES** of metal- and persimmon-headed drivers were made less than 20 years apart and are indicative of how far technology has come. The change in size, weight, and materials used is marked.

Aerodynamic design contributes to faster clubhead speed

Screws fix the metal sole plate to the clubhead

Persimmon is treated with oil to increase its resistance to impact

Woven strapping binds the clubhead to the shaft

Turnkey determines a single set of launch conditions

Despite having a much larger clubhead, the metal driver weighs less than the wooden alternative

Metal heads can be produced on a mass scale, unlike wooden drivers, so they dominate the market

Shaft is molded into the clubhead and set fast

▲ **A PERSIMMON DRIVER FROM 1980s**

▲ **A TITANIUM DRIVER**

On the Tee

The tee shot should be one of the easiest shots in golf; after all, you have the advantage of raising the ball off the ground using a tee peg. However, more often than not, for the amateur golfer, this advantage is countered by the player adopting a poor setup. All good golf swings start with a good setup. There are three golden rules to follow: a neutral grip on the club; parallel alignment of the feet, knees, hips, and shoulders with the target line; and an athletic and comfortable posture. It is well worth making the effort to adopt these fundamentals.

a Arms hanging, palms facing   **b** Club runs diagonally across palm   **c** Two knuckles on show   **d** Soft trigger

FORMING THE GRIP

To assume the perfect neutral hold requires some careful application.

a Start by letting your arms hang down free from tension, with your hands on either side of the grip, palms facing one another.

b Now feed the club into your left hand, so the club runs diagonally from the first joint of your forefinger up into the fleshy pad at the top of your palm. Close your fingers around the grip.

c Your left thumb should rest on top of the grip, just right of center. In a mirror, only two knuckles on your left hand should be visible to you.

d To apply the right hand to the club, keep in mind the all-important palms-facing principle. Bring the right hand in toward the grip and wrap the fingers around it. The right hand should fit snugly on top of the left, the right thumb and forefinger forming a soft trigger around the grip.

Start by letting your arms hang down free from tension, with your hands on either side of the grip, palms facing one another.

TYPES OF GRIPS

The hands should now feel bonded together, as if one. How you join the hands together is a personal choice. Most top players adopt the Vardon grip, whereby the little finger of the right hand sits in the ridge created between the forefinger and middle finger of the left hand (left). Other players, including Tiger Woods, choose to entwine the little finger of the right hand with the left forefinger (right). Only you will know which feels most comfortable. Go with that.

RELAXED SHOULDERS
Your shoulders should be relaxed (with your arms hanging freely) and aligned parallel with the target

HIP ALIGNMENT
Bend your upper body forward from your hips. Your hips should be aligned parallel left of the target

FLEXED KNEES
Your knees should be primed and flexed. They should be in direct alignment with your shoulders, feet, and hips

FEET
The line formed by your feet should be in parallel alignment to the target. Feet should be shoulder-width apart, and the weight should be on the balls of the feet in readiness for the swing

PERFECT ALIGNMENT

On the tee, good alignment is paramount. The principle of perfect aim and alignment could not be simpler. Imagine a railroad track running down the fairway. The golf ball rests on the outer track, which points straight at the target. This is where you aim the clubface. The inner track runs parallel left of that target line. This is where you align your feet, hips, and shoulders. Collectively, this is known as perfect parallel alignment; it determines the path of your swing and is thus an essential requirement of powerful, straight driving.

PERFECT POSTURE

To hit perfect drives, your feet should be shoulder-width apart with the toes splayed out slightly. The ideal ball position for the driver is opposite the inside of your left heel, as that encourages a sweeping angle of attack, striking the ball slightly on the upswing. The weight should slightly favor your back foot—a ratio of about 60/40 is about right. This primes you for a good weight shift into the right side in your backswing, essential for generating maximum power in your swing.

The Drive

The drive is a big shot in more ways than one. The driver is, of course, the longest club in the bag and the club that we hit the farthest. It sets the tone for a hole, even for an entire round. A good drive puts you in the perfect position to attack a green and boosts your confidence. A good drive off the tee makes you believe you can shoot your best score ... today! For all of these reasons, good driving is as much about the position as it is about power. Although, of course, it is far better to have both.

ⓐ THE FOUNDATIONS OF A GOOD SWING

The driver swing generates the most power, so the need for good foundations is paramount. Balance and posture need to be perfect. Think "shoulders over toes, hands under the chin." That should help get your posture in great shape every time you set up to hit a drive. Also, parallel alignment should be achieved; the feet, hips, and shoulders all parallel to the target line (see pp.50–51). Good alignment promotes an on-line swing path.

ⓑ GIVE YOURSELF TIME

Do not be in a hurry to get to the top; just keep your rhythm and tempo nice and smooth. Give yourself time to make a good shoulder turn and, more important, time to complete your backswing. For the perfect combination of arm swing and body turn, think, "turn your back on the target and point the club straight at the target."

> Do not be in a hurry to get to the top; just keep your rhythm and tempo nice and smooth.

ⓐ Strong foundations   ⓑ Keep your rhythm smooth   ⓒ Shift your weight with the club   ⓓ Swing through and finish

ⓒ LET YOUR WEIGHT FLOW

Poor weight shift drains the power out of your swing like nothing else. The key thing to remember is that you should let the weight move in the direction of the swinging clubhead. So as you swing the club back, the weight moves on to your right foot; then as you swing the club down, the weight moves on to your left foot. Now you can punch your weight off the tee.

ⓓ SWEEP THROUGH AND HOLD YOUR FINISH

Let the club swing through. Keep your head down until the right shoulder comes through and raises it naturally. The intention to complete the swing with a well-balanced finish has knock-on benefits for your entire swing. It instills in your mind the need to keep your balance, a key requirement of solid ball-striking. Also, in doing that, you are less inclined to lose control or hit at the ball too aggressively. The swing stays smooth, which helps promote a pure and solid hit.

STAY IN CONTROL

- Many golfers feel that they should try to hit their drive shots as hard as they can. However, position, not power, is the most important factor off the tee. A shot of 250 yards (230 m) that finds the middle of the fairway is always preferable to a shot of 300 yards (275 m) that ends up in heavy rough.
- Most professional players hit their drives at 70 to 80 percent capacity. Less is often more when it comes to the golf swing; smooth rhythm is preferable to brute force. By employing this technique, you will discover that not only does your rhythm improve, but your distances are likely to be greater, too.
- For even greater control off the tee, try gripping the club down the shaft a little and then make your normal swing. By "choking down" on the grip, your swing will automatically become abbreviated—and a shorter swing results in greater control.

SWING SECRETS

Fully rotate the left shoulder under the chin

Keep the head down through impact

Ensure a smooth, one-piece takeaway

Align the ball with the left heel at address

Tee it high to maximize the driver's sweet spot

FREE-WHEELING
You should feel that the club is almost free-wheeling as it approaches the "hitting zone." It has little to do with brute force

WRIST ANGLE
Retain the angle in your wrists into your downswing, as this helps store the power in the swing

LEFT SHOULDER
As you start the downswing, feel that you pull the left shoulder away from the chin

WEIGHT FORWARD
Keep your weight moving to the left as you swing into and through impact; do not under any circumstances allow yourself to fall backward away from the shot

THE MAGIC MOVE
There is no single part in the golf swing that could be said to be the key to great driving—golf is not that simple. If there is such a thing as a "magic move," then it is the split second transition from the completion of the backswing to the start of the downswing. The weight shifts on to the left side, the hips start to unwind, the right elbow drops down to the right side, and the shoulders stay back. The player is primed for the impact position.

PRACTICE MAKES PERFECT
Rehearse the "magic move" in slow motion and practice it in front of a mirror. Try to ingrain it into your practice swings until it starts to feel comfortable and you feel you can replicate it in your actual swing. Repetition is a wonderful thing. Practice this move to train good driving habits.

STABLE BASE
Both feet should feel planted as the downswing starts, proving the stable base that is essential for making a controlled and well-balanced swing

BALL POSITION
With the ball correctly positioned opposite the left heel, it is easier to achieve the desired sweeping angle of attack, promoting dead-solid contact

Big Hitters: A Master Class

Nothing receives greater admiration than a well-struck monster drive. It is the shot the galleries want to see. It is the shot club golfers want to hit most. New golf-club technology means that, when we get it right, we can achieve great distances, if not accuracy, but, given that we will probably never be able to hit the ball as far as the world's best drivers, every golfer can learn from what they do.

ANGEL CABRERA'S FREE SWING

The tendency to hit at the ball with the driver is one of the biggest obstacles to achieving golf's Holy Grail—good distance and respectable accuracy. The trouble is, an overly aggressive approach tends to rob the swing of coordination and timing, which leads to poor distance and a loss of accuracy.

So if you struggle with the driver, take a leaf out of 2007 US Open champion Angel Cabrera's book. The big Argentine was famed for hitting the ball a country mile when he was at the height of his game between 2005 and 2010. In 2007, his average driving distance according to PGA Tour statistics was 303.2 yards (276 m), but it looked relatively easy. The secret lies largely in the freedom of motion.

Cabrera sets the club beautifully in his backswing and makes a big turn, which stores the power in his swing. Then in the downswing, he just lets it go; he swings the club down and almost freewheels straight through the ball. It is a free swing, with the ball merely getting in the way of the club. That is a far more useful swing than trying to hit the ball as hard as possible and then having to deal with the problems associated with such a philosophy.

Make sure that you generate enough clubhead speed so the ball will spend enough time in the air to achieve a decent length

Driver shafts are generally made from graphite, because it is a light and very strong material

Big hitting does not come from brute force alone, but strong forearms, for example, will help generate a large amount of power and distance

▶ **CABRERA'S BIG SHOULDER** turn enables him to freewheel into the ball. This freedom of motion gives him great distance.

THE GREATEST DRIVE

At the 1960 US Open at Cherry Hills in Denver, Arnold Palmer trailed leader Mike Souchak by seven shots going into the last round. Cue one of the greatest last-round charges in the history of golf. Palmer smashed his drive on to the green at the 346-yard (316 m) 1st hole and two-putted for birdie, the first of six birdies in the first seven holes. Palmer went on to shoot 65, at the time the lowest score ever in the final round by a winner, to win by two shots. It all started with that sensational drive on the 1st hole—surely the greatest drive ever.

Palmer lays down a marker

VIJAY SINGH'S RHYTHM

Rhythm in your golf swing is the key to consistent shotmaking. Poor rhythm is debilitating with any club, but with a driver—the most unforgiving club in the bag—the effects are catastrophic. You will miss fairways and lose balls all day long.

Vijay Singh has always been a great scholar of the golf swing, and a man with a great swing himself. He advocates an old Bobby Jones adage that you "start your downswing at the same speed as you took the club back."

It helps make smooth that crucial split-second transition from completing the backswing to starting the downswing. It gives you the time to coordinate the various moving parts in your swing so that everything arrives at impact working in harmony. That is the essence of good timing. It is the way to hit drives long and straight, just like Vijay does.

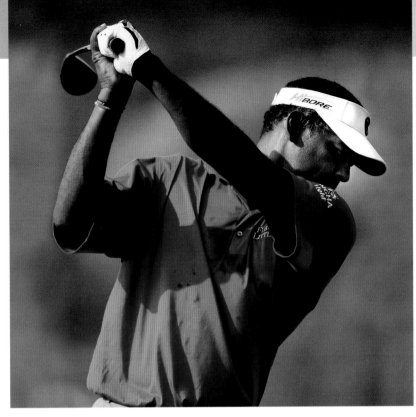

▶ **VIJAY HAS A GREAT SWING** and excellent tempo, which is the same with every club in the bag. He is a great student of the game and renowned for the time he spends working on his swing.

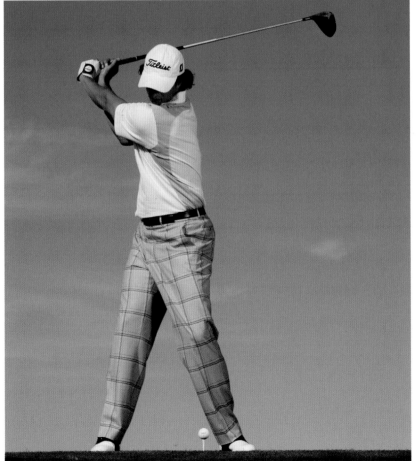

ADAM SCOTT'S SHOULDER TURN

Adam Scott is not the strongest man in golf. He does not have the raw physical power of some of the bigger men on Tour, but he is a great driver of the golf ball, who has the ability to generate a lot of speed and distance, with good trajectory and a high level of consistency. A look at his PGA Tour statistics reveals that he averaged 308 yards (282 m) from the tee in 2020, placing him inside the world's top-20 in that classification. The position he achieves at the top of the backswing is picture perfect, and it is one of the main reasons he drives the ball so well.

Scott makes a full shoulder turn, winding his body up like a coiled spring. All the time, he is resisting with his lower body, the hips turning only half as much as the shoulders do. This action generates a lot of resistance—in essence, latent energy waiting to be unleashed.

From the top of the swing, he can then basically recoil his upper body—like a spring unwinding—which drives his downswing forward at pace. He converts all of that power into the back of the golf ball with a good hand and arm action.

Again, with Scott and the other big hitters, the secret is that the hands, arms, and body work together toward impact. One does not reach its target before the other, meaning that every part of the swing is well coordinated and complements each other.

◀ **SCOTT'S TECHNIQUE AND ABILITY** enable him to play and be successful no matter where in the world he plays. He won the Masters in 2013 and came second at the Open in 2012.

Metals and Hybrids: The Design

Fairway metals are the distance clubs that do not bite. Like the driver, they have a relatively long shaft that helps generate distance. Unlike a driver, however, which has a relatively straight face, a fairway metal has a greater degree of loft on the clubface. This helps generate more height and more backspin, which in turn counteracts sidespin. This means that a fairway metal is easier to hit straight than a driver. It is more forgiving, too.

LOFTED METALS

Lofted metals come in a range of different designs. Aside from aesthetic considerations, which are of course important to any golfer, the focus of the club designer is on similar playability issues to that of the driver—maximum ball speed off the clubface, forgiveness, and moment of inertia (resistance to twisting at impact).

Versatility is also a key factor for this type of club, because a fairway metal will be required to perform in a greater variety of on-course situations—off the tee, from the fairway, and from light rough. There is much to gain—at least from the club golfer's perspective—in carrying more than one fairway metal, as it increases the range of shots at one's disposal.

In recent years, there has been a revolution in the role of the lofted metal. It has in many ways been superseded by a new innovation that offers even greater playability.

THE HYBRID REVOLUTION

The hybrid or rescue club differs in appearance and design from the traditional fairway metal. It has a smaller clubhead, like an oversize long iron with a bulbous back edge, and it produces the ball-flight characteristics of a long iron without any of the hardships. The hybrid is incredibly versatile.

▼ FAIRWAY METALS WITH HIGH LOFTS were traditionally the preserve of women and senior golfers until the revolution in hybrid clubs. Nowadays, they feature in the bags of many professional players, too.

Steel and graphite composite clubhead offers the perfect blend of distance and ease of use

Smooth sole area reduces drag and offers improved playability from a variety of different lies

Deep face and enlarged sweet spot forgives off-center strikes

▲ VIEW FROM THE ADDRESS POSITION

COMPARING THE SWEET SPOT

Fairway metals, hybrids, and long irons are interchangeable on the golf course. Each has its own advantages and disadvantages, but they travel similar distances. The key when considering your options is to think about the gap in distance between your 3-wood and the longest iron that you intend to keep in your bag—a 5-iron, for example. There will be a hybrid to fill that gap. Use the conversion chart below to build a set that best fits your game.

CONVERSION CHART			
210–230 YDS	3-metal	1 hybrid	1-iron
190–210 YDS	4-metal	2 hybrid	2-iron
170–190 YDS	5/7-metal	3 hybrid	3-iron
160–180 YDS	9-metal	4 hybrid	4-iron
150–170 YDS	N/A	5 hybrid	5-iron

The rounded, compact clubhead makes light work of clingy rough. It is a superb club to use off the tee on tight par-4s—the generous loft and relatively short shaft optimize accuracy without any significant drain on distance.

Its performance advantages can be attributed to clubhead design and weight distribution. With a long iron, the capability to distribute weight around the clubhead is limited. The rounded and slightly chunkier hybrid design, however, offers greater potential for redistributing the mass of the clubhead; this boosts the size of the sweet spot on the face and lowers the center of gravity, the dual effects of which make it more forgiving. It also increases the launch angle, enabling golfers to get the ball airborne far more easily. High-flying long shots—not a realistic proposition with a long iron in the hands of the majority of amateur golfers—are very much back on the agenda.

GAME IMPROVEMENT

These clubs sit very nicely behind the ball, and this in itself gives golfers a great deal more confidence than if they were looking down at a long iron. These psychological benefits combined with the tangible advantages in playability add up to a huge difference.

What is surprising is not that the hybrid has found its way into the golf bags of millions of golfers around the world but that the world's best players are using them, too. One would have assumed that they hit their long irons so well that they did not need help from a hybrid, but the hybrid simply makes too compelling a case for itself to be ignored. The world's top-50 players have embraced this new concept club wholeheartedly.

An early fan of the hybrid was 2007 Open champion Pádraig Harrington (see p.186). He said there was a case for some golfers—especially seniors and those who perhaps do not generate much power in the swing—to carry only the irons numbered 6 and above. The 2-, 3-, 4-, and 5-irons can therefore be replaced by the equivalent hybrid, which is easier to hit and offers more height, distance, and accuracy—a potent combination.

The bulbous clubhead results in a relatively low center of gravity

▲ **COMPACT AND FORGIVING,** the hybrid is suitable for a wide range of shots; it is even used for chipping around the greens.

Perimeter weighting increases the club's resistance to off-center strikes

▲ **THE TRADITIONAL** lofted metal features a wide clubhead. Not as versatile as the hybrid, it is best deployed from the tee or fairway.

CONTROL FROM THE ROUGH

Before the invention of the rescue club, it was hard to gain good distance from the rough. The clubheads of long irons get tangled by the grass, and the resulting shot is dragged off line. However, the larger clubhead and round sole of utility clubs scythe through the grass. This makes a long, straight shot much more achievable for the club golfer.

Narrow clubhead and exposed hosel results in twisting impact

Bulbous clubhead and rounded sole cuts through grass

● Iron from rough   ● Hybrid from rough

The smooth "speed plate sole design" reduces turf drag and promotes versatility from all lies

▲ **AN ULTRA-LIGHTWEIGHT** titanium head can be incorporated into the design of a utility metal. This element allows the designer to lower the club's center of gravity.

The center of gravity is positioned relatively far forward and close to the face to promote a low, penetrating ball flight

▲ **A PRESET FADE OR DRAW BIAS** may be included in the features of a utility metal. If a player has a persistent slice, a club with a draw bias will lead to straighter shots.

Tungsten-nickel weight lowers and deepens center of gravity for high launch and low spin

▲ **SOME HYBRIDS** offer a degree of forgiveness via a combination of shock absorption technology, a high launch angle, and soft landing.

The Fairway Metal Shot

Mastering the art of hitting solid fairway metal shots gives you more strategic options on the golf course and ultimately makes you a more complete golfer. When you really need to hit a tight fairway, you can depend on a fairway metal to give you more accuracy than a driver, and with good distance. A fairway metal brings the green into play in two shots on those tough par-5s and helps you generate good distance out of light rough. Fairway metals can be a golfer's best friends, if you know how to use them.

a STATIC BUT ATHLETIC POSTURE

Your posture at address is integral to your chances of hitting a good shot because it determines the shape and quality of your body motion during the swing. It is easy to fall into bad habits, so when you practice, recreate perfect posture with this simple routine.
- Stand up straight with your feet shoulder-width apart, your hands placed on the grip, and your arms extended comfortably around chest height.
- Bend over from the hips until the clubhead rests on the turf.
- Flex your knees, feeling some athletic tension in the thighs. Try to feel that your back is relatively straight, and hold your chin high.

The golf swing is a fluid motion, and it is hard to make a good start from a totally static position. Waggle the club back and forth as you prime yourself to start the swing; this helps banish tension from the hands, arms, and shoulders.

a Address routine

b LEFT SHOULDER OVER RIGHT KNEE

Starting from the address position, begin the takeaway. Your body motion is the engine of the golf swing. Your body needs to move correctly and efficiently in order to drive your swing. Think of turning your left shoulder over your right knee, to promote a full turn. Make sure you keep that right knee flexed, just as it was at address, because that gives you a firm base from which to wind and unwind your body in the swing.

c FULL ROTATION

As you swing your hands and arms through, the body needs to continue to unwind. The momentum of your swing will carry you through impact to a finish, but it helps if you think of completing your swing with your chest facing the target. This will get you "through the ball" better than ever.

Waggle the club back and forth as you prime yourself to start the swing; this helps banish tension from the hands, arms, and shoulders.

b Address position   Smooth takeaway   Left shoulder over right knee   c Rotate down and through the ball

PERFECT PLANE

There are several key checkpoints you can rehearse as you practice hitting balls; this is one of the best. As your left arm reaches parallel with the ground in the early stages of the backswing, make sure that the wrists are fully hinged, thus setting the club on the perfect plane.

Check it in a mirror—your hands should be right in front of your chest, and the shaft of the club should be at an angle that hits the ground roughly equidistant between the golf ball and your toes. This is perfect plane. From there, you just keep turning your shoulders to complete the backswing.

KEEP IT TOGETHER
Feel that the arms swing at the same time as the body rotates

CHIN UP
Maintain your height, to make room for that shoulder turn, and keep your chin up

TURNING SHOULDERS
Turn your shoulders on a flat plane to complete your swing

FLEXED KNEE
Maintain the flex in your right knee

KNEES AND HIPS
Let your left knee work toward the ball as your hips turn

KEEP THE RHYTHM

You can expect good distance with fairway metal shots—they are the second-longest clubs in the bag—but do not push it. Maintaining a smooth rhythm and focusing on dead-solid contact is the way to go, as that will promote sweet timing and the distance you seek, without sacrificing accuracy.

SWING SECRETS

Hands stay in front of chest in backswing

Weight moves to the right as backswing progresses

Right foot stays planted in backswing

Left arm rotates to keep clubface neutral

The Hybrid Shot

The hybrid is a key stage in the evolution of club design. The neat clubhead and relatively short shaft makes a hybrid comparatively easy to hit and very forgiving, and it promotes a high launch angle. Because it also glides through rough better than the equivalent long iron, it is incredibly versatile, too. To hit perfect hybrid shots from the rough, you need to keep in mind a few important factors that will determine the success of the shot.

ⓐ SETUP RULES

You can never ignore the setup; it has a huge bearing on the quality of your shotmaking. A poor setup almost invariably leads to a poor shot; a good setup massively improves your chances of making a good swing and hitting a solid golf shot.

When hitting a hybrid from the rough, move the ball a little farther back in your stance than you would for a shot from the fairway or off the tee. Somewhere around two balls'–width inside the left heel is perfect. Also, make sure that your hands are slightly in front of the golf ball. Combined, these two measures will help promote the slightly descending angle of attack, which is necessary to generate good contact and a strong ball flight.

BE SMART

Smart shot selection is one of the keys to good scoring, which is one of the reasons a hybrid is such a useful tool to have in your bag. While attempting to hit a long iron out of rough can lead to disaster, a hybrid is relatively easy to hit and, therefore, constitutes a smarter club selection. Do not be too ambitious, though. If you feel you would struggle to hit a 7-iron from a particular lie, then you should not contemplate a hybrid, either.

ⓐ Focus on setup

ⓑ Compact swing

ⓒ Drive through

ⓑ THE PERFECT BLEND

A three-quarter backswing is more than enough for this type of shot—indeed it has its advantages in the sense that a compact swing is easier to control and can help deliver a crisp blow to the back of the ball, but you must complete that full shoulder turn, allied to the appropriate arm swing. To arrive at the ideal top-of-the-backswing position, think in terms of making a "flat shoulder turn and an upright arm swing."

Do not have a wide stance—a slightly narrow base is best

ⓒ PUNCH AND DRIVE

Hit down into the back of the ball, as though you are trying to hit a punch shot under the wind. This again reinforces the need, partly initiated in the nature of your setup, to deliver a slightly descending strike. That helps make sure that the minimum amount of grass gets trapped between the clubface and the ball. It helps you make the best possible contact.

ⓒ Descending strike

The Hybrid Chip and Run

The hybrid is much more than the default option from the fairway or rough from 150 to 200 yards (137 to 183 m). It is also an excellent chipping club, frequently used by professionals. If you have a nice lie on the closely mown green fringe and a lot of green to work with, it is a smart play that produces neat chip-and-run shots. You can nudge the ball on to the putting surface with finesse and far more consistency than a lofted wedge shot.

ⓐ CHOKE DOWN AND SET YOUR HANDS HIGH

You need to preset a few changes in your setup in order to execute the hybrid chip-and-run well. First, place the ball in the middle of your stance, with your weight slightly favoring your front foot. Second, choke down on the grip, almost to the metal—you want to avoid any wrist hinge with this shot. Then stand as close to the ball as you comfortably can, with your hands a little higher than would be the case for a regular full shot.

> If the ball is nestling in a tricky lie, the hybrid is the best choice since there is no risk of the dreaded mishit.

ⓑ Rock the shoulders

ⓒ Sweep through

Keep your feet narrower than you would normally

ⓐ Choke down

ⓑ ROCKING SHOULDERS

Now, you need to swing the club almost as you would a putter on a long-range putt across the green. Feel as though the stroke is controlled by a rocking motion of the shoulders combined with a simple arm swing. The hands should stay relatively passive in the stroke.

ⓒ SWEEPING PATH

Executed correctly, you should find that the clubhead stays relatively low to the ground, back and through. You want to feel that the clubhead almost sweeps the ball on its way with a smoothly accelerating forward swing. You should find that the ball is lofted gently forward and, because there is no backspin generated at impact, it runs out toward the hole just like a putt. You may find you overhit the shot the first few times you play it, but with practice, you will soon find it is easy to judge distance.

Fairway Metal: A Master Class

If you watch a golf tournament on television, especially a Major championship, where the golf courses tend to be set up with additional demands on accuracy as well as distance, you will see how frequently the top players rely on their fairway metals. Placement shots off the tee on tight par-4s, advancement shots on superlong par-5s, and shots into distant greens—these clubs are absolutely indispensable.

TIGER WOODS'S ANGLE OF ATTACK

The fairway metal is a different animal to the driver, but it needs very similar treatment to bring out its best qualities. The ball needs to be struck with a sweeping, shallow angle of attack. Many club golfers fail to achieve this all-important goal. They tend to think that, because the ball is sitting on the fairway and not on a tee peg, it is necessary to hit down into impact—just like an iron shot. Wrong. It needs to be swept away.

Watch Tiger. He practices a very rounded swing motion when he is shaping up to hit a fairway metal. He knows the value of that sweeping angle of attack through impact; it is how you optimize ball flight, distance, and accuracy.

Try to feel that the club works around your body in the backswing, allied to a good shoulder turn. This helps put you in the ideal position at the top of your backswing to approach the ball from the inside and on a shallow angle of attack. You will sweep the ball away, with solid contact.

Upper body rotation and a rounded swing are key when using a fairway metal

Neither hand should become dominant at any point of the swing—otherwise, a loss of clubhead control will result

Do not get greedy with this club—it is about placement, not distance

GREATEST SHOT

On the final day of the 1983 Ryder Cup at PGA National, Florida, Seve Ballesteros had driven into the fairway bunker on the 18th hole in his singles match against Fuzzy Zoeller. The situation looked lost, but Seve hit a 3-wood fully 240 yards (220 m) on to the fringe of the green, an astonishing stroke of genius, to secure an unlikely half. The US Ryder Cup captain Jack Nicklaus described it as one of the greatest shots he had ever witnessed. Praise comes no higher.

● Unbelievable Seve

▶ **USING A METAL REQUIRES** the golfer to round out their swing and sweep it away, for position play; it is how Tiger Woods generates the perfect ball flight, coupled with accuracy.

JIM FURYK'S POSITION PLAY

The fairway metal off the tee is a smart play; it gives you respectable distance and the extra loft on the face offers a greater level of accuracy than a driver. You can hit more fairways, which is a positive thing.

The key, once you have decided to hit a fairway metal off the tee, is making sure you do not try to make up the distance that in the back of your mind you know you are losing through not hitting a driver. That is an easy mistake to make, but not one made by Jim Furyk.

Furyk's swing may not be picture-perfect, but there is no one better at maintaining good rhythm and playing for position rather than for power. He believes in his swing, he knows exactly how far he hits the ball with that club, and he never pushes for more distance. That is why he hits more fairways than probably any other top player in the game.

So when you are hitting a fairway metal off the tee, think position, not power. That is the whole point of the club.

◄ **JIM FURYK MIGHT NOT HAVE THE** most elegant swing on tour, but he is renowned for his consistency. Being able to keep the ball on the fairway is one of his greatest strengths.

PAUL CASEY'S WIDE ARC

It is astonishing the distances England's Paul Casey can generate with every club in the bag. The fairway metal is no exception. This swing trait, however, disguises the real source of Casey's power. He sweeps the club away on a wide arc in the backswing and makes a superb upper-body rotation. It is a potent combination, one that any golfer would do well to try to emulate.

Relaxed hands, arms, and shoulders at address is a crucial starting point. Tension is a total killer. Casey then sweeps the club away low to the ground for the first 30 in (76 cm), and at the same time, the left shoulder starts to turn in behind the golf ball. That is the first power move. From here, the swing just flows.

He sweeps the club away on a wide arc in the backswing and makes a superb upper-body rotation.

▶ **CASEY HAS THE ABILITY** to create effective width in his backswing with a wide takeaway. This, coupled with a full shoulder turn, serves to store up power for the downswing.

Irons: The Design

Choosing a set of irons used to be a choice between two distinct options. Were you drawn to the purity and classic look of blades, or did you prefer the forgiveness of a peripherally weighted set with its trademark cavity-back? Times have changed—and immeasurably for the better as far as the golfer is concerned. The advancements in club technology mean that golfers of all levels have the potential to improve.

CAVITY-BACK IRONS

The main focus for golf club manufacturers is centered around game improvement. This is largely achieved by manipulating a club's center of gravity and weight distribution in order to optimize performance and forgiveness. In recent years, the means by which they have strived to achieve this goal has become more varied.

Innovative and more sophisticated methods in the manufacturing and forging processes mean that cavity-back iron clubheads are stronger, easier to hit, better balanced, more consistent, and more forgiving than ever before. There are so many excellent cavity-back irons on sale, especially at the premium end of the market, that selection almost comes down largely to aesthetics.

▶ **THE DESIGN OF THE CAVITY-BACK IRON** is concerned with redistributing the weight of the clubhead around the edge, leaving a cavity in the center. This weight transference means the clubhead is less likely to twist at impact with off-center strikes.

"Inverted Cone" technology ensures a high level of energy transfers from the clubhead to the ball at impact, imparting increased distance

The moderate offset of the clubhead from the hosel promotes a relatively square face at impact, which leads to improved ball control

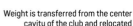

Weight is transferred from the center cavity of the club and relocated around the perimeter—the essence of cavity-back technology

IN THE MAKING

As recently as the 1960s, many touring professionals spent their time between tournaments working in their club shop, making and refining their own golf clubs and servicing the needs of the club's members. Today the world's leading professionals receive around-the-clock service from golf equipment manufacturers and are given various sets of irons tailored specifically to their needs. Times have changed.

● Sam Snead in his pro shop, 1949

Grooves should be kept free from dirt and grass to maximize backspin

Steel shafts are usually standard for irons, especially for talented golfers, as they stress accuracy over distance

▲ **IRON FACE**

MULTI-MATERIALS AND MOVABLE WEIGHTS

Multi-material clubhead construction is a new technology. Some irons now feature lightweight titanium clubfaces, allowing more of the clubhead's weight to be located around the outer edges, specifically the sole of the club. Forgiveness is the major payoff.

Other companies adopt a similar principle, involving specially constructed metal composite inserts, designed to help create a low center of gravity and high launch angle.

Movable weights are another method used by designers of club heads. Progressive tungsten weights, which alter the playing characteristics of the club depending on loft, are the big selling point on some of the 21st century's newest irons. This innovation offers benefits in terms of the level of forgiveness and the optimization of the ball's launch angle.

Two shock absorption discs in the back of the clubhead produce a softer feel off the face at impact

Tungsten-nickel weight lowers the center of gravity for a relatively high launch angle and reduced spin

▲ **CAVITY-BACK IRONS** such as these are typical of the latest developments in club design. They feature a "WS system"—essentially a tungsten weight and shock absorption discs—as well as a cavity-back element.

The muscle-back design (a partial cavity-back) helps concentrate the club's center of gravity in the middle of the clubhead

Clubhead is finished in double nickel chrome plating for a durable and classic appearance

▲ **BLADED IRONS AND MUSCLE-BACKS** are aesthetically pleasing but difficult for beginners to use due to a lack of peripheral weighting.

THE BEST OF BOTH WORLDS

For those who cannot decide between blades or cavity-backed irons, there is another option known as a "progressive" set, which provides the best elements of both. The long irons, for years the bane of many an amateur golfer's life, feature a cavity-back design and slight offset to help you flight your shots properly; these also offer a good level of forgiveness.

However, rather than the whole set of irons featuring the same degree of cavity-back, the progressive set is different. Basically, as the loft increases, each club is progressively more bladelike in design and appearance and features less offset.

It is the best of both worlds. The cavity-backed long irons have a slightly bigger hitting area, and the design is such that it goes through light rough a lot better than a traditional long iron. Also, the offset head helps square the face at impact so there is less of a tendency to slice, yet you do not have to compromise with the short irons—you still get the enhanced feel and playability of a blade at that end of the set.

TRADITIONAL BLADES

As well as the revolution in the design of game-improvement irons, there is also a wide choice of blades on the market. The leading manufacturers have in recent years successfully upgraded the forging process of the mild carbon steel typically used in the construction of blade clubheads. The purity of the forged steel results in supreme consistency and performance throughout the set to help optimize distance control.

The muscle-back appearance of 21st-century blades is an attractive design, but it also has a practical application, helping to concentrate the clubhead's center of gravity in the middle of the blade for solid hits and neutral shot bias throughout the set. It allows the more accomplished player a greater degree of shotmaking control, to work the ball both ways through the air.

For many players, there is nothing to beat a top-grade set of blades. These clubs are not very suitable for beginners, however; a player needs to be able to strike the ball well to get the best out of them.

THE PERFECT BLEND

The progressive set of irons is a great innovation in club design. By combining elements of the traditional cavity-back and classic blade in the same set, a player benefits from a cavity-back with the long irons yet retains the pleasing features of the blade with the short irons.

8-iron, 9-iron, and pitching wedge are bladelike

Medium irons (5-, 6-, and 7-irons) have a partial cavity-back

Long irons feature a pronounced cavity-back

IRON LOFT AND LENGTH

Loft is the essence of creative play on the golf course. If all clubs were of the same loft, even the best players in the world would struggle to shoot low scores. There is a distinct variation between the loft of a 3-iron (approximately 22 degrees) and a pitching wedge (approximately 48 degrees). Similarly, the length of the shaft in a standard set of 9-irons differs—longer shafts are better for distance; shorter shafts more suited to precision play.

▶ **BLADED IRONS AND MUSCLE-BACKS** are aesthetically pleasing but difficult for beginners to use due to a lack of peripheral weighting.

▼ **THE SHAFT LENGTH** of a 3-iron is approximately 4 in (10 cm) longer than a pitching wedge, with increments of half an inch for all clubs in between.

A 3-iron is 38.75 in (98.5 cm) long—a longer shaft promotes distance

A 6-iron has a shaft length of 37.25 in (94.5 cm)

A 9-iron is 35.7 5in (91 cm) long—a shorter shaft is conducive to precision play

22 degrees of loft

25 degrees of loft

28 degrees of loft

Loft is calculated as the angle between the face and center of the hosel

Leading edge is lower to the ground at the bottom end of the set

▲ 3- IRON

▲ 4- IRON

▲ 5- IRON

IRON DISTANCES

The distance that a player can hit a golf ball with irons of different lofts varies somewhat according to the player's swing and physical strength. However, there is one factor that does not vary— a long iron will have a lower trajectory and carry through the air approximately 80 yards (73 m) more than a pitching wedge.

A ball struck with a pitching wedge flies on a steep trajectory and lands softly

A shot with a 6-iron flies on a medium trajectory and carries approximately 150 yards (137 m)

A ball struck with a 3-iron flies on a shallow trajectory and bounces forward on landing

DISTANCE IN YARDS

		PW	9	8	7	6	5	4	3
110		130	130		150	150	160	170	170	180	190
	120		130	140	140	150	160	160	170	180	180	190	200

32 degrees
of loft

36 degrees
of loft

40 degrees
of loft

44 degrees
of loft

48 degrees
of loft

▲ 6- IRON   ▲ 7- IRON   ▲ 8- IRON   ▲ 9- IRON   ▲ PITCHING WEDGE

CUSTOM FITTING

Custom fitting provides the player with clubs tailored exactly to their specification. Fitting the perfect set is determined by various dynamic factors such as swing speed, angle of attack, launch angle, and so on, but it also takes account of various static measurements such as height, the size of a golfer's hands, and other considerations such as age and sex. The key measurements in the perfect set are as follows:

● **Length**: The ideal length of a club shaft is determined by a player's height and, to a lesser degree, the distance from the tips of their fingers to the ground. Shafts can be shortened or lengthened accordingly.

◀ **AN ARRAY** of different clubheads can be fitted to an equally diverse number of shafts to find the perfect combination for a player.

▲ **CLUB TECHNICIANS** are constantly on hand at major tournaments to make any adjustments required to the equipment supplied by the manufacturers to the professional players they sponsor.

● **Lie angle**: This is the angle formed by the shaft and the bottom edge of the clubhead. Broadly speaking, short golfers require a flat-lie angle on their irons; tall golfers require an upright-lie angle.

● **Shaft type**: There will typically be a range of shafts available from each manufacturer, with different weight, flex, and bend profile characteristics. As a rule, the stronger the hitter, the stiffer the shaft required.

● **Grip size**: Grips should be the correct size so that the hands can work properly during the swing. If grips are too thin, the hands tend to be overactive, which causes problems. If grips are too thick, then it can lead to inactive hands where there is no zip to the swing in the hitting area.

The Iron Shot

There is an art to great iron play. The clubs vary enormously in terms of loft, shaft length, and of course the distance the ball flies, yet they are all categorized in the same way. The great iron player must be able to cope with all these elements—control their ball flight, gauge distance, and control spin—using clubs as diverse as a 3-iron and a 9-iron. This is an art that can be learned, and every golfer can quickly improve their iron play. It is just a question of knowing where to look and how best to turn theory into practice.

UNDERSTANDING BALL POSITION

Ball position is a fundamental aspect of iron play. Any confusion or lack of awareness of this part of the setup can, and probably will, have dire consequences on the state of your approach play.

a Here is a useful rule to work on. Play your wedge shots with the ball in the middle of your stance; then move the ball progressively farther forward in your stance as the club gets longer. As a guide, the 5-iron is just over a ball's-width forward of center; the 3-iron farther forward still, inside your left heel.

The reason for doing this is that it helps encourage the correct angle of attack as the clubhead approaches the ball—relatively steep with the wedge and progressively more shallow as the club gets longer. It is one of the keys to solid iron play.

b In terms of how far away from the ball you stand, again depends on the club you are using. Quite simply, you stand progressively closer to the ball as the shaft of the club gets shorter. Use the posture drill at the start of the section of fairway metals to help you determine the distance you stand from the ball with every club in the bag.

a Ball position varies by club   **b** Club length is key

LEARN GOOD DISTANCE CONTROL

Good distance control is the foundation of successful iron play. What you need to do is try to establish your own personal yardages for each club. Use your time on the practice ground to establish how far you hit each club—on the fly, that is—by hitting 20 balls and discarding the longest five and the shortest five. That middle cluster of 10 balls represents your average distance with that club. Write down a number for each club. When you are on the golf course, get into the habit of using a yardage chart. That professional approach will pay off. Then learn to control your swing.

c Always make a smooth, well-balanced swing. You still need to commit to the shot through impact, but the overall motion of your swing must be within your own physical limits. Most top players swing at about 80 to 85 percent of full power. It is the only way you can achieve the necessary consistency of strike and distance control.

WRAP THE SHAFT AROUND YOUR NECK

Anyone who tells you that the follow-through makes no difference to the quality of your iron shots is missing the point. Of course, the ball is gone and on its way, but if you have in your mind's eye a positive image of how you want to finish the swing, you can improve the execution of your iron shots.

d Here is a good image to have in mind. Wrap the shaft of the club around the back of your neck as part of a balanced finish to your swing. What this does is encourage a really positive release of the club into and through the ball. You will hit consistently better iron shots as a result.

c Poised follow-through

d Practice with purpose and make a smooth swing

SWING SECRETS

Attention is focused on the back of the ball

Right arm stays close to side coming into impact

Right knee moves in toward the ball

Left knee stays braced and does not collapse

ROCK STEADY
Head stays behind the ball, representing a fixed axis point for the swing

SHOULDER LINE
Right shoulder stays "under" to promote good swing path into impact

HANDS LEAD THE CLUBHEAD

It is common for many amateurs to flick at the ball with their iron shots, in the belief that this will help the ball into the air and lead to better shots. It does not; it is one of the worst faults in the game.

Look at the top players. Their hands lead the clubhead into the ball, generating a downward angle of attack. The key aspect to have in mind is making sure that there is a degree of forward lean in the shaft at the moment of impact. This compresses the golf ball and means that your shots will have a much more effective trajectory.

KEEP THE ARC
Left arm straightens to maintain the arc of the swing

CLEAR A PATH
Left hip clears out of the way to make room for a free swing of the arms

DESCENDING BLOW
Club approaches the golf ball on a slightly descending angle of attack

Shaping Shots

Most amateurs assume that intentionally shaping shots in different ways through the air is a game best left to the top players, but that need not necessarily be the case. Simple rules can help you shape shots—either with a draw or a fade, high or low—and anyone with ambition to improve their game can quickly develop these skills. It all comes down to practice and application. You will find that there are many on-course situations in which your game will benefit hugely.

HOW TO HIT A DRAW

Shaping a draw involves moving the ball through the air from right to left for the right-hander and left to right for the left-hander.

ⓐ Aim the clubface straight at the target, as if you are hitting a straight shot. Then align your feet in the direction that you want your ball to start off, without adjusting the clubhead.

ⓑ Now make a normal backswing following the line of your feet.

ⓒ Through the hitting area, pay extra attention to rolling your right hand over your left to encourage a good release of the clubhead.

ⓓ Then follow through to a well-balanced finish. The opposing angles at address and the resulting path of attack and clubface positioning at impact, impart the necessary sidespin and cause the ball to start off in one direction and curve away through the air.

ⓐ Aim at the target   ⓑ Swing normally   ⓓ Follow through

Your weight shifts normally from the back foot to the front

ⓒ Roll the hands

HOW TO HIT A FADE

Hitting a fade involves moving the ball through the air from left to right for the right-hander and right to left for the left-hander.

ⓐ Aim the clubface where you want the ball to finish—that is, straight at the target. Then align your feet in the direction you want the ball to start, while maintaining the position of the clubhead.

ⓑ Make a normal swing along your aim lines.

ⓒ As you approach impact, delay the release of your hands—the opposite of rolling your hands, shown above—to make sure that the face stays open through the hitting area.

ⓓ Proceed with your follow-through to a balanced finish. With this shot and the draw, the key is to practice it enough that you can control the amount of movement through the air. Your ultimate aim is to be able to shape the ball to suit different situations.

Make your usual full body turn

ⓐ Aim at the target   ⓒ Delay the hands   ⓓ Hold your finish

ⓑ Swing normally

a Ball back, weight forward

Backswing reaches to only three-quarters of its normal length

c Stay back

d Punchy follow-through

b Abbreviated backswing

HOW TO HIT IT LOW

For the low shot, where you need to keep the ball under an obstacle, such as a tree branch, a couple of adjustments at address are essential.

a To begin with, choke down on the grip an inch or two. Place the ball farther back in your stance and hold your hands ahead of the ball; this de-lofts the clubface. You are effectively presetting a lower-than-normal ball flight. Place extra weight on your front foot.

b There is no need to make fancy moves in your swing. Make a three-quarter length backswing, with a full shoulder turn.

c In the downswing, try to feel as though your chest "covers" the ball through the hitting area. You should drive the club through low to the ground, with your hands very much ahead of the point of impact. Cultivate a sense that the clubhead stays low to the ground through the ball.

d The abbreviated follow-through is a sign of a controlled, well-balanced, and punchy swing.

Do not be tempted to hit the ball harder. Just hit it better. Dead-solid contact is the real key with this shot. Remember, a lower ball flight will result in extra run of the ball upon landing, so allow for this when choosing your club.

b Get the hands high

c Hold your weight back

d Balanced finish

Hands are level with the ball at address

Through the swing, weight remains on the right side longer

a Ball forward, hands back

HOW TO HIT IT HIGH

Hitting a high ball is probably not a shot you will need to call on all that frequently, but if you have an obstruction in your way, such as a tree, or you need to attack a very tight pin position over a bunker, this is a useful shot to know.

Drastic changes to the setup and swing are not advisable. It is far better in this case to keep things subtle.

a You need a higher-than-normal ball flight, so it is necessary to preset a little more loft on the clubface at address by positioning the ball farther forward in the stance. Rather than the hands being ahead of the ball, as was the case with the low shot, this time place them level with the ball.

b Now make a slightly more upright backswing, getting the hands high at the top.

c The feeling through impact is of staying behind the ball, your weight just hanging on the right side a fraction longer than normal.

d With the ball on its way, proceed through to a well-balanced finish with the weight slightly more on the right side than usual.

Iron Shots: A Master Class

The simplest yardstick of good iron play is the number of greens hit in regulation. The players at the top of the rankings hit as many as 80 percent of the greens they aim at. As with other areas of the game, there is much we can learn from the professionals, but there is more to great iron play than hitting greens. Strategy comes into play, as does the ability to move the ball through the air and to hit shots pin high.

Keep the clubhead online with the target through the shot

The right arm should be fully extended through impact

The legs provide a solid platform for the powerful unwinding of the body and a free swing of the arms

ERNIE ELS'S EXTENDED ARMS

Ernie Els is one of the greatest ball strikers in the game, his seemingly effortless and beautifully rhythmic swing disguising serious power and great compression of the golf ball at impact. It is one of the many reasons why his iron shots fly so pure, straight, and far.

There is much in Ernie's swing that every golfer can learn from, such as the way his arms are fully extended as he swings the clubhead into and through the ball. This helps him carry good speed into the ball and deliver that all-important descending blow.

To emulate Ernie's positive move through impact, visualize your right arm extending fully toward the target and the clubhead traveling low to the ground after the ball. This will encourage you to swing freely through the ball and extend your arms like Ernie does.

◀ **THE ELS STYLE IS LEGENDARY** and the envy of many players. His seemingly effortless swing and rhythmic tempo are complemented by the way he extends his arms through the ball.

THE GREATEST IRON SHOT

Sergio García was playing in the final round of the 1999 USPGA when he hit an iron shot of pure genius. His drive on the 16th came to rest against the roots of a large oak tree, 189 yards (173 m) from the pin. Initially he thought he would have to chip out, but then he saw an opening. He grabbed a 6-iron, opened the face, and hit it as hard as he could with his eyes closed. When he opened them, he could see it going exactly where he wanted and slicing. It made the green, some 35 ft (10 m) from the hole, and he almost holed the putt for birdie.

García goes for broke on the 16th

COLIN MONTGOMERIE'S CONTROL

Scotland's Colin Montgomerie, a record-breaking eight-time winner of the European Tour's Order of Merit, may not have the most conventional-looking golf swing, but few in the modern era could be said to have better controlled the distance of their iron shots into greens. Monty has hit the ball pin high probably more times than any golfer in the last 30 years.

One of Monty's great strengths, which is something that every amateur or club golfer can easily carry into their own game, is the way his swing maintains its rhythm no matter which club he is using, from the 3-iron to the 9-iron—specifically, the way he maintains the same rhythm in that crucial transition from finishing his backswing to starting his downswing. He does not snatch the club down; he gives himself time. Therein lies a lesson for every golfer. Keep that first move down silky-smooth.

▶ **WHILE THERE MAY BE FLAWS** in his character, in terms of his temper and his concentration, the same cannot be said of Monty's iron play, which is smooth, free-flowing, and accurate.

▼ **SORENSTAM HAD A POLICY** of attacking the pin wherever possible and rarely laid up to get out of trouble. Her approach play was considered, and she made very few mistakes.

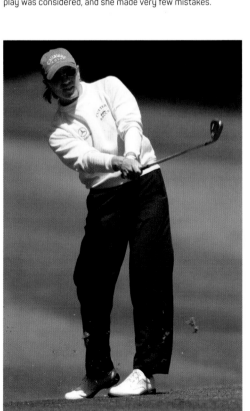

ANNIKA SORENSTAM'S GOOD ROTATION

Annika Sorenstam is the greatest woman golfer of the last 30 years and certainly one of the greatest players in golf history. She has set new standards in the women's game—much like Tiger Woods has in the men's game. She is very much the complete golfer and has no real weakness to speak of.

Sorenstam has one little quirk to her swing, however, which is unconventional. She turns her head markedly to the left as she delivers the clubhead to the ball. It is perhaps a dangerous move to mimic precisely, as every player will have a unique element to their swing that works just for them, but there are elements of this that would help improve many golfers' impact position. It is a case of taking a little, rather than a lot, of what Annika does and using it to the benefit of your own swing.

With a subtle turn of the head, Annika encourages good rotation of the upper body through the ball; it also helps her clear the left side out of the way, and in doing so, she gives herself enough room to enable her arms to swing freely.

Sorenstam has one little quirk to her swing, however, which is unconventional. She turns her head markedly to the left as she delivers the clubhead to the ball.

Sloping Lies

No golf course is completely flat. In fact, the only time you can guarantee a totally level lie is on the tee and that accounts for a small percentage of the shots you will play in a round of golf. Whether uphill, downhill, or sidehill, you have to be able to cope with various sloping lies because the fact is you will face them every time you set foot on the golf course.

BALL ABOVE YOUR FEET

The first thing to understand when the ball lies above the level of your feet is that you will have a tendency to pull the ball down the slope. There are a few swing changes to adopt to compensate for this.

a First, aim to the right of your target. Then, choke down on the grip. This shortens the club and thus compensates for the fact that the ball is effectively higher than it would be on a level lie. Also, stand a little more upright with slightly less knee flex.

b The combined effects of the slope and the nature of your stance will encourage a slightly more rounded swing plane—the feeling being that you are swinging the club more around your body. That is how it should feel; just try to maintain your original height and spine angle as best as you can.

c Then rotate your body through to a finish, all the while maintaining your balance.

a Aim right, choke down, stand tall

c Keep your balance

Maintain solid foundations through the swing

b Maintain your height

BALL BELOW YOUR FEET

Once again, the slope influences the ball flight and you must accept that the awkward nature of this lie and your stance tends to limit your body rotation.

a The ball will tend to fly right, so aim to the left of the target. At address, bend from the hips more than you would normally, to get yourself down to the level of the ball. Plenty of knee flex is also advisable, as is a wider stance, to give you more stability.

b Due to your inhibited turn, your backswing will be more arms-dominated and therefore shorter and more upright. You will generate less power, so club-up accordingly, and maintain a nice smooth rhythm.

c Swing through as freely as possible within the confines of the slope.

The key to this shot is maintaining your original height and spine angle until the ball is struck. Any tendency to gain height, an easy mistake given the nature of the situation, will result in a topped or thinned shot.

Grip the club toward the end of the shaft

b Shorter, upright swing

c Make a free follow-through

a Aim left, bend knees and hips

a Align shoulders with slope

c Keep your head down

b Maintain your balance

Steady backswing works in harmony with the slope

BALL ON AN UPSLOPE

This is probably the easiest of all the shots from sloping lies, because there is a sense of being able to launch the ball into the air. However, there are a few ways to make sure you play it well.

a Your right shoulder should be markedly lower than your left and your weight favoring the back foot. Adopt a slightly wider stance and aim right of the target, because the ball tends to hook from an upslope.

b Try to swing in harmony with the slope and maintain your balance. Do not get thrown back onto your right foot or lean into the slope.

c Keep your weight stable and your head down through impact. Let the natural momentum of your swing pull you into the finish position.

UNDERSTANDING LAUNCH ANGLES

Club selection is not as straightforward when you are playing from an upslope or a downslope. The main thing to keep in mind is the change in the initial launch angle. On a downslope, it will be significantly lower, so you can afford to take less club—say, a 6-iron instead of a 5-iron. On an upslope, the opposite is true. The launch angle is higher, which means you can take more club—for instance, a 7-iron instead of an 8-iron. Do not fight that slope effect—just go with it. Remember: less club on a downslope, more club on an upslope.

a Ball back in stance

b Early wrist hinge

c Stay down through impact

Keep your head down through impact

Try your best to maintain your balance throughout the swing

BALL ON A DOWNSLOPE

This is the toughest of all the sloping lies, because the downslope gives you the sense that it is very difficult to get the ball airborne. It is not imagined. The nature of a downslope means that you are deprived of loft, and it is all too easy to scuttle the ball straight along the ground.

a Make sure your shoulders and hips are as close to parallel with the slope as possible—your left shoulder feeling lower than the right. Place the ball back in your stance. This is a very important point. You will tend to want to put the ball forward in your stance, as it feels natural to generate some elevation from there, but this will prevent you from getting the ball airborne.

b Pick the club up a little steeper in your backswing with an early wrist hinge. This sets the club in a position from which you can more easily generate the necessary steep angle of attack into impact. Make sure you maintain your weight distribution all the way to the top of the backswing.

c As you swing down into impact, try to feel as though you are chasing after the ball down the slope, staying well down through impact so that the clubhead follows the contours of the ground. Never try to help the ball into the air.

Problem Shots

When you play a round of golf, you are taking on Mother Nature, a skilled golf course architect, and the capricious nature of the game itself. The accomplished player knows how to cope with the varied challenges that are thrown at them. Whether you are battling with a gusty wind, trying to excavate your ball from clinging rough, or have found a bunker with your drive, there are ways you can use the elements or improve your chances of recovery.

USE THE WIND, DO NOT FIGHT IT

The wind is an ever-present challenge virtually every time you play golf. Whether it is merely a gentle breeze or a strong and gusting wind, you have to know how to play it.

Playing into the wind, you should take a bigger club and swing it easier; the ball flight will penetrate the wind far more effectively. Do not make the common mistake of taking the same club and just trying to hit it harder—that never works.

When playing downwind, take less club and again swing easier. Do not take the same club and try to ease up on the shot; you will probably mishit it. Also, consider taking a 3-wood off the tee rather than a driver. The extra height will allow you to benefit more from the tailwind and thus gain distance.

ⓐ Playing with a crosswind, tour professionals will often work shots into the wind—for instance, hit a draw into a left-to-right wind—as they feel it gives them more control over distance and spin. This is the advanced option. Most times, however, it is easier to use the wind rather than fight it. In a right-to-left wind, simply shift your aim focus to the right of the target. Then hit a straight shot and let the wind do the rest for you.

ⓐ Aim right and use the crosswind

PLAYING OUT OF THE ROUGH

In the rough, the main problem is grass getting trapped between the clubface and ball. This drains the power out of the shot and loses you distance. The key is to train a steeper angle of attack into impact, as this gives you the best possible contact with the golf ball, which leads to a more "normal" iron shot.

ⓑ Put the ball back in the middle of your stance, with your hands ahead of the ball. Hinge the wrists a little sooner in the backswing.

ⓒ Hit down into the back of the ball, with your hands leading the clubhead through impact, and make sure you make a full follow-through.

> The key is to train a steeper angle of attack into impact, as this gives you the best possible contact.

ⓑ Hands ahead, break wrists early

ⓒ Steep angle of attack, full follow-through

THE LONG BUNKER SHOT

Rule No. 1 from any fairway bunker is to take a club with sufficient loft to clear the front lip. If it so happens that the club has the distance to also reach the green, consider that a bonus. Clean contact is everything with this shot, because sand soaks up the energy in the swing and, therefore, even slightly heavy contact results in catastrophic loss of distance.

a Choke down on the grip about an inch. This will hold the clubhead up off the sand and help promote a clean contact with the ball.

b Shuffle your feet into the sand to give yourself a secure footing. This will lower the base of your swing, so choking down on the club is key.

c Make a smooth, well-balanced swing and make sure you hit down into the back of the ball instead of trying to help it into the air.

d You should strike the back of the ball, not the sand. If you catch the sand before the ball, it will feel "heavy."

a Shorten the club

b Shuffle down

c Strike the ball, not the sand

A secure footing will enable you to make a balanced swing

GREAT PRACTICE

Finding yourself in a fairway bunker during the course of a normal round of golf might rightly be considered a negative, but you can use this scenario very much to your advantage in a practice environment.

One of Vijay Singh's favorite practice drills is hitting full iron shots from a fairway bunker. It is a wonderful way to train clean, pure contact with the golf ball. Vijay, of course, is one of the best ball strikers in the world, so if it works for him ...

d Make a smooth swing

Wedges: The Design

As recently as the 1990s, the scope of the wedge in any golfer's bag was very narrow. There was simply the pitching wedge and the sand wedge. If a player wanted to produce extra loft on a shot, they had to open the clubface and improvise. Today, these two staple clubs have been largely replaced in the market by a series of wedges ranging from 52 to 64 degrees and offering players of all levels greater versatility.

PRECISION TOOL

Although it does not promise booming tee shots, like the driver, or holed putts and tumbling scores, like the putter, the wedge does have its own charms. It is a precision tool, and it wins its place in a golfer's bag by offering an alluring combination of feel, high spin, and maximum control. From a playing perspective, that is plenty for any golfer to get excited about. Perhaps it is just that the wedge does not get the hard sell, like drivers, putters, and hybrids. This is partly because, for designers, there is a limited window of opportunity in terms of how they can maximize the performance of a wedge. A club's performance is, therefore, influenced by more basic considerations, such as the groove configuration and the type of metal used. None of this has quite the same "tech appeal" as "moment of inertia" and "center of gravity."

These considerations matter a great deal. A large percentage of the shots you play in a round of golf are from inside 100 yards (91 m). Aside from putts, then, it means the wedges in your bag get plenty of action.

▶ **THE DESIGN OF WEDGES** tends to be more bladelike in appearance than long irons because they are easier to hit. The sole is more rounded and the leading edge higher off the ground. Peripheral weighting is of secondary importance to feel and the pursuit of precision striking.

Black nickel finish is softer than chrome and affords the player more feel around the greens

The rounded sole helps the player execute shots from sand or lush grass

Clubhead is made of grain flow forged carbon steel for distance control and a pure feel

IN THE GROOVE

The R&A and USGA, who together govern golf worldwide, set rules relating to grooves in golf clubs, including the width, depth, and distance between each groove. Spin is the name of the game with wedges so club manufacturers take groove sizes to the extremes of legality. Amateur golfers who struggle to spin the ball probably wish there were no restrictions.

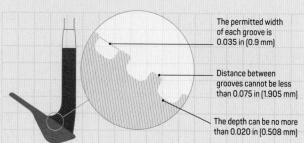

The permitted width of each groove is 0.035 in (0.9 mm)

Distance between grooves cannot be less than 0.075 in (1.905 mm)

The depth can be no more than 0.020 in (0.508 mm)

The loft of a pitching wedge, measured from the center of the hosel, is approximately 46 degrees

Rounded sole with relatively low bounce angle

▲ **TOE-END VIEW**

BELIEVING THE SPIN

High spin rate is the key selling point of any wedge. The finish on the face of the club and the groove pattern are both designed to create friction when the clubface meets the ball, and to produce increased spin. Grooves on the faces of the modern wedge are so effective that professional golfers are able to generate amazing amounts of spin even from the rough, although of course the strike needs still to be precise.

HEAD CONSTRUCTION

The type of metal used in the construction of the wedge clubhead has not only a practical application—in the sense that some metals are softer than others and therefore offer greater potential for feel—but also an aesthetic quality. The classic chrome finish is still the most popular option, although a light satin finish is also available as, too, is an "oil can" finish, which eliminates glare and also gives a slightly softer feel.

Other companies offer a "rusty" or "vintage" finish. The effect is the same; these clubheads rust over time, affording the player greater control. There are also jet-black clubheads in many manufacturers' wedge range. The choices are wide; the decision is an entirely personal one.

▼ WEDGES COME IN A RANGE of finishes—from chrome and black to copper, "oil can," and rusty.

Copper and bronze finishes are favored because they have a softer feel than other metals

A jet-black finish is achieved via a complex oxidization process. The effect is to reduce glare at address

▲ GROOVE DETAIL

► BY CARRYING A RANGE of wedges in a set, players give themselves different options on the course. Players should carry at least two—or ideally three—wedges.

The lob wedge is typically the most lofted club in the bag

Every golfer should carry a sand wedge (56 degrees)

The "gap" wedge fills the distance gap between pitching wedge and sand wedge

LOFTY MATTERS

No golfer should ever carry just one wedge in their set. Two is the absolute minimum; three is advisable. In terms of "building" a set of three wedges, the key is to make sure you have an evenly spaced loft progression, aiming for approximately four degrees between each club. Use your 9-iron as a starting point and work your way up to whatever maximum loft you feel is appropriate for your needs.

The most lofted club in many golfers' bags is a 60-degree lob wedge, which is sensible. Phil Mickelson has been known to carry a 64-degree wedge, which is probably too extreme for the average player.

THE WEDGE BOUNCE

Bounce is the term used to describe the relationship between the leading edge of the clubhead and the sole. It determines how easy it is to strike the ball effectively from a given lie. The bounce angle is the distance off the ground of the leading edge when the sole is at address. Different bounce angles suit different shots, so when you are buying a wedge, it is essential to consult your local pro and get a bounce angle that is fit for your purpose, whether that is to play from closely mown grass (low bounce) or a bunker (high bounce).

Low bounce angle of 0–10 degrees

Tight lie on firm ground

High bounce angle of 10–18 degrees

Lie in soft sand or lush grass

● Low bounce angle   ● High bounce angle

The Pitch Shot

One of the greatest skills you can have as a golfer is the ability to pitch well. On par-4s, it helps you save par if you have been in trouble off the tee. On par-5s, it can help set up birdie chances when the green is out of reach in two. That ability to turn three shots into two will have a dramatic effect on your average scoring. It is a wonderful skill to have and one that is definitely worth working on.

a Setup secrets

SMOOTHLY DOES IT

There is no place for ego in the world of pitch shots. It is not about how far you can hit your pitching wedge; it is about how close the ball finishes to the flag. That is the only meaningful measure of success. For that reason, leave aside any thoughts of trying to force your pitch shots. A smoothly accelerating swing is far more effective. If you feel you need to hit a pitch shot hard to reach the target, then you are using the wrong club.

a FOUR SETUP ESSENTIALS

Poor quality pitching often stems from a poor setup. Here are four steps to a better setup and more successful pitching action.

- Make sure that your feet are only slightly open and that your shoulders are square.
- Choke down on the grip. This gives you maximum feel and clubhead control as you swing.
- Put the ball back in your stance and hold your hands forward.
- Keep your chin up. This simple move tends to lead to a better posture, with the spine angle more erect, and it gives you space under your chin to turn your left shoulder. Try to feel as though you are almost looking down your nose at the golf ball.

b MAINTAIN THE TRIANGLE

The wedge swing is often a difficult one to master, partly because a lot of amateurs view this shot as less than full and therefore assume they have to do something different. The most common tendency is to get a little too "handsy" in the swing, with the body almost going to sleep. That leads to poor strikes and distance control.

This may not be a power shot, but you should still endeavor to make the perfect blend of arm swing and body turn as you start the club away from the ball. A useful swing thought is to visualize the triangle formed by the shoulders and the arms then to maintain that for the first 30 in (75 cm) of the backswing. Let your body turn in harmony with the swinging arms, your left shoulder moving behind the ball as the backswing continues.

c CRISP CONTACT

The ideal pitch shot is one where the ball rises steeply to the top of its flight and then lands softly with little or no run. With this in mind, on the downswing, you should encourage a slightly descending angle of attack. The goal is crisp, ball-turf contact and lots of backspin. However, you must not quit on the shot at impact; this will result in too large a divot and a loss of distance. Instead stay focused on making a positive swing through the ball to a neat finish.

b Keep your hands, arms, and body in unison during the backswing   **c** Make crisp ball-turf contact and hit through the shot

SWING SECRETS

Position the ball in the middle of your stance

Point the butt end of the club at the ground

Hands lead the clubhead into impact

Head stays over the point of impact to stabilize swing

Keep your left arm fairly straight

SHAFT ANGLE
Take the club back just beyond the vertical position

LOW HANDS
The hands swing to shoulder-height in the backswing then through to shoulder height in the follow-through

HANDS AND CHEST
To help promote a synchronized golf swing, think of the hands staying in front of the chest throughout

BODY ROTATION
Body rotates in harmony with the arm swing

NARROW STANCE
Legs are only slightly apart, creating a narrow stance

SHOULDER-TO-SHOULDER SWING

One of the most common mistakes that amateurs make when hitting pitch shots is to make a full swing and try to hit the ball too hard. The ball tends to balloon into the air, with no control of spin or trajectory.

Remember, pitch shots are all about control. It is not a contest of how far you can hit it. So think in terms of making a "shoulder-to-shoulder swing"—that is, the hands travel to shoulder height in the backswing and shoulder height in the follow-through.

Your only other focus should be on maintaining a smooth rhythm in your downswing and a sense of "natural acceleration" into and through impact. This encourages a sweet and consistent strike, making it easier for you to judge line, length, and spin.

Pitching: A Master Class

The great pitchers in golf can control the spin of their shots, the trajectory, the distance, and the accuracy. It is why, faced with 100 yards (91 m) or less, they will more often than not get down in just two shots. Many amateurs, on the other hand, will tend to miss greens with pitch shots and often take three, even four shots, from 100 yards (91 m) and in. By studying the best players, you too can learn to pitch like a pro.

Keep a firm left arm
through impact

Hands lead the
clubhead into the ball

Focus on the
back of the ball
for solid ball-turf
contact

LUKE DONALD'S OPEN CLUBFACE

On most pitch shots, it is advisable to adopt a slightly open clubface at address. The reason being, it is easier to control your ball flight and have some finesse in your game if there is some loft on the clubface. Also, it allows you to commit to striking down and through the shot, without the fear of overshooting the green.

Look at the greatest pitchers of the ball—players such as England's Luke Donald. His swing is blessed with a wonderful sense of rhythm and timing right through the bag. It does not matter if he is pitching from 80 yards (73 m) or half that distance; he always commits to the shot fully through impact.

Keep in mind that it is not a hard hit—rather, a positive and committed strike delivered with a sense of the arms and body working together. It is controlled.

◀ **A GOOD PITCHING ACTION** affords you the chance to hit the ball close and save strokes on your score. With an action that commits fully to the shot, Luke Donald has one of the best in the game.

THE GREATEST PITCH SHOT

The 1995 Ryder Cup at Oak Hill was a typically close contest. What became evident as the last day progressed was that the singles match between Nick Faldo and Curtis Strange would probably be pivotal. The pair came to the 18th hole all square, and, having driven into deep rough, Faldo had punched his ball out to within 100 yards (91 m) of the green. Faldo hit a sublime pitch to 5 ft (2 m). He holed the putt for par, Curtis made bogey, and the Ryder Cup was soon in European hands again, after the 1993 defeat at The Belfry.

Faldo's pitch wins the Ryder Cup

RETIEF GOOSEN'S ANGLE OF ATTACK

Retief Goosen is very much his own man in the sense that he did not have a swing coach for much of his career, but that has not stopped him from developing one of the soundest and most admired swings in the game. His pitching action is a joy to watch, and, naturally, it is blessed with one of the key requirements of a successful technique—namely, a relatively steep angle of attack coming into the ball that pinches the ball cleanly, thus generating lots of spin and optimum control of distance.

Here is a useful swing thought to help you emulate "The Goose." As you play the shot, imagine hitting the ball under a park bench right in front of you. This encourages a downward strike, with the hands leading the clubhead into the ball. Try it in your next practice session. It helps get you into a much better impact position, and consequently you will strike the ball with far greater authority.

▶ **BY ADOPTING A STEEP ANGLE OF ATTACK** on the downswing, Goosen generates good backspin and distance control. It is one of the attributes that has made him a two-time US Open champion.

▼ **DECELERATION INTO IMPACT** is one of the worst faults among amateur golfers. In contrast, all the world's best players, including Thomas Bjørn, accelerate into the ball for better pitching.

THOMAS BJØRN'S ACCELERATION

It has been proven by short-game guru Dave Pelz that an accelerating clubhead is far less prone to mishits. On pitch shots, a positive hit is required, with good acceleration through impact. There is no better exponent than Dane Thomas Bjørn, a wonderful pitcher of the golf ball; his action through the ball is sublime.

Think along these lines. The length of your backswing should always be such that you can accelerate smoothly through impact to send the ball the required distance. Too short a backswing and you need to force the hit; too long a backswing means you have to decelerate to not hit the ball too far.

There is no better exponent than Dane Thomas Bjørn, a wonderful pitcher of the ball; his action through the ball is sublime.

The Chip Shot

It would be nice to think that we could all one day play to a standard where we hardly ever missed a green, thus eliminating the need to play any chip shots at all, but the game of golf just is not like that. Even the best players in the world miss greens—on average, perhaps three or four a round. Part of the reason they are so successful in the game is that they can so often clean up with a neat chip and a single putt, or often, just a chip. It is a wonderful skill to have, one that every golfer should spend some time working on.

ⓐ SETUP RULES

It is an oversimplification to say that bad chipping always stems from a bad setup, but it is certainly true to say that a lot of golfers make life extremely difficult for themselves by neglecting this important aspect of the chip shot. The correct setup for 99 percent of all chip shots can be expressed in one simple phrase: "ball back, hands and weight forward." This promotes a shape of swing that makes the clubhead approach the ball on a slightly descending angle of attack, leading to crisp ball-turf contact.

"SEE" THE SHOT

A good imagination is an absolute prerequisite of an all-around successful chipping game and something that all the top professionals employ to great effect. You need to be able to visualize the flight of the ball, landing position, and amount of run in different situations to match the club to the job and then execute the shot with conviction.

ⓐ Ball back, hands forward   ⓑ Hands lead the clubhead through the hitting area   ⓒ Maintain a smooth rhythm

ⓑ HOLD HANDS FORWARD

One of the golden rules of chipping is to make sure that the hands lead the clubhead through the hitting area, thus guaranteeing that all-important descending angle of attack. That is a crucial point of understanding for amateur golfers; if the hands stay ahead, a clean and consistent strike is far more likely. If, however, you allow the clubhead to overtake the hands coming into impact, the arc of the swing effectively bottoms out before it reaches the golf ball. In that instance, a mishit is virtually assured.

ⓒ KEEP FOREARMS SOFT

As you may have learned from previous sections in this book, any tension in your hands, arms, or body destroys your chances of hitting solid, consistent golf shots. So is the case with chipping. To prevent this insidious fault from creeping into your action, try to make sure your forearms stay soft as you swing the club back and through. That thought alone effectively "oils" the swing with a lovely smooth rhythm. It also helps keep the acceleration smooth through the hitting area so that the ball comes off the face not too "hot" but on a soft and easily controllable ball flight.

CLUB SELECTION

The setup and the simple swing required to hit neat chip shots can be applied to different clubs. When you need to play a chip to carry some rough or a bunker between you and the flag—go with lots of loft, such as a wedge. If a low-running chip shot is required, go with less loft—a 7- or 8-iron. The swing stays the same. All you have to do is make sure that in your setup the ball is back and your hands and weight are forward and that your hands lead the clubhead into the ball. Trust your swing and just let the loft do the rest.

SWING SECRETS

The left wrists stays firm as the club swings through

Legs stay flexed, supporting the swinging motion

Spine angle stays constant to promote good contact

Wrists stay "quiet" with no excessive hand action

Loft on the club does the work

HEAD POSITION
Head only comes up long after the ball is on its way

UPPER BODY MOVEMENT
Hands, arms, and torso should work as a unit, turning together

SOFT GRIP
Grip pressure remains soft, for maximum feel

FOLLOW-THROUGH
Clubhead travels through farther than it traveled in the backswing

FLEXED
Adopt a narrow stance with flexed knees

LOW CLUB
Clubhead stays low to the ground through impact and rises only at the end of the swing

TURN YOUR BODY

The typical chip shot involves a relatively short swing, but that does not mean to say that the body can stop working. Indeed, poor contact with the ball is often the result of the body not turning as the arms swing down, which often causes the clubhead to overtake the hands. So always think of turning your chest back and through in harmony with your arm swing.

This gives the swing some nice momentum and, providing you keep your hands in front of the ball, helps keep the club on the correct downward angle of attack.

Chipping: A Master Class

One of the real pleasures of watching the best players in action is admiring their skill around the green. They play chip shots of such great variety, and with wonderful touch and feel, that it is a joy to behold. Great chipping is within the compass of every golfer in the world because there are no physical limitations. You do not need to be incredibly strong—this is a short and relatively simple swing.

◀ **OLAZÁBAL IS NOT AFRAID** to hit the ball with pace because he knows that the spin imparted on the ball will make it stop.

The upper body must remain as still as possible as you swing from the shoulders and arms

At the point of impact, the hands should be in front of the ball

JOSÉ MARIA OLAZÁBAL'S ACCELERATION

Spain has, through the years, had a great reputation for producing golfers with exquisite short games; two-time Masters champion José Maria Olazábal is among the very best. He is sometimes let down by his driving, which means that his ability to scramble at times has to make up for it.

A golfer who can chip (and putt) will always be dangerous, and Olazábal is blessed with a chipping action that imparts wonderful acceleration through the ball, with the hands very much in front of the clubhead throughout the stroke. It is a very crisp, positive action, which produces low-flying shots that tend to skip forward and then spin and stop.

This is a good image to have in mind when you chip. Indeed, conjuring a mental picture of the Olazábal style of chipping has a number of benefits for the golfer who sometimes struggles with chipping. It prevents any deceleration into the ball. It also encourages the hands to stay ahead of the clubhead at the point of impact.

His chipping action is blessed with a wonderful sense of acceleration through the ball, with the hands very much in front of the clubhead throughout.

KJ CHOI'S CONSISTENT ACTION

South Korea's KJ Choi, a regular winner on the PGA Tour, has done well throughout his career in the "scrambling" statistics—a figure based on the number of times during the year that a player has a chip and a single putt, or just a chip, to secure at least par.

One of Choi's great qualities as a player is the way he keeps his chipping action essentially the same for every chip shot, simply varying the club selection in order to conjure the trajectory, height, and spin required for any given situation. For any amateur, this is a good example to follow, as you will quickly become more comfortable with your chipping technique and better able to repeat consistently.

The alternative method, adopted by some top players, is to mostly use the same chipping club but vary the technique in order to manipulate the loft on the clubface and thereby produce shots of varying heights. It has its merits and will improve your range of shots, but bear in mind it requires considerably more skill and practice.

▶ **FOR A BIG MAN** (before becoming a professional golfer, he was a powerlifter), Choi has soft hands and a great touch around the greens.

THE GREATEST CHIP

In the 1987 Masters, local boy and rank outsider Larry Mize made it into a playoff with Seve Ballesteros and Greg Norman. Seve bogeyed the first playoff hole and was eliminated. On the par-4 11th, Mize missed the green to the right. Norman, meanwhile, hit the green in regulation and was two putts away from the Masters title. However, Mize played a deft pitch and run; the ball skipped on to the green, trickled down toward the hole ... and in! Norman missed his birdie putt, meaning Mize had won.

○ Mize chips in to win the Masters

SEVE BALLESTEROS'S IMPROVISATION

Seve Ballesteros was the most creative golfer of his generation and he also had by far the best short game. These two qualities are inextricably linked. A good imagination is a prerequisite of a successful short game. You first have to be able to visualize different chip shots around the green and then develop the touch and feel to turn those shots into reality. Chipping is not a one-dimensional affair. It demands variety.

So always practice your short game with a selection of clubs by your side and make sure you constantly vary your target from one shot to the next. Each time, visualize in your mind's eye the flight of the golf ball— where you want it to land and how much run is required to get it close to the hole. Remember, every shot is different. Once you have a picture in your mind of the shot you want to play, select the club that best performs that function. The key is to change the club to vary the shots that you play—some high with very little run; others low with lots of run.

Never stand by the side of the practice green and simply hit the same shot to the same target for long periods—there is no real challenge in that—and thus your short game will not benefit in any meaningful fashion.

◀ **BALLESTEROS** was one of the most imaginative shotmakers of his generation. He was always able to think around a problem and invent an improbable solution.

The Bunker Shot

The sand wedge is a unique piece of equipment designed entirely on the principle that form should follow function. We have Grand Slam winner Gene Sarazen (see p.109) to thank for this, for it was he who first identified the need for a broader sole on the wedge. Up until that point, the implements used to extricate a golf ball from sand had not been entirely fit for the purpose. The straight leading edge and narrow sole, much like a classic blade in profile, tended to dig too deep into the sand, meaning that too much of the energy in the swing was dissipated.

HOW A SAND WEDGE WORKS

Gene Sarazen's inspiration for creating the sand wedge was part that of a golfer frustrated with his equipment and part that of a man with a lively imagination. He claimed he had been studying ducks landing on water, observing the way that their rounded underbellies skimmed across the surface. He designed a sand wedge that had a similar rounded underbelly, what we now call the flange or sole of the club, and found that such a clubhead would slide through the sand very efficiently.

When you play a bunker shot, the flange of the club works in such a way that, when the clubhead is delivered on a shallow and slightly descending angle of attack, it slides through the sand. This creates a splash of sand at impact, which propels the ball forward and out of the bunker. This is why the perfect escape from a bunker is sometimes referred to as a "splash shot."

ⓐ ADOPT AN OPEN SETUP

In order for you to utilize the bounce effect of the sand wedge, you must adhere to a couple of simple setup rules that will affect the shape of the swing.
- The stance must be open—that is, the feet aligned to the left of the target.
- The clubface must be open—that is, aimed to the right of the target.

ⓑ SWING ALONG YOUR AIM LINES

By addressing the ball correctly, the swing becomes immeasurably easier. The secret is to swing along the lines of your body—in other words, across the line on an "out-to-in" path.
- Focus on a spot in the sand roughly 2 in (5 cm) behind the ball; this is the intended point of entry for the clubhead.
- Swing back and through, combining your arm swing with your body turn.
- Strike down into the sand on your intended spot and accelerate the club through the sand under the ball, with the feeling of swinging the club to the left of the target through impact.
- Always follow through on every bunker shot.

GRIP IT RIGHT

Once you have opened your stance, you can form your grip. Remember, the sand wedge does its best work when the clubface is open. This aspect of the setup is paramount, which is why it is wise to adopt this simple routine to ensure that the clubface is indeed open as you address the ball and then start your swing.

Hold the club out in front of you, just in your right hand, and swivel the grip counterclockwise in your hands until the clubface is open (below left). Then, without altering that position, form your grip (below right). That way, the clubface will more than likely stay open during the swing, which is perfect—just what you need to play great bunker shots.

ⓐ Open stance and clubface

ⓑ Swing along your aim lines, strike the sand behind the ball, and remember to follow through

SHUFFLE, THEN PICK YOUR SPOT

When you are standing in a bunker, you are not on solid ground, so it is important to create a secure footing. Shuffle your feet into the sand to give yourself a solid base. Then pick a spot behind the ball and commit to striking the sand at that point.

Strange as it sounds, the short-range bunker shot is the only shot in golf where you should not actually hit the ball. The club glides under the ball and the ball flies onto the green on an explosion of sand. Remember: shuffle into the sand, then strike it.

Fear of bunker play is common among amateur golfers, but it is easily banished once you adhere to the fundamentals.

SWING SECRETS

Ball should be positioned forward of center

Shoulders, feet, and hips open to the target line

Strike the sand behind the ball

Feel the heel of the club entering the sand first

Spine angle remains constant into impact

FORMING THE GRIP
It is hugely important that you open the clubface and then form your grip. If you do it the other way around, the clubface will tend to return to square at impact, completely ruining the shot

FLEXED KNEES
Knees are flexed at address and should stay that way during the swing

LOFT AND BOUNCE

The choice of loft on a wedge is, to some extent, determined by the nature of the bunkers on a golf course. A course with shallow bunkers and big greens has no real call for a highly lofted wedge; whereas on a links course, where the bunkers are typically deep and require escape shots of maximum elevation, a lot of loft is desirable.

It is also imperative that the sand wedge should have a fair degree of bounce angle, certainly more than eight degrees and as much as 12 to 14 degrees. This bounce angle helps ensure that the clubhead slides through the sand instead of digging in to it (see pp.78–79).

HANDS ALIGNMENT
The hands can be slightly ahead of, or even level with, the golf ball for a regular greenside bunker shot

WEIGHT DISTRIBUTION
The weight should favor the front foot but only slightly

CLUBFACE
You can afford to open the clubface on a sand wedge more than you realize

Bunker Play: A Master Class

All of the game's top players display sublime greenside bunker skills. Indeed, there are some critics of the modern professional game who say, rather churlishly, that bunkers are no longer proper hazards, such is the dizzying array of skills on show at a typical tournament. We should continue to observe in wonderment the way the world's best players splash the ball out to within inches of the flag.

Both the shoulder turn and the follow-through must be as full as possible

Concentrate on a spot about 2 in (5 cm) behind the ball, and strike the clubhead through the sand

GARY PLAYER'S PRACTICE METHODS

South Africa's Gary Player, the self-styled Black Knight, is the greatest bunker player who ever lived. He once famously proclaimed that the more he practiced, the luckier he became. The man did himself an injustice. Yes, he practiced his bunker play probably more than any other golfer in his day, but there was nothing lucky about the results. The man was a genius in the sand.

There is a lot we can learn from Player's approach to practicing his bunker play. Some lesser players would always practice shots from the perfect lie. Not Gary Player. He would randomly throw handfuls of golf balls into the sand and then simply play each ball wherever it came to rest. Some would be in a good lie, others would not. It meant Player developed an incredible imagination and skill for hitting great bunker shots from all manner of different situations. He was prepared for any eventuality.

He would even set goals, say, challenging himself to hole three bunker shots before he could go in and join his wife or guests for dinner.

◀ **AS ONE OF THE HARDEST** working men in golf, Gary Player spent a lot of time working on his technique. The result was brilliant bunker play and nine Major championships.

THE GREATEST BUNKER SHOT

The European side was on the brink of victory on the last day of the 2002 Ryder Cup. Three times Paul Azinger had trailed Niclas Fasth by a margin of two holes, but the American produced one of the shots of the year on the par-4 18th, holing from a greenside bunker to keep this Ryder Cup contest alive.

High fives all round after Azinger holes from the sand

PHIL MICKELSON'S WRIST HINGE

Phil Mickelson has probably the most creative short game of any player at the top of the game and can produce a range of magical shots from around the green, including bunker shots. Mickelson often carries an exceptionally lofted sand wedge, often as much as 64 degrees, and uses this to generate greenside bunker shots where the ball climbs almost vertically skyward and stops abruptly on landing. It is not all down to the equipment he uses, though. The skill is in the hands, too.

Michelson hinges the wrists early in the takeaway to set the club on a very steep angle of attack; this in effect presets a swing arc that is distinctly U-shape in profile. So the club goes back steeply and then comes down steeply, too. Mickelson then zips the clubhead through the sand under the ball with a fast and aggressive hand action; that is the key, fast hands through the ball. The ball pops straight up in the air and stops virtually dead in its tracks. This is a shot to practice before attempting it on the course.

Every golfer can learn from the soft hold he applies to the grip.

▲ **MICKELSON HAS THE ABILITY** to exert terrific control over a golf ball, so he can afford to have an aggressive short game. His recovery shots from greenside bunkers is unique because of his choice of lofted sand wedge.

◄ **GARCÍA IS AN INTUITIVE AND IMAGINATIVE** golfer who has great technique around the greens. He is a touch player, and his soft hands complement his great feel.

SERGIO GARCÍA'S SOFT HANDS

Sergio García is another in a long line of Spanish golfers blessed with a sensational short game. He has a technique very much his own invention, one which might best be described as "handsy." Overall, it is an extremely difficult method to teach because of its individual nature. However, every golfer can learn from the soft hold he applies to the grip.

A soft hold on the club effectively spreads into the arms and shoulders as well. It helps endow your swing with an "oily" rhythm back and through. Only by swinging in this fashion can you develop the wonderful sense of touch and feel that is characteristic of all great bunker players.

Increasing your touch is a difficult concept to grasp, but by gripping the club softly the way García does, you will start to become a much better bunker player.

Putters: The Design

The interesting thing about putters is that there is a greater variation in aesthetics than for any other club in the bag. Designs vary from the original blade putter, to heel-and-toe, mallet heads, and futuristic deep-backed putters with a high moment of inertia. Literally, almost anything goes, obviously within the limits of what the governing bodies will allow.

PRINCIPLES OF DESIGN

The principle of peripheral weighting is fundamental to the design of many of the putters on the market today. By placing weight in both the heel and the toe of the putter and toward the back of the putter-head, its dynamic stability is increased. This means that the face stays square at impact, so the ball goes where you want it to, even with off-center strikes.

The two-ball and three-ball putters, for instance, have white discs the size of golf balls perpendicular to the face, which are used as alignment aids at address. There are many different interpretations of this basic design principle, each with the intention of being not only forgiving to off-center strikes but also easy to aim. A golfer needs to make a decision based on personal preference.

WEIGHT AND TWIST

The key factor with a lot of these radical, deep-faced designs is moment of inertia, or MOI. The center of gravity is moved way back from the face, deep behind the ball, which promotes a high MOI and therefore improves the putter-head's built-in resistance to twisting at impact. The fact that a lot of tour pros are using putters of this type adds a good deal of credence to the manufacturers' bold claims.

▶ **THIS PUTTER** by Robert J. Bettinardi is a classic modern example of the heel-and-toe weighting first developed by Ping in the 1960s. The purpose of peripheral weighting is to counter the propensity of the face to twist at impact.

Black line marks the sweet spot on the face

▲ **THIS SIMPLE, CLASSIC** design, the Bettinardi "C Series," is forged from a single piece of carbon steel.

Movable weights enable the player to alter the club's balance

▲ **MALLET-HEADED** putters work on the principle of moving weight back in the putter-head to reduce twisting at impact.

The offsetting of the putter-head at the hosel helps sighting at address

Weighting the putter at the heel and toe reduces twisting of the putter face at impact

Bettinardi's patented honeycomb face promotes consistent ball-striking and a smooth roll

Carbon steel material is soft enough to promote good feel, but the metal makes a solid "click" sound at impact

Weight is set back away from the face

▲ **TWO- AND THREE-BALL PUTTERS** help players line up putts by placing the ball directly in front of the "virtual" balls.

THE PUTTER-FACE

Feel is a major factor with any shot—none more so than putting, where judgment of distance is everything. In reality, feel probably has as much to do with the sound of the putter-face contacting the ball as anything physically felt through the hands.

This is why face inserts have become so popular in modern-day putters. These synthetic inserts are softer than the metals used in the construction of the putter-head. They sound different and therefore offer a greater "feel" at impact; in a sense, more feedback, which helps the golfer judge the speed of the ball off the face more easily.

◄ **SOME PUTTERS** are made from light aluminum for a better feel. The mallet head can also be heavily weighted and given a degree of loft.

▼ **PUTTERS WITH HIGH MOI** can also be given a face insert that promotes maximum forward spin for a truer roll on the ball.

The vertical milling process results in a putter face flat to one-thousandth of an inch

Bent shafts are used in putter technology to create offset or a specific lie angle

Weight set back from the face encourages a smooth stroke

Face inserts such as plastic compounds or titanium promote a better feel

Polymer-filled grooves reduce backspin

Perfectly flat for true ball-striking

▲ **GROOVE TECHNOLOGY**

▲ **HONEYCOMB FACE**

SHAFT LENGTH

Which length putter-shaft you choose comes down to personal preference. The standard length is approximately 35 to 36 in (89 to 91 cm), but it is not uncommon for some of the world's best players to have a putter cut down to as little as 32 to 33 in (81 to 84 cm).

Some leading golfers take the matter of length to the other extreme, using one of the many different long-handled putters available. In addition to the broomhandle putter, for example, which is braced against the chin or breastbone, there is also the belly-putter—or baby-broomhandle—that is secured in the midriff. These long-shafted models are available with a variety of putter-head designs, so a golfer can pick a model that best suits their game.

Grip is held by your lower hand to guide the stroke

Top grip is secured under the chin

Shafts are usually at least 50 in (1.27 m) long

▲ **THE BROOMHANDLE PUTTER** became popular as a way to execute a smooth stroke. The putter is held under the chin and swung in a pendulum motion.

PUTTER TOPSPIN

As strange as it sounds, some putters impart a notable amount of backspin on the ball. This leads to a period of skidding shortly after impact, which affects the roll of the ball. Top-of-the-range putters are instead designed to promote topspin. This feature, coupled with a putting stroke that strikes the ball on an ascending angle of attack, results in a pure roll. Provided that the putt is on line, a ball that hugs the surface of the green with topspin will find the target more surely than one that skids (with backspin) off the putter-face.

Initial skid off the clubface

Grooves impart forward spin and ball hugs the surface

Skid | Forward roll

PAYING THE PRICE

Many golfers find it hard to swallow the high price tags of today's leading models, yet the putter is such an important club—if you do not hole out consistently, your scores will never improve. There is a further justification for these prices. In a typical round of golf, you will use your putter probably three times more often than your driver—a club that may have cost you twice the money of the putter. On a "cost per usage" basis, then, a putter is six times better value for money than a comparable driver.

The Putting Stroke

Putting is the most individual aspect of the game. Just look at any tour event and you will see a multitude of different styles of putting strokes. So there is more than one way to get the ball into the hole on a consistent basis. There are, however, certain characteristics that are common to the majority of very fine putters. This is the conventional wisdom of great putting. You may have your own style, but if you want to make a lot of putts, it pays to integrate these core elements into your technique.

ⓐ EYES OVER THE BALL

Ball position is as important in the putting stroke as it is in the full swing. There are two factors to bear in mind. First, the ball should be forward in your stance to encourage a slightly ascending blow when the putter-face meets the ball. That imparts a good roll on your putts. Second, your eyes should ideally be directly over the ball, as this gives you the best perspective of the line from the ball to the hole.

One simple routine helps give you the perfect ball position. Adopt a comfortable posture and then drop a golf ball from the bridge of your nose.

The spot on which it lands represents the perfect ball position for you.

ⓑ SHOULDERS AND EYES PARALLEL

Once you have the ideal ball position in your stance, the next key requirement is to have your shoulder line and eye line parallel to the path on which you want the ball to start. You can check very easily that these two crucial checkpoints are maintained.

Hold the shaft of the putter along the top of your chest. The line of the shaft should match the target line; if so, it will help promote an on-line stroke.

Also hold the shaft along your eye line and see whether it corresponds with the target line. If so, it further improves your perspective to help you visualize the path the ball must take on its journey to the hole.

ⓐ Drop a ball from your nose

ⓑ Shoulders square

ⓒ TAKE DEAD AIM

The aim of the putter is a crucial determining factor in how many putts you make. After all, if you do not aim correctly, how can you be expected to hit your target?

One method that should help you eliminate the likelihood of poor aim is to place the golf ball on the green in such a way that the manufacturer's name corresponds exactly with the line on which you want the ball to start its journey. You should then set the putter-face behind the ball so that it is exactly perpendicular to that line. Alternatively, draw a line on the ball. This is a very effective method, adopted by many of the leading players, because it provides you with a visual image of the perfect aim and path to the hole.

ⓒ Taking aim

KEEP YOUR HEAD STILL

Any head movement before the ball is struck knocks the shoulders—and therefore the putter—out of its natural path; this leads to a crooked stroke and a missed putt. It is particularly common (and damaging) on short putts, where there is a tendency for golfers to take an anxious peek and see whether the ball is heading toward the hole.

One of the key objectives for any good putter, therefore, must be to keep the head rock still throughout the stroke. The simplest way to achieve this is to commit to keeping your head down until you hear the sound of the ball dropping in the hole.

MAINTAIN THE PERFECT TRIANGLE

You should try to maintain the triangle formed at address by the shoulders and arms throughout the putting stroke. The stroke should never be wooden, but neither should it have too many independently moving parts. It should be a soft yet coordinated motion that involves the hands, arms, and shoulders all working together.

To encourage this harmony of movement, think of the stroke being controlled predominantly by the rocking motion of the shoulders. The hands and arms then respond to the momentum created by this rocking motion so that the putter tracks a neat path back and through. It helps if you focus on maintaining throughout the stroke the triangle formed at address by the shoulders and the arms. Once again, it is worth stressing that the hands should stay soft on the putter and that, while some softness in the wrists is desirable, there should not be too much independent wrist action as that can lead to an erratic stroke and lack of consistency.

KEEP STEADY
The head stays rock steady until the ball is on its way

MAINTAIN THE UNIT
A slightly fatter-than-standard grip is popular with many top players, as it tends to help keep the hands and wrists "quieter" during the stroke

NO MOVEMENT
From the waist down, everything stays still during the stroke. Imagine your legs are set in concrete

KEEP ON TRACK
From short range, imagine the face of the putter looks at the hole through impact

SOLID BASE
Your weight should be evenly spread between both feet, with a sense that they are very much planted for a secure base to the stroke

SWING SECRETS

Maintain the angle in the back of the left wrist

Hands stay soft on the putter throughout the stroke

Think "left shoulder down" in the backstroke

Think "left shoulder up" in the through-stroke

Keep the head down until your hear the ball drop

The Art of Putting

Putting is often described as the game within a game. It may be something of a cliché, but it captures the essence of putting better than any other single phrase. A bad ball-striking round can be saved by good putting as surely as a potentially good score can be ruined by poor putting. There are many different facets to the art of putting, and the fundamentals explained here will stand you in good stead as you strive to improve.

READING GREENS AND MAKING PUTTS

No green is totally flat. Thus, most putts have a degree of break on them—often subtle, sometimes severe. The best way to deal with breaking putts and sloping greens is to treat every putt as if it is straight. This is how it works.

a Identify how much break there is on a putt—for example, a 3 ft (1 m) break from the left. The hole itself now ceases to be your target. Your new target is an imaginary hole positioned 3 ft (1 m) to the left of the actual hole.

b As you go through your preshot routine, aiming the putter-face and aligning your stance, your focus should continue to be the imaginary target.

c Now hit a dead-straight putt at your imaginary target to the left of the hole, and the slope on the green takes care of the rest.

The advantage of this method is that you are far more likely to make a pure stroke when hitting a straight putt than you are when trying to guide the ball on a breaking putt.

> The best way to deal with breaking putts and sloping greens is to hit the putt straight and let the green take care of the rest.

a Identify a target to the side of the hole

b Adopt your stance and aim at the imaginary target

c Strike a normal putt and let the slope do the work

a Make your preparations

b Stroke through the pegs

THE PERFECT SHORT-PUTT DRILL

This is one of Tiger Woods's favorite putting drills. Once during a tournament, he practiced it for 30 minutes every day and during the four rounds made 59 out of 60 putts from inside 8 ft (2.5 m).

a It is best when practiced on a relatively flat portion of the green; the straighter the putt, the better. Place your putter on the ground and stick two tee pegs on either side of the heel and toe of the putter-head, leaving about a ½ in (1.25 cm) gap on either side (you can reduce the gap as your confidence grows).

b Now place a ball down and simply hit putts, trying to swing the putter-head through the gate formed by the two tee pegs.

If your stroke is crooked, then either the heel or the toe of the putter will collide with one of the tee pegs through impact. In this way, the drill forces you to make an on-line stroke. If you miss a lot of putts during this practice drill, check the aim of the putter-face at address. It could be that it is not square.

AROUND THE CLOCK

Another fun, and extremely useful, putting drill to try is as follows. Line up 12 golf balls in a circle around the hole, one for each point on the clockface. Then putt the golf balls one at a time into the hole; each time you miss one, you must start again until all 12 are holed consecutively. Start at a distance of about 3 ft (1 m) from the hole, then gradually increase the distance as you gain confidence and your putting stroke improves.

a THE PERFECT LONG-PUTT DRILL

Good long putting is all about speed and rolling the ball stone-dead. If the putt drops, so be it. That is a bonus. From 40 ft (12 m) or more, every golfer, even the best, is satisfied with a safe two-putt. One of the best ways to improve your judgment of pace on long putts is to rehearse this practice drill.

Place a handful of tee pegs in the ground, starting at about 20 ft (6 m) and working away from you at intervals of about 3 ft (1 m). Use as many tee pegs as space on the green permits.

Now putt the first ball to the first tee peg, the second ball to the second tee peg, and so on. The idea is that you get one chance at each putt, just as is the case on the golf course during a real round of golf. You can mix things up a bit, too, by hitting putts randomly to the various tee pegs.

This drill is so effective because it trains you to see a putt and then translate those visual messages into the feel for distance.

a Refine your feel for distance

Putting: A Master Class

The professional game is all about making birdies, and that means making putts. The best players in the world average around 28 or 29 putts per round over the course of an entire season, which means they will typically single putt probably seven or eight greens per round. That is impressive. As we already made clear, there is more than one way to putt well.

TIGER WOODS IS SOLID

Next time you watch Tiger Woods putt, ignore for a moment where the ball goes and focus instead on his hips and legs. You will notice that they stay absolutely rock still throughout the stroke. This is hugely significant and one of the major points of difference between top players and many amateurs.

By keeping the hips and legs steady, Woods establishes a solid foundation as he swings the putter back and through. It makes it easier to produce an on-line stroke on a more consistent basis, which leads to sweet strikes. This feature of Woods's putting stroke is well worth copying.

THE GREATEST PUTT

The 1999 US Open at Pinehurst will go down as one of the most poignant tournaments in US Open history: Payne Stewart's last win before he lost his life in a plane crash, and the scene of arguably the greatest putt ever. Having holed a 25 ft (7.5 m) putt to save par on the 16th, Stewart then knocked a 6-iron to 3 ft (1 m) for birdie on the 17th, which meant he needed a par on the 18th to win his second US Open title. After driving into trouble, he played out into the fairway and hit a lob wedge to 15 ft (4.5 m). "That putt to win the US Open." Stewart rolled the ball into the hole, right in the middle.

Stewart's last Major win

The size of the swing should be in proportion to the length of the putt. Too much swing will result in a loss of accuracy

Woods uses the reverse overlap putting grip. It is thought to be the best way to control the putter

The putter meets the ball on a slight upward arc, imparting a smooth roll

▲ **WOODS HAS THE KNACK** of being able to sink the putts at the most crucial of times. He is a firm striker of the ball, secure in his ability to judge any putt to perfection. It is believed the ideal pace for holing a putt is such that, if the ball misses, it would travel 18 in (45 cm) past the hole.

PÁDRAIG HARRINGTON'S GRIP

The 2007 Open champion Pádraig Harrington, one of the finest all-around putters in the pro game, has used the same putting grip since he was a boy—a grip whereby the left hand sits below the right. He is not alone in that regard, either. Jim Furyk and Thomas Bjørn are just two of several other notable players who prefer this style of grip.

Positioning the left hand below the right has the effect of leveling the shoulders at address, which promotes a pendulum-type putting stroke. It helps maintain a firmer left-wrist position as the putter is delivered to the back of the ball, which eliminates any tendency to twitch putts to the left, a fault suffered by some. Other players find it also helps keep the putter closer to the ground on the way back and through, for a good roll.

If you feel frustrated with your performance on the greens, often it pays to try something different. The so-called "cack-handed" grip is not for everyone, but the benefits are real and it should not be dismissed.

▶ **HARRINGTON** is one of the most reliable putters on the professional tour. He averages about 28 putts per round, which has helped push him up the world rankings.

▼ **THE FREE-FLOWING** putting action of David Toms means that he is a great long putter. Leaving the ball very close to the hole from long range—"lag putting"—is a great attribute.

DAVID TOMS'S DEAD-WEIGHTED PUTTS

Rolling the ball stone-dead—and very occasionally into the hole—from long distance is a wonderful skill that all top golfers possess. Former USPGA champion David Toms demonstrates this skill better than most of his contemporaries. He is a superb lag putter.

Of particular note to anyone wishing to learn from Toms's technique is the free and uninhibited swing of the putter. It stems from a very natural, upright address position where the arms hang comfortably. This allows him to swing the putter on a lovely flowing arc. It is almost as though there is no hit, just a sweeping motion with the ball simply getting in the way.

One other useful exercise, which Toms himself often replicates in his own putting strategy, is making practice putting strokes while looking at the hole. This helps give you a feel for the length and pace of stroke required and should improve your judgment of distance on long putts.

Of particular note to anyone wishing to learn from Toms's technique is the free and uninhibited swing of the putter.

Course Management

If the shots you hit are the tools of the trade, then course management is perhaps best described as the manner by which you use those tools. It relates to the strategy you employ on the golf course and covers such areas as club selection, percentage play, staying out of trouble, getting out of trouble, and much more. The final section of this chapter provides a window into the mind of golf's great strategists. It should hopefully help you plot a less troubled path around the golf course.

If you have a fade, teeing up on the right and playing down the left gives you a wider margin for error.

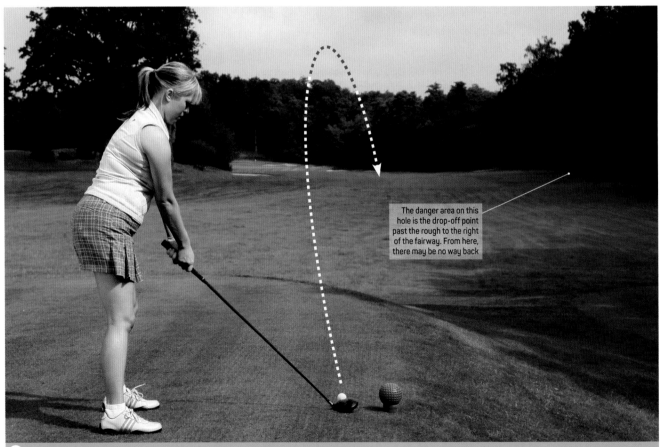 AVOID TROUBLE OFF THE TEE

Three-quarters of the world's amateur golfers flight their long shots on a left-to-right trajectory (right-to-left for the left-hander)—a fade or slice. Therefore, trouble down the right-hand side of the fairway tends to be the biggest danger area for most golfers. If your typical ball flight fits this description, a useful strategy to minimize the risk is to tee up the ball on the very right-hand edge of the teeing area, then aim down the left-hand side of the fairway.

If the shot goes according to plan, the ball will assume its normal left-to-right flight and finish in the middle of the fairway. The great thing is that you have also got a wide margin for error, for if the ball flies dead straight, it will finish only in the left rough, and if the ball slices a little more than anticipated, probably the worse you can expect is to finish in the right rough.

The danger area on this hole is the drop-off point past the rough to the right of the fairway. From here, there may be no way back

a The shot starts on the line of the left rough and finishes in the middle of the fairway

SHAPE YOUR SHOTS

If you find yourself in a position whereby an obstruction blocks your way to the green and you intend to play a shot with shape, it is important to bear in mind the simple rules of impact ballistics (see pp.70–71).

ⓐ With a short shot that requires a lofted club, it is easier to hook or draw the ball than it is to fade or slice the ball.

ⓑ With a longer shot that requires a less lofted club, it is much easier to fade or slice the ball than it is to hook or draw the ball.

Keep these factors in mind when considering which shape shot best gives you a route to the target. One option may be considerably easier than the other.

MAKE A GOOD START

However many warm-up exercises and practice swings you make before a round, you will probably still be nervous on the first tee. Follow these rules to increase the likelihood of hitting a good shot and to start the round as you mean to go on:
- Choose a club you are confident with; do not feel compelled to hit a driver
- Take a few deep breaths to lower your heartbeat
- Grip the club lightly
- Make a smooth swing

ⓐ Draw with a short iron

ⓑ Fade with a long iron

Although it is tempting to aim for the green and take a chance on missing the trees, the sensible shot is to play out to the fairway

ⓐ Playing it safe limits the risk of mistakes

ⓐ TAKE YOUR MEDICINE

Every golfer, even the best player in the world, makes mistakes. This is not the end of the world, but it is when you compound that initial mistake with another, and then another, that it becomes serious. A lot of players are simply too ambitious; they will hit the ball into trouble and then try to play a heroic recovery shot and land themselves in more trouble. They basically turn a five into a possible seven or eight.

If you find yourself in trouble—say, you have hit it into trees—make sure you get your next shot back in play. That is all. Do not try to punch the ball through tiny gaps in the trees or go for broke. Just play the simplest shot available to you. That way, your mistakes only ever cost you one shot.

ABOVE ALL, ENJOY IT

All golfers naturally want to play their best every time they set foot on the golf course, but do not let your ambition blinker you from the simple enjoyment to be gained from playing this game.

The great Walter Hagen, an 11-time Major champion, played the game with a joie de vivre that is unparalleled in the modern game, yet he was one of the greatest champions who ever lived. Hagen proved that you could have fun and win (see p.108).

Hagen sets a great example to us all. If you can maintain a state of equanimity, take the bad shots as they come, and above all keep your composure. You will in all probability not only enjoy the game more but play better, too. It is one of the game's delicious ironies.

3

THE GREATEST GOLFERS

Old and Young Tom Morris

Among the early pioneers of the game, two families stand supreme. If your name was not Park or Morris, then winning the Open Championship in its formative years was almost impossible. Willie Park Senior and Old Tom Morris made the new Open into their personal duel—until Tommy, or Young Tom, arrived as the game's first star.

OLD TOM MORRIS STATS

BORN June 16, 1821; St .Andrews, Scotland
DIED May 25, 1908

MAJORS 4
THE OPEN: Won 1861, 1862, 1864, 1867

HONORS
Oldest winner of the Open Championship, aged 46

YOUNG TOM MORRIS STATS

BORN April 20, 1851; St. Andrews, Scotland
DIED December 25, 1875

MAJORS 4
THE OPEN: Won 1868, 1869, 1870, 1872

HONORS
Kept championship belt after hat trick of victories

▲ **ST. ANDREWS GOLFERS,** including resident club and ball maker Allan Robertson (third from the right), in 1859. Old Tom Morris was Robertson's apprentice in the 1850s.

▲ **MORE THAN A CHAMPION** golfer, Old Tom Morris designed the original courses at Muirfield, Prestwick, and Carnoustie.

Old Tom Morris is generally regarded as the first professional golfer. A year after he became the Open's oldest winner at the age of 46 in 1867, his fourth title in seven years, his son Tommy became the youngest at 17. Both records stand to this day. Young Tom was a prodigy who was beating a number of the leading professionals by the age of 13. After winning his first Open, Young Tom retained the title the next year and again in 1870, playing 36 holes at Prestwick in a score of 149 and winning by 12 strokes. Having won three times in a row, Young Tom received the championship belt outright. There was no event the following year, but a new trophy, the Claret Jug, was presented in 1872, and Young Tom won for the fourth time in a row.

But in 1875, at the age of just 24, his short life came to a heart-broken end when Young Tom's wife and child died in childbirth. Young Tom fell into a mighty depression and died of a burst artery in his lung on Christmas morning.

Old Tom had been an apprentice ball maker for Allan Robertson at St. Andrews before becoming Keeper of the Green at Prestwick, where he laid out the original 12-hole course; he also had a hand in designing the courses at Carnousite and Muirfield among many others. During his time at Prestwick, the first Open was played at the club, and Old Tom was beaten by Willie Park. He had his revenge by winning the next two, finished second to Park again in 1863, then won again in 1864 and 1867. It is thought that Morris was responsible for modern greenkeeping development; was partly responsible for the standardization of the rules of golf and the number of holes to be played; and helped design many of the hickory clubs that were used at the time. He returned to St. Andrews in 1865 to be the greenkeeper and remained in that role until he finally retired to his workshop by the 18th hole in 1904. Golf's founding father died four years later.

John Ball and Harold Hilton

Only three men have won the Open Championship as an amateur, and one of them was the legendary Bobby Jones. The other two were both Englishmen and both members of Royal Liverpool Golf Club at Hoylake. John Ball and Harold Hilton were not just contemporaries but two of the finest players of their generation.

John Ball was the first Englishman to win the Open when he triumphed at Prestwick in 1890. A hugely determined man of few words, he was a joy to watch. Bernard Darwin wrote, "I have derived greater aesthetic and emotional pleasure from watching John Ball than from any other spectacle in the game." Ball was the most dominant force in British golf; much the same as Bobby Jones was in the US. He won a record eight Amateur titles between 1888 and 1912 (when he was 51), his most successful year being 1890, when he won both the Amateur and the Open titles. This victory in 1890 made him the only man other than Bobby Jones to hold the Open and Amateur titles in the same year.

Harold Hilton also matched Jones in being the only other golfer to hold the Amateur Championships of both Britain and America at the same time. The year was 1911. After winning the third of his four British Amateur titles, Hilton was victorious in the US version at Apawamis at Rye, New York, winning the matchplay competition at the 37th hole against Fred Herreshoff of the US. He also won the Open twice, first in 1892 at Muirfield when the championship was extended to two days and 72 holes for the first time. He won again on his home links of Hoylake five years later.

DIFFERENT STYLES

Ball, a shy, modest man, was not the greatest putter to ever play the game, but he more than made up for this by being peerless with his long approach shots. Where others tried merely to find the green, he utilized his shot-making ability to get as close to the hole as he possibly could. In contrast, Hilton went after the ball in a ferocious manner. "A little man jumping on his toes and throwing himself and his club after the ball with almost frantic abandon," wrote Darwin of Hilton's swing. A great enthusiast of the game, even after retiring from competitive golf, Hilton became the first editor of Golf Monthly magazine in 1911.

JOHN BALL STATS

BORN December 24, 1861; Hoylake, England
DIED December 2, 1940

VICTORIES 8
BRITISH AMATEUR: 1888, 1890, 1892, 1894, 1899, 1907, 1910, 1912

MAJORS 1
THE OPEN: Won 1890

HAROLD HILTON STATS

BORN January 14, 1869; West Kirby, England
DIED March 5, 1942

VICTORIES 5
BRITISH AMATEUR: 1901, 1911, 1913
US AMATEUR: 1911

MAJORS 2
THE OPEN: Won 1892, 1897

▼ **HAROLD HILTON** was the first non-American-born player to win the US Amateur championship.

▲ **JOHN BALL** playing the Amateur Championship at Royal St. George's, England, in 1914. In 1927, at the age of 66, Ball played his last British Amateur game.

Great Triumvirate

Long before the Big Three—Palmer, Nicklaus, and Player—there was the Great Triumvirate. At the turn of the century, the careers of Harry Vardon, JH Taylor, and James Braid had a profound effect on the development of the game, not just in Britain but around the world.

Vardon, Taylor, and Braid were all born within a year of each other, and from the age of 25, they dominated the nascent professional golf scene. They won the Open Championship 16 times in a 21-year period (1894–1914). It is a feat that will never be equaled.

Harry Vardon's six victories at the Open remains the largest haul in the history of the event. He was regarded as the best player of his time, and his fame spread far and wide. He made three long exhibition tours of America and helped the game gain in popularity rapidly. In 1900, he won the US Open at the Chicago Golf Club, while on his other two appearances in the championship, he was second on both occasions. Accuracy was the key to Vardon's game. He was a consistent driver and, playing from the fairway more than anyone else, honed his iron play to relentless perfection. It was said that if he played the same course twice in a day, he would be playing from the same divots in the afternoon. He wrote extensively about the swing, and the overlapping grip that he adopted became known as the "Vardon grip"; where the so-called "St. Andrews" swing was flat, with the club swung around the body, Vardon favored a more upright action.

Born in Jersey, Vardon started caddying at a young age and quickly became besotted with the game. His first Open win came at Muirfield in 1896 after a playoff against Taylor. His last came in 1914. The second half of his career was afflicted by ill health; he suffered from tuberculosis. He also designed courses, including South Herts, the club to which he was affiliated for his last three Open wins. Two trophies bear Vardon's name: for

JH TAYLOR STATS

BORN March 19, 1871; Devon, England
DIED February 10, 1963
TURNED PRO 1890

MAJORS 5
THE OPEN: 1894, 1895, 1900, 1909, 1913

HONORS
Ryder Cup Captain: 1933

JAMES BRAID STATS

BORN February 6, 1870; Fife, Scotland
DIED November 27, 1950
TURNED PRO 1890

MAJORS 5
THE OPEN: 1901, 1905, 1906, 1908, 1910

HARRY VARDON STATS

BORN May 9, 1870; Jersey, Channel Islands
DIED March 20, 1937
TURNED PRO 1896

MAJORS 7
THE OPEN: 1896, 1898, 1899, 1903, 1911, 1914
US OPEN: 1900

● JH Taylor wins the first Open outside Scotland

◀ **THE GREATEST GOLFER OF** his time, Harry Vardon won an unmatched six Open titles and the US Open in 1900.

Vardon played as if he was enjoying the game, Braid as if he were going through his day's work, and Taylor, in certain moods at any rate, as if he hated it.

BERNARD DARWIN, GOLF WRITER

▲ **JH TAYLOR WAS MADE AN** honorary member of the Royal and Ancient Golf Club in 1947 and of Royal North Devon 10 years later.

◄ **THE 1902 OPEN CHAMPION**, Sandy Herd, joins JH Taylor (back right), James Braid (front left), and Harry Vardon (front right).

the winner of the European tour's Order of Merit, and for the stroke average title in America.

JH Taylor learned the game at Westward Ho! and, playing with the then-traditional flat swing, was a master in the wind. He won two Opens before Vardon had won his first and totaled five in all. His first, in 1894, came at the first Open held outside Scotland at Royal St. George's at Sandwich, Kent. He was a runner-up no less than six times in the Open, but his most satisfying achievement was winning at St. Andrews in 1900, when he produced the lowest score in every round to win by eight shots from Vardon. He became the professional at Royal Mid Surrey, one of the many courses he designed and was instrumental in setting up the Professional Golfers' Association (PGA).

James Braid was a tall and powerful Scotsman who smashed the ball as far as he could, then looked for it. He was not the straightest-hitting player, but he possessed a fine short game, making him a flamboyant and exciting player to watch. Like Taylor, Braid won five Opens, and although he was a later starter than his contemporaries—he gave Vardon a three Open start—he got to five titles first. Braid was the first professional at Walton Heath, Surrey, and became a distinguished course designer, with the Kings and Queens courses at Gleneagles being among his finest work.

Walter Hagen

Golf's first great showman, Walter Hagen was colorful and flamboyant, brash and, to some, arrogant. But if he could talk the talk, then he could certainly walk the walk. "Sir Walter," or "The Haig," as he was known, gave golf a higher profile during the Roaring Twenties and, in winning 11 Major titles, was also one of the game's greatest championship winners.

PLAYER STATS

BORN December 21, 1892; Rochester, New York
HEIGHT 5ft 11in (1.80m)
TURNED PRO 1912

DEBUT WIN 1915 Massachusetts Open
TOUR WINS 51
PGA TOUR: 44
OTHER: 7

MAJORS 11
MASTERS: T11TH 1936
US OPEN: WON 1914, 1919
THE OPEN: WON 1922, 1924, 1928, 1929
USPGA: WON 1921, 1924, 1925, 1926, 1927

HONORS
Ryder Cup Team: 1927, 1929, 1931, 1933, 1935

He was an irresponsible playboy; and at the same time a keen and determined competitor.

GRANTLAND RICE SPORTS WRITER

Walter Hagen won the US Open twice, the USPGA Championship five times in six attempts, and crossed the Atlantic to win the Open Championship on four occasions. But his greatest and most lasting achievement was in inventing the role of the touring professional, showing that it was possible to make a fortune playing exhibitions all over the world. Before Hagen, there were only club professionals; he was the first to go "unattached."

The son of an immigrant family, Hagen began caddying at Rochester's first golf club at the age of seven. He left school to become an assistant professional, but his own game was entirely self-taught. He had the stance of a baseball player—and tended to lunge at the ball—but he played the game with the same gusto with which he lived his life. He enjoyed scrambling to recover a bad shot, he holed the putts that mattered, and was at his best when competing at match play. He lost only once—in the final to Gene Sarazen in 1923 at the second extra hole—in six outings at the USPGA, then a matchplay championship. When the Ryder Cup started, he was a natural first US captain, and he won seven of his nine matches.

Hagen raised the stature of the golf professional in America at a time when the game was growing fast, but Britain lagged behind. At his first Open, at Royal Cinque Ports in Kent in 1920, Hagen arrived in a chauffeur-driven Austro-Daimler limousine and dressed in a Saville Row overcoat. Told he could not enter the clubhouse, he changed his shoes in the car. Two years later, he celebrated his first Open win by giving the check of £50 ($221) to his caddie. In 1923, at Troon, where he was the runner-up, the presentation ceremony was the only occasion that professionals were allowed in the clubhouse. Hagen declined the offer and bought drinks for the gallery at the local pub.

● Cigarette card from 1920

◄ **WALTER HAGEN WAS PART OF A US TEAM** that traveled to Gleneagles, Scotland, in 1921 to play against Great Britain and Ireland. This event was the forerunner of the Ryder Cup.

Gene Sarazen

A short man, always dapperly dressed in plus fours, Gene Sarazen was an engaging character whose enthusiasm for the game was infectious. He won seven Major championships, invented the sand wedge, and later in life helped pioneer "Shell's Wonderful World of Golf" matches on television. Sarazen was one of the game's great ambassadors.

PLAYER STATS

BORN February 27, 1902; Harrison, New York
HEIGHT 5ft 5in (1.68m)
TURNED PRO 1920

DEBUT WIN 1922 Southern Spring Open
TOUR WINS 41
PGA TOUR: 39
OTHER: 2

MAJORS 7
MASTERS: WON 1935
US OPEN: WON 1922, 1932
THE OPEN: WON 1932
USPGA: WON 1922, 1923, 1933

HONORS 8
Bob Jones Award: 1992
Won a career Grand Slam
Ryder Cup Team: 1927, 1929, 1931, 1933, 1935, 1937

GENE'S SAND IRON

Sarazen invented the sand wedge, a club with a high degree of loft and a raised leading edge. When using a sand wedge, the player strikes the sand behind the ball to lift the ball out of the trap.

● Sarazen shows off his sand technique

Born Eugenio Saraceni, he changed his name at the age of 17 after a newspaper reported that he had made a hole in one. "When I saw my name in print, I thought it looked like a violin player," he explained. "I wanted something that sounded more like a golfer."

It was a name that would soon become well known. In 1922, at the age of 20, he won the first of two US Open Championships and a month later won the first of three USPGA titles. He retained the USPGA Championship a year later, but in the era of Walter Hagen and Bobby Jones, he eventually found success hard to find. What helped rekindle his career was his innovative mind. At the time, playing out of bunkers was regarded as a tricky business. Sarazen fiddled around with the loft and lie of his wedge clubs and eventually refined not only the implement now known as the sand wedge but also the method of playing a bunker shot. These changes allowed him to get up and down in two strokes with much greater regularity. Sarazen was not the best driver of a ball. He had a homemade swing and an unusual grip, with four knuckles showing on his left hand. But with his recovery play from bunkers hugely improved, confidence flowed through the rest of his game, and he won the US Open again in 1932. During that same summer, he returned to Britain—where he had first attempted to play in the Open in 1923 but failed to qualify—and won the only Open ever to be played at Prince's in Kent. He won two more Major championships, the second of them the Masters in 1935, which meant that he became the first player to win all four of the modern Grand Slam tournaments. Known as the "Squire," he remained an honorary starter at the Masters until shortly before his death at the age of 97.

All men are created equal. I'm just one stroke better than the rest.

GENE SARAZEN

▲ **SARAZEN IS CARRIED** on the shoulders of enthusiastic fans after winning the US Open at Skokie Country Club, Illinois, in 1922. He beat Bobby Jones by one stroke.

Bobby Jones was the greatest championship golfer in the history of the game, amateur or pro.

CHARLES PRICE, GOLF WRITER

Bobby Jones

Perhaps no one can ever be definitively hailed as the greatest golfer to have played the game, but Bobby Jones was undoubtedly one of the very best and probably the most popular. His feat of winning the Grand Slam in 1930 is rivaled only by Ben Hogan's three titles in 1953 and Tiger Woods winning four consecutive Majors in 2000–2001, but neither could be more beloved than Jones.

PLAYER STATS

BORN March 17, 1902; Atlanta, Georgia
HEIGHT 5ft 8in (1.72m)
DIED December 18, 1971

TOUR WINS 9
PGA TOUR: 7
OTHER: 2

MAJORS 7
US OPEN: Won 1923, 1926, 1929, 1930
THE OPEN: Won 1926, 1927, 1930
US AMATEUR: Won 1924, 1925, 1927, 1928, 1930
BRITISH AMATEUR: Won 1930

HONORS
Grand Slam Winner: 1930
Walker Cup Team: 1922, 1924, 1926, 1928, 1930
Founded the Masters at Augusta National

◀ **FEW MEN, LET ALONE GOLFERS,** have been as beloved as Bobby Jones—admirers followed his every shot on the course.

BOBBY ON FILM

Jones made a number of coaching films. Here he is shown (third from the left) looking at the results of a recent shoot. In his series *Bobby Jones: How I Play Golf* (1931), Jones is seen coaching some of the top celebrities of the time, including WC Fields and Loretta Young.

A master golfer on film

Robert Tyre Jones was introduced to the game at an early age at the East Lake golf club in Atlanta. A sickly child, the fresh air was considered good for him, but the youngster took to the game immediately—in fact, he proved to be a prodigy. He won his club's junior title at the age of nine, beating a 16-year-old in the final, and by 12, he was the club champion. Two years later, he was the Georgia State champion and played in the US Amateur for the first time.

Jones was as enthralled with the mechanics of the game as he was with actually playing it, learning his trade under the guidance of Stewart Maiden, a native of Carnoustie, at East Lake. But he was never just a golfer. He earned degrees in engineering from Georgia Tech and English literature from Harvard, then studied law and passed his bar exams after just a year. Although his professional career would be as a lawyer, it was on the golf course that he was to become a hero.

By the time of his 21st birthday, Jones had been playing in national championships for seven years but had won nothing significant. He had all the physical attributes necessary for playing the game to a level never seen before, but his temper often let him down. There were club-throwing incidents and verbal outbursts, and the president of the US Golf Association wrote a letter threatening to ban him from the main championships if his antics continued.

Jones suffered from nerves and anxiety and hardly played tournament golf outside the big events. "He was a fascinating personality," wrote American sports writer Al Laney. "Outwardly so gentle, so intelligent and pleasingly charming in a remarkably mature way; underneath lay concealed a furious often uncontrolled temper. In the young Bobby Jones, the emotions, the temperaments were a chaotic mixture with the fiercely choleric threatening to take control at times." Yet Jones learned to manage these elements of his personality and become a fearsome match player—no one ever beat him twice in championship play—and from 1923 to 1930, he had an astonishing run of success. He won 13 of the 21 championships he entered—the Majors of the day for the amateur. He won the US Amateur five times, the US Open four times, the Open Championship three times, and the British Amateur once. From 1922 to his retirement, he played in the US Open and Open Championship 12 times, won on seven occasions, and finished runner-up in four of the other five tournaments.

His breakthrough came at the US Open in 1923 when he looked a comfortable winner before finishing bogey, bogey, double bogey, to end up in a playoff. "I didn't finish like a champion," he said. "I finished like a yellow dog." But the playoff came down to the 18th hole, and this time Jones did finish like a champion. From a sandy lie and over 200 yards (183 meters) away, Jones hit a 2-iron over the water and on to the green to 6ft (1.8m). It was one of the greatest shots he ever hit, and the legend was born.

▲ **BOBBY JONES WITH THE IMPRESSIVE ARRAY** of trophies won during the 1930 season: (left to right) the Open, the US Amateur, the British Amateur, and the US Open.

BOBBY'S WAR

Robert T. Jones Jr. reports for duty as an officer of the Army Air Corp during World War II. He was initially assigned to the Aircraft Warning Service, an organization of civilian volunteers who manned observation posts along the Atlantic Coast but later served overseas. During the war, he allowed the US military to graze cattle on the grounds at Augusta National.

Jones trades his plus fours for military uniform

THE MAKING OF A LEGEND

Part of the legend that grew up around Jones was his willingness to call penalty shots on himself, for example, during the 1925 US Open when, unseen by anyone else, his ball moved after being addressed. He ended up losing a playoff for the title but when asked about it he said, "There is only one way to play this game and that is by the rules. You might as well praise a man for not robbing a bank."

Jones won the Open for the first time in 1926 at Lytham, becoming the first man to win both the US and British titles in the same year. In preparation for the Open, he played a round of near perfection at Sunningdale. He shot 66 with 33 strokes to the turn and 33 home. There were 33 strokes from tee to green and 33 putts, only one of them a long one. There were even a handful of missed chances as well.

PLANNING THE SLAM

In 1930, he planned an assault that became known as the Grand Slam—the Amateur and Open titles of both the US and Britain (see pp.212–213). The British Amateur, which involved head-to-head matches, came first at St. Andrews. It was the only time he won the title and was the key, he felt, to winning all four. Then came the Open at Hoylake, where he survived a double bogey seven at the final hole to win. The US Open was at Interlachen, where he holed from 40ft (12m) on the final green for the victory. The last leg of his mission was the US Amateur, which was, like the British equivalent, a matchplay event, but he again defeated all comers. One report named the achievement the Impregnable Quadrilateral, but it was the phrase "Grand Slam" that stuck.

Later that year, at the age of 28, he announced his retirement to concentrate on his family and business interests. With a group of investors, he bought land in Augusta, Georgia. Along with Alister Mackenzie, Jones created the Augusta National Golf Club and, from 1934, the Masters (see pp.214–125 and pp.296–299). In 1948, he played his last round of golf and was later diagnosed with the neuromuscular wasting disease, syringomyelia. Over the next 23 years, he became increasingly incapacitated, deciding he would simply "do the best I could."

Pat Ward-Thomas wrote: "Jones was the champion of champions. No golfer has achieved or is ever likely to achieve a supremacy of all the players in the world for as long as he did. No golfer will command more lasting affection and respect for his qualities as a person."

▲ JONES IS ESCORTED back to the clubhouse after winning the British Amateur at St. Andrews, the first leg of his Grand Slam.

1916
Wins the Georgia State Amateur title at the age of 14.

1923
Secures his first Major, the US Open, at Inwood Country Club, at the 18th hole in a playoff.

1927
Defends his Open title at St. Andrews with a record low score of 285.

1929
Wins his third US Open at Winged Foot after a playoff against Al Espinosa.

BOBBY JONES AT ST. ANDREWS

On first seeing the Old Course in 1921, Jones was less than impressed. In the third round of the Open, he went to the turn in 43, double bogeyed the 10th, visited a bunker on the par-3 11th, and was about to make another six when he picked up his ball. He did not tear up his card or storm off the course, but he had quit the tournament. Over the years, his opinion of it changed significantly. "The more I studied the course, the more I loved it ... the more I loved it the more I studied it," he said. In 1927, at St. Andrews, he won his second Open title, and in 1930, he won the first leg of the Grand Slam, the British Amateur, on the Old Course.

In 1936, on a short visit to Scotland en route to the Olympics in Berlin, Jones played a game at the Old Course, and 5,000 people turned out to watch, even though there had been no official announcement of his visit. The rest of the town was deserted. "Our Bobby is back," the cry went up. In 1958, Jones added to his honorary memberships of the Royal and Ancient, St. Andrews, and New golf clubs by being awarded the Freedom of the Royal Burgh of St. Andrews in an emotional ceremony. "If I could take out of my life everything but my experiences in St. Andrews, I would still have had a rich, full life," Jones said. In 1972, there was a memorial service for Bobby in the town where Roger Wethered, the defeated finalist in the 1930 British Amateur, delivered an address describing, "A golfer matchless in skill and chivalrous in spirit." The 10th hole on the Old Course is named "Bobby Jones."

▲ **GENE SARAZEN** (left) and Jones (right) were great rivals. By winning the Masters in 1935, Sarazen helped Jones's new tournament become established.

◄ **JONES REPRESENTED** the US in his fifth and final Walker Cup in 1930, at Royal St. George's. Here he is playing against Britain's RW Hartley.

● A cigarette card from 1930

> ## No one will ever replace Bobby Jones in the hearts of those to whom golf means more than a game.
>
> **GRANTLAND RICE,** SPORTS WRITER

1930
Seals victory at the British Amateur Championship, beating Roger Wethered by seven shots.

1930
Wins his third Open Championship—and the second part of the Grand Slam—at Hoylake.

1930
Holes a 40 ft (12 m) putt on the final green to win the US Open at Interlachen.

1930
Completes the Grand Slam of Amateur and Open titles by winning the US Amateur at Merion.

1934
Comes out of retirement to play in the inaugural Masters tournament in 1934 at his new course in Augusta, Georgia.

1958
Is made a Freeman of St. Andrews, only the second American—after Benjamin Franklin—to be so honored.

Joyce Wethered

Joyce Wethered was to the women's game what Bobby Jones was to the men's. She was the dominant player of the 1920s, virtually unbeatable in her short career. Jones was her hero. But the admiration was mutual, and it was Jones who described Wethered as the best golfer, man or woman, that he had ever seen. She was also a leading force in founding the Curtis Cup.

Wethered took up the game while on vacation in Scotland and was encouraged by her brother, Roger, one of the best amateur players of the era. She entered the English Ladies Championship at Sheringham in 1920, merely to keep a friend company, and ended up beating the then-star Cecil Leitch in the final. Subsequently, she went on to win five consecutive English titles and the British Amateur four times. In the latter championship, she played 38 matches and won 36 of them. After winning her third British title in 1925, she retired from competitive golf but made a comeback in 1929 at St. Andrews where she beat America's best player, Glenna Collett. After her famous win at the Old Course, she retired again from championship golf at the age of 28, as Bobby Jones would do at the same age a year later. She would be the first British captain in the Curtis Cup in 1932, having helped establish the competition.

Jones often competed against Joyce's brother, Roger, and beat him in the final of the British Amateur at St. Andrews in 1930. A week later, Bobby and Joyce partnered each other in a fourball match off the back tees on the Old Course. Jones had a round of 75 to Joyce's 76, but Jones said he felt "utterly outclassed." "It was not so much the score as the way she made it," Jones said. "It was impossible to expect Miss Wethered would ever miss a shot—and she never did." As identified on film during her US tour of 1935, the pair shared a remarkably similar free-flowing swing. On that tour, Wethered played at Jones's home club of East Lake in Atlanta. Her partner, Charlie Yates, a future British Amateur champion, was outscored by Wethered for the first 14 holes. "I would have been pretty embarrassed but I was hypnotized by watching her play", said Yates.

PLAYER STATS

BORN November 17, 1901; Surrey, England
DIED November 18, 1997

WINS 9
BRITISH WOMEN'S AMATEUR CHAMPIONSHIP: Won 1922, 1924, 1925, 1929
ENGLISH LADIES' CHAMPIONSHIP: Won 1920, 1921, 1922, 1923, 1924

HONORS
Curtis Cup Player/Captain: 1932

▼ **JOYCE WETHERED** leads fellow players and spectators across a bridge at St. Andrews during the English Ladies' Championship in 1929.

▲ **WETHERED'S ELEGANT SWING** was captured on film in 1932, three years after her last triumph in the Women's Amateur.

I never played golf with anyone, man or woman, amateur or professional, who made me feel so utterly outclassed.

BOBBY JONES

Henry Cotton

Although he died before being able to attend Buckingham Palace for the investiture, Sir Henry Cotton was golf's first knight. Cotton became a patriarch of the European Golf Tour, authored a number of books, designed golf courses, and was the most respected British instructor of his time. He was Britain's finest golfer between the Great Triumvirate and Nick Faldo.

While most professionals of his time had been caddies or the sons of golf professionals, Henry Cotton broke the mold. He was educated at public school in London, and his middle-class background would have suggested a career as an amateur. But Cotton wanted to make the most of his golfing abilities, and to him that meant turning professional.

His first Open triumph ended an 11-year run without a British winner. It came at Royal St. George's in 1934, where he sprinted ahead of the field with opening rounds of 67 and 65. The latter score was a record that would stand for 43 years and was so amazing that a golf ball manufacturer wanted to commemorate the feat: the Dunlop 65 became the ball of choice for years to come. Cotton stuttered to a final round 79 but still won by five strokes. Three years later, he won again at Carnoustie, against the full might of the American Ryder Cup team. The American writer Al Laney described Cotton as

"a strange, forbidding man in those days, but he could handle a golf club with his three-quarter swing more expertly than anyone I have seen since except Ben Hogan. When Cotton hit an iron to the green with chilling, humorless concentration it seemed magic. Like Hogan ... he gave the impression of coldness, but there was also the same feeling ... that the ball had been given no option, that there was nothing he could not achieve."

Always one to winter in the sun, Cotton and his wife, Toots, lived in Penina, Portugal, where professionals would make a pilgrimage for advice and guidance.

PLAYER STATS

BORN January 26, 1907; Holmes Chapel, England
DIED December 22, 1987
TURNED PRO 1924

TOUR WINS 16

MAJORS 3
THE OPEN: Won 1934, 1937, 1948

HONORS
Ryder Cup Team: 1929, 1937, 1947
Ryder Cup Captain: 1947, 1953
Harry Vardon Trophy Winner: 1938

● Cotton speaks at the London Coliseum

▼ **COTTON CHIPS** on to the green during a match at the Royal Mid Surrey Course, England, in 1947, the year of his final Ryder Cup appearance.

Byron Nelson

Although he became famous for "The Streak" (see pp.216–217), Byron Nelson will be remembered as the first gentleman of golf. His death, in 2006, came as Tiger Woods was compiling a run of seven successive wins on the PGA Tour. In his historic season of 1945, Nelson won 11 in a row. However, 60 years after his retirement, the obituaries spoke more of the man than the golf.

PLAYER STATS

BORN February 4, 1912; Waxahachie, Texas
HEIGHT 6ft 1in (1.85m)
TURNED PRO 1932

DEBUT WIN 1935 New Jersey State Open
TOUR WINS 63
LPGA TOUR: 52
OTHER: 11

MAJORS 5
MASTERS: Won 1937, 1942
US OPEN: Won 1939
THE OPEN: 5th 1937
USPGA: Won 1940, 1945

HONORS
Vardon Trophy Winner: 1939
PGA Tour Money Winner: 1944, 1945
Ryder Cup Team: 1937, 1947
Ryder Cup Captain: 1965
PGA Player of the Year: 1945

▼ **"LORD" BYRON'S** 11 straight tournament victories in 1945 still stands as one of golf's most remarkable records.

Nelson had only a short career, but he remained close to the game long after he finished playing. He was the first star golfer to become a television commentator, and he mentored promising professionals, including Tom Watson and Ken Venturi. He served as a long-time honorary starter at the Masters, and since 1968, the Dallas Open has been known as the Byron Nelson Classic—the only US tour event named after a player. "Lord Byron," as he was affectionately nicknamed, was never less than a much-loved legend of the game, and the hand-written notes of congratulation or commiseration he sent to players became treasured keepsakes. Venturi, talking of their time playing exhibitions around the country, said Nelson would always check the course record and who held it. If it was the local club pro, they would leave it intact.

Nelson was born in the same year as Sam Snead and Ben Hogan and in the same state (Texas) as Hogan. They contested the final of the Glen Garden Country Club caddies' championship in 1927 with Nelson winning narrowly—a result that was repeated in their playoff at the 1942 Masters. Nelson won two Masters, two USPGA titles, and the US Open (after yet another playoff)—but never the Open Championship.

As a player, he was the first big-name golfer to truly adapt to the new, larger ball and clubs with steel shafts. His iron play was robotic—in the 1939 Open, he hit the pin six times during the regulation 72-hole play. In testament to his consistency, the USGA's equipment-testing machine was named "Iron Byron," and at a time when only the leading 15 or 20 players received prize money each week, Nelson was "in the money" for 113 consecutive tournaments.

ABOUT THAT STREAK

A blood disorder prevented Nelson from going to war, and in 1944, he left his club job at Inverness in Toledo and played only on tour. He won eight times that year but was not happy with his chipping and a number of careless shots. Every round was noted in a diary and analyzed at length. The following year, he won 18 times on the tour. His stroke average for the season was 68.34, a figure beaten only by Tiger Woods in 2000. The 11-tournament winning streak began at a fourball event in Miami, in March 1945, and ended when he lost at the Memphis Invitational in August. It was said, unfairly and inaccurately, that the courses were easy and that the opposition limited—despite the fact that Sam Snead and Ben Hogan both won a number of tour events that year. "I don't care if he was playing against orangutans," said Jackie Burke. "Winning eleven straight is amazing".

He was victorious six times in 1946 but virtually retired at the end of the year, aged only 34. He bought a ranch near Fort Worth with his first wife, Louise, and freely admitted that his main motivation for every

● Nelson featured on a cereal-packet advertisement

victory in the previous two years had been to earn money to buy another cow or more land for his ranch. "I was tired and I'd accomplished everything I'd set out to do in golf," he explained. "It was time to move on. Once the ranch belonged to us, nothing else mattered."

> I don't know very much. I know a little bit about golf. I know how to make a stew. And I know how to be a decent man.

BYRON NELSON

▶ **NELSON RETURNS TO THE CADDIESHACK,** where he started his career, beating rival Ben Hogan for the caddies' championship at Glen Garden in 1927.

▶▶ **BING CROSBY** is excited to capture the first gentleman of golf on film at Crosby's tournament at Pebble Beach in 1951. Nelson won with a 54-hole total of 209.

▼ **NELSON MODERNIZED** the art of the golf swing, taking advantage of steel shafts and the larger ball. His iron play, in particular, was metronomic.

Sam Snead

Known as "slammin' sammy," or simply "slammer," Sam Snead was blessed with one of the sweetest swings the game has ever seen. That sweet swing had such balance and rhythm, such touch and timing that he was one of the longest hitters of his time. It was the hallmark of a career that spanned six decades and encompassed 162 tour victories, seven of them Majors.

PLAYER STATS

BORN May 27, 1912; Ashwood, Virginia
DIED May 23, 2002
HEIGHT 5ft 11in (1.80m)
TURNED PRO 1934

DEBUT WIN 1937 Oakland Open
TOUR WINS 165
LPGA TOUR: 82
SENIOR TOUR: 13
OTHER: 70

MAJORS 7
MASTERS: Won 1949, 1952, 1954
US OPEN: 2nd 1937, 1947, 1953/T2nd 1949
THE OPEN: Won 1946
USPGA: Won 1942, 1949, 1951

HONORS
PGA Tour Money Winner: 1938, 1949, 1950
PGA Player of the Year: 1949
Vardon Trophy Winner: 1938, 1949, 1950, 1955
Ryder Cup Team: 937, 1947, 1949, 1951, 1953, 1955, 1959
Ryder Cup Captain: 1951, 1959, 1969

Snead's origins were very humble indeed. He grew up and lived his whole life in Hot Springs, Virginia, in the foothills of the Blue Ridge mountains—huntin' and fishin' country. The youngest of five sons, Sam saw his elder brother Homer playing in the family pasture and copied his style, using homemade clubs fashioned from broken branches. He was a phenomenal athlete, his party tricks being one-armed press-ups and kicking cans off the top of doors. His golf may have been self-taught, but his big break came when he became the assistant professional at the Greenbrier in North Carolina, a club that he remained associated with until he died, four days short of his 90th birthday.

Snead's driving dramatically improved only after Henry Picard gave him a club that had a stiffer shaft and suited his swing better than the old more flexible drivers. He became known as the longest, straightest driver of the ball on tour. Putting became his only weakness, as he tried many different styles, but to make up for it, he was a demon pitcher and hit wonderful long-iron shots.

COUNTRY BOY
Snead became the greatest winner on the US tour, with 82 official victories—the last when he was 52—and more besides when traveling outside the US, something he generally disliked. Snead was always a country boy at heart, and his agent, Fred Corcoran, unashamedly promoted his humble roots. Snead had a wicked sense of humor but could be crude and definitely not politically correct, and the press reveled in his unpolished sayings. Asked once

about the winning score in a US Open, Snead said: "Oh, I'll take 280, sit in a clubhouse, eat hot dogs, drink Cokes, and fart."

Snead won seven Major championships—three Masters, three USPGAs, and the Open, in 1946—but finished runner-up no less than four times at the US Open. At times others did better, but on other occasions he simply fell apart. A triple bogey at the final hole lost it

◀ **SNEAD HOLDS THE RECORD** for most victories at one event, winning the Greater Greensboro Open eight times.

Any guy who would pass up the chance to see Sam Snead play golf would pull the shades driving past the Taj Mahal.

JIM MURRAY, SPORTS WRITER

▲ **SNEAD BECAME THE GREATEST** winner on the PGA Tour with 82 victories, the last of them coming at the age of 52. Tiger Woods equaled the tally in 2019.

for him in 1937, as did a three-putt at the last hole of a playoff in 1947, while in 1949 and 1953, he had final rounds of 76 and even an 81. On one of those occasions, he was asked if he had felt tight, and Snead replied, "Tight? I was so tight you couldn't a drove a flax seed up my ass with a knot maul."

Rather against his better judgment—the traveling expenses were greater than the first prize—Snead traveled to the Open Championship at St. Andrews in 1946, and on the train that was entering the town,

he said to a companion: "That looks like an abandoned golf course." Of course, it was the Old Course and news of the insult got around. "Snead, a rural American type, undoubtedly would think the leaning tower of Pisa is a structure about to totter and crash to his feet," wrote a correspondent from *The Times*. Nevertheless, Snead mastered the course, plotting his way around brilliantly in the gusty conditions, and took the title by four strokes. It was said of Snead's swing: "He just walked up to the ball and poured honey all over it." Nothing was sweeter.

SAM'S BIG BREAK

Sam Snead's big break came when he played a foursome at the Greenbrier in West Virginia. He was offered the post of teaching professional but almost lost it when he drove the green at the short par-4 5th and hit a hotel guest on the backside. The guest was a director of the railroad company that owned the hotel, but after seeing Snead do it again the next day, he made him his personal teacher.

⬤ Snead in the Greenbrier pro shop

◀ **SNEAD WAS A PHENOMENAL** athlete whose swing was as elegant at the end of his career as it was at the start.

Ben Hogan

"You have to dig it out of the dirt," Ben Hogan said. No one enjoyed practicing or improved his swing as much as Hogan did. After a slow start compared to his contemporaries Byron Nelson and Sam Snead, Hogan dominated the game immediately after World War II, despite suffering a near-fatal car crash. In 1953, he won three Major championships, including triumph at the Open in his only appearance.

PLAYER STATS

BORN August 13, 1912; Stephenville, Texas
DIED July 25, 1997
HEIGHT 5ft 7in (1.70m)
TURNED PRO 1929

DEBUT WIN 1940 North and South Open
TOUR WINS 64
LPGA TOUR: 64

MAJORS 9
MASTERS: Won 1951, 1953
US OPEN: Won 1948, 1950, 1951, 1953
THE OPEN: Won 1953
USPGA: Won 1946, 1948

HONORS
PGA Tour Money Winner: 1940, 1941, 1942, 1946, 1948
Vardon Trophy Winner: 1940, 1941, 1948
PGA Player of the Year: 1948, 1950, 1951, 1953
Ryder Cup Team: 1947, 1951
Ryder Cup Captain: 1947, 1949, 1967

Ben Hogan was a complex man. At the age of only nine, he had to deal with the death of his father, who died by suicide. He came through the caddie ranks at Glen Garden in Fort Worth, Texas, along with Byron Nelson, but struggled when he turned professional. He found himself broke at least a couple of times and did odd jobs in the winter—at one time working as a croupier. However, hours on the practice range eventually gave him a powerful but soft-landing fade. This replaced his natural violent hook, which he once said was like having a "rattlesnake in your pocket."

Although his putting was not the best and did let him down later in his career, few have perfected the game from tee to green as Hogan did. Like a "machine stamping out bottle caps," said *Time* magazine.

He lost three years to military service, but in 1946, when he won 13 times, he discovered the key to success was to concentrate on a few fundamentals. He won the first of nine Majors in 1946 at the USPGA, but it was when he won the US Open for the first time that he started an incredible run of success: he won eight out of the 11 majors he entered between 1948 and

● A Phoenix Open program

▶ **HOGAN WAS RENOWNED** for his steely resolve and was reportedly unapproachable. But he was all smiles after the 1951 US Open.

HOGAN'S LUCKY ESCAPE

In 1949, driving along a road in Texas, Hogan's car ran into a Greyhound bus that was overtaking a truck. At the moment of impact, Hogan threw himself across the car to protect his wife. Both survived, but Hogan suffered a broken collarbone and fractures of his hip, ribs, and left ankle. He also suffered a blood clot and never had normal circulation in his legs again.

○ Hogan in a critical state after the car accident

1953. After his car accident (see above and pp.220–221), playing golf meant dealing with pain. In the most remarkable victory of his career, at the US Open in 1950, he struggled through 36 holes on the final day and then won an 18-hole playoff the following day. In 1951, he brought the monster Oakland Hills course to its knees to win the US Open once again; then two years later, he won a second Masters and a fourth US Open. In 1953 Hogan traveled for the first and only time to Britain for the Open. He had stopped playing the USPGA due to its long matchplay format, and in any case, the events overlapped. At Carnoustie, he triumphed with a course record of 68 in the final round. The "Wee Ice Mon" was immediately taken to the hearts of the Scots gallery.

He remains one of only five players to have won all four Major titles and, with Tiger Woods, the only other player to have won three Majors in the same season (see pp.222–223).

▲ **HOGAN'S SWING** was the envy of his fellow professionals, and his methods live on. His technique is central to the teachings of many modern-day coaches, including David Leadbetter.

You hear stories about me beating my brains out practicing, but the truth is, I was enjoying myself. I couldn't wait to get up in the morning, so I could hit balls.

BEN HOGAN

Babe Zaharias

Babe Zaharias was the first woman athlete to become a national hero in America. A brilliantly gifted all-around sportswoman, she was already a successful Olympic track and field athlete before she turned to golf, where she found lasting success. She also helped found the Ladies Professional Golf Association (LPGA) in 1950.

PLAYER STATS

BORN November 20, 1917; Port Arthur, Texas
DIED September 27, 1956
TURNED PRO 1947

DEBUT WIN 1940 Western Open (as an amateur)
TOUR WINS 31
LPGA TOUR: 31

MAJORS 10
WESTERN OPEN: Won 1940, 1944, 1945, 1950
WOMEN'S US OPEN: Won 1948, 1950, 1954
TITLEHOLDERS CHAMPIONSHIP: Won 1947, 1950, 1952

HONORS
British Amateur Championship: Won 1947
US Amateur Championship: Won 1947
Winner of two gold and one silver medal for track and field at 1932 Los Angeles Olympics

Mildred Didrikson changed her surname to Zaharias in 1938 after marrying professional wrestler George Zaharias. She had already become simply "Babe," after legendary baseball player Babe Ruth, following a baseball game in which she hit five home runs. In fact, she was gifted at many sports, including basketball, tennis, diving, skating, bowling, and billiards, not to mention athletics. At the US Olympic trials in 1932, she won six out of eight events, and at the Olympic Games in Los Angeles later that summer, she won gold medals in the javelin and the 80-meter hurdles. At the same Games, she, albiet briefly, established a new high jump world record but was later demoted to the silver-medal position because her technique was considered to be illegal.

AN OUTSTANDING AMATEUR
When she turned to golf on a full-time basis, she could hit the ball vast distances but took time to learn the game. After winning the Texas Amateur title in 1933, she was barred from playing in amateur events since she was considered to be a professional for earning money at other sports. She went on exhibition tours but eventually regained her amateur status and went on a brilliant winning streak. She won the US Amateur in 1946 and the British Amateur at Gullane the following year.

Zaharias turned professional in 1947 and won the Women's US Open three times while heading the prize money list on the LPGA Tour in the first two years of its existence. In 1953, she was diagnosed with cancer, but after surgery, she returned to win the 1954 US Open by 12 strokes. It was her last great triumph, because in 1955, the cancer reappeared. On her hospital bed, her final words to her husband were, "Honey, I ain't going to die."

▲ **ZAHARIAS WAS A LATECOMER** to the game and was introduced to it by the sports writer Grantland Rice during the 1932 Olympics in Los Angeles. In between events, Rice maintains she shot a round of 91.

▲ **FROM OLYMPIC STAR** to golfing champion, Babe Zaharias was a sensational athlete blessed with a natural gift and rhythm.

She is the Ultimate Amazon and the greatest athlete of all mankind for all time.

GRANTLAND RICE SPORTS WRITER

Max Faulkner

At a time when the Open Championship became dominated by visitors from Australia, South Africa, and, of course, America, Max Faulkner was a beacon of hope, the last British champion for almost two decades until Tony Jacklin. Faulkner was a flamboyant character, a British version of Walter Hagen, who brightened up postwar golf. Portrush in 1951 was his lasting memorial.

PLAYER STATS

BORN July 29, 1916; Bexhill, England
DIED February 26, 2005
TURNED PRO 1946

TOUR WINS 18
European Seniors Tour: 2

MAJORS 1
THE OPEN: WON 1951

HONORS
Ryder Cup Team: 1947, 1949, 1951, 1953, 1957

▼ **FAULKNER ESCAPES** from the rough at Royal Portrush on his way to winning the 1951 Open, his sole Major success.

It was said in a newspaper column, penned by the sports journalist Ian Wooldridge, that Max Faulkner went around signing autographs at the 1951 Open with the addendum "Open Champion 1951." In fact, Faulkner had signed an autograph prior to the final round for a small boy whose father asked for the words to be added. Having obliged, Faulkner thought, "What have I done! I'd better win now."

He was six strokes ahead and duly took the crown and the £300 ($840) prize money with a final score of 285. A straight driver and iron player, Faulkner's putting that week was also superb. He had only 24 putts in the second round, but the especially light putter he used that week was just one of 300 he collected and used, most of which he'd made himself.

TEAM PLAYER

At the 1957 Ryder Cup at Lindrick in Yorkshire, England, Faulkner was left out of the singles but still had a vital role to play. Ken Bousfield, who claimed the winning point, recalled: "Those were the days before scoreboards out on the course and walkie-talkies. All of us playing out there have no idea what was happening in the other matches if it wasn't for Max. He was marvelous. And he seemed to bring good news every time I saw him. He'd nip up to me [and say], 'Rees is winning'; 'Brown's four-up'; 'We've got them on the run, Guv'nor'; 'Go on! You can beat this boy.' Then he'd dash off and come back ten minutes later with more good news. We might have won without him, but he was magnificent that day—I'll never forget what he did."

Bobby Locke

Bobby Locke was the first great player to emerge from South Africa, starting a dynasty that continued with Gary Player and has progressed into the modern era with Ernie Else, Retief Goosen, Louis Oosthuizen, and Charl Schwartzel. Locke was also one of the finest putters the game has ever seen, his success on the greens bringing him four Open Championships between 1949 and 1957.

He was the greatest putter I have ever seen.

PETER ALLISS

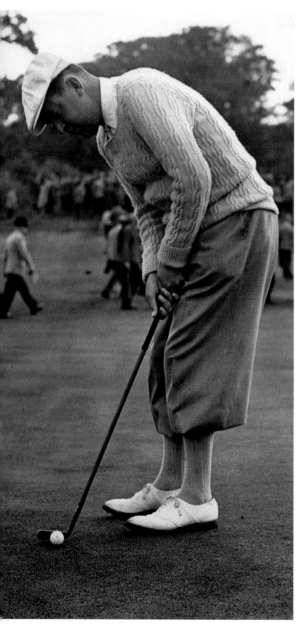

Locke used the same hickory-shafted, rusty-bladed putter for most of his career. Gripping the club very lightly, Locke had marvelous touch and was a firm believer in easing the ball into the hole at "dead pace." His exceptional feel also showed in his distance control with his irons and in his accurate chipping.

When Sam Snead traveled to South Africa, he came up against Locke and was defeated 12-2 in a series of exhibition matches. But Snead was happy nonetheless to give him some career advice. The younger man once asked Snead if he could make a living in America. "Make a living?" replied Snead, "you'll get rich and very quickly." Locke did indeed win regularly in the US, but because many American players disliked a foreigner plundering their tour, he was resented and was briefly banned on the pretext of missing a couple of events he had entered. During his ban in the US, he played mainly in Britain, winning the Open for the first time in 1949, when he beat Harry Bradshaw in a playoff. It was when he started playing in Britain that he decided to change his natural fade to a draw, aiming away to the right and bringing the ball back. The change had a positive impact on his already impressive game.

The fourth and last of Locke's Open titles came at St. Andrews in 1957 when, on the final green, he moved his marker for another player but did not move it back to its original position. This was the first televised Open and replays showed the error, but the committee ruled that the result should stand. Three years later, Locke was injured in a car accident; he lost some of his sight in one eye and was never quite the same player again.

◀ **FOR MUCH OF HIS CAREER,** Locke dressed almost exclusively in gray flannel trousers, white buckskin shoes, linen dress shirts with neckties, and white Hogan caps.

PLAYER STATS

BORN November 20, 1917; Germiston, South Africa
DIED March 9, 1987
TURNED PRO 1938

DEBUT WIN 1938 South African Open
TOUR WINS 72
LGPA TOUR: 11
EUROPEAN TOUR: 23
SOUTHERN AFRICA TOUR: 38

MAJORS 4
MASTERS: 10th 1948
US OPEN: 3rd 1947, 1951
THE OPEN: WON 1949, 1950, 1952
USPGA: T33rd 1947

HONORS
Named an honorary member of the Royal and Ancient Golf Club in 1976

▲ **LOCKE HOLDS THE CLARET JUG** Jug at Royal St. George's in 1949; it was the first of four Open victories.

Peter Thomson

With Bobby Locke flying the flag for South Africa, Peter Thomson arrived on the scene to do the same for Australia. The pair dominated the Open in the 1950s, with Thomson winning the title four times, and five overall. He became a writer, commentator, and course architect and went on to become a tour winner all over again on the Seniors Tour.

PLAYER STATS

BORN August 23, 1929; Melbourne, Australia
DIED June 20, 2018
TURNED PRO 1949

DEBUT WIN 1950 New Zealand Open
TOUR WINS 70
LGPA TOUR: 11
AUSTRALASIA TOUR: 20
EUROPEAN TOUR: 2
SENIOR TOUR: 11
OTHER: 7

MAJORS 1
MASTERS: 5th 1957
US OPEN: T4TH 1956
THE OPEN: Won 1954, 1955, 1956, 1958, 1965
USPGA: DNP

HONORS
Presidents Cup Captain: 1998
President of Australian PGA: 1962, 1963, 1994

Thomson was a cerebral player. He never believed in hours and hours of ball-beating on the practice range. It was said that if he had a problem with his game, he would sit in a chair, analyze the possible causes and solutions, and then head for the range only to confirm his theory with a dozen or so balls. He had a simplistic approach to the game; he would play for position and run the ball onto the green along the ground. In this way, his game was ideally suited to the fast-running courses of Australia and the summer links of Britain. Having perfected his game, he considered the knack of competing to be the key ingredient of winning tournaments. Between 1952 and 1958, he finished either first or second at the Open.

▲ **THOMSON'S SON HOLDS** the Australian Open trophy in 1967. Thomson was a prolific champion, winning the national championships of 10 different countries.

CHAMPION OF THE OPEN

His first victory came at Royal Birkdale in 1954, and he would go on to become the first player since Young Tom Morris to win three consecutive Open Championships. A fourth title arrived in 1958 and the fifth in 1965 back at Royal Birkdale. By this time, the Open had been "rediscovered" by the best US players, and among his opponents were Arnold Palmer, Jack Nicklaus, Phil Rodgers, and Tony Lema, the defending champion. It was his finest hour and finally cemented his reputation in America. His ventures to the US had been brief and brought him only one victory, but when the Seniors Tour started up in the 1980s, he returned and plundered the circuit for a couple of years before finally retiring to television commentary and his course design business.

◄ **THOMSON BELIEVED** that careful planning, calm and clear thinking, and common sense were the most important facets of golf.

Billy Casper

Anyone would look a little less exciting when put alongside Arnold Palmer, but Billy Casper showed there was another way to forge a successful career. A conservative, patient, disciplined man compared to Palmer's aggressive and charismatic showman, Casper nonetheless showed that patience is a virtue. The 1966 US Open was his greatest triumph.

PLAYER STATS

BORN June 24, 1931; San Diego, California
DIED February 7, 2015
TURNED PRO 1954

DEBUT WIN 1956 Labatt Open
TOUR WINS 66
LPGA TOUR: 51
CHAMPIONS TOUR: 9
OTHER: 6

MAJORS 3
MASTERS: Won 1970
US OPEN: Won 1959, 1966
THE OPEN: 4th 1968
USPGA: 2nd 1958, 1971/T2nd 1965

HONORS
Ryder Cup Team: 1961, 1963, 1965, 1967, 1969, 1971, 1973, 1975
Ryder Cup Captain: 1979
PGA Tour Money Winner: 1966, 1968
Vardon Trophy Winner: 1960, 1963, 1965, 1966, 1968

Inevitably, perhaps, the 1966 US Open became known as the championship Arnold Palmer lost rather than the championship Casper won. Palmer led at the Olympic Club in San Francisco by seven strokes with nine holes to play, but his swashbuckling style suddenly suffered a huge collapse and Casper's steady consistency was rewarded. Palmer came home in 39, Casper in 32, to force a playoff.

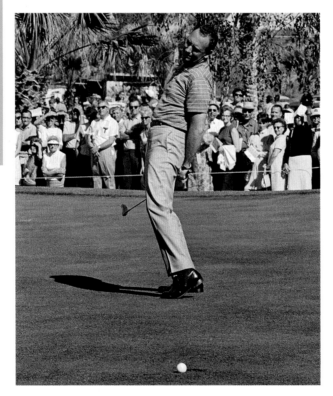

▶ **THE PUTTS** usually dropped for Billy Casper, but on this occasion, at the Bob Hope Desert Classic in 1968, the birdie putt stayed out.

The following day, Palmer was again four ahead at the turn but again capitulated. "I had seen other guys tense up, panic under pressure, but not Arnie," Casper said. "Once it looked like I was getting into his lead, his swing got shorter and faster."

Casper was an experienced winner. He won 51 times on the US tour between 1956 and 1975, including three Major championships. His 1966 win was his second US Open title, and he took the 1970 Masters in another playoff, this time against his fellow San Diegan Gene Littler. Later he was successful on the Seniors Tour winning two Senior Majors (in 1983 and 1988) and seven other titles.

STEADY AS HE GOES

Casper's game was based on steadiness, straight driving, and wonderful putting. He said he was too lazy to go to the range so perfected his chipping and putting instead. But his peers knew of his great qualities. "To be a winner you have to have heart," said Jack Nicklaus. "You really have to control your emotions and your golf game. Billy Casper was wonderful at this and does not get the credit he deserves. He didn't have all the shots that others had, but he was able to will the ball into the hole." On the course, he based his demeanor on Ben Hogan's "iceman" image. Off it, it was reckoned that he was "so austere ... that by contrast a Franciscan monk looks like a swinger," while Dave Hill wrote in his autobiography that he had "as much personality as a glass of water." Members of the Mormon Church, Casper and his wife had 11 children, many of whom were adopted from poorer backgrounds overseas.

> You must have the ability to control your mind and your heart. The golf swing is really a small part.
>
> **BILLY CASPER**

Julius Boros

A late starter as a professional golfer, Julius Boros still enjoyed a long and successful career. When he won the USPGA Championship in 1968, he became, at the age of 48, the oldest-ever winner of a Major championship. Not bad for a former accountant who turned to professional golf at the age of 30.

PLAYER STATS

BORN March 3, 1929; Bridgeport, Connecticut
DIED May 28, 1994
TURNED PRO 1949

DEBUT WIN 1951 Massachusetts Open
TOUR WINS 22
LPGA TOUR: 18
OTHER: 4

MAJORS 3
MASTERS: T3rd 1963
US OPEN: Won 1952, 1963
THE OPEN: DNP
USPGA: Won 1968

HONORS
Ryder Cup Team: 1959, 1963, 1965, 1967
PGA Player of the Year: 1952, 1963
PGA Tour Money Winner: 1952, 1955

Boros was of Hungarian descent and lived in Connecticut. He played a lot of golf with Sam Snead and Tommy Armour, who was the professional at his local club, before he turned pro himself. When Boros decided to make a living from the game, Armour was not particularly encouraging, although he admired his superb bunker game. However, Boros made an immediate impact. He placed ninth at his first US Open in 1950, finished fourth the following year, and then won at Northwood in 1952.

His game suited the US Open as he drove the ball straight and always managed to maintain a relaxed demeanor. Lee Trevino once said of him, "I'm telling you, of all the guys up there on that leaderboard, he scares me more than anybody. When he putts, you can't tell by looking at him whether he's just practicing or that it's for fifty grand if he sinks it." He did not practice much, and, concerned that he might lock up over a shot, he would walk casually up to his ball, shuffle into his stance in a distinctive manner, and then swing. Perhaps it all helped his longevity; 11 years after his first US Open victory, he triumphed at Brookline in 1963 after a playoff with Arnold Palmer and Jacky Cupit. Palmer was also involved five years later when Boros won the USPGA at Pecan Valley by one stroke from Arnie and Bob Charles.

Boros won the 1977 PGA Seniors' Championship, and two years later, in partnership with Roberto De Vincenzo, he won the Legends of Golf tournament after holing a birdie putt on the sixth hole of a sudden death playoff. It is widely acknowledged that this putt provided the impetus for the formation of the Senior PGA Tour in 1980.

▼ **BOROS TEES OFF** in the Los Angeles Open, the first tournament of the 1956 season, having ended the previous year as the tour's leading money winner.

▲ **BOROS CONTEMPLATES** from the rough at Royal Portrush on his way to winning the 1951 Open, his sole Major success.

▲ **NICKLAUS AND PALMER** line up a putt at the 1971 Ryder Cup. Their rivalry generated much drama and interest throughout the 1960s.

◀ **ARNOLD PALMER BROUGHT** a new audience to golf and inspired spectators around the world throughout his career.

Arnold Palmer

Arnold Palmer was golf's working-class hero. If Bobby Jones received the sort of hero worship reserved for an untouchable god, Palmer was a man of the people. He was golfing royalty but adored by all—men and women, rich and poor, golfer and nongolfer. He won seven Major championships, often dramatically, within a span of six years, and his timing was perfect—television was just starting to broadcast the sport, and Palmer was its first star.

PLAYER STATS

BORN September 10, 1929; Latrobe, Pennsylvania
DIED September 25, 2016
HEIGHT 5ft 10in (1.78m)
TURNED PRO 1954

DEBUT WIN 1955 Canadian Open
TOUR WINS 9
PGA TOUR: 62
SENIORS TOUR: 10
OTHER: 23

MAJORS 7
MASTERS: Won 1958, 1960, 1962, 1964
US OPEN: Won 1960
THE OPEN: Won 1961, 1962
USPGA: T2nd 1964, 1968, 1970

HONORS

US Amateur Winner: 1954
PGA Tour Money Winner: 1958, 1960, 1962, 1963
PGA Player of the Year: 1960, 1962
Ryder Cup Team: 1961, 1963, 1965, 1971, 1973
Ryder Cup Captain: 1963, 1975
Presidents Cup Captain: 1996
PGA Senior Championship: 1980, 1984
US Senior Open: 1981
Senior Players Championship: 1984, 1985

Palmer grew up on the Latrobe course on the outskirts of Pittsburgh, where his father, Deacon, was the greenkeeper and professional. From the start, Palmer married natural ability with innate aggression. This aggression was channeled positively after an early club-throwing incident earned a reprimand. When Palmer was three, his father placed a club in his hands and showed him the right grip, which he never changed. His father said, "Just hit the ball as hard as you can and then go and find it." And that's how he played all his career.

Palmer went to college at Wake Forest and completed military service in the Coast Guard. He won the US Amateur in 1954, then turned professional the following year, traveling in an RV with his young wife, Winnie. He won a few tournaments and played in the Masters, but his style did not impress some of the veterans such as Ben Hogan. In 1958, that all changed, as Palmer was tied with Sam Snead going into the last round at Augusta and won by four shots. At the 12th hole, his ball was over the green and plugged in the bank. There was confusion about how to proceed, but a rules official told him to play it as it lay but to drop another ball and play that, too. He got a five the first time and then a par 3 with the free drop. Mad as hell, Palmer made an eagle 3 at the 13th hole and was only then told that the free drop at the 12th was allowable and his par 3 would stand.

ARNIE'S GOLDEN YEARS

At 28, the same age that Bobby Jones was when he retired, Palmer was only just starting to win Majors. Although Jack Nicklaus would eclipse his four titles, it was at Augusta that Palmer was at his best. It was

FASTEST AROUND THE WORLD

A keen private aviator, Arnold Palmer has held several flying records during his life. In 1976, he flew around the world in 58 hours in a Learjet 63. In 1996, he bought the first-ever Cessna Citation X plane and promptly set a speed record with that over a closed 3,000-mile (5,000km) course. His local airport was renamed The Arnold Palmer Regional Airport in his honor.

● Palmer stands ready to pilot a bi-plane

here that Arnie's Army, a loyal band of supporters (see p.131), was founded. He won the title in alternate years between 1958 and 1964. In 1960, he birdied the last two holes to win by one shot. The following year, walking up the 18th fairway, he was distracted by a friend congratulating him. He took a double-bogey six and lost by one shot to Gary Player. In an 18-hole playoff in 1962, he beat Player and Dow Finsterwald by shooting the inward nine in 31.

Perhaps his greatest triumph came at Cherry Hills in 1960, the only time he won the US Open. Palmer was seven shots behind Mike Souchak with a round to play. Having a hamburger in the locker room with a couple of players and journalist friends, Palmer suggested that a 65 might still win. "That would get me to 280, and 280 always wins the Open," Palmer said confidently. "Only when Hogan shoots it," someone replied. Taking this comment as a slight, Palmer promptly drove the short, par-4 1st hole and two-putted for a birdie. In fact, he birdied six of the first seven holes, scored 65, and won by two shots. Two years later, he lost to Nicklaus in the US Open at Oakmont and suddenly the task of anyone other than "the Bear" winning Majors became difficult.

> There has never been anyone like him before in the game ... and there probably won't be another like him again.

JACK NICKLAUS, WRITING ABOUT PALMER IN HIS AUTOBIOGRAPHY

However, the pair would enjoy a friendly rivalry, both on and off the course, for the rest of their lives.

Having won the Masters and the US Open in 1960, Palmer headed to the Open at St. Andrews. On the plane, he was thinking that there should be some professional equivalent of Jones's Grand Slam of the two Open and Amateur championships of the US and Britain. Palmer and Bob Drum, a journalist friend, came up with the idea for the modern Grand Slam—the Masters, the US Open, the Open, and the USPGA. Palmer came second to Kel Nagle at the 1960 Open but won the title at Birkdale the following year, playing a shot from horrendous rough on what is now the 16th hole. There is now a plaque celebrating the wondrous thrash. He won again the following year at Troon, where the crowds overwhelmed the course. And it was Palmer who rekindled interest in the Open when it was flagging and encouraged his countrymen to travel to Britain each summer.

FINAL FAREWELLS

As well as the triumphs, there were also disappointing days on the course. One such included the 1966 US Open at the Olympic Club in San Francisco, where he was seven ahead with nine to play but ended up losing a playoff to Billy Casper the following day. Palmer was not a perfect golfer, but, as with Seve Ballesteros, seeing him trying to get out of the trouble he had created was part of the wonder. "Trouble is bad to get into but fun to get out of," he said. "I suppose there is a place to play it safe, but as far as I'm concerned it is not on a golf course." Without Palmer, modern-day players would not be competing for the millions they do, and the Seniors

> # Success in golf depends a lot less on strength of body than upon strength of mind and character.
>
> **ARNOLD PALMER**

circuit certainly would not exist to the same extent had Palmer not so enthusiastically embraced the idea in the early 1980s. He simply loved to play golf.

Arnold Palmer, like other celebrities unwilling to leave the stage, was legendary for his farewells. There was the Open at St. Andrews, in 1990 and again in 1995. There were several at Augusta, where the officials did not put up his scores on the last few appearances. Then there was the US Open at Oakmont, in his home state of Pennsylvania, in 1994. He was applauded every step of the way for 36 holes, with much of the crowd oblivious to the rest of the tournament. In the press room afterward, a towel around his shoulders, there were no questions. Palmer tried to speak but dissolved into tears. Eventually, he said, "It's been 40 years … When you walk up the 18th and get an ovation like that,

1954

Having spent three years in the Coast Guard, Palmer returns to win the US Amateur title.

1958

Palmer receives the Masters winner's medal from Bobby Jones—the first of four wins at Augusta.

1961

Wins the first of his two Open Championships, at Royal Troon.

1962

Claims the Open for a second time. His appearances in Britain breathed new life into the tournament.

1962

Palmer wins seven other PGA Tour events during the season, and his rivalry with newcomer Jack Nicklaus begins in earnest.

1963

Palmer is playing captain for the victorious US Ryder Cup team at East Lake, Atlanta. He featured in eight competitions as a player.

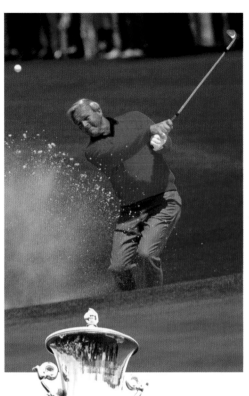

ARNIE'S ARMY

By the late 1960s, Palmer found himself being eclipsed by a new star, Jack Nicklaus. Even when he began to lose regularly to his great rival, Palmer's huge fan base, known as "Arnie's Army," never left him. His popularity was instrumental in establishing the US Seniors Tour, for which he became eligible in its inaugural season. He won 10 tour events between 1980 and 1988, including five senior Majors.

Arnie with his adoring fans

▲ **THE COMPETITION BETWEEN** Arnie and Jack was the rivalry to end all rivalries— golf's greatest hero, Palmer, versus the game's greatest player, Nicklaus.

▲ ▶ **PALMER KNEW ONLY ONE WAY TO PLAY,** and his swashbuckling style continued on to the Seniors Tour, which would not exist without him.

I guess that says it all. I think you all know pretty much how I feel. It's been 40 years of work, fun, and enjoyment. I haven't won all that much. I won a few tournaments. I won some Majors. I suppose the most important thing is the game has been so good to me. I think that's all I have to say." He buried his head in the towel and then departed.

▲ **ONE FINAL WAVE** to the gallery at the Masters as the four-time champion makes an emotional farewell from Augusta.

1973

Palmer competes in his last Ryder Cup as a player, as the US win 19–13 at Murifield.

1980

Brings his considerable presence to bear on the Seniors Tour, winning the PGA Championship in his first season.

1981

Palmer becomes the first person to win the US Open and US Senior Open.

1984

Wins two of his five senior Major titles, the Senior PGA (pictured) and the Senior Players titles.

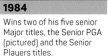

1994

Palmer makes his 32nd and final appearance in the US Open at Oakmont Country Club. He also bids farewell at the USPGA.

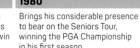

1995

On his 35th appearance, Palmer bids farewell to the Open Championship, fittingly at St. Andrews.

▲ **PLAYER WAS AS SUCCESSFUL** on the Champions Tour as he was on the PGA Tour, winning nine Majors on each.

◀ **KISSING THE OPEN TROPHY** in 1968 the "Black Knight," as he was nicknamed, was a distinctive character on the golf course.

Player, golf's Little Big Man, is of course a phenomenon. He rants about his religion, his dedication, and the searing nature of difficulties he has mastered. But there is no doubt about his place in the deity of the game.

JAMES LAWTON, SPORTS WRITER

Gary Player

Gary Player was part of the "Big Three," with Arnold Palmer and Jack Nicklaus (see pp.224–225). He won nine Major championships, more than any other golfer born outside the US, and he did it the hard way. He is said to have traveled approximately 15 million miles during his career, and while not as naturally talented as many other elite players, his dedication and belief took him to the very top of the game.

PLAYER STATS

BORN November 1, 1935; Johannesburg, South Africa
HEIGHT 5ft 7in (1.70m)
TURNED PRO 1953

DEBUT WIN 1955 East Rand Open
TOUR WINS 163
PGA TOUR: 24
CHAMPIONS TOUR: 19
OTHER: 120

MAJORS 9
MASTERS: Won 1961, 1974, 1978
US OPEN: Won 1965
THE OPEN: Won 1959, 1968, 1974
USPGA: Won 1962, 1972

HONORS
PGA Tour Money Winner: 1961
Presidents Cup Captain: 1995, 2003, 2007
Nine-time Senior Major Champion

▼ **GARY PLAYER WAS AS** fierce a competitor as they come, and his drive brought him nine Majors.

Player appeared in the Masters for the 50th time in 2007 and, into his 80s, still travels the globe playing golf. No one in golf has clocked up more air miles. In the early days of his career, international travel was more difficult than it is now, but Player would fly and tee up in virtually every continent. With his wife, Vivienne, his staunchest ally, there was a time when Player traveled with all six of his children, more than 30 pieces of luggage, and would need a fleet of taxis once he arrived at his destination.

When Player first left South Africa to play golf in Britain in 1955, his game was not ready. He broke even on the trip but was often told by his British peers that he might be better off heading back to Johannesburg and finding some other occupation. "It did me a great service to my drive and determination," he said. In 1956, he won the South African Open for the first time, and his game began to blossom. When he returned to England, he beat Arthur Lees, the local professional, in the 90-hole Dunlop tournament at Sunningdale and a year later headed for the PGA Tour.

MAJOR BREAKTHROUGH

All the time, Player worked on improving his game, and his big breakthrough came at the Open at Muirfield in 1959. With one day (36 holes) to go, he was behind by eight shots but told his equipment representative, "You're going to see a small miracle tomorrow. In fact, you are going to see a big miracle. I'm going to win." And he did, with a final round 68.

Two years later, Player won the Masters in somewhat fortunate circumstances. Arnold Palmer could have won the title, but he took a double bogey at the last to let Player sneak the victory. Player claimed the USPGA the following year, and then at the US Open at Bellerive in 1965, he beat Kel Nagle in a playoff. In doing so, he joined Gene Sarazen and Ben Hogan as the only golfers to have won all four of the modern Major championships. He achieved this Grand Slam before Jack Nicklaus, who completed it the following year. Tiger Woods is the only other golfer to join this highly prestigious and exclusive list.

From the early '60s, Player's off-course affairs were looked after by agent Mark McCormack, who also boasted Palmer and Nicklaus as clients, but on the course, he faced the sternest of tests. While Player was winning his nine Major titles, Palmer was winning six of his seven Majors, and Nicklaus 14 of his 18. There were also the likes of Lee Trevino, Johnny Miller, and Tom Watson to contend with in one of the most competitive golfing eras ever. Player was skillful with

▼ **PLAYER LOVED THE FORMAT** of matchplay golf. He won the World Match Play at Wentworth five times, making him the second most successful winner of the title.

the irons, pitched well, and was aggressive when chipping and putting. If there was one aspect of his game that singled him out, it was his sand play; he is one of the greatest bunker players ever. While other competitors were often happy simply to give themselves a chance at a putt to save par, Player would be looking to hole out from the sand.

Player won his second Open at Carnoustie in 1968, when he played a superb 3-wood shot at the par-5 14th to two feet for an eagle to hold off Nicklaus. It had been a superb duel between the two, but, try as he might, the Bear could not catch the South African over the closing stretch. He won a third Claret Jug in 1974 at Royal Lytham, where he played a magical 9-iron from the rough at the 17th. He won by four strokes from Peter Oosterhuis and by five from Nicklaus.

There were three green jackets in total, with further wins coming in 1974, and famously in 1978, when he closed with a brilliant 64 on the last day, coming home in only 30 strokes. A second USPGA title was secured in 1972 at Oakland Hills, where at the 16th hole he again hit a great 9-iron shot, from the rough, over trees and water to help secure victory.

▲ **TOM WATSON HELPS PLAYER** into a Masters green jacket in 1978. It was his third victory at Augusta and his last Major win.

BODY AND SOUL

Faith was always of great importance to Player, and he was always eager to acknowledge his God-given ability as a golfer. He was the first golfer to manage his diet and eat healthy foods, and he would always take bananas and raisins on to the course to snack on during a round. He was also the first to employ a strict fitness regime at a time when golfers did not consider themselves athletes and did not believe that physical fitness was something to concern themselves with. There is no doubt that Player was ahead of his time.

As well as being a pioneer, he courted controversy regarding his views on South Africa's political stance. He found himself much criticized when he wrote that he

was a proud South African and supported apartheid. In a later autobiography, he retracted what he had once wrote and worked to overcome the system by setting up a foundation educating underprivileged children.

In his book, Grand Slam Golf, Player described himself as "Small, dark, deliberate, painstaking ... a man without talent who has done it all by sheer hard work and nothing else, a highly-strung faddist who bores

> # You should look after your body. If you do, it could last you a lifetime.
>
> **GARY PLAYER**

1959
At Muirfield, Player becomes the youngest golfer to win the Open Championship.

1961
Player becomes the first non-American to win the Masters at Augusta.

1965
Wins the World Series of Golf when it was an invitation event rather than a PGA Tour event.

1965
Wins the US Open to complete a career Grand Slam, at the age of 29.

1965
Wins the first of five World Match Play titles, beating Peter Thomson 3 and 2 at Wentworth.

1969
At the USPGA Championship, black militants, perceiving him to be a racist, throw a cup of ice in his face on the 10th tee.

There was a time when Player wore only white clothes, to reflect the sun. But for most of his career he wore all black—better to absorb the sun and keep his muscles warm. At the 1960 Open, he wore trousers with one white leg and one black leg. However, worried that this could be perceived as a political statement, he only did so on one further occasion, very late in his career.

Player tees off at the Old Course

▲ **PLAYER WAS A MASTER IN THE BUNKER**, and whenever possible, he would play aggressively from the sand rather than merely seeking a safe exit from a trap.

the ears off you with weight-lifting and diets and nuts and raisins and talk of God, dark clothes, sombre under big peaked cap, and, above all, a little fellow, a little man."

Player won more than 150 titles around the world. From the very beginning, he was convinced that his determination and industrious nature could overcome any disadvantage or suffering. No one worked harder at all aspects of his game than Player, and the harder he worked, the more successful he became. He said, "You know, I'll tell you something. The more I practice, the luckier I get." It was a winning mantra.

1974
Becomes the only golfer of the 20th Century to win the Open in three different decades.

1978
The last of Player's nine Majors comes at the Masters where he wins by just one shot.

1998
Becomes the oldest player to make the cut for the final rounds at the Masters.

2003
Captains the International Team in the first Presidents Cup held in South Africa.

2007
Plays in his 50th Masters, tying Arnold Palmer's record for the most appearances at Augusta.

▲ ▲ **NICKLAUS STRIKES** a short iron to the green during a round at the 1969 Open at Royal Lytham.

▲ **NICKLAUS TAKES POSSESSION** of the Open Claret Jug for the second time, at St. Andrews in 1978.

◄ **PUTTER RAISED** in celebration, Nicklaus holes a birdie 3 on Augusta's 17th green en route to victory in 1986.

Jack Nicklaus

Decades before anyone started planning for a millennium party, Jack Nicklaus was considered the best golfer of the 20th century. His haul of 18 Major titles remains an Everest yet to be scaled, although Tiger Woods is gaining ground. During a run of 154 consecutive Majors, Nicklaus finished in the top 10 in half of them and came second 19 times. The "Golden Bear" was not only a prolific winner but also one of the most gracious players the game has seen.

PLAYER STATS

BORN January 21, 1940; Columbus, Ohio
HEIGHT 5ft 10in (1.78m)
TURNED PRO 1961

DEBUT WIN US Open 1962
TOUR WINS 113
PGA TOUR: 73
CHAMPIONS TOUR: 10
OTHER: 30

MAJORS 18
MASTERS: Won 1963, 1965, 1966, 1972, 1975, 1986
US OPEN: Won 1962, 1967, 1972, 1980
THE OPEN: Won 1966, 1970, 1978
USPGA: Won 1963, 1971, 1973, 1975, 1980

HONORS
US Amateur Champion: 1959, 1961
PGA Tour Money Winner: 1964, 1965, 1967, 1971, 1972, 1973, 1975, 1976
PGA Player of the Year: 1967, 1972, 1973, 1975, 1976
The only player to have won all four Majors at least three times
Finished 2nd in Major championships 19 times
Eight senior Major championships
Ryder Cup Team: 1969, 1971, 1973, 1975, 1977, 1981
Ryder Cup Captain: 1983, 1987
Presidents Cup Captain: 1998, 2003, 2005, 2007

▼ **NICKLAUS THROWS HIS BALL** in celebration, having become the first player to retain the Masters, in 1966.

Nicklaus grew up in Columbus, Ohio, and was encouraged in his golf by his father, Charlie, at the Scioto Country Club. An early club-throwing incident was the last of its kind, as his father instilled in young Jack the values of the game—to act graciously, win or lose. Once, when Jack was about to break 70 for the first time, Charlie insisted that they went home, as they were expected for dinner. They later returned, and Jack eagled the 18th for a 69.

At the age of 16, Nicklaus won the Ohio State Open. The event was over four rounds but only three days, with 36 holes on the final day. After his round on the afternoon of the second day, Nicklaus flew across the state to play in an exhibition match with Sam Snead. Nicklaus lost but was so inspired at having seen Snead play that he was determined to win the next day—which he did.

THE FUNDAMENTALS

Nicklaus's long-time teacher was Jack Grout, who had grown up in Texas playing with Ben Hogan and Byron Nelson. Grout preached the importance of performing the fundamentals correctly, particularly keeping the head still. He would even take hold of Nicklaus's hair and make him swing, which made for a painful lesson.

Nicklaus could thunder the ball off the tee and brought the idea of powerful driving to a new level. He also hit magnificent iron shots, and he could putt. He once said that he did not hole many really long putts, but then he rarely missed any of the short ones.

In fact, he holed more putts in the 10–15ft (3–5m) range than anyone else in the game. He was not the most naturally gifted player, but his head and his course management were better than anyone else's. He always played the right shot at the right time. He was deliberate and almost slow as a player, but in the Majors he figured out that the more he hung around without doing anything silly, the more everyone else would fall away. Some thought that he played really aggressive golf only when he absolutely needed to.

▼ **ARNOLD PALMER BROUGHT** a new audience to golf and inspired spectators around the world throughout his career.

Jack knew he was going to beat you. You knew Jack was going to beat you. And Jack knew that you knew he was going to beat you.

TOM WEISKOPF

THE CONCESSION

Jack Nicklaus had a profound effect on the Ryder Cup, and in 1969, his act of sportsmanship was rejoiced all over the world. Tony Jacklin had a short putt to win their match, but Nicklaus conceded it, saying, "I don't think you would have missed that putt but under the circumstances I would never give you the opportunity." It meant that the overall match was tied, but the US, as the holders, kept possession of the Cup.

Nicklaus and Jacklin share a moment

Whether he would have won even more if he had pushed harder, we will not know, but, as he said, "I guess I could keep playing my game longer than they could keep playing theirs."

OUT OF HIS CAGE

Nicklaus won the US Amateur twice, in 1959 and 1961, and might have won the 1960 US Open, where he played the last 36 holes with the veteran Ben Hogan. "Today I played with a kid who could have won this Open by 10 shots if I'd be thinking for him," said Hogan. Two years later, Nicklaus's first professional title was no less than the US Open. If that was not already a mighty statement in itself, he defeated, after a playoff, the great Arnold Palmer in Palmer's home state of Pennsylvania. On the slick Oakmont greens, Nicklaus had only one three-putt in 90 holes. "Now that the big guy is out of the cage, everybody better run for cover," said Palmer. Nicklaus, just out of college with a crew cut and on the tubby side, was the subject of abuse from the gallery, most of them Palmer fans. "Ohio Fats," and worse, was called out, but he never let it affect him. After a few years, Nicklaus also became a crowd favorite.

In 1966, Nicklaus became the first player to win successive Masters titles, and he also won the Open at Muirfield—he liked the place so much he named his famed course in Ohio "Muirfield Village." The Open win gave him a complete set of the four Grand Slam titles, something he would achieve three times over. He won the Masters six times, the USPGA five times, the US Open four times, and the Open three. He considered

> I think when I play golf, yes, I have to make the world revolve around me. If you want to be the best at something, you have to make it revolve around what you are doing.

JACK NICKLAUS

1961
Claims his second US Amateur title with an 8 and 6 victory over Dudley Wysong. The tournament at that time was match play.

1962
Wins the first of his 18 Major championships at the US Open. It is his first victory as a professional golfer.

1966
Wins at the Masters, becoming the first golfer to successfully defend the title.

1969
Makes his Ryder Cup debut at Birkdale. He makes his concession to Tony Jacklin (see above).

1972
Becomes the first golfer to record a double career Grand Slam.

1978
Named "Sportsman of the Year" by *Sports Illustrated* magazine.

▲ **FOR A RECORD SIXTH TIME,** Nicklaus is presented with a green jacket at Augusta, on this occasion by Bernhard Langer, in 1986. At 46, Nicklaus remains the oldest winner.

◄ **NICKLAUS ACKNOWLEDGES** the crowd's applause at Palm Beach Gardens, Florida, as he wins the USPGA for the second time in 1971.

winning the Open at St. Andrews a necessary part of any complete golfing CV, and he did it twice, in 1970 and 1978. On the first occasion, Doug Sanders missed a short putt on the 18th green to allow Nicklaus into an 18-hole playoff the next day. With the outcome still to be decided at the short par-4 last, Nicklaus removed his sweater and belted his drive through the green. He chipped and putted for a three.

Nicklaus's last two Masters wins were special. In 1975, he held off Johnny Miller and Tom Weiskopf in a remarkable three-way battle, which was settled when

Nicklaus holed from 45ft (13m) at the 16th. In 1986, on the most exciting Sunday in Masters history, Nicklaus swept to the title at the age of 46 (see pp.230–231).

Nicklaus kept winning when he went on to the Seniors Tour but didn't have the appetite for "ceremonial" golf, as he put it. Yet the farewells were inevitable, and it all ended on the Swilken Burn bridge on the 18th hole at St. Andrews in 2005.

1986
Wins the Masters for a record sixth time—his last Major victory—in his 25th year as a golf professional.

1993
Comes back to win the US Senior Open for the second time after a win-free year in 1992.

1998
At 58, achieves a top-10 finish at the Masters. A plaque commemorating his career is unveiled at the Masters.

2002
Teams up with Tiger Woods at the made-for-TV "Battle of Bighorn." The pair win and split the $1.2 million prize money.

2005
Nicklaus retires and is also presented with the Presidential Medal of Freedom by President Bush.

Mickey Wright

Mickey Wright was not just the Annika Sorenstam of her time, she possessed what is generally regarded as one of the best swings of any golfer, ever. Having left Stanford University at the end of her first year to pursue a golfing career, her early learning of the game and her sheer ruthlessness helped her become the dominant player of her generation, winning a career Grand Slam by the time she was 27.

Mickey Wright was a modest character who simply let her clubs do the talking. Growing up in San Diego, she broke 100 at age 11, 90 a year later, and 70 at 14. When she arrived on tour, she knew how to hit the ball exactly as she wanted.

Betsy Rawls, a friend and rival, suggested that "Mickey was able to move the clubhead so fast and hit the ball a very long way because her mechanics were so good. She was strong but she had no wasted movement in her swing so that everything contributed to moving the clubhead."

Getting used to traveling and tour life didn't come easily to Wright. However, she threw herself into the golfing community, acting as secretary, treasurer, and president of the LPGA. Her first win came in 1956, but she had to learn one more important lesson before she could truly dominate, ironically from her rival Rawls. "Betsy taught me the most important thing of all: to take responsibility for everything that happens to you on the golf course; not to blame the greens for bad putting, the caddie for bad club selection, or the fates for a bad day."

Between 1956 and 1973, Wright won 82 times, including 13 Major championships. There were four US Open titles—her fourth in 1964 in San Diego in front of her parents being her personal favorite. In a four-year stretch between 1961 and 1964, she won 44 times, including 13 events in 1963 and 11 the following year. But the pressure was too great for her; if she didn't play, the sponsors would threaten to withdraw their support, and she burnt herself out playing too many tournaments. However, by the time she cut back her playing commitments, she had won everything there was to win, and her success raised the profile of the women's game. Judy Rankin said, "Mickey's golf made the golf world sit up and take notice."

▶ **TALL AND STRONG,** Mickey Wright had a classical swing and a sense of perfection that drove her to so many victories.

PLAYER STATS

BORN February 14, 1935; San Diego, California
DIED February 20, 2020
HEIGHT 5ft 9in (1.75m)
TURNED PRO 1955

DEBUT WIN 1956 Jacksonville Open
TOUR WINS 82 (all LPGA TOUR)

MAJORS 13
LPGA CHAMPIONSHIP: Won 1958, 1960, 1961, 1963
WOMEN'S US OPEN: Won 1958, 1959, 1961, 1964
TITLEHOLDERS CHAMPIONSHIP: Won 1961, 1962
WESTERN OPEN: Won 1962, 1963, 1966

HONORS
LPGA Tour Money Winner: 1961, 1962, 1963, 1964

▲ **WRIGHT SHOWS OFF** the Women's Titleholders Golf Tourney trophy in April 1961. She posted a score of 299, finishing one stroke ahead of the field.

Perfection motivated me, doing it better than anyone who had ever done it, just as simple as that.

MICKEY WRIGHT

Bob Charles

Bob Charles was a pioneer and, in his time, was golf's greatest left-handed player. Until Mike Weir won in 1993, Charles was the first left-hander to have won a Major championship. Before Michael Campbell was victorious at the US Open in 2005, Charles was the only New Zealander to have won a Major. He is also the only golfer to become a Knight Companion of the New Zealand Order of Merit.

Like Mickelson, Bob Charles is naturally right-handed, at least at everything except two-handed sports. His parents were both left-handed and so he learned the game that way, using some of their spare clubs. The availability of left-handed equipment has become much wider, which was not always the case, and as a result, there are many more successful left-handed golfers than there once were. Charles's success, and endorsement of left-handed clubs, was a significant step in developing the market.

Charles won the New Zealand Open, for the first of four times, as an 18-year-old amateur, in 1954. But it was not until 1960 that he turned professional, having spent his time honing his game while working as a bank clerk. His greatest triumph came after only three years as a professional when he won the Open at Royal Lytham & St. Annes in 1963. In the last-ever 36-hole playoff in the Open championship, Charles defeated American Phil Rodgers by eight strokes. He had singled-putted 11 times in the morning round, and it was his success on the greens that became the hallmark of his career. At the time, a *Sunday Telegraph* reporter wrote: "When he was on the green, the hole was never safe. Keeping his wrists unbroken and moving the club head more slowly under pressure than the game's case-hardened chroniclers had ever seen, Charles dropped putt after putt from any distance."

He soon started winning consistently, and after a career of remarkable longevity and including his many years of winning on the Champions tour, he had collected more than 66 titles on five continents. On the 30th anniversary of his Open win almost to the day, he claimed a second Senior British Open win, coming from one behind Tommy Horton on the last hole to win with a birdie. *Golf Weekly* reported: "If you had to put your life on someone sinking the winning putt in a Major, that someone would be Charles. When it comes to testing seven-footers, there is no one better."

▶ **IN 1993, THE NEW ZEALANDER** returned to Royal Lytham, the scene of his Open triumph 30 years earlier, and won the British Seniors Open.

◀ **BOB CHARLES WAS THE FIRST** left-hander to win a Major championship. Here, he lifts the Claret Jug, following his Open triumph.

PLAYER STATS

BORN March 14, 1936; Carterton, New Zealand
HEIGHT 6ft 1in (1.85m)
TURNED PRO 1960

DEBUT WIN 1961 New Zealand PGA Championship
TOUR WINS 66
LPGA TOUR: 6
AUSTRALASIAN TOUR: 8
CHAMPIONS TOUR: 36
OTHER: 16

MAJORS 1
MASTERS: T15th 1963
US OPEN: 3rd 1964/T3rd 1970
THE OPEN: Won 1963
USPGA: T2nd 1968

HONORS
Knight Companion of the New Zealand Order of Merit: 1999

I'm an introvert. I take things seriously, particularly my golf. That's my business and the golf course is my office.

BOB CHARLES

Lee Trevino

One of the great characters of golf, Lee Trevino was an entertainer and a golfer of the highest order. He won six Major championships—the Open championship, the US Open, and the USPGA twice each—chatting and wisecracking all the way. And all of this after growing up in poverty in Dallas and not starting on the tour until he was 28 years old.

PLAYER STATS

BORN December 1, 1939; Dallas, Texas
HEIGHT 5ft 7in (1.70m)
TURNED PRO 1960

DEBUT WIN 1968 US Open
TOUR WINS 85
LGPA TOUR: 29
CHAMPIONS TOUR: 29
OTHER: 27

MAJORS 6
MASTERS: T10th 1975, 1985
US OPEN: Won 1968, 1971
THE OPEN: Won 1971, 1972
USPGA: Won 1974, 1984

HONORS
Vardon Trophy Winner: 1970, 1971, 1972, 1974, 1980
Ryder Cup Team: 1969, 1971, 1973, 1975, 1979, 1981
Ryder Cup Captain: 1985
Champions Tour Rookie of the Year: 1990

● Cover star, July 1971

In 1967, Trevino challenged as an unknown at the US Open in his first season on tour. He did so well that he finished fifth (winning $6,000) and later that year was named Rookie of the Year.

Before becoming a professional on the PGA Tour, Trevino made his living from working at golf courses and by hustling in and around Dallas, Texas. In one of the numerous stories told about Trevino in his early days, he is said to have won many matches for money at the par-3 pitch-and-putt course where he worked. But instead of using a club, he would use a Dr Pepper bottle. His golf may have been entirely self-taught, but his dedication to his sport was Hoganesque.

One of Trevino's first jobs was as the assistant professional at Horizon Hills in El Paso. Here, he took part in money matches and came into contact with professional golfers. When Ray Floyd visited the club, he was flabbergasted when he was told that he was playing the kid who took his clubs from the car to the locker room. But Floyd trailed after each of the first two rounds of the 54-hole match and needed an eagle at the last to win. When he got back on tour, he told his peers, "Boys, there's a little Mexican kid out in El Paso. When he comes out here, you'll have to make way for him."

When he did eventually make it on to the tour, Trevino put down a marker by beating Jack Nicklaus by four strokes at the 1968 US Open. However, his big year—when he was christened the "Super Mex"—came in 1971, when in successive starts he won the US Open, the Canadian Open, and the Open Championship at Birkdale. A year later at Muirfield, with Nicklaus trying to win a fourth major in a year and when Tony Jacklin was at his very best, Trevino won again. During the final round, he saw off Nicklaus but became involved in

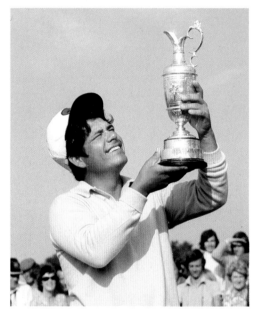

▲ **WINNING A SECOND** successive Open in 1972, at Muirfield, was joy for Trevino but misery for England's Tony Jacklin when the American chipped in at the 17th hole in the final round.

▼ **TREVINO WON** his first Major title (and first-ever Tour title) in 1968 at Oak Hill, beating Jack Nicklaus by four strokes.

Pressure? These guys don't know what pressure is. Pressure is when you're playing some hard-nosed gamblers for $25 and you've only got $10 in your pocket.

LEE TREVINO

THE HIGH ROLLER

Lee Trevino was one of golf's great showmen. He loved spending the money he won, reportedly losing two fortunes but luckily gaining three. He won two Major titles in 1971—indeed, it was his most prolific year in terms of titles won—and by the early 1980s, he was second on the PGA Tour career money list, behind Jack Nicklaus.

● Trevino enjoyed traveling in style

a furious duel with Jacklin. He made a mess of the par-5 17th but salvaged it with a chip-in for par. However, it seemed that he had lost his chance as Jacklin appeared certain to birdie the hole. Instead, apparently unnerved by Trevino's recovery, Jacklin three-putted for a bogey, thus handing Trevino an unlikely victory.

Trevino won the USPGA in 1974 and 1984, but by that time, he was suffering from severe back problems—in 1975, he had been hit by lightning at the Western Open and was never quite the same again. However, on turning 50, his career experienced a revival, and Trevino enjoyed several good seasons competing on the Seniors Tour, winning four of the tour's Major titles, two of them in 1992. He was indomitable of spirit throughout. "How can they beat me?" he said, alluding to his life's misfortunes. "I've been struck by lightning, had two back operations and been divorced twice."

Off the course, he was a private man; on it, he was every bit the "Merry Mex." At the World Match Play in 1972, Jacklin made a simple request, "Lee, is it all right if we don't talk today?" Trevino replied, "Sure, Tony. You don't have to talk, just listen."

▶ **"MERRY MEX" ONCE SAID,** "I played the tour in 1967 and told jokes and nobody laughed. Then I won the Open ... told the same jokes, and everybody laughed like hell."

Tony Jacklin

From the vibrancy of the 1960s came a golfer to excite Britain like never before. Tony Jacklin was a product of his age, and although his spell at the very top was brief, he was the brightest of stars. He won the Open and the US Open, but perhaps his greatest gift to European golf was masterminding the Ryder Cup revival in the 1980s, turning it into a genuine contest.

PLAYER STATS

BORN July 7, 1944; Scunthorpe, England
HEIGHT 5ft 10in (1.78m)
TURNED PRO 1960

DEBUT WIN
Coombe Hill Assistants 1964
TOUR WINS 28
EUROPEAN TOUR: 8
LGPA TOUR: 29
CHAMPIONS TOUR: 2
OTHER: 14

MAJORS 2
MASTERS: T12th 1970
US OPEN: Won 1970
THE OPEN: Won 1969
USPGA: T25th 1969

HONORS
European Tour Money Winner: 1973
Ryder Cup Team: 1967, 1969, 1971, 1973, 1975, 1979
Ryder Cup Captain: 1983, 1985, 1987, 1989

◀ **JACKLIN EMERGED** as one of the biggest names of the Swinging Sixties, and for a time, he eclipsed even Jack Nicklaus.

▼ **AT ROYAL LYTHAM IN 1969** Jacklin became the first Englishman for 18 years to raise the Open Championship Claret Jug.

Jacklin was from northern England but headed south to develop his golf at the Potters Bar Golf Club in Hertfordshire. He was taught by hard taskmaster and former Australian rugby league player–turned-golfer Bill Shankland. Jacklin was a style-conscious character. For an interview early in his career, he turned up wearing gold lamé trousers, a gold cashmere sweater over a white polo neck, and gold shoes. Scotland's Eric Brown

said of his first encounter with Jacklin, "I thought he was a big-headed so-and-so. But he has all the shots. Guts. Dedication. And he's cocky. He has a chance to win any tournament, including the Open."

Two years later, in 1969, Jacklin did just that, winning the Open at Royal Lytham. He was the first home champion since Max Faulkner in 1951, and it showed that the dominance of American golfers was

SCUNTHORPE MOTORCADE
....

In honor of his victory at the 1970 US Open at Hazeltine, Tony Jacklin was driven in a white Cadillac through the streets of his hometown of Scunthorpe, Lincolnshire. Jacklin led from the start of the tournament and eventually secured a seven-shot victory over Dave Hill. This was the greatest winning margin for almost 50 years.

The US Open champion returns home

not absolute. The next year, he won the US Open at the new venue of Hazeltine in Minneapolis. He led after every round and won by seven shots to become the first British winner since Ted Ray in 1920. He was also the first Briton since Harry Vardon, in 1900, to hold both the British and US Opens at the same time.

Jacklin was a regular contender at the Open until 1972 at Muirfield, when Lee Trevino chipped in on the 71st hole for an unlikely par. Jacklin, shocked at the sudden turnaround, three-putted for a bogey. He was never quite the same player again. Off the course, his wife, Vivienne, died of a brain hemorrhage in 1988, and in business, he was never as successful as he would have liked.

As a player, he was always battling against greater opposition, but it was the Ryder Cup that cemented his place in the history of the game. In 1969, he was involved in the famous incident when Jack Nicklaus conceded Jacklin's putt at the last to tie the match (see p.264). When he was offered the captaincy in 1983, Jacklin did it his way. He demanded first-class treatment for the players, and they flourished under his inspirational leadership. With Seve Ballesteros leading the team on the course, Jacklin made light of a narrow defeat in 1983, and then in 1985, he guided Europe to their first Ryder Cup victory for 28 years. A first-ever

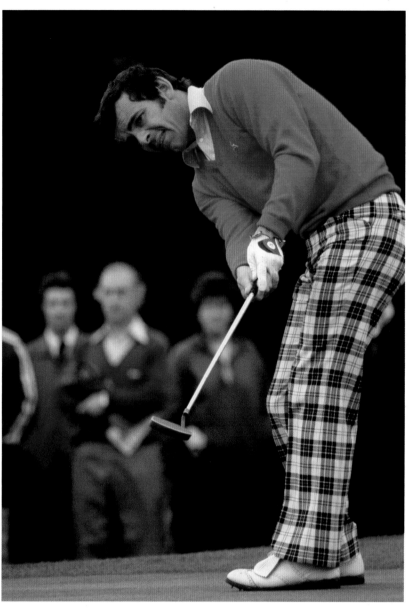

win on American soil followed at Muirfield Village in 1987. Jacklin retired after the tied match at the Belfry in 1989, having played his part in reestablishing the Cup as a viable contest and as one of the world's most exciting sporting events.

▲ **JACKLIN STRUGGLED** in the late 1970s and early 1980s but found a new role as an inspirational Ryder Cup captain.

This was my Everest, and no one can take away ... that moment when I sat on its peak.

TONY JACKLIN ON WINNING THE 1969 OPEN

Raymond Floyd

Raymond Floyd won a few times very early in his career but was much more successful later on. He went from being a playboy of the tour—the heir to Walter Hagen—to being a family man and one of the game's revered elder statesmen. In 1993, he became the oldest man to play in the Ryder Cup, winning three points out of four at the Belfry.

PLAYER STATS

BORN September 4, 1942; Fort Bragg, North Carolina
HEIGHT 6ft 1in (1.85m)
TURNED PRO 1961

DEBUT WIN
1963 St. Petersburg Open Invitational
TOUR WINS 66
LPGA TOUR: 22
CHAMPIONS TOUR: 14
OTHER: 30

MAJORS 4
MASTERS: Won 1976
US OPEN: Won 1986
THE OPEN: T2nd 1978
USPGA: Won 1969, 1982

HONORS
Vardon Trophy: 1983
Byron Nelson Award: 1983
Ryder Cup Team: 1969, 1975, 1977, 1981, 1983, 1985, 1991, 1993
Ryder Cup Captain: 1989

> After you have won a tournament, you have a warm glow. When I was a bachelor, I used to celebrate some after I'd won.

RAYMOND FLOYD

Floyd was the son of a military man who opened a driving range when he left the army. He arrived on tour in 1963, aged 20, and four months later had his first victory. But winning came too easily. "Winning tournaments meant nothing to me," he said later. "I thought the tour was just one big ball, traveling from Miami to Los Angeles to New York, and all those other exciting places."

Floyd won the first of four Major titles at the USPGA in 1969. It was still party time, but in 1973, he met, fell in love with, and married Maria Primoli. She was to have the most profound affect on his life and his career. When Ray withdrew from a tournament midround, two days of soul-searching followed. "Maria jumped on me like a tiger," Floyd explained. "It helped put my life in proper focus. From that moment on, I was a more mature, patient, and responsible man."

Floyd's best golf was still to come. In 1976, he won the Masters by eight strokes, tying Jack Nicklaus's then-tournament record of 271. A second USPGA title arrived in 1982, after an opening 63 at Southern Hills, the best round of his career, which included nine successive threes. In 1986, he won the US Open at Shinnecock Hills with a last round of 66, aged 43. Four years later, he almost won the Masters again but lost in a playoff to Nick Faldo.

When Floyd learned how to focus on the scent of victory during a round, he would get a fixed look in his eyes, concentrating on nothing but the next shot. Fellow competitors called it "the stare." "When he gets that look in his eyes," said Lanny Wadkins, "he's hard to handle."

▼ **FAMILY MAN RAY FLOYD** found lasting success late in his career, winning the US Open in 1986.

▲ **FLOYD COMBINED GREAT POWER** with a soft touch and is generally recognized as one of the best chippers the game has ever seen.

Hale Irwin

He missed one of the shortest putts in the history of Major championships—he actually missed the ball—but made one of the longest, at least one of the longer, important putts. Hale Irwin, three-time US Open winner, and the Tiger Woods of the Senior Tour, was as intense a competitor as you could hope to find in any sporting arena.

Irwin learned the game on a sand-greens course in Kansas. His first love was baseball, but in college he starred as a defensive player on the football field. "I was undersized, under speed, under everything," Irwin recalled. "But I had the determination to get it done. The intensity that I had to play at allowed me to compete with others with better skills."

His game was solid, but his strength, that of consistently hitting fairways and greens, got its greatest reward at the US Open. The setup for the 1974 championship at Winged Foot was so difficult it became known as a "massacre." Battling a young Tom Watson and an old Arnold Palmer, Irwin won at seven-over par. He won again at Inverness five years later, despite a poor final round in which he admitted "choking from the first tee."

That same year, in the 1979 Open at Royal Lytham, Irwin fought out the last two rounds with Seve Ballesteros and came off second-best. Here was a

clash of styles and personalities. Irwin was the "anti-Seve" and could not believe that driving the ball so waywardly could earn rewards. In 1983, at Royal Birkdale, Irwin finished runner-up to Tom Watson but was left ruing a bogey at the 14th in the third round where he went to tap-in from two inches and hit an air shot—the putter hit the ground first and went over the ball.

But in 1990 at Medinah, a hat trick of US Open titles arrived, as he had dreamed it would two weeks earlier. He played the last eight holes in five-under and holed from more than 50 feet at the last hole, celebrating by circling the green slapping hands with spectators. The putt got him into a playoff, and he beat Mike Donald the following day.

Irwin qualified to play on the Champions Tour in 1995, when he reached the age of 50, and enjoyed great success. Having won 45 times, including seven senior Major victories, he tops the all-time Champions Tour money list, with earnings of more than $25 million.

PLAYER STATS

BORN June 3, 1945; Joplin, Missouri
HEIGHT 6ft (1.83m)
TURNED PRO 1968

DEBUT WIN
1971 Sea Pines Heritage Classic
TOUR WINS 87
LPGA TOUR: 20
CHAMPIONS TOUR: 45
OTHER: 22

MAJORS 3
MASTERS: T4th 1974, 1975
US OPEN: Won 1974, 1979, 1990
THE OPEN: T2nd 1983
USPGA: T5th 1975

HONORS
Ryder Cup Team: 1975, 1977, 1979, 1981, 1991
Presidents Cup Captain: 1994

▼ **HALE IRWIN'S CONSISTENT PLAY** made him an ideal contender at the US Open, which he won on three occasions.

▶ **IRWIN CELEBRATES** the huge putt that got him into a playoff at the 1990 US Open at Medinah; he won the following day.

Nancy Lopez

As a star whose success and personality helped massively raise the profile of her sport, Nancy Lopez stands alongside Arnold Palmer and Seve Ballesteros. She arrived in the late 1970s like a ray of sunshine and maintained a long career while also raising a family. She enjoyed great success, winning a host of awards and three Major championships.

PLAYER STATS

BORN January 6, 1957; Torrance, California
HEIGHT 5ft 5in (1.70m)
TURNED PRO 1978

DEBUT WIN Bent Tree Classic 1978
TOUR WINS 52
LPGA TOUR: 48
OTHER: 4

MAJORS 3
LPGA CHAMPIONSHIP: Won 1978, 1985, 1989
ANA INSPIRATION: T3rd 1995
US WOMEN'S OPEN: 2nd 1975, 1977, 1989, 1997
DU MAURIER CLASSIC: 2nd 1979, 1996

HONORS
LPGA Player of the Year: 1978, 1979, 1985, 1988
Rookie of the Year: 1978
Curtis Cup Team: 1976
Solheim Cup Team: 1990
Solheim Cup Captain: 2005

Lopez was one of the best women golfers of all time. She showed promise at an early age by winning the New Mexico Amateur, aged 12. Lopez turned professional in 1977, and in her first full season on the tour, in 1978, she was a sensation. She won nine tournaments in all, including the LPGA Championship, but it was a run of five successive victories that captured the imagination of media and public alike.

It helped that she possessed a charming manner and a dazzling smile. She was a star but seemingly so down-to-earth. Her father, Domingo, was a three-handicap golfer who had encouraged her talent but never pushed. Her mother, Marina, died unexpectedly just as she was about to go on tour, a devastating blow that only strengthened her will to succeed. "I wanted to win for my parents because they sacrificed a lot for me to play golf," Lopez said. "They were always there when I needed them and I wanted them to be proud of me. I couldn't do anything except play golf to repay them."

AMERICAN IDOL

The great Mickey Wright said of the young Lopez: "Never in my life have I seen such control from someone so young." However, success could not last forever, and the wins became less frequent after she married baseball player Ray Knight and started a family.

She was runner-up at the US Open on four occasions, the first in 1975 as an amateur. In 1997, she won for the 48th time on tour but yet again finished runner-up at the US Open, beaten by England's Alison Nicholas, who had grown up idolizing the American. "I probably won't sleep tonight because I'll be thinking about every shot ... and what I could have done," Lopez sighed. But she was no loser. She was a great competitor and a great champion.

▲ **A SIGHT THAT WAS SEEN** time and again in her early days as a sensational new star on tour—Lopez smiling in celebration of victory.

▲ **LOPEZ LEADS AMERICA** to victory at the 2005 Solheim Cup, along with Christina Kim (left) and Natalie Gulbis (right).

My image reflects on me, my husband, my family, my life. Everyone should be good in public.

NANCY LOPEZ

Johnny Miller

Back in the mid-1970s, you might have been considered crazy to suggest that Johnny Miller would become better known as a golf broadcaster than as a player. For a brief spell, the lanky, blond bombshell from California played the finest golf you could wish to see and won two Major championships. He became one of the finest golf commentators of all time, before hanging up his microphone in 2019.

PLAYER STATS

BORN April 29, 1947; San Francisco, California
HEIGHT 6ft 2in (1.88m)
TURNED PRO 1969

DEBUT WIN
1971 Southern Open Invitational
TOUR WINS 30
LPGA TOUR: 25
OTHER: 5

MAJORS 2
MASTERS: T2nd 1971, 1975, 1981
US OPEN: Won 1973
THE OPEN: Won 1976
USPGA: T11th 1977

HONORS
PGA Tour Money Leader: 1974
PGA Tour Player of the Year: 1974
Ryder Cup Team: 1975, 1981

When I get going it's like I'm in a trance ... I can black everything out.

JOHNNY MILLER

What a show Miller put on between 1973 and 1976. He won the US Open at Oakmont in 1973 with a final round of 63, the first time anyone had scored so low during a Major championship, let alone en route to victory. Oakmont possesses the fastest and most devilish greens imaginable and is a beast of a course. There was a storm prior to the final round that softened the greens, but still Miller produced one of the finest rounds ever compiled. The 26-year-old Californian, who had learned his golf at Olympic Club in San Francisco and Pebble Beach, opened with four straight birdies but still appeared to be a long way back. Having gone out in 32, Miller came home in 31 and set a target no one could beat.

In 1974, Miller won the first three tournaments he played in and eight in all. The following year, he won four more titles and was involved in a thrilling contest at the Masters in which Jack Nicklaus beat Miller and Tom Weiskopf. In 1976, Miller won the Open at Royal Birkdale with a final round of 66, leaving Nicklaus and a young Seve Ballesteros in his wake. Victories were sporadic after the Open, because he struggled on the greens. By the end of the 1980s, he had essentially retired from the tour and became a commentator for NBC television, where he was always known to speak his mind. One of the few events he still played in was the AT&T Pebble Beach Pro-Am. In 1994, in a final-day tussle involving Tom Watson and Tom Kite, Miller pulled off a remarkable victory. "This isn't right; this is a fluke," he said. "I'm not a golfer; I'm a television announcer."

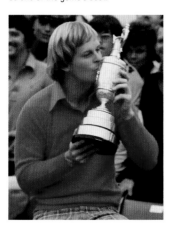

▼ **WINNING THE OPEN** at Birkdale in 1976, ahead of Jack Nicklaus and Seve Ballesteros, confirmed Miller as one of the game's best.

▶ **MILLER AT THE OPEN** at Royal Birkdale in 1971, the scene of his triumph five years later. He had top-five finishes at the Masters and US Open in 1971.

◄◄ **TOM WATSON HOLDS** aloft the Open Claret Jug for the fifth time at Birkdale in 1983. He beat Andy Bean and Hale Irwin by one stroke.

◄ **IN PARTNERSHIP** with Jack Nicklaus, Watson was a member of the greatest-ever American Ryder Cup team in 1981.

▼ **ON HIS WAY TO WINNING** his first green jacket at Augusta in 1977, Watson is watched by Ben Crenshaw as he tees off at the 4th.

Tom Watson

By winning the Open Championship five times, Tom Watson proved himself one of the greatest golfers of all time and endeared himself permanently to the British galleries. In the mid-1970s, he took over from Jack Nicklaus as the game's best player and, starting with the Open in 1975, won eight Major championships in as many years.

PLAYER STATS

BORN September 4, 1949; Kansas City, Missouri
HEIGHT 5ft 9in (1.75m)
TURNED PRO 1971

DEBUT WIN 1974 Western Open
PROFESSIONAL WINS 62
LPGA TOUR: 39
CHAMPIONS TOUR: 10
OTHER: 13

MAJORS 8
MASTERS: Won 1977, 1981
US OPEN: Won 1982
THE OPEN: WON 1975, 1977, 1980, 1982, 1983
USPGA: 2nd 1978

HONORS

PGA Tour Money Winner: 1977, 1978, 1979, 1980, 1984
Vardon Trophy Winner: 1977, 1978, 1979
PGA Tour Player of the Year: 1977, 1978, 1979, 1980, 1982, 1984
Ryder Cup Team: 1977, 1981, 1983, 1989
Ryder Cup Captain: 1993

It was **Watson's great play** that forced Jack Nicklaus to say, "I'm tired of giving it my best shot and coming up short." Some players briefly got the better of Nicklaus, but Watson managed it on a regular basis (see pp.228–229). Between 1975 and 1983, he won eight Majors and matched the achievement of James Braid, JH Taylor, and Peter Thomson by winning five Opens. He also led the money list in America for four years in a row. But when Watson, who grew up in Kansas City and has lived there ever since, graduated from Stanford University, he was unsure about what to do as a career. He had been introduced to the game by his father and turned professional in 1971 with the flimsiest of games. What held him together was his brilliant scrambling skills, his short game, and his bold putting. Initially, he could not win and was written off as a choker, but he worked with Byron Nelson, and once he started winning, he could not stop.

Watson won the Open on his first appearance, at Carnoustie in 1975. Two years later, he beat Nicklaus in the final round of the Masters and then again at Turnberry in the Open. They played together over the weekend, shooting 65s in the third round to distance themselves from the field before Watson edged out Nicklaus by one shot, shooting 65 on the final day. It was a round of electrifying golf as they pushed each other all the way. One ahead playing the last, Watson hit his approach to two feet. But Nicklaus, who had been in trouble off the tee, holed from more than 30ft (9m) for a birdie to keep the pressure on. They left the green arm-in-arm to wild scenes.

HITTING THE WALL

Watson won again at Muirfield in 1980, Troon in 1982, and Birkdale in 1983. He had also taken the Masters again in 1981 and won the US Open at Pebble Beach in 1982, where he had played as a student. But in 1984 at St. Andrews, where he

◀ **THE VICTORIOUS RYDER CUP CAPTAIN** at the Belfry in 1993, when the US retained the trophy they won in dramatic circumstances at Kiawah Island in 1991.

THE LOSS OF A FRIEND

Watson was Player of the Year in 2003, but the year also was marked by sadness. His long-time caddie, Bruce Edwards, was diagnosed with the progressive neurodegenerative disorder Lou Gehrig's disease. Watson donated $1 million to help found the organization Driving 4 Life to help fight the disease.

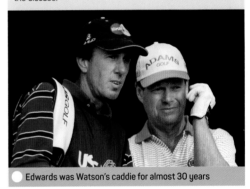

● **Edwards was Watson's caddie for almost 30 years**

was trying to tie Harry Vardon's record of six Open titles, he went over the green at the 17th in the final round and finished against a stone wall. He lost to Seve Ballesteros and was never quite the same again. However, at the 2009 Open at Turnberry, the 59-year-old Watson seemed to roll back the years and came close to his sixth tournament triumph—his first since 1983. One off the lead, at five-under, after the first round, Watson was tied for the lead after day two and led the field by one shot going into Sunday. Sadly, cruelly, it wasn't to be, and Watson failed to make par on the 18th to win the Claret Jug and lost to Stewart Cink in a playoff.

Not as good as a few, but better than most. Let's put it that way.

TOM WATSON, SUMMING UP HIS CAREER

◀ **SEVE IN FULL FLOW** was the most awe-inspiring sight European golf had ever seen—fans remained enraptured for three decades..

▼ **SEVE SHOWS OFF** his brilliant short-game skills at the Spanish Open in 1991. He won the title in 1981, 1985, and 1995.

▼▼ **HIS MOST FAMOUS** celebration— Seve winning the second of his three Open successes, at St. Andrews in 1984.

Severiano Ballesteros

It was not just what "Seve" Ballesteros did, but the way that he did it. He was thrilling, he was charismatic, he was swashbuckling, and he never gave up. He might play an awful shot one minute but follow it with a brilliant recovery the next. He was the Arnold Palmer of Europe. Golf in Spain, across Continental Europe, and the whole European Tour owes him so much.

He's probably the most creative player who has ever played the game. He was a genius.

TIGER WOODS

Ballesteros was the leader. He was the first to be born of the "Big Five"—Nick Faldo, Bernhard Langer, Sandy Lyle, and Ian Woosnam were the others—and he was the first at everything else, too. He was the first to win a Major, to win in the US, to win an American Major, and to realize that the Americans could be defeated in the Ryder Cup.

His uncle, Ramon Sota, was Spain's most famous player before Seve. All four of his elder brothers caddied and played golf at the club in the small fishing village of Pedrena, near Santander in northern Spain. Seve followed suit but spent much of his early days playing with only a rusty 3-iron on the beach. There he learned not only the skill but also the art of improvisation.

Ballesteros turned professional just before his 17th birthday, but it was at the Open Championship at Royal Birkdale in 1976 that the world discovered him. He led for the first three days, then Johnny Miller overtook him on the final day. But the youngster stole the show. He eagled the 17th, then played an audacious chip and run between two bunkers, over the bumps and hollows, to tie with Nicklaus for second place. Between 1976 and 1995, he won 87 times around the world. He won the World Match Play Championship five times, loving the head-to-head contests, and he thrived in Britain, where both the galleries and the press adored him.

OPEN GLORY

In 1979, he won the Open at Royal Lytham, playing alongside Hale Irwin over the weekend (see pp.226–227). Irwin was a two-time US Open champion, adept at hitting the fairways and the greens, and was playing steady golf. The contrast was absolute. Ballesteros blasted the ball with all his might off the tee, and the brilliance of the next shot was usually in direct correlation to the amount of trouble he was in. At the 16th hole in the final round, his drive found a temporary parking lot, but he played a remarkable recovery shot and birdied the hole. "Car Park Champion," they said in America. It only motivated him to win more.

At St. Andrews in 1984, Ballesteros fought a brilliant duel with Tom Watson, who was going for a sixth Open title. With the American in trouble on the road hole, Ballesteros rolled in a birdie putt on the 18th green that sparked a joyous and triumphant fist-pumping

▼ **IT WAS LOVE AT FIRST SIGHT** as the young Ballesteros became an instant hit with the British gallery at the 1976 Open at Birkdale.

PLAYER STATS

BORN April 9, 1957; Pedrena, Spain
DIED May 7, 2011
HEIGHT 6ft (1.83m)
TURNED PRO 1974

DEBUT WIN 1976 Dutch Open
TOUR WINS 94
EUROPEAN TOUR: 49
PGA TOUR 9
OTHER: 36

MAJORS 5
MASTERS: Won 1980, 1983
US OPEN: 3rd 1987
THE OPEN: Won 1979, 1984, 1988
USPGA: 5th 1984

HONORS
Ryder Cup Team: 1979, 1983, 1985, 1987, 1989, 1991, 1993, 1995
Ryder Cup Captain: 1997
European Tour Order of Merit winner: 1976, 1977, 1978, 1986, 1988, 1991
European Player of the Century: 2000

celebration that became his trademark. Four years later, back at Royal Lytham once more, Seve scored a blistering 65 in the final round to beat both Nick Price and Nick Faldo. "I told him afterwards it was the greatest round of golf I had ever seen," Faldo recalled.

The three Open titles were joined by two Masters green jackets. In 1980, he led by 10 strokes with nine holes to play, eventually winning by four. Three years later, he shot a final-round 69 and won by four again from Ben Crenshaw and Tom Kite. His European contemporaries saw Ballesteros winning the biggest prizes and followed suit. At Augusta, six Europeans won a collective 11 green jackets between 1980 and 1999.

Seve had further chances to win the Masters but without success, notably in 1986 when in the last round he hit an awful 4-iron into the pond at the 15th hole and lost to Jack Nicklaus. Furthermore, a long-term back complaint ultimately shortened his career. His body could not stand up to the punishment of his violent swing, and, always an instinctive player, he could not refine the technique. He won for the last time in Madrid, at the Spanish Open, at the age of 38 and, following years of struggling with his game, he retired on the eve of the 2007 Open at Carnoustie.

RYDER CUP COLOSSUS

During Seve's last years on tour, his short game was still magnificent, but he could not get the ball on the fairway. However, the Ryder Cup brought out the best in Ballesteros. In his last Ryder Cup singles match, against Tom Lehman in 1995, he barely hit a fairway or a green in regulation, but, using almost magical powers, he managed to extend the match to the 15th hole.

Under Tony Jacklin's captaincy in 1983 in West Palm Beach, Europe lost, but only narrowly. Ballesteros played an awesome shot—the best Jack Nicklaus had ever seen—from a bunker more than 200 yards from the green, with a 3-wood from a lie that most would struggle to play with a 6-iron. It was his third shot, but it helped him escape with an unlikely half against Fuzzy Zoeller. Afterward, his European

teammates were disconsolate, but Seve, recognizing a major shift in the balance of power, was upbeat. He encouraged the team to celebrate as if they had won. The next time, they did win. In 1987, Europe was victorious for the first time in the US, and a legendary partnership between Seve and José Maria Olazábal began. They won 11 times together, halving two matches and losing only two. They had a "no sorrys" policy and never admitted that any precarious situation was irretrievable. "When Seve gets his Porsche going not even San Pedro in heaven could stop him," Olazábal said. His driving style was certainly in evidence when he charged around Valderrama on a buggy as captain in 1997. Victory on the only occasion the match has been played on Spanish soil was his destiny, just like everything else in his remarkable career.

◄ **DARK AND BROODING,** sometimes Ballesteros was at his best with the world—particularly the Americans—against him.

▼ **SEVE CELEBRATES VICTORY** at St. Andrews in 1984. The joy is unconfined after an epic final-round duel with Tom Watson.

1976
Shoots to prominence by finishing runner-up to Johnny Miller in the 1976 Open at Royal Birkdale.

1979
Seve wins his first Open in 1979 at Royal Lytham, becoming the youngest winner of the century.

1980
Cruises to victory at the Masters. Aged 23, Seve becomes the second non-American and the first European to wear the green jacket.

1983
At the Ryder Cup at West Palm Beach, Seve plays the shot of his career, but Europe loses narrowly.

1984
At St. Andrews Seve claims a second Open Championship—and fourth Major in all—after a duel with Tom Watson.

Seve was golf's Cirque du Soleil. The passion, artistry, skill, drama.

NICK FALDO

THE SEVE TROPHY IN IRELAND

Great Britain and Ireland captain Nick Faldo receives the Seve Trophy from the captain of Continental Europe, Seve Ballesteros, after winning at the Heritage in Ireland in 2007. The event was started in 2000 to celebrate Seve's love of international team matchplay golf, with Seve himself lifting the trophy in the first year.

Faldo receives the Seve Trophy from Ballesteros

NOTHING IS IMPOSSIBLE

Throughout his career, Seve was renowned for taking on high-risk shots. At the European Masters in Switzerland in 1993, he displayed a brilliant final-round charge, but all appeared lost when he sliced his drive at the last. He lay between two trees, with a 6-foot wall just in front of him. He had to go over the wall, under the branches, then over a swimming pool, some tents, four more trees, and a bunker to reach the green. His caddie, Billy Foster, told him it was impossible, but Seve was determined. He played the shot, and the ball found the tiniest of gaps and landed just in front of the green.

He then chipped in for his third successive birdie but ultimately lost by one stroke. "It was difficult," he admitted later, "but I wanted to make a three, I wanted to win. I am always looking to go forwards not backwards."

1985

Seve is an integral part of the first European Ryder Cup victory at the Belfry, winning 3.5 points.

1988

Wins a third Open Championship at Royal Lytham. His final-round 65 is too good for Nick Faldo and Nick Price.

1991

Wins two of his five senior Major titles, the Senior PGA (pictured) and the Senior Players titles.

1997

Captains the European Ryder Cup team to victory on home soil at Valderrama.

2000

Captains Europe to victory in the inaugural Seve Trophy.

Ben Crenshaw

Ben Crenshaw was one of the best putters of his generation, and twice he conquered the greens at Augusta National to win the Masters. He was nicknamed "Gentle Ben," but ironically, he was an emotional character who was given to bouts of temper. This trait was highlighted when he captained the US team to victory at one of the most fiery Ryder Cup competitions of recent years.

PLAYER STATS

BORN January 11, 1952; Austin, Texas
HEIGHT 5ft 9in (1.75m)
TURNED PRO 1973

DEBUT WIN 1973 San Antonio Texas Open
TOUR WINS 27
PGA TOUR: 19
OTHER: 8

MAJORS 2
MASTERS: Won 1984, 1995
US OPEN: T3rd 1975
THE OPEN: T2nd 1978, 1979
USPGA: 2nd 1979

HONORS
Ryder Cup Team: 1981, 1983, 1987, 1995
Ryder Cup Captain: 1999
Bob Jones Award: 1991

▼ **SEVE BALLESTEROS HELPS** a delighted Crenshaw into a Masters green jacket at Augusta for the first time in 1984.

Crenshaw became a star of college golf and quickly made an impact when he won his first event on the PGA Tour at the Texas Open in 1973. He was from Austin, Texas, just as Tom Kite was, and the pair enjoyed a long-standing friendly rivalry. At least a rivalry was perceived. They were very different characters: Kite, organized, consistent, a more mechanical swing; Crenshaw, an emotional, more go-with-the-flow, feel player.

In 1984, Crenshaw won the Masters for the first time, coming from two behind Kite on the final day with a 68 to win by two from Tom Watson. Throughout his career, apart from brief periods of banishment from his bag, Crenshaw used "Little Ben"—a putter his father bought for him when he was 16 years old. "I leaned on that putter hard to bail me out," Crenshaw said. "It did some extraordinary things."

THE GREAT REVIVAL

Crenshaw's second Masters victory came at Augusta in 1995 in the most emotional circumstances. His life-long coach from Austin Country Club, Harvey Penick, had died the previous Sunday, so he and Tom Kite went back midweek for the funeral. On the following Sunday, Crenshaw beat Davis Love III with a final round of 68 to take the title. "I had a 15th club in the bag and it was Harvey," an emotional Crenshaw said afterward. "It was like someone had their hand on my shoulder this week and guided me through."

In 1999, at Brookline, Crenshaw was the captain of the US Ryder Cup team. The US trailed by four points after the first two days, but at a press conference on the Saturday night, Crenshaw simply said, "I'm a big believer in fate. I have a good feeling about this. That's all I'm going to say." The following day, the American players won the singles by 8½ points to 3½. Passions boiled over, however, and celebrations at the 17th green, when José Maria Olazábal was still to putt, made for a controversial finale (see p.236).

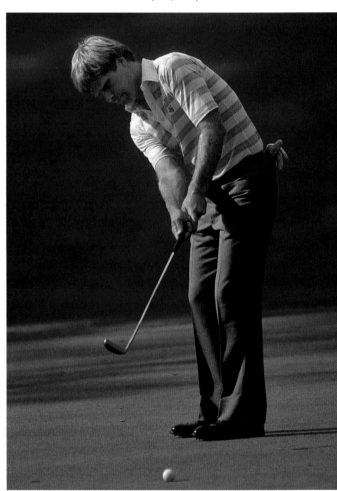

▲ **CRENSHAW WAS ONE** of golf's finest putters, and his philosophy was simple: "The ball which arrives at the hole with the proper speed has an infinitely greater chance of falling in the hole from any entrance."

Bernhard Langer

Bernhard Langer is a man of patience and perseverance. Overcoming the yips on multiple occasions and yet still conquering the greens at Augusta illustrates this. Twice he was Masters champion, and both times this devout Christian donned the green jacket on Easter Sunday. He also enjoyed a spectacular triumph as Ryder Cup captain on US soil.

PLAYER STATS

BORN August 27, 1957; Anhausen, Germany
HEIGHT 5ft 9in (1.75m)
TURNED PRO 1972

DEBUT WIN German National Open 1974
TOUR WINS 112
EUROPEAN TOUR: 42
PGA TOUR: 3
CHAMPIONS TOUR: 41
OTHER: 26

MAJORS 2
MASTERS: Won 1985, 1993
US OPEN: T4th 1987
THE OPEN: 2nd 1981/T2nd 1984
USPGA: T21st 1987

HONORS
European Tour Order of Merit Winner: 1981, 1984
Ryder Cup Team: 1981, 1983, 1985, 1987, 1989, 1991, 1993, 1995, 1997, 2002
Ryder Cup Captain: 2004

▼ **THOUGH BEST KNOWN** for using a broom-handled putter, Langer twice mastered the greens at Augusta with a conventional club.

Langer's Czech-born father escaped from a Siberia-bound prisoner-of-war train in 1945 and settled in Anhausen, Germany. From the age of eight, Bernhard, with his brother Erwin, cycled the five miles to Augsburg Golf Club, where he started caddying. He fell in love with the game and went on to become his country's best and most famous player, winning the World Cup for Germany in 1990 and again 16 years later at the age of 49.

Langer's talent became evident when he won the Cacharel Under-25s title in 1979 by a remarkable 17 strokes. He suffered a number of near misses in the Open but twice won the Masters. In 1985, he was six behind before he eagled the 13th in the penultimate round. The next day, four birdies in six holes on the back nine sealed the win. In 1993, he eagled the 13th again to take the title.

WHATEVER IT TAKES

Although he would always go to whatever lengths necessary (see right), the hallmark of Langer's career has been an attention to detail and precision. Playing with him in the Ryder Cup, Colin Montgomerie revealed that when giving him a yardage, Langer had responded: "Is that from the front of the sprinkler head or the back?" He suffered from bouts of the yips (a nervous twitch), but each time he fought back: using the left-below-right putting method; then moving his left hand down the shaft and clamping his forearm to the shaft with his right hand; then going to the long putter. "I don't care what it looks like," he said, "We don't get paid for looking good." Which is just as well, as at the Masters in 1985, he wore a red top and admitted looking like a Christmas tree when he put on the green jacket. He went on to win the Masters again in 1993, and this time he wore yellow.

▲ **LANGER LEAVES NOTHING** to chance, but at Fulford, England, in 1981, he decided his best option was to climb a tree before chipping to safety.

His Ryder Cup career was a mixed bag. His worst moment came in 1991, when he missed a 6ft (2m) putt on the last green to lose his match, and the Cup. It was a devastating blow, but a week later, he won the German Masters in a playoff. Under his captaincy in 2004, Europe recorded a record nine-point win at Oakland Hills.

Good things can come out of everything. When you go through bad times, good can follow, because you learn more in bad times than in good times.

BERNHARD LANGER

Sandy Lyle

Blessed with so much natural talent and such an amiable character, Sandy Lyle is one of the most beloved British golfers. In 1985, at Royal St. George's, he became the first British player to win the Open since Tony Jacklin in 1969, and in 1988, he became the first Briton ever to win the Masters. That victory included one of the greatest shots in championship golf.

PLAYER STATS

BORN February 9, 1958; Shrewsbury, England
HEIGHT 6ft (1.83m)
TURNED PRO 1977

DEBUT WIN 1978 Nigerian Open
TOUR WINS 28
EUROPEAN TOUR: 17
PGA TOUR: 6
OTHER: 5

MAJORS 2
MASTERS: Won 1988
US OPEN: T16th 1991
THE OPEN: Won 1985
USPGA: T16th 1991

HONORS
European Tour Order of Merit Winner: 1979, 1980, 1985
Ryder Cup Team: 1979, 1981, 1983, 1985, 1987

▼ **IN 1988, LYLE** became the first Briton to win the Masters at Augusta, leading the way for Nick Faldo and Ian Woosnam to follow.

No one who was at Augusta that Sunday afternoon, or watching late at night in Britain, will ever forget the final round of the 1988 Masters. Needing a 3 to win at the sharply uphill 18th hole, Lyle's drive found a bunker. "I'm dead," Lyle thought as he walked off the tee, but the moment he saw the ball with a good lie on the upslope of the face of the bunker, his mood improved. He hit a 7-iron, easily reaching the green and rolling beyond the pin. The ball almost stopped on the top tier, but then it ever so slowly began to roll back down the green, accompanied by a huge roar from the gallery. Lyle was left with a 15-footer to win, and he holed the putt, before celebrating with a quirky jig. It was to be the start of an amazing run of four successive British winners of the green jacket.

Lyle was literally born to golf. His Scottish father, Alex, had moved to Shropshire to become the professional at Hawkstone Park when Sandy was born. By the age of three, he was hitting golf shots. Always tall and strong for his age, he proved to be a prodigy. He was successful at boy, youth, and full amateur levels, playing for England as an amateur but switching his allegiance to Scotland when he turned professional. Ian Woosnam was a local rival, but once on tour another adversary appeared in the form of Nick Faldo. They could not have been more different: Faldo mightily driven; Lyle just naturally talented (see opposite).

His gift was revealed most in his ability to hit the hardest club in the bag: the 1-iron. His ball-striking with the long-irons was so pure that he hit his 1-iron as far as most players hit their driver, and his short game was sublime. These qualities combined to overcome the odd disastrous shot and his perennial laid-back manner.

CHAMPION GOLFER OF THE YEAR

At Royal St. George's in 1985, Lyle found himself in contention for the Open on the final day. But he duffed a chip in Duncan's Hollow, beside the 18th green, and everyone watching experienced the anguish with him. He made a bogey and, after a long wait for the remaining players to finish their rounds, it turned out that no one had beaten him. The next day, he threw a party for his friends, and most of the players on the tour turned up.

He rushed out to get mountains of Chinese food and spent most of the party cleaning up. That was Sandy. His hospitable nature seemingly knew no bounds. "I'll tell you what my life's like with Sandy," his long-term caddie Dave Musgrove once remarked. "My wages must be the best on tour ... and when I stay at his house at Wentworth, he brings me tea in the morning. That can't be bad, can it?"

Three years after his triumph at Royal St. George's, he won the Masters. It was far from a one-off victory on

His record as a golfer is truly brilliant, but what always made him stand out was his naturally spontaneous personality and humanity.

SEVE BALLESTEROS

the US tour. The year before, Lyle had won the Players Championship at Sawgrass, the only British player to do so. Asked how the event compared with the Open Championship, the Scot replied: "About 100 years of history." After winning the Masters in 1998, Lyle returned to the UK and won the World Match Play Championship at Wentworth, beating Faldo in the final after falling at the last hurdle in previous years. He played in five successive Ryder Cups matches from 1979 and contributed to the victories in 1985 and 1987. But then his game deserted him. There were flashes of form, but he was rarely able to put four good rounds together. Not one to emphasize technique, he was unable to piece his swing back together. In 2006, he returned to the Ryder Cup as an assistant to the captain, Ian Woosnam, and tasted victory again at The K Club. Yet through the bad times, as in the good times, he remained the same old Sandy Lyle.

▼ **LYLE PLAYED SOME** of his best golf in the worst conditions, and his long-iron play was one of his greatest strengths.

On-course rivals, Faldo and Lyle

▼ **LYLE CELEBRATES WINNING** the Open at Royal St. George's in 1985. The victory made him a hero of British golf.

▲▲ **IT WAS AT AUGUSTA** that Norman was christened the "Great White Shark," but it was also the scene of far too many near misses for the Australian.

▲ **NORMAN PARTNERS HIS SON,** Gregory, in the 2006 Father and Son event in Orlando. More businessman than golfer these days, Norman now plays in few tournaments.

◄ **NORMAN CELEBRATES MAKING** the putt that got him into a playoff at the 1984 US Open at Winged Foot. He lost the next day to Fuzzy Zoeller.

Greg Norman

When the most severe criteria to judge a player (Majors won) is used, the name of Greg Norman is not among those at the top of the list, but, by sheer force of his personality, the "Great White Shark" dominated golf for a decade, from the mid-1980s until the arrival of Tiger Woods. Norman twice won the Open, but he could—and with better fortune would—have won the Grand Slam.

PLAYER STATS

BORN February 10, 1955; Queensland, Australia
HEIGHT 6ft (1.83m)
TURNED PRO 1974

DEBUT WIN 1976 West Lakes Classic
TOUR WINS 90
PGA TOUR: 20
EUROPEAN TOUR: 15
AUSTRALASIA TOUR: 39
OTHER: 16

MAJORS 2
MASTERS: T2nd 1986, 1987/2nd 1996
US OPEN: 2nd 1984, 1995
THE OPEN: Won 1986, 1993
USPGA: 2nd 1986, 1993

HONORS
Australia Tour Order of Merit Winner: 1978, 1980, 1983, 1984, 1986, 1988
PGA Tour Money Winner: 1986, 1990, 1995
PGA Player of the Year: 1995
Vardon Trophy Winner: 1989, 1990, 1994
Presidents Cup Team: 1996, 1998, 2000
Presidents Cup Captain: 2009, 2011

I hate failure. The idea of failure is, I think, my driving force.

GREG NORMAN

A native of Queensland, Australia, Norman grew up on the beach and in the wild—surfing, fishing, and hunting. His mother, Toini, was an enthusiastic golfer for whom Norman caddied. He learned from her, too, but he didn't take up the game until he was 16. He was a scratch golfer just two years later, and, just before turning professional in 1976, he assured his club teammates that he would be a millionaire by the time he was 30. This he achieved easily.

First in Australia, then in Europe, and finally in the US, the strong, blond Aussie charmer captivated the galleries with his smash-it-and-find-it attitude. A local paper in Augusta gave Norman his distinct nickname on his Masters debut. He won 90 tournaments worldwide and could have won the Grand Slam; instead he became the second man, after American Craig Wood, to lose playoffs at all four Majors.

THE SATURDAY SLAM

Norman should have won at Augusta, a course ideally suited to his attacking game, but it just never happened for him. Against Jack Nicklaus in 1986, he fired his approach to the last hole into the crowd on the right. In 1987, on the second hole of a playoff, Larry Mize chipped in from 40 yards at the 11th to deny him victory. In 1996, he led rival Nick Faldo by six shots, but his game fell apart and he finished five strokes behind Faldo.

If the Mize shot was a blow, at the 1986 USPGA, Norman lost in outrageous circumstances when Bob Tway holed a bunker shot at the last. That year, he did the "Saturday Slam," leading after 54 holes at each Major but winning only one of them: the Open at Turnberry. After reining in his swing under the tuition of Butch Harmon, he became the longest, straightest driver in the game and the world No 1. In one of the

greatest final days of them all, Norman beat Nick Faldo and Bernhard Langer to win the Open for a second time at Royal St. George's in 1993. Norman shot a final-round 64, and his four-round total of 267 remained the lowest in the Open until Henrik Stenson's 264 in 2016.

With back surgery hampering any Seniors Tour ambitions, Norman turned increasingly to his many business interests, which include course design, winemaking, clothing, and restaurants.

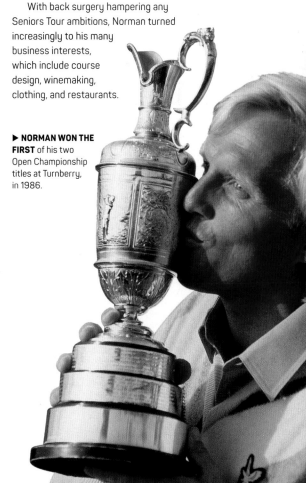

▶ **NORMAN WON THE FIRST** of his two Open Championship titles at Turnberry, in 1986.

FLYING SHARK

In 1995, Norman fulfilled a dream of flying in a Navy jet and landing on an aircraft carrier. He loves to travel in style and is no stranger to commuting by private boat, helicopter, or jet in order to manage his varied business interests around the world.

Norman has a lifelong love of flying

There was something quietly beautiful about the relentless,
slow-burning courage with which he played golf. Among British
sportsmen, Nick Faldo ranks with the greatest of the great.

HUGH MCILVANNEY, SPORTS WRITER

Nick Faldo

Not just the greatest British golfer of the modern era, Nick Faldo is also one of the greats of all British sports. His achievement in winning six Major championships brought respect and admiration. To succeed at the highest level, he kept his emotions under close control, which meant he appeared cold and clinical at times. Golf is Faldo's passion, and this became increasingly apparent over the years—especially when he began work as a commentator.

PLAYER STATS

BORN July 18, 1957; Welwyn Garden City, England
HEIGHT 6ft 3in (1.91m)
TURNED PRO 1976

DEBUT WIN 1977 Skol Lager Individual
TOUR WINS 46
EUROPEAN TOUR: 30
PGA TOUR: 9
OTHER: 7

MAJORS 6
MASTERS: Won 1989, 1990, 1996
US OPEN: 2nd 1988
THE OPEN: Won 1987, 1990, 1992
USPGA: T2nd 1992

HONORS
PGA Tour Player of the Year: 1990
European Tour Player of the Year: 1989, 1990, 1992
European Tour Order of Merit Winner: 1983, 1992
Eleven consecutive Ryder Cup team appearances: 1977–1997
Ryder Cup Captain: 2008

▼ **IT MIGHT HAVE TAKEN** 18 pars in the final round to do it, but victory in the 1987 Open at Muirfield was still sweet for Faldo.

Faldo always pursued individual sports—he ran, he cycled, he swam—and he did them all pretty well. But one night after watching Jack Nicklaus at the Masters, he switched his attention fully and irrevocably to golf. He was 13 and a slower starter compared to Sandy Lyle, who was hitting balls at the age of three. But Faldo more than made up for that with his determination to succeed. A school careers officer suggested professional sport was to be avoided since only one in 10,000 make it. "Well, I'll be that one, then," Faldo replied. He won the English Amateur at the age of 18, in 1975, and turned professional a year later—having worn out the practice range at Welwyn Garden City (where he first learned to play). A debut in the Ryder Cup followed in 1977, and his first big win, the PGA Championship, came at Royal Birkdale in 1978. The wins continued, and he had chances in the Majors. However, although he was a tall man with an aesthetically pleasing swing, he felt his willowy action was not consistent enough under pressure.

Faldo sought out David Leadbetter, an aspiring coach, and they worked on a tighter, more consistent swing. It took almost two years out of his career, but the reward was knowing that he could hit the shots he needed to when the pressure was greatest. In 1987, at Muirfield, Faldo won the Open with a final round of 18 pars. This sounds monotonous, but given the poor weather conditions, the round was pure brilliance. After this triumph, he never looked back. He won the Masters in 1989 after a playoff with Scott Hoch and repeated the feat the next year, winning in near darkness on the 11th green following a playoff against Ray Floyd.

Later that summer, Faldo arrived at St. Andrews as the world's best player, and his golf justified this label as he went on to win a second Open crown. He fought off

▲ **FALDO AND DAVID LEADBETTER** made one of the great pupil-teacher relationships, with Faldo completely remodeling his swing before finding Major success.

the challenge from Greg Norman in the third round and enjoyed a victory walk down the 18th on the final day. In 1992, he won again at Muirfield. Leading for much of the championship, he was suddenly two behind John Cook with four to play. "I've got to play the greatest four holes of my life," he said to himself, and he did. Afterward, in a less-than-gracious speech, he broke into a rendition of "My Way" and thanked the media "from the heart of my bottom." Faldo never had an easy relationship with the press; they thought he was boring, and he mistrusted them.

MAJOR FOCUS
A complex character, Faldo's whole approach was to employ tunnel vision—his focus was on the golf and nothing else. He was never an easy teammate in the Ryder Cup, but, apart from a couple of matches in which his game was in trouble, he always gave his all. He was

A DIFFERENT PURSUIT

His passion for fishing began even before Faldo became interested in golf. His father introduced him to the sport, and it became a lifelong enjoyment—the perfect way to relax away from the golf scene. His fishing trips have taken him all over the world, from Sweden to New Zealand and, in the company of musician Huey Lewis, to Montana.

 A successful day's fishing

particularly effective in partnership with Ian Woosnam, a pairing that rivaled Ballesteros and Olazábal for reliability. By the end of his then-record 11th Ryder Cup appearance, in 1997, he had won more points than anyone else on either side. In 1995, at Oak Hill, Faldo rallied over the last three holes to secure a vital point against Curtis Strange.

If that moment helped turn admiration for Faldo into a warmer appreciation, so did his last great victory, at the Masters in 1996. Faldo started the final round six strokes behind his playing partner, Greg Norman. He knew he could not afford to make a single mistake if he was to claim a third green jacket, and he did not. The relentless excellence of his play finally told on the Australian, who started to fritter away strokes. Faldo's 67 enabled him to come from six behind to win by five. On the 18th green, Faldo took Norman in his arms and said, "I don't know what to say. I just want to give you a hug."

A NEW CHAPTER

With six Majors, Faldo stood head and shoulders above his contemporaries, but from the late '90s, Tiger Woods was the new golfing force, and Faldo put the first green jacket on the young champion in 1997. Interested in course design, with his Chart Hills course in Kent being well received, Faldo also started working in other areas of the game. A particularly fulfilling project was setting up the Faldo Junior Series, which includes tournaments and mentoring from Faldo himself. The program has flourished, and in 2005 Nick Dougherty became the first former winner to become a champion on the European Tour. Rory McIlroy, the 18-year-old winner of the Silver Medal as the leading amateur at the 2007 Open, is also a graduate of the program. Then along came television, which helped reveal Faldo's true love of the game. Faldo turned 50 on the eve of the 2007 Open Championship at Carnoustie. He missed the cut but the following week made his debut in

▲ **FALDO LEAPS FOR JOY** after holing a putt for victory in the World Match Play Championship at Wentworth in 1989. He also lifted the crown in 1992.

1977
Faldo becomes the youngest player to appear in the Ryder Cup to date, at the age of 21.

1978
Wins his first big tournament: the PGA Championship at Royal Birkdale.

1983
Takes the European Order of Merit, winning five times during the season.

1987
At the Open at Muirfield, Faldo manages to beat American Paul Azinger by one shot, with a historic final round of 18 pars.

1989
Wins the first of three green jackets at Augusta after a playoff with American Scott Hoch.

1990
Becomes the first player since Jack Nicklaus to successfully defend the Masters title.

the Senior Open Championship at Muirfield. He had a good first day but could not sustain the challenge. "Thank goodness I have a day job," he said, referring to his television work. After a few years commentating for ABC television, Faldo was offered a huge contract to work almost weekly for CBS and the Golf Channel in America. When his course-design interests, the Faldo Series (which expanded from Britain to Asia and the US), and his four children are also factored in, he said that playing golf became his fifth priority.

Being made captain of the European Ryder Cup team for 2008 was an inevitable honor, although Europe struggled that year and were beaten at Valhalla. It took until 2018 for his Ryder Cup points total to be beaten, when Sergio García pipped him by half a point when he reached 25.5 points. Faldo's career saw him collect his 25 Ryder Cup points across 11 appearances.

Faldo was never the machine some made him out to be. He once said, "I'm just playing for the love of the game. And for the little cups." If he had been a fairways-and-greens plodder, he would probably have won either the US Open or the USPGA, instead of suffering near misses in those events. Winning at Augusta and on the links of the Open rota requires flair. It was Faldo himself who hoped people would say of him: "I saw Nick Faldo play golf. He wasn't bad." He was the best of British and rightly received a knighthood in 2009.

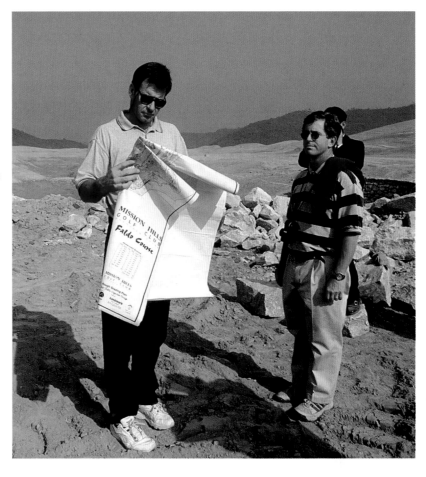

▶ **FALDO VISITS MISSION HILLS** in China, another course-design project. Faldo's design company has produced courses all over the world—from Cyprus, Turkey, and Egypt to Dubai, Mexico, and Ireland.

> I went there with the intention of winning that Major, not just turning up and saying this feels good and I wonder what's going to happen.
>
> **NICK FALDO**

1990	1992	1996	1997	1998	2004	2004
Claims a second Open title with an emphatic triumph at St. Andrews.	Victorious again at Muirfield claiming his third Open after playing "the greatest four holes of my life."	Seals a famous victory at the Masters, defeating Greg Norman, to collect his sixth and final Major title.	Plays in a record 11th Ryder Cup.	Accepts an MBE at Buckingham Palace, in recognition of his golfing exploits.	Begins commentating regularly for US television after retiring from the tour.	Turns 50 and becomes eligible for the Seniors Tour. Shoots 68 in his first competitive round.

Curtis Strange

At a time when European golf was at its strongest in the second half of the 1980s, Curtis Strange was the dominant American golfer. He won the US money list three times in the space of four years. In 1988 and 1989, he became the first player since Ben Hogan in 1951 to win consecutive US Open titles. Then, suddenly, golfing success deserted him.

PLAYER STATS

BORN January 30, 1955; Norfolk, Virginia
HEIGHT 5ft 11in (1.80m)
TURNED PRO 1976

DEBUT WIN Pensacola Open 1979
TOUR WINS 25
PGA TOUR: 17
OTHER: 8

MAJORS 2
MASTERS: T2nd 1985
US OPEN: Won 1988, 1989
THE OPEN: T13th 1988
USPGA: T2nd 1989

HONORS
Ryder Cup Team: 1983, 1985, 1987, 1989, 1995
Ryder Cup Captain 2002
PGA Player of the Year: 1988
PGA Tour Money Winner: 1985, 1987, 1988

▼ **WITH A REPUTATION** for methodical play, Strange found that grinding out pars was crucial to his US Open wins.

The son of a club professional from Virginia, Strange won 17 times on the American circuit between 1979 and 1989. For much of that period, he was known as a money-making machine, winning the money title in 1985, 1987, and 1988. He was also the first player to win $1 million in a single season (1988).

Strange was the quintessential grinder and once said that making only one birdie in 35 consecutive holes during a US Open was "as exciting as watching paint dry." He also disliked that he was described as a fiery competitor. That said, his day in, day out tenacity was sometimes accompanied by lapses in behavior (he was fined for using bad language) and stubbornness (he declined to make several trips to Britain for the Open, partly because everyone told him he should go). He later admitted that not competing at the Open more often was the "biggest mistake of my career. It didn't bother me then but it bothers me now. I should have gone. Sitting in your rocking chair you don't want to have any regrets. That's one of mine."

Another regret may be how he started at the 1985 Masters. Strange recovered from an opening 80 with rounds of 65 and 68 and led by four with nine to play. Unfortunately, he then went in to Rae's Creek at the 13th and in the pond at the 15th to lose to Bernhard Langer. Three years later, however, he made a superb up-and-down from a bunker to tie with Nick Faldo at the US Open at Brookline and won the 18-hole playoff the next day. The following year at Oak Hill, he beat Ian Woosnam, Chip Beck, and Mark McCumber by one shot. Going for three in a row at Medinah in 1990, he finished six shots back and then suffered health problems, causing his play to deteriorate. Afflicted with headaches and lethargy, the intensity seeped from his game. The worse he felt he was playing, the more he tinkered with

his swing. "Maybe I lost enthusiasm because I knew my game was going south. I couldn't stop it for a while. The pressure to play well every day was part of it. We only have so much energy, mentally and physically, to be the best. The first thing that goes is the mental edge. Except for Jack Nicklaus, it's only for seven or eight years."

Strange never won again. He did make his fifth Ryder Cup appearance in 1995 at Oak Hill but bogeyed the last three holes to lose an important singles to Nick Faldo.

▼ **AT THE BROOKLINE COUNTRY CLUB** in 1988, Strange won the first of his two successive US Open titles after beating Nick Faldo by four shots in an 18-hole playoff.

> ## I wasn't playing well ... and I was getting worse and said, "To hell with it."
>
> **STRANGE ON SWITCHING TO THE CHAMPIONS TOUR AGED 50**

Ian Woosnam

Of Europe's "big five," who were all born within a year of each other, Ian Woosnam was the youngest. The others—Nick Faldo, Sandy Lyle, Seve Ballesteros, and Bernhard Langer—all won Major championships, on both sides of the Atlantic. Although wee "Woosie" was not able to emulate this feat, he possessed both a huge heart and one of the sweetest swings in the game.

PLAYER STATS

BORN March 2, 1958; Oswestry, Wales
HEIGHT 5ft 5in (1.65m)
TURNED PRO 1976

DEBUT WIN 1982 Ebel Swiss Open
TOUR WINS 45
EUROPEAN TOUR: 29
PGA TOUR: 2
OTHER: 14

MAJORS 1
MASTERS: Won 1991
US OPEN: T2nd 1989
THE OPEN: 3rd 1986/T3rd 2001
USPGA: 6th 1989

HONORS
Ryder Cup Team: 1983, 1985, 1987, 1989, 1991, 1993, 1995, 1997
Ryder Cup Captain: 2006
PGA Player of the Year: 1988
European Tour Order of Merit Winner: 1987, 1990
European Senior Tour Order of Merit Winner: 2008

▲ **IAN WOOSNAM WON** his only Major championship at the Masters in 1991. He celebrated the winning putt with passion, before being lifted off the ground by his caddie.

CADDIE TROUBLE

First caddie Miles Byrne (head bowed) cost Woosnam a two-stroke penalty in the 2001 Open after an extra club was discovered in the bag. Then, in the next tournament, he missed an early tee off, forcing Woosnam to break into his own locker. This time, Byrne was sacked.

● A bad day for player and caddie

His swing was a thing of beauty. It was a swing that drew admirers even among his peers, who would stop and watch him on the range. It allowed this short man to smash the ball to kingdom come, and it matched his character—Woosie has always been a straightforward man who enjoys a beer and a smoke.

Woosnam's strength came from working on the family farm, and his early golf was played at Llanmynech, which has 15 holes in Wales and three in England. Golfing success did not always come easily. He attended the Qualifying School three times and later, as a struggling pro, traveled the circuit in an RV, eating baked beans. Sandy Lyle, the same age, was an early rival. "One day I'll beat you," Woosnam said to Lyle after losing the 1969 Hereford Boys' Championship. "You'll have to grow a bit first, Woosie," replied Lyle. In 1987, the pair met in a brilliant final at the World Match Play tournament, and Woosnam took his revenge. After the final, reminded of the earlier exchange, Lyle added, "If he ever grows up, he'll hit the ball 2,000 yards."

Winning the Order of Merit and the World Cup for Wales in 1987 capped Woosie's first great season. He won the Order of Merit again in 1990 and then claimed his biggest triumph at Augusta, in 1991—winning by a shot from Olazábal. However, his one weakness was his putting, which may have prevented him from winning more Majors. During the Open at Royal Lytham in 2001, he birdied the par-3 1st in the final round to take the lead but then discovered that there was an extra driver in his bag and was penalized two shots for having 15 clubs (one too many). He lost to David Duval but later in the summer became the first player to win the World Match Play in three different decades. His courage and determination made Woosnam a vital Ryder Cup player for Europe, and his passion as captain drove Europe to a third successive victory at The K Club in Ireland in 2006.

Payne Stewart

Payne Stewart's death in a plane crash in 1999 at the age of 42 came at the end of his most rewarding season. He had just won the US Open for the second time—his third Major—and, off the course, the man known for his brashness and his outrageous clothing was more content than at any time in his life.

PLAYER STATS

BORN January 30, 1957; Springfield, Missouri
DIED October 25, 1999
HEIGHT 6ft 1in (1.85m)
TURNED PRO 1982

DEBUT WIN 1981 Indian Open
TOUR WINS 23
PGA TOUR: 11
OTHER: 12

MAJORS 3
MASTERS: T8th 1986
US OPEN: Won 1991, 1999
THE OPEN: 2nd 1985/T2nd 1990
USPGA: Won 1989

HONORS
Ryder Cup Team: 1987, 1989, 1991, 1993, 1999

Stewart hailed from the heart of America and was known on the US Tour for his individualism. He wore plus-twos, and for many years had a clothing contract with the National Football League to wear the colors of the local teams. Unashamedly patriotic, Stewart was easily labeled "cocky" in the conservative world of American golf. He had won in Asia and Australia before making it in the US. His first Major title came at the 1989 USPGA, and two years later, he won the US Open at Hazeltine, after an 18-hole playoff against Scott Simpson.

However, by 1999, he had not won for four years. He was runner-up twice in the Open Championship and was pipped on two occasions in the US Open by Lee Janzen, losing at Olympic Club in San Francisco in 1998. When asked to describe what it was like playing with Stewart at the US Open, Janzen said, "He's more outgoing than most people on tour but his style of play is exactly the opposite. Nothing fancy, hit the fairways, hit the greens and try and make a few putts."

Stewart said he never minded making a bogey at the US Open. This was probably because he had an excellent short game and was blessed with great imagination. At Pinehurst in 1999, he defeated Phil Mickelson, Tiger Woods, David Duval, and Vijay Singh, holing from 15ft (4m) at the last for the victory. To Mickelson, the runner-up whose wife was expecting their first child, Stewart said, "You'll win the Open but now you have more important things to do. You'll be a great daddy." Age mellowed Stewart, and he traded his cocksure image for that of a fine family man, active at a Baptist church in Orlando. "This walk I am having in Christianity is being led by my children," he said.

Shortly after a fifth Ryder Cup appearance, where he had a spectator who was heckling Colin Montgomerie removed from the venue, he set out to visit a course he was designing. His private jet depressurized after takeoff, and all on board suffocated. The plane, on automatic pilot, finally ran out of fuel and crashed in South Dakota.

▲ **STEWART HOLDS ON** tightly to the US Open trophy at Pinehurst in 1999. His third Major championship would, tragically, prove to be his last.

▲ **IN A TYPICALLY COLORFUL OUTFIT,** the young Stewart won his first US Open at Hazeltine in 1991 after a playoff against Scott Simpson. His clenched-fist celebration became a common sight on the tour.

SMILING IRISH EYES

Payne Stewart enjoyed visiting Ireland, particularly Waterville, on golf trips, and the Irish loved him. "If I ran for mayor ... it would be a landside," he said. After his death, the residents of Waterville erected a statue in his honor.

● Stewart's statue at Waterville

John Daly

Golf's "Wild Thing" has enjoyed a turbulent life, both on and off the golf course. His massive hitting, combined with a delicate touch around the greens, brought him two Major championships. The first, at the 1991 USPGA at Crooked Stick, Indiana, was one of the most surprising in the game's history; his second at the Open in 1995 at St. Andrews was no surprise at all.

PLAYER STATS

BORN April 28, 1966; Carmichael, California
HEIGHT 5ft 11in (1.80m)
TURNED PRO 1987

DEBUT WIN Ben Hogan Utah Classic 1990
TOUR WINS 20
PGA TOUR: 5
EUROPEAN TOUR: 3
OTHER: 12

MAJORS 2
MASTERS: T3rd 1993
US OPEN: T27th 1997
THE OPEN: Won 1995
USPGA: Won 1991

HONORS
Rookie of the Year 1991
PGA Tour Comeback Player of
the Year: 2004

WILD SING

A talented singer and guitarist, Daly produced an album entitled *My Life*, which includes a track called "All My Exes Wear Rolexes." "Music is my therapy," Daly says. "I think for all of us it is therapy, whatever style of music you are into. If I am driving my bus, I can't do it with no sound. The world can't exist without music."

Daly relaxes by playing the guitar

Daly's "Grip it and Rip it" style of golf astonished the world when he came from nowhere to win the USPGA at Crooked Stick in 1991. Daly, a rookie on the US Tour who had been playing on mini-tours and in South Africa before that season, was the ninth reserve for the event. He drove for seven hours, arriving at his hotel at midnight before the first round, and didn't even have a practice round. But he played brilliantly, hitting long drives and putting superbly to win by three strokes. Suddenly his life became very public.

He grew up in Dardanelle, Arkansas; he started playing golf at the age of four and drinking at the age of eight. In his teens, he was heavily into Jack Daniel's. He was already divorced once when he won at Crooked Stick. After the win, he discovered his fiancée was 10 years older than she said, had a 13-year-old son, and was not yet divorced. They split up and then got married when she became pregnant. Later, he was served divorce papers during the Masters. Throughout four marriages, he fought addictions to alcohol, gambling, chocolate, and Diet Coke—sometimes getting through 18 cans during a round. He has attended clinics and wrecked hotel rooms but has always strenuously denied accusations of wife-beating. "I play golf aggressively," explains Daly. "I like to go for it on the course but now I'm better at not going for it off the course."

No matter what problems befall him—whether he has just walked off the course or been disqualified—he has always retained the loyalty of his many fans. In 2004, he won for only the fifth time on the US Tour, and the highlight of his career came when he won at St. Andrews in 1995, overpowering the Old Course with his length off the tee and making low scores with a superb touch on the huge double greens. In windy conditions, he tied with Italian Costantino Rocca and then won a four-hole playoff comfortably. Despite his Majors, he has never played in the Ryder Cup; he has not qualified by right nor been picked by a captain as the ultimate wild card.

▶ **GRIP IT AND RIP IT,** the Daly philosophy, produced big hitting but also gained the "Wild Thing" two Major championships and a fan base to rival any of the game's top players.

Fred Couples

Fred Couples did not set out with the ambition of being the best player in the world, but for a short spell in 1992, that is exactly what he was. Winning the Masters and topping the money list was the pinnacle of his golfing career, but his laid-back approach to the game and his humility made him hugely popular, especially in the US.

▲ **FRED COUPLES BECAME** one of the most popular American golfers in the 1990s with his wonderfully fluid swing and his laid-back approach to the game and to life.

Fred Couples learned to play at a municipal course in Seattle. "I was playing with guys 60, 65-years-old, and having a blast," he recalled. "It was a good atmosphere; if I screwed around, some of the older guys let me know about it." Obviously talented, he was soon known as "Boom Boom" on tour for his great length, but although he won regularly, some critics wondered whether he really had the ruthless streak to be a great champion. It did not help when Couples revealed he liked nothing better than being a television couch potato.

The turning point in his career was playing with Raymond Floyd in the 1991 Ryder Cup. "You can be friendly with them another time," Floyd told his partner when Couples started complimenting their opponents' shots. "For one week we are trying to beat these guys." They won two of their three matches together and some of Floyd's competitiveness must have rubbed off. He won twice early in 1992, arriving as a hot favorite at Augusta where he beat none other than Floyd by two strokes. His play more than justified the victory, but he profited from a moment of fortune at the short 12th; his tee short started to roll back toward the water but implausibly stayed on the bank. In the prime of his career, Couples joined up with Davis Love III to win the World Cup four times in a row from 1992. But in 1994, he suffered a back injury that never really went away.

Off the course, there was the sadness of his parents dying within three years of each other, and a very public divorce, with his ex-wife later dying by suicide. In 2003, five years after his previous win, came a popular victory at the Houston Open. But his attitude was simple. "Is it really important how many trophies you wind up with? I love golf, don't get me wrong, but there are other things I want out of life."

PLAYER STATS

BORN October 3, 1959; Seattle, Washington
HEIGHT 5ft 11in (1.80m)
TURNED PRO 1980

DEBUT WIN 1983 Kemper Open
TOUR WINS 47
PGA TOUR: 15
EUROPEAN TOUR: 3
OTHER: 29

MAJORS 1
MASTERS: Won 1992
US OPEN: T3rd 1991
THE OPEN: T3rd 1991, 2005
USPGA: 2nd 1991

HONORS
PGA Tour Player of the Year: 1991, 1992
USPGA Tour Money Winner: 1992
Vardon Trophy: 1991, 1992
Ryder Cup Team: 1989, 1991, 1993, 1995, 1997
Presidents Cup Team: 1994, 1996, 1998, 2005
Presidents Cup Captain: 2009, 2011, 2013

> Fred would rather do his own thing than get involved in the business of being a celebrity. He is a very modest person.
>
> **DAVIS LOVE III**

▶ **COUPLES WON REGULARLY** on the US Tour before claiming his only Major at the 1992 Masters. He is also king of the Skins, winning five times between 1995 and 2004.

Laura Davies

Laura Davies became far more than the finest British woman player of the modern era. In 1994, she was the first European golfer to be ranked No. 1 in the world, helping make the women's game truly international. She hit the ball farther than any other woman, she won around the globe, including four Major championships, and she earned friends everywhere she traveled.

PLAYER STATS

BORN October 5, 1963; Coventry, England
HEIGHT 5ft 10in (1.78m)
TURNED PRO 1985

DEBUT WIN 1985 Belgian Open
TOUR WINS 91
EUROPEAN TOUR: 45
LPGA TOUR: 20
OTHER: 26

MAJORS 4
ANA INSPIRATION: 2nd 1994
LPGA CHAMPIONSHIP: Won 1994, 1996
US WOMEN'S OPEN: Won 1987
DU MAURIER CLASSIC: Won 1996
WOMEN'S BRITISH OPEN: T8th 2004

HONORS
European Tour Order of Merit Winner:
1985, 1986, 1992, 1996, 1999,
2004, 2006
LPGA Tour Money Winner: 1994
LPGA Tour Player of the Year: 1996
Curtis Cup Team: 1984
Solheim Cup Team: 1990, 1992, 1994,
1996, 1998, 2000, 2002, 2003, 2005,
2007, 2009, 2011

In 2007, more international players than Americans teed off in the US Women's Open. Two decades earlier, that would have been unthinkable, and it certainly would not have been possible without Laura Davies winning the 1987 US Open as a nonmember of the LPGA Tour. For six days, Davies held both Open titles and only just failed to defend her Women's British Open—not then classed as a Major—the following weekend.

Davies was an instant success on the fledgling European circuit, winning the money list in her first two seasons in 1985 and 1986. Sensitive about her size, she used it to her advantage by hitting the ball huge distances, and as a natural gambler, on and off the course, she would attempt the most audacious shots in the manner of Ballesteros or Palmer. She also had the delicate touch around the greens to recover when

▲ **DAVIES IS UNQUESTIONABLY** Britain's most successful, golfer. She has won many golfing honours and holds the record for the most eagles in a season: 19 during 2004.

necessary. The putts did not always fall, and more than one putter finished up in a waste bin, but the victories rolled in. Between 1994 and 1996, she won 24 times around the world, in 1994 becoming the first player, male or female, to win on five different tours; she won three more Majors in that time to add to her US Open.

Davies has also been instrumental in making the Solheim Cup a competitive match. When the women's version of the Ryder Cup was introduced, the US dominated the inaugural match. At Dalmahoy in 1992, however, Davies inspired a young European team to victory, and the transatlantic rivalry started in earnest.

▲ **DAVIES HAS BEEN ONE** of Europe's most inspirational Solheim Cup players, picking up a record 25 points in 12 appearances.

José Maria Olazábal

José Maria Olazábal not only followed his countryman Seve Ballesteros in winning Major championships but also formed with him perhaps the greatest partnership in the history of the Ryder Cup. Blessed with fierce determination, majestic iron play, and a brilliant set of recovery shots, he also overcame serious injury to continue his illustrious career.

Olazábal grew up with golf on his doorstep. He was born the day after the Real Golf Club de San Sebastian opened and practically lived on the course. First his grandfather and then his father worked as greenkeepers, and "Ollie" was introduced to the game with a cut-down club. He enjoyed success as an amateur, winning the triple crown of the British Boys, Youths, and Amateur titles. He won the tour qualifying school in 1985 and went on to win his first title the following year. In 1987, he played in the Ryder Cup for the first time, at the age of 21, and began his inspirational partnership with Ballesteros. They won 11 of their matches together, halving two, and losing only two. Their sheer presence intimidated the opposition.

They were never out of a hole, one of them conjuring up an unlikely escape. They had a policy of "no sorrys"; they just got on with the next shot. At first, Ballesteros was the senior man, but soon Olazábal proved the rock of the partnership. Although his driver could be erratic, his quick swing produced wonderful long-iron shots, and his putting was deadly, which complemented his magic around the greens.

Olazábal won the Masters in 1994 and again, more emotionally, in 1999. In between, he feared he would not play again, or might even end up in a wheelchair. For 18 months, from late in 1995, he was absent from the game and for six months in 1996 could barely walk, crawling from his bed to the bathroom. He was diagnosed with rheumatoid polyarthritis but, remarkably, returned to play his part in the Ryder Cup win at Valderrama in 1997. Having not played since 1999, Olazábal returned to the Ryder Cup in 2006 at The K Club, winning three matches out of three, and while hoping to play in 2008, he was named as a vice captain designate by Nick Faldo, who marveled at the Spaniard's "great passion and incredible determination."

PLAYER STATS

BORN February 5, 1966; Fuenterrabia, Spain
HEIGHT 5ft 10in (1.78m)
TURNED PRO 1985

DEBUT WIN 1986 Ebel European Masters Swiss Open
TOUR WINS 31
PGA TOUR: 6
EUROPEAN TOUR: 23
OTHER: 2

MAJORS 2
MASTERS: Won 1994, 1999
US OPEN: T8th 1990, 1991
THE OPEN: 3rd 1992/T3rd 2005
USPGA: T4th 2000

HONORS
The Amateur Championship Winner: 1984
Ryder Cup Team: 1987, 1989, 1991, 1993, 1997, 1999, 2006, 2012
Ryder Cup Captain: 2012

▲ **OLAZÁBAL HAS AMASSED** a collection of trophies over his career. The highlights of his collection remain his two Masters green jackets.

▲ **OLAZÁBAL WAS ALWAYS** at his inspired best in the Ryder Cup. He captained Europe to victory in 2012, which was dubbed the "Miracle at Medinah."

There are no sorrys between us if either of us hits a bad shot. We just make sure we get the next one right.

SEVE BALLESTEROS, ON PLAYING WITH OLAZÁBAL IN THE RYDER CUP

Nick Price

Nick Price is so nice that he does not even mind being called nice. He is also downright talented and a great iron player. A long-term student of David Leadbetter, his crisp and efficient golf swing propelled him to three Major championship victories in as many years in the early 1990s. He proved the phrase "nice guys don't win" was nonsense.

PLAYER STATS

BORN January 28, 1957; Durban, South Africa
HEIGHT 6ft (1.83m)
TURNED PRO 1977

DEBUT WIN 1979 Asseng TV Challenge Series
TOUR WINS 46
PGA TOUR: 18
EUROPEAN TOUR: 7
OTHER: 21

MAJORS 3
MASTERS: 5th 1986
US OPEN: 4th 1992/T4th 1998
THE OPEN: Won 1994
USPGA: Won 1992, 1994

HONORS
PGA Tour Money Winner: 1993, 1994
Vardon Trophy: 1993, 1997
Jim Murray Award: 2002
Bob Jones Award: 2005
Presidents Cup Team: 1994, 1996, 1998, 2000, 2003

Price was born to an English father and a Welsh mother in South Africa. His mother told him, "I don't care how successful you are, what you've done in life, how much money you make—it doesn't matter. All I want to see every time I see you is a smile on your face." He grew up in what was then Rhodesia and went into the air force for his military service, which coincided with the civil war of the late 1970s. The experience gave him a new perspective on the life of a professional golfer.

Price played in South Africa and Europe before heading to America, where his first big win was beating Jack Nicklaus at the 1983 World Series of Golf. The year before he had started a career-long association with David Leadbetter. Although he had a quick rhythm, Price became a great striker of the ball. If anything let him down, it was his putting, which was one reason why he started to win the biggest titles only in the early 1990s. In 1992, he won the USPGA, and two years later, he won both the Open and the USPGA and became the world's best player.

Twice Price had come close to winning the Open; in 1982, he shot a final-round 73 to lose by one to Tom Watson, but in 1988 at Lytham, he saw Seve Ballesteros rip the title away with a brilliant 65 to Price's 69. However, at Turnberry in 1994, his time had come. Jesper Parnevik led by one on the 18th tee but bogeyed the last; Price then eagled the 17th to win a fascinating duel. His caddie for all three of his Major wins was Jeff "Squeeky" Medlen, who died from leukemia at the age of 43 not long afterward. "He was diligent and conscientious and humble and simple and honest and all the good things any man should be," Price wrote in tribute.

In 2002, the Golf Writers Association of America inaugurated an award in the memory of the late *Los Angeles Times* writer Jim Murray to honor a player who, in being approachable and accessible, "reflects the most positive aspects of the working relationship between athlete and journalist." The first winner was Nick Price; the second was Arnold Palmer.

◀ ▼ **NICK PRICE HOLES** a long eagle putt at the 17th hole at Turnberry on the way to winning the 1994 Open Championship.

Colin Montgomerie

If Major championships are the measure of greatness, and they have to be, Colin Montgomerie does not register. But the Scot's achievements in the game defy such a bleak assessment. His Ryder Cup successes and Order of Merit titles make him one of Europe's best-ever golfers, and "Monty" is an always enthralling, if unpredictable, individual.

After the bountiful Majors success of Europe's big guns, such as Nick Faldo, Sandy Lyle, and Seve Ballesteros, a vacuum was left that Colin Montgomerie, aka "Monty," filled. His record of winning the Order of Merit eight times from 1993 to 2005 will surely never be bettered. This achievement revealed his determination not to relinquish his crown as Europe's No. 1, and he achieved this—he will be the last person that needs reminding—without adding the biggest prizes of all.

At his best, Monty rarely practiced. He just showed up and hit precise and consistent fades down the middle of the fairway—and into the green—every time. In the first half of his career, he was a magnificent putter, which meant that he was often able to capitalize on the birdie opportunities his accurate iron play afforded.

A COMPETITIVE PLAYER

The son of a former military man who worked for Fox's Biscuits in northern England and then became secretary at Royal Troon, Monty was a good amateur player but not the best. José Maria Olazábal had beaten him in the final of the 1984 Amateur Championship. Nevertheless, he improved simply by being more competitive than anyone else, even though he could be irascible and was easily distracted by noise from the gallery or by a photographer in the wrong place.

At the Majors, Monty always came up just short. He lost playoffs at the 1994 US Open and the 1995 USPGA and then finished behind Ernie Els for the second time, at the 1997 US Open. Later, more chances appeared, although Tiger Woods was never going to be beaten at the 2005

Open, the year Monty added an eighth Order of Merit. A double bogey on the final hole at the 2006 US Open ruined his best chance of a Major success.

Yet throughout his career, Monty has proved an inspirational figure at the Ryder Cup. He first played in 1991, and in 1997 at Valderrama, he was Europe's main man, securing the winning point. At Brookline in 1999, the heckling—which so obviously got under his skin—was at its worst, but he rose above it. In 2002 and 2006, he led off the singles matches and secured yet another winning point at Oakland Hills in 2004.

> ## The Ryder Cup brings out the best in me and I'm grateful it does.
>
> **COLIN MONTGOMERIE**

▶ **MONTY CELEBRATES** yet another Ryder Cup triumph, at Oak Hill in 1995. He beat Ben Crenshaw 3 and 1 in the singles to help Europe secure a one-point victory.

Ernie Els

A big man blessed with such wonderful natural rhythm, Ernie Els became South Africa's next golfing superstar after Gary Player. At his best, the nickname of the "Big Easy" is a perfect fit. Any suggestion that there is not also the will to win, the loathing of losing, and the hard work and dedication must be refuted. The rewards have been well earned.

PLAYER STATS

BORN October 17, 1969; Johannesburg, South Africa
HEIGHT 6ft 3in (1.90m)
TURNED PRO 1989

DEBUT WIN 1991 Amatola Sun Classic
TOUR WINS 69
PGA TOUR 19
EUROPEAN TOUR 28
OTHER 22

MAJORS 4
MASTERS: 2nd 2000, 2004
US OPEN: Won 1994, 1997
THE OPEN: Won 2002, 2012
USPGA: 3rd 1995, 2007

HONORS
PGA Tour Rookie of the Year: 1994
European Tour Order of Merit Winner: 2003, 2004
Sunshine Tour Order of Merit Winner: 1992, 1993, 1994, 1995
Presidents Cup Team: 1996, 1998, 2000, 2003, 2007, 2009, 2011, 2013
President's Cup captain: 2019

Els was a naturally talented sportsman throughout his school days. He played rugby, cricket, and tennis, becoming the Eastern Transvaal junior tennis champion at the age of 13. However, by the age of 14, he was a scratch golfer, and at the World Junior Championships in San Diego in 1984, he beat Phil Mickelson to the title in the 13–14 age group (Tiger Woods won the 9–10 age group).

After becoming South African Amateur Stroke Play Champion in 1989, Els completed his military service and—having had surgery on his hand after a car accident—made his big breakthrough in 1992. He won six times in South Africa that year, including the triple crown of the South African Open, the PGA, and Masters titles. This was also the year that he moved to Europe, and he has played all over the globe ever since. Now based at Wentworth (in England), he still competes in the US, Europe, Asia, and in South Africa every year.

Five years after turning pro, he won the 1994 US Open at Oakmont. He announced himself to the world by beating Loren Roberts and Colin Montgomerie in a playoff. Monty always had trouble with Els. He was again on the losing end of an Els victory in the US Open of 1997 when the South African's wonderful approach at the 17th hole ended a terrific duel.

A PEERLESS MATCH PLAYER

Els had to wait until 2002 to win his third Major, the Open Championship at Muirfield. The old motto—"swing easy in the wind"—helped him survive the blustery conditions throughout the third round, but he still had to recover over the closing holes before winning a playoff against Thomas Levet, Stuart Appleby, and Steve Elkington. No one can win at Muirfield without being

◄ **ELS ANNOUNCES HIMSELF** as a world player by winning at Oakmont in 1994 after a playoff against Loren Roberts and Colin Montgomerie.

ALL-AROUND SPORTSMAN

The "Big Easy" is equally comfortable with a golf club or a cricket bat in his hands. In his early years, Els showed enormous talent in a range of sports, but eventually the time came when he had to choose which to pursue professionally. His love of golf won over, and this decision has certainly been more than justified over the years.

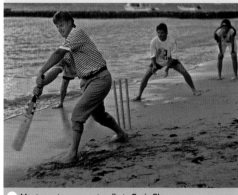

● Most sports come naturally to Ernie Els

a master bunker player, and Els is every bit as good as compatriot Gary Player in this department.

One record Els took from Player, and from Seve Ballesteros, was in winning the World Match Play Championship at Wentworth seven times. He has proved a dominant force in the 36-hole format, winning his first 11 matches before losing to Vijay Singh in the 1997 final. But he was victorious in 26 out of 31 matches by the time of his seventh title in 2007.

In the Majors, Els has not had it his own way. He was the distant runner-up to Tiger Woods in the US Open and in the Open of 2000. In 2004, he had chances to win all four Majors but won none. And a knee injury has had a lasting effect on his swing, but he remains one of the most popular professionals in the game. Indeed, in 2012, he ended his 10-year wait for another Major by lifting the Claret Jug at Royal Lytham & St. Annes. Els finished one shot ahead of Australia's Adam Scott.

Annika Sorenstam

At a time when the women's game was becoming genuinely global, Annika Sorenstam proved herself the best in the world and the outstanding candidate as the greatest player of all time. A friend and "rival" of Tiger Woods, during the 2001 and 2002 seasons, she was even more dominant on the women's circuit than Tiger. After each Major win, the pair exchanged text messages of congratulations.

PLAYER STATS

BORN October 9, 1970; Bro, Sweden
HEIGHT 5ft 6in (1.68m)
TURNED PRO 1992

DEBUT WIN 1994 Holden Australian Open
TOUR WINS 94
LPGA TOUR: 72
OTHER: 22

MAJORS 10
ANA INSPIRATION: Won 2001, 2002, 2005
LPGA CHAMPIONSHIP: Won 2003, 2004, 2005
US WOMEN'S OPEN: Won 1995, 1996, 2006
WOMEN'S BRITISH OPEN: Won 2003
DU MAURIER CLASSIC: 2nd 1998

HONORS
Rookie of the Year: 1994
LPGA Tour Money Winner: 1995, 1997, 1998, 2001, 2002, 2003, 2004, 2005
Solheim Cup Team: 1994, 1996, 1998, 2000, 2002, 2003, 2005, 2007
Solheim Cup Captain: 2017

▼ **SORENSTAM CAUSED A SENSATION** when she played in a men's event, the 2003 Colonial. It was a one-time occurrence and a personal challenge.

▲ **SORENSTAM HOLDS** the Kraft Nabisco trophy in 2002 after taking the traditional leap into the lake by the 18th green.

Sorenstam was a talented young sportswoman who played and skied to a high standard but found her single-minded approach best suited golf. She became a pupil of Pia Nilsson, who encouraged players not to limit themselves to two putts a hole but to think about birdieing every hole. Sorenstam's initial run of success would have made for a satisfying career in itself (see p.240). She was the Rookie of the Year in Europe in 1993 and in the US the following year. In 1995, she topped the money lists on both sides of the Atlantic and won the US Open, which she would retain at Pine Needles the following year.

WINNING STREAK

More wins followed, and Sorenstam led the LPGA money list again in 1997 and 1998, but then she was overtaken by the likes of Karrie Webb and Se Ri Pak. Her determination to regain her top billing and start winning Majors again came to fruition in 2001. She won the Kraft Nabisco Championship, plus seven other events, and broke or tied 30 LPGA records, including shooting a round of 59. After working tirelessly on her fitness, she became one of the longer hitters on the women's circuit while at the same time retaining her remarkable accuracy. In 2002, she won 13 times around the world, including the Kraft Nabisco Championship again. In 2003, she won the two Majors she had not yet won, the LPGA Championship and the Women's British Open at Royal Lytham. The following year, she won 10 times, and in 2005, she won 11 times in 21 starts, including a third successive LPGA Championship (the first person in LPGA history to achieve this) and a record eighth LPGA Player of the Year award. In 2006, after a wait of 10 years, she won a third US Open—her 10th Major. Her other achievements included being the first player in LPGA or PGA history to win the same event five consecutive years at the Mizuno Classic. Sorenstam's game was based on a clinical precision from tee to green, while she also played occasional practice rounds with Tiger Woods in order to learn some of his short-game secrets. In the Solheim Cup, the women's equivalent of the Ryder Cup, she has been supreme. She played in eight cups and was the record points maker until Laura Davies moved past her in 2011. Although she was just one of a number of Swedish players to reach the top of the game, her influence led to the Solheim Cup being played twice in her home country, in 2003 at Barseback, where Sorenstam helped Europe to a famous victory, and at Halmstad in 2007, where the US retained the trophy.

SILENT ASSASSIN

Initially shy early in her career, as an amateur Sorenstam might three-putt at the last hole to avoid giving a winner's speech. When a coach decided that both the winner and the runner-up were required to speak, she started to win. Something of a silent assassin on turning professional, she gradually developed a more expressive personality, as comfortable in front of a microphone as out on the fairways. Her locker-room speech at the 2000 Solheim Cup at Loch Lomond, sharing her passion and determination to succeed, helped Europe to victory that week.

COMPETING WITH THE MEN

In 2003, Sorenstam became the first woman for 58 years to play in a men's PGA Tour event, at the Colonial. The news that she was playing drew much attention, and she prepared as if it was a Major championship. Not one of the longer courses on the men's tour, her accuracy worked in her favor, but it was not her best putting week. Some critics suggested that this was a fundamental flaw in her game, but the number of times she has holed important putts in her many victories suggests this is incorrect. She narrowly missed the cut at the Colonial, but she firmly believed the one-off experience—unlike others, she never saw it as a regular happening—helped her when she was trying to win women's Majors. Two of her next three victories were Majors. One of those victories came at the Weetabix Women's British Open at Royal Lytham, where she beat Se Ri Pak in a thrilling duel. "I believe I have become a better player since playing at the Colonial," she said that night. "There were times today when I felt the pressure and then I thought it was not as bad as the Colonial."

TOP PLAYER, HEAD CHEF

One of Sorenstam's favorite hobbies is cooking. With more of a winter break in the women's schedule than on the men's tour, Sorenstam was able to develop her culinary skills. She spent her time off before the 2003 season working eight-hour shifts in the kitchens at the Lake Nona restaurant in Florida, near her home. She has talked of enrolling at a cooking school, and she often participates in cooking demonstrations at tournaments, including with Robert Wegman, sponsor of the LPGA event in Rochester, New York.

○ Sorenstam at ease in the kitchen

I love to crunch numbers. I look at how many fairways I hit, how many greens I hit. I plan my way around the golf course.

ANNIKA SORENSTAM, ON HER APPROACH TO THE GAME

▲ **ANOTHER PUTT FINDS THE BOTTOM** of the cup for Sorenstam. Initially not the most emotive on the course, Annika developed into a more charismatic figure as her career progressed and the wins flowed. She retired from the pro game in 2008.

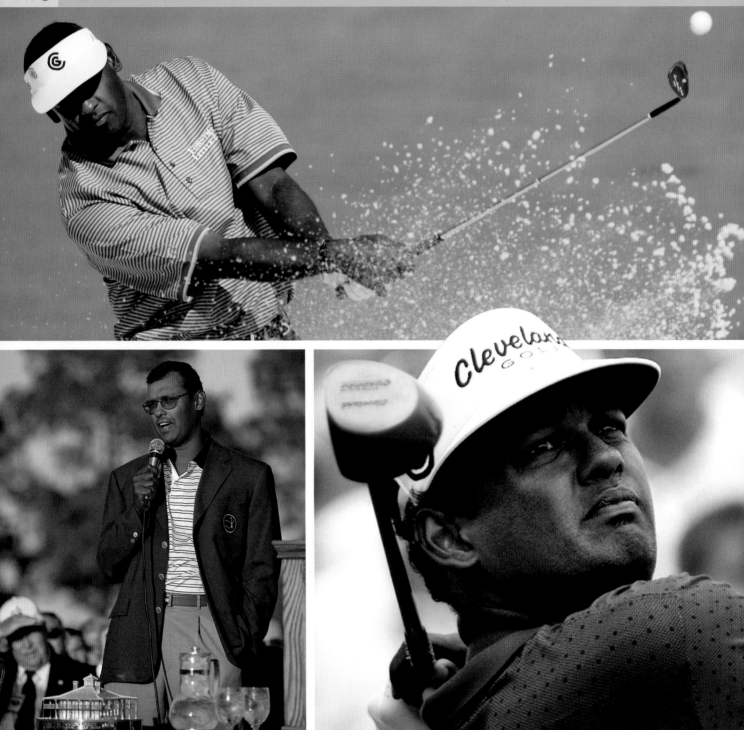

I'm from the old school ... Practicing is how I learned the game.
To practice and build a swing is a victory in itself.

VIJAY SINGH

Vijay Singh

It was a long and unlikely journey that took Vijay Singh to the top of the game. He grew up in Fiji, was outcast to Borneo, and even briefly acted as a nightclub bouncer in Edinburgh. He went on to win in every continent (except Antarctica), claiming three Major championships along the way. Vijay achieved his success by practicing more than anyone else.

PLAYER STATS

BORN February 22, 1963; Lautoka, Fiji
HEIGHT 6ft 2in (1.88m)
TURNED PRO 1982

DEBUT WIN 1984 Malaysian PGA Championship
TOUR WINS 64
PGA TOUR: 34
EUROPEAN TOUR: 13
OTHER: 17

MAJORS 3
MASTERS: Won 2000
US OPEN: T3rd 1999
THE OPEN: T2nd 2003
USPGA: Won 1998, 2004

HONORS
Rookie of the Year: 1993
PGA Tour Money Winner: 2003, 2004, 2008
Vardon Trophy Winner: 2004
Presidents Cup Team: 1994, 1996, 1998, 2000, 2003, 2005, 2007, 2009
FEDEX Cup: 2008

◄◄ **AS BRYON NELSON NOTED,** Vijay never appears to rush—he swings fast through the ball, but his rhythm does not change.

◄ **DEDICATION ON THE DRIVING RANGE** and in the gym paid off for Vijay when he became the world No. 1 in 2004.

◄◄ **VIJAY THANKS** the gallery in his newly presented green jacket after winning the Masters at Augusta in 2000.

Vijay was the son of an airport technician. He had to sprint across the runway to get to his local course, and he studied the golf magazines that were flown into the airport—focusing particularly on American Tom Weiskopf, a similarly tall man. There were only approximately 200 golfers in Fiji at the time, but, by the age of 15, Singh was the best of them. Although his father helped teach Vijay the game, Vijay angered his father by neglecting his schoolwork to practice golf.

Eventually, Vijay turned professional and, with no backing, went to Australia. He won the Malaysian Open in 1994 but a year later was accused of doctoring his scorecard at the Indonesian Open. He claimed the marker had made the mistake, which he had not noticed, but he was still suspended from the Asian Tour. He felt harshly treated, since such an offence—even if he had committed it—should have resulted in disqualification from the event rather than a ban from the Tour.

EUROPEAN SUCCESS

Needing to make his living, Vijay took a job as the club professional at a course in Malaysian Borneo and continued to hone his skills. His breakthrough was winning the Nigerian Open in 1988 and the Safari Tour Order of Merit. He earned his card on the European Tour in 1988, having failed to gain access to the Tour the previous year, and immediately became a regular winner. In 1993, he finished second at Bay Hill and then won the Buick Classic to secure his card in the US. In 2008, he won the Deutsche Bank Championship to claim his 34th PGA Tour victory, with an event record of 262 and 22-under.

On the circuit, Vijay was known for being the first man on the practice range and the last to leave. When he was not hitting balls, he was working on his fitness. His work ethic was extraordinary, although he always said golfers have far more vacations than other people do. "I have a family but golf was always me. I go to sleep thinking about it and wake up thinking about it. My mind is consumed with my career."

He experimented with different putting styles but won his biggest tournaments putting cross-handed

▲ **VIJAY HOLDS ALOFT** the huge Wanamaker Trophy after winning the USPGA Championship for the first time, at Sahalee in 1998.

with a conventional putter. He won the USPGA at Sahalee in 1998 at the age of 35 and then claimed the Masters at Augusta in 2000 by three strokes from Ernie Els. Into his third decade as a pro, Vijay's rate of success actually increased, and he has won more titles than anyone else in their 40s—beating the previous record set by Sam Snead. His second USPGA title came at Whistling Straits in 2004, where he won a playoff against Justin Leonard and Chris DiMarco. It was one of nine victories that season, which briefly put him above Tiger Woods as the world No. 1 and earned him an astonishing $10 million in prize money. Vijay means "victory" in Hindu, and he has certainly lived up to the name—he has won more titles on the PGA Tour than any other non-American golfer.

Paul Lawrie

Paul Lawrie was a slow starter to the game of golf. Then in 1999, he shocked himself and the whole golfing world by winning the Open at Carnoustie. When Jean van de Velde stumbled, Lawrie seized his chance and took home the Claret Jug. He was the first Scot to win the title in Scotland for 68 years and the last European to win a Major until Pádraig Harrington won in 2007.

PLAYER STATS

BORN January 1, 1969; Aberdeen, Scotland
HEIGHT 5ft 11in (1.80m)
TURNED PRO 1986

DEBUT WIN 1996 Catalan Open
TOUR WINS 15
PGA TOUR: 1
EUROPEAN TOUR: 8
OTHER: 6

MAJORS 1
MASTERS: T15th 2003
US OPEN: T30th 2002
THE OPEN: Won 1999
USPGA: T34th 1999

HONORS
Ryder Cup Team: 1999, 2012

It was not that Lawrie was unknown—he had won twice on the European Tour in the three years prior to winning the Open and won twice more in the following three years—but his route to becoming the "champion golfer of the year" was improbable. He turned professional at the age of 17, with a handicap of five, and worked as an assistant professional in the pro shop at Banchory Golf Club in Aberdeenshire, Scotland. He did not get on to the European Tour for another six years. In 1996, Lawrie secured his first victory—the Catalan Open. Then, several months before his Major triumph, he won in the wind in Qatar. Nevertheless, he still had to qualify for the Open at Carnoustie.

Lawrie was outside the world's top 150 and started the final round 10 strokes behind the leader but produced a brilliant 67. Jean van de Velde, on the other hand, teed off at the last hole with a three-shot lead but took a triple-bogey seven and limped into a playoff with Lawrie and Justin Leonard. In the playoff, Lawrie birdied the last two holes in the cold rain to claim the crown.

Lawrie had taken his opportunity. He was the leading points-scorer for Europe in the Ryder Cup later that year, and he won the Dunhill Links Championship in 2001. With the media stuck on the Van de Velde story, Lawrie never got the credit he deserved—not that he was seeking attention. "I didn't want to be a celeb in the papers every day saying 'look at me.' I am very much a person who does his work and then goes home," he said. Yet at the age of 30, he had suddenly achieved his life's dream. As a result of winning the Open, Lawrie set up a junior program that has introduced hundreds of children in his hometown to the game.

▲ **ALL SMILES AFTER** winning the Open Championship at Carnoustie—a brilliant but shocking victory after a four-hole playoff.

▶ **LAWRIE STARTED** as an assistant in the pro shop at Banchory, but years of hard work took the Scot to the very heights of the game.

Jesper Parnevik

Three times in five years, Jesper Parnevik came close to winning the Open and becoming the first Swedish player to win a Major championship. Although it never quite happened for him at the very highest level, Parnevik did become an inspirational Ryder Cup player and with his unconventional style was one of the most popular players of his generation.

PLAYER STATS

BORN March 7, 1965; Stockholm, Sweden
HEIGHT 6ft (1.83m)
TURNED PRO 1986

DEBUT WIN 1993 Bell's Scottish Open
TOUR WINS 9
EUROPEAN TOUR: 4
PGA TOUR: 5

MAJORS 0
MASTERS: T20th 2001
US OPEN: T14th 1998
THE OPEN: 2nd 1994, 1997
USPGA: T5th 1996

HONORS
Ryder Cup Team: 1997, 1999, 2002

CRAZY GOLF

Whether on or off the course, Jesper Parnevik stands out as unique. Known for his outrageous fashion sense, he has been known to change outfits during the course of a round, and when he appeared in the Ryder Cup, he received a customized upturned team cap. His style and individualism have made him hugely popular with the galleries.

Parnevik supporters

▲ **THREE TIMES PARNEVIK** came close to winning the Open Championship, but his dream of becoming Sweden's first Major winner was never fulfilled.

Parnevik is a famous name in Sweden because his father, Bo, was one of the country's foremost comedians. Parnevik learned to play by hitting floating golf balls into a lake behind the family house, and he developed into a great striker of the ball.

An early trademark developed after leaving the Swedish winter to practice in Florida for the start of the season. To improve his suntan, Parnevik flipped up the peak of his cap. He found his putting improved; he got into a playoff with Seve Ballesteros in his next event; the gallery loved it; and sponsors competed for the underside of the peak.

Parnevik, dubbed "the spaceman," is regarded as quite the eccentric both on and off the course. He has tried a diet of volcanic sand and fruit; has used stroboscopic glasses; had his metal tooth fillings replaced with ceramic fillings; and named his children Peg (he had a tee peg in his pocket), Penny (his favorite marker was a penny), Phillipa (she was almost Pebble Peach), and Phoenix (where Parnevik had his first win in

the US). He launched a vitamin company, and he has led the way in fairway fashions thanks to the Swedish designer J.Lindeberg. He also once missed a 2ft (60cm) putt at Loch Lomond because he was thinking about how much extra rope it would take to encircle the world on 3ft (1m) high stakes. He has a wandering mind. He also took up magic.

Aside from all of that, Parnevik can play golf. He almost won the Open at Turnberry in 1994 but did not look at the leaderboard on the 18th tee. Thinking he needed a birdie, he bogeyed instead; Nick Price eagled the 17th and claimed victory. At Troon in 1997, Parnevik led by two with a round to play but lost to Justin Leonard. His best chance, he believed, came a year later at Birkdale, when he finished two strokes outside the playoff won by Mark O'Meara.

Retief Goosen

One of the best golfers to emerge from the rich breeding ground of South Africa, Retief Goosen overcame extreme circumstances to win the US Open in 2001 and 2004. His liking for tough conditions and ability to stay calm make him well suited to the most mentally demanding Major championship courses. This, after all, is a man who survived being hit by lightning.

Goosen has no memory of the moment he was struck by lightning. Standing on the 12th green at Polokwane Golf Club, a lightning bolt hit a tree before striking the youngster, just a few days away from his 16th birthday. His playing partner was knocked to the ground but found Goosen unconscious. His clothes had been burned away and his rubber shoes had melted.

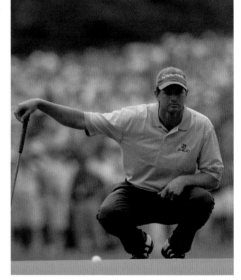

▲ **A QUIET ACHIEVER,** Retief Goosen's low-key personality has not prevented him from winning some of the game's biggest prizes—on both the European and the PGA Tours.

Goosen simply remembers waking up in the hospital "feeling sore and covered in skin burns. There is nothing left of it now but at the time I was a bit of a mess." There were related health issues for a time, and his mother, Annie, believes that the incident left him more introverted than he had been before.

Nevertheless, Goosen was one of South Africa's finest amateurs, and after winning on his home circuit, he won the European Tour Qualifying School in 1992. Since 1996, he has been a regular winner in Europe and the US. A man of few words, he admits to being less intense after marrying English wife, Tracy, and becoming a family man. On the course, he was initially overlong and displayed a bit of a temper. He successfully reined in both and learned how to plot his way around the most difficult courses while maintaining a calm equilibrium.

In the 2001 US Open at Southern Hills, Goosen had two putts from 12 feet to win at the last but missed from 18 inches for the victory, in what commentator Johnny Miller called the "worst three putt in the history of golf." Contrary to expectation, and thanks to assistance from sports psychologist Jos Vantisphout, Goosen did not crumble after the miss and won an 18-hole playoff against Mark Brookes the next day. Three years later, on the baked-out, glassy greens of Shinnecock Hills, Goosen put on a brilliant display of putting and overcame a New York crowd desperate for Phil Mickelson to claim the title again. He has also won the European Order of Merit in 2001 and 2002.

PLAYER STATS

BORN February 3, 1969; Polokwane, South Africa
HEIGHT 5ft 11in (1.80m)
TURNED PRO 1990

DEBUT WIN 1991 Iscor Newcastle Classic
TOUR WINS 33
EUROPEAN TOUR: 14
PGA TOUR: 7
OTHER: 16

MAJORS 2
MASTERS: 2nd 2002/T2nd 2007
US OPEN: Won 2001, 2004
THE OPEN: T5th 2005, 2009
USPGA: T6th 2005

HONORS
European Tour Order of Merit Winner: 2001, 2002
Presidents Cup Team: 2000, 2003, 2005, 2009, 2011

▼ **TWICE GOOSEN HAS TRIUMPHED** at the US Open, with his second win coming at Shinnecock Hills in 2004.

Who knows what it would have been like if I didn't win the US Open, but you know, my life has gone down this way now and I've done pretty well.

RETIEF GOOSEN

David Duval

For a brief period, David Duval was the best player in the world. He won prolifically, shot 59 to claim one title, topped the world rankings, and claimed his first Major championship title at the 130th Open at Royal Lytham & St. Annes (winning by three strokes). Then due to injuries, he lost his swing, and apparently his passion for the game faded, too. However, in 2009, he stormed back to almost take the US Open.

PLAYER STATS

BORN November 9, 1971; Jacksonville, Florida
HEIGHT 6ft (1.83m)
TURNED PRO 1993

DEBUT WIN Michelob Championship 1997
TOUR WINS 19
PGA TOUR: 13
OTHER: 6

MAJORS 1
MASTERS: 2nd 1998/T2nd 2001
US OPEN: T7th 1998, 1999, T2nd 2009
THE OPEN: Won 2001
USPGA: T10th 1999, 2001

HONORS

PGA Tour Money Winner: 1998
Vardon Trophy Winner: 1998
Ryder Cup Team: 1999, 2002
Presidents Cup Team: 1996, 1998, 2000

▲ **DAVID DUVAL** overtook Tiger Woods as the world's best player in 1999, and the success continued when he won the 2001 Open.

Golf seemed to be David Duval's salvation. A star in college golf, Duval never dropped out of the top 11 on the money list in his first seven seasons in the US. At first, however, the wins would not come: he was a runner-up seven times and third on four other occasions before his first victory. Then, having shown great tenacity and belief, he found the way to win, tallying 11 victories between 1997 and 1999. He won four times early in 1999, including the Bob Hope Chrysler Classic, where he shot a 59 in the final round. Having started the round seven strokes off the lead, he made 11 birdies (and an eagle at the final hole). None of the putts holed were more than 10 feet; he missed only from 12 feet and 15 feet for birdies.

Duval's was the third official 59 in the US but the first to win a tournament on the last day. Two months later, on the same day that his father won on the Seniors Tour, he claimed victory at the Players Championship in his hometown of Jacksonville.

Early in 2000, however, Duval suffered a ligament sprain in his back that led to years of problems on the course. Initially overweight when he arrived on tour, he

▲ **THE WRAPAROUND SHADES** suited a man who showed little emotion on the golf course.

slimmed down with a relentless exercise regime. After a number of near misses at the Majors, a 65 in the third round put him in contention for the 2001 Open at Royal Lytham. He swept imperiously to victory with a closing 67 and a 10-under-par total. Often perceived as a cold, prickly character of few words, he removed his hat and wraparound sunglasses at the prize-giving and smiled, finally allowing his personality to shine through. "My existential moment was right there," he said.

However, Duval won only once more—in Japan later that year. Winning a Major was not the life-changing event he had imagined. Injuries led to a loss of confidence, and, having revamped his swing, his game fell away. At the 2009 US Open, the Duval of old seemed to come roaring back. He was in contention for the prize on the final round, until a 17th hole bogey saw him eventually finish second. It was his first top-10 at a Major since 2001.

Karrie Webb

From one of the most remote areas of the world, Karrie Webb emerged to become the best woman golfer in the world. Peter Thomson even suggested she was the best golfer, male or female, with a better swing than Tiger Woods. At the age of 30, Webb joined Thomson and Greg Norman as Australia's representatives in the World Golf Hall of Fame.

PLAYER STATS

BORN December 21, 1974; Ayr, Queensland, Australia
HEIGHT 5ft 6in (1.68m)
TURNED PRO 1994

DEBUT WIN 1995 Weetabix Women's British Open
TOUR WINS 56
LPGA TOUR: 41
EUROPEAN TOUR: 15

MAJORS 7
ANA INSPIRATION: Won 2000, 2006
LPGA CHAMPIONSHIP: Won 2001
US WOMEN'S OPEN: Won 2000, 2001
DU MAURIER CLASSIC: Won 1999
WOMEN'S BRITISH OPEN: 2002

HONORS
European Tour Rookie of the Year: 1995
LPGA Rookie of the Year: 1996
LPGA Tour Money Winner: 1996, 1999, 2000

> I look back at my career sometimes and can't believe how fast everything has gone and how much I've been able to accomplish.

KARRIE WEBB ON BEING INDUCTED INTO THE WORLD GOLF HALL OF FAME

Webb grew up in Ayr, around 1,000 miles (1,600km) from Brisbane, not exactly a hotbed for golf. Most of the town's population of 8,600 are involved either in the production of sugar cane or providing services for it. Webb's parents owned a toy and gift shop, right next door to the newsdealers.

Kevin Haller, whose parents owned the newsdealers, used to study the golf magazines, and, since the local golf club didn't have a professional, he became Webb's coach. Webb turned pro in 1994 and was Rookie of the Year in Europe. She also won the British Open for the first of three times (the first two did not count as official LPGA Majors). A year later, she was Rookie of the Year in the US, becoming the first woman to earn more than $1 million in a season. Webb herself does not know where her greatest strength comes from. "I think I was given a gift to play golf and to be mentally strong," she said. "You know, I don't see a sports psychologist. I've somehow just known what to do." Off the course, Webb is uncomfortable in the limelight and happy to let her clubs do the talking.

Her finest spell was between 1999 and 2002 when she won six Majors. Webb won the US Open in 2000 and 2001, and fellow golfer Meg Mallon said of her, "Sometimes when a player makes it look as easy as she does, it's hard to appreciate how good she is." By winning the British Open at Turnberry in 2002, Webb became the first player to win all five LPGA Majors, the so-called Super Grand Slam. By 2000, she had earned enough points to be inducted into the World Golf Hall of Fame but was unable to take up her place until 2005, by which time she had completed her 10th season on the tour.

After a lull, Webb won her seventh Major, the 2006 Kraft Nabisco Championship (now called the ANA Inspiration), in spectacular fashion. She holed a 116-yard shot to eagle the 18th hole and then birdied the same hole in a sudden-death playoff to beat Lorena Ochoa.

◀ **WEBB ESCAPES FROM** a bunker during the 2000 Women's British Open at Royal Birkdake. She has won the championship three times.

Se Ri Pak

In 1998, Se Ri Pak made the sort of splash in the women's game not seen since Nancy Lopez arrived two decades earlier. Pak won two Major championships in her first season on the LPGA tour, including the US Women's Open, and at a stroke signaled the arrival of South Korea, and other less familiar nations, at the top of the women's game.

PLAYER STATS

BORN September 28, 1977; Daejeon, South Korea
HEIGHT 5ft 6in (1.68m)
TURNED PRO 1996

DEBUT WIN LPGA 1998
TOUR WINS 30
LPGA TOUR: 24
OTHER: 6

MAJORS 5
ANA INSPIRATION: T4th 2014
LPGA CHAMPIONSHIP: Won Won 1998, 2002, 2006
US WOMEN'S OPEN: Won 1998
DU MAURIER CLASSIC: T7th 2000
WOMEN'S BRITISH OPEN: Won 2001

HONORS 5
LPGA Tour Rookie of the Year: 1998

Pak was not the first player from South Korea to make it onto the LPGA circuit in the US, but her remarkable rookie season led many more to follow her lead. Her success changed the face of women's golf, with players from other nontraditional golfing nations like Mexico and Paraguay enjoying success.

Pak displayed an incredible work ethic when first taking up the game. Although she was a sprinter at school, by the age of 14, she had turned seriously to golf. Her father, a top amateur golfer, employed training methods perhaps not approved of in other cultures. He had Pak running up and down the staircases of their 15-story apartment building at 5:30 in the morning and sometimes took her to a cemetery in the middle of the night "to develop courage and nerve." He recalled how he "wanted to teach her that to win in golf, she first had to win the battle within herself."

TOO MUCH, TOO SOON

Pak won 30 times as an amateur in Korea, and then as a professional on the Korean Ladies Professional Golf Association (KLPGA) circuit, she won six times and was second seven times in her first 14 events. In 1998, she arrived in America, winning four titles as a 20-year-old. Her first two wins were Major championships: the LPGA followed by the US Open, which she won after a 20-hole playoff against amateur Jenny Chuasiriporn. At the end of a long season, she returned home to South Korea and was awarded the Order of Merit, the country's highest honor for an athlete. So exhausting was the attention and fame that she collapsed and spent four days in the hospital. Her cool demeanor on the course, compounded by her little English in the early days, masked an emotional character off the course.

◀ **PAK HAS LED AN INVASION** of talent from South Korea onto the world stage in women's golf.

▲ **WINNING THE LPGA CHAMPIONSHIP** and the US Women's Open made for a memorable introduction to American golf for Se Ri Pak.

Her first experiences of links golf, in horrid weather, was less than enjoyable, but when the British Open moved to Sunningdale in 2001, Pak claimed her third Major. In 2005, she suffered from shoulder, neck, back, and finger injuries and took a break from the game, but in 2006, she followed up her 2002 victory by winning her third LPGA crown, beating Karrie Webb in a playoff. In 2007, she surpassed Webb once again by virtue of being the youngest living entrant to be inducted into the World Golf Hall of Fame. At the 2016 KEB Hana Bank Championship in South Korea, she made an emotional farewell and retired from the pro scene.

Pádraig Harrington

At Carnoustie in 2007, Pádraig Harrington became the first European golfer to win a Major championship since Paul Lawrie at the same venue eight years before. After a dramatic playoff with Sergio García, Harrington claimed the Claret Jug, and Ireland had its first Open champion since Fred Daly 60 years previously. For Harrington, all the years of hard work had finally paid off.

PLAYER STATS

BORN August 31, 1971; Dublin, Ireland
HEIGHT 6ft (1.83m)
TURNED PRO 1995

DEBUT WIN 1996 Peugeot Spanish Open
TOUR WINS 31
EUROPEAN TOUR: 15
PGA TOUR: 6
OTHER: 10

MAJORS 3
MASTERS: T5th 2002, 2008
US OPEN: T4th 2012
THE OPEN: Won 2007, 2008
USPGA: Won 2008

HONORS
PGA Tour Player of the Year: 2008
European Tour Order of Merit
Winner: 2006
Ryder Cup Team: 1999, 2002, 2004, 2006, 2008, 2010

▲ **WITH HIS TRIUMPH** at Carnoustie in 2007, Harrington became only the second Irishman ever to win the Open Championship.

After a glittering amateur career, Harrington won the Spanish Open in his first season as a pro. He had to wait until 2000 for his next victory, but all the time he was improving his game, having begun work with the legendary coach Bob Torrance. Harrington has never stopped trying to better himself, combining the work ethic of a Vijay Singh with the discipline and management skills of a Bernhard Langer.

So often Harrington would finish as a runner-up, occasionally because he had a chance to win and slipped up but more often because of a stronger finish from others. From 2000, however, he began to win regularly, including twice in the US in 2005, and in 2006 he won the Dunhill Links Championship for the second time. This victory helped secure the European Tour's Order of Merit, although it arrived only thanks to a strong finish at Valderrama and García's bogey on the

▲ **HARRINGTON IS A CONSISTENT** performer. He has finished in the top 10 on the European Tour's Order of Merit nine times.

last hole. In 2007, he won what he called his "fifth Major," the Irish Open. If the celebrations were great then, they were nothing compared to what was to follow in July at the Open, when Harrington beat Sergio García by one shot in a four-hole playoff.

In both 2007 and 2008, Harrington rose to the very top of the game, reaching number three in the world rankings. The likable Dubliner defended his Open title at Royal Birkdale, becoming the first European to do so since James Braid in 1906. Barely a month later, Harrington was at it again, collecting his third Major by holding off García and Ben Curtis. That season he also pocketed a career-best $4.3 million in prize money.

Sergio García

Bursting on to the golfing scene with such a whirlwind of energy, it seemed inevitable that Sergio García would become Spain's next great golfer. After several near misses over the first 15 years of his career, he finally landed a Major in 2017. His brilliant record in the Ryder Cup continues the magnificent tradition of Seve Ballesteros and José Maria Olazábal for the European team.

PLAYER STATS

BORN January 9, 1980; Castellón, Spain
HEIGHT 5ft 10in (1.78m)
TURNED PRO 1999

DEBUT WIN 1999 Murphy's Irish Open
TOUR WINS 36
EUROPEAN TOUR: 16
PGA TOUR: 11
OTHER: 9

MAJORS 1
MASTERS: Won 2017
US OPEN: T3rd 2005
THE OPEN: 2nd 2007, T2nd 2014
USPGA: 2nd 1999, T2nd 2008

HONORS

Ryder Cup Team: 1999, 2002, 2004, 2006, 2008, 2012, 2014, 2016, 2018
European Tour Golfer of the Year: 2017
Vardon Trophy: 2008

García started playing golf at the age of three, guided by his father, Victor, a professional himself. Nicknamed El Niño, he won regularly as an amateur, including claiming the British Amateur at Muirfield in 1998. He was the leading amateur at the Open in 1996 and at the Masters in 1999, after which he turned professional. In only his third start on the European Tour, he won the Irish Open. Then, at that year's USPGA Championship at Medinah, he lost narrowly to Tiger Woods. At the 16th hole, he played an extraordinary "Seve-esque" shot from behind a tree and then sprinted and jumped his way down the fairway to see the ball land on the green.

MATCHPLAY MASTER

García exhibited his characteristic flamboyance on his Ryder Cup debut at the age of 19 at Brookline later that season and immediately formed a brilliant partnership with Swede Jesper Parnevik. His tears at the end of the contest encapsulated the pain of defeat for the European team (see p.236). Throughout his Ryder Cup career, where he has won a record 25½ points from nine matches, his putting has been brilliant and his enthusiasm irrepressible. Here, he is once more the young kid who emerged so gloriously at the end of the 1990s.

Destined to be a nearly man at the Majors, after two second places at the US Open and USPGA, the stars finally lined up for García at Augusta in 2017. It was his 74th start at a Major and 19th appearance at the famous event in Georgia, but the Spaniard kept pace with the pack and pulled out a stunning eagle at the 15th to help force a playoff with Justin Rose. A birdie on the first hole of the sudden death matchup was enough to see him slip into the green jacket. A worthy winner indeed that April.

▲ **LIKE HIS COMPATRIOTS** Ballesteros and Olazábal, García has a tremendously effective game around the greens.

▲ **GARCÍA'S STYLE AND FLAIR** on the fairways always delights the crowd.

▲ ▲ **ALONE WITH HIS THOUGHTS** at the 2003 USPGA at Oak Hill, as another Major championship slipped away—before his win at Augusta.

▲ **WINNING THE USPGA CHAMPIONSHIP** at Baltusrol in 2005 gave Mickelson a second Major title in two years.

◄ **MICKELSON JUMPS FOR JOY** after winning a breathtaking duel with Ernie Els to claim his first Masters title in 2004.

Phil Mickelson

For many years, the only thing missing from Phil Mickelson's career was a Major championship. Then at the 2004 Masters, the left-hander finally claimed a green jacket. He then won the USPGA in 2005 and the Masters for the second time in 2006. By 2013, Mickelson had boosted his Major haul to five to secure his spot as a true legend.

PLAYER STATS

BORN June 16, 1970; San Diego, California
HEIGHT 6ft 3in (1.91m)
TURNED PRO 1992

DEBUT WIN 1991 Northern Telecom Open
TOUR WINS 58
PGA TOUR: 44
OTHER: 4

MAJORS 5
MASTERS: Won 2004, 2006, 2010
US OPEN: 2nd 1999, 2002, 2004/T2nd 2006, 2009, 2013
THE OPEN: Won 2013
USPGA: Won 2005

HONORS
Presidents Cup Team: 1994, 1996, 1998, 2000, 2003, 2005, 2007, 2009, 2011, 2013, 2015, 2017
Ryder Cup Team: 1995, 1997, 1999, 2002, 2004, 2006, 2008, 2010, 2012, 2014, 2016, 2018

▼ **MICKELSON IS HELPED** into his green jacket by rival Tiger Woods after his second victory in three years at Augusta.

Mickelson was always supremely talented. He grew up in San Diego, the son of a pilot, and it was while watching his father play—mirroring his motion while standing alongside him—that Phil started to play the game left-handed. He is naturally right-handed, and his father tried to turn him around, but the youngster refused. By the age of six, he was playing all day at a par-3 course, and it was there and in his backyard that he developed a stellar range of short-game skills.

At the age of 20, Mickelson became the US Amateur champion. He was the National College champion three years out of four, and even before he turned professional, he won the Northern Telecom Open in Tucson in 1991—the first amateur to win on the US Tour since Scott Verplank's victory six years beforehand.

The victories accumulated but so did the near misses at the Majors: in Mickelson's first 46 Majors, he was runner-up twice at the US Open and once at the USPGA and was third three times at the Masters. "The frustrating part is not that I am trying to win a Major; I'm trying to win a bunch of them," he said. At Augusta in 2004, he adjusted his game slightly by shortening his swing and reining in his all-out aggression. The changes still produced birdies—in the final round, he birdied five of the last seven holes and shot a 31 to beat Ernie Els in a classic contest.

Two months later, Mickelson lost to Retief Goosen at the US Open, but suddenly he was putting himself in contention. The game adjustments and a new preparation routine were paying off. He would go to the tournament site and spend hours and hours studying the course alongside his short-game guru and one-time NASA scientist Dave Pelz. He won the USPGA in 2005 and the very next Major, the 2006 Masters. It

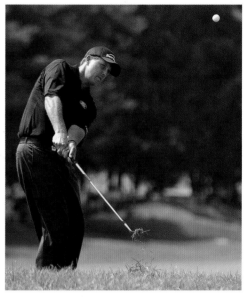

▲ **MICKELSON BECAME THE THIRD** left-handed golfer to win a Major championship, after Bob Charles and Mike Weir.

was Augusta, again, that would be the stage for Mickelson's fourth Major, in 2010. That year, he clawed back at Lee Westwood, who led after 54 holes, and his amazing 6-iron from 207 yards on the 13th on Sunday gave him an easy birdie and a shot at yet another Masters.

While the US Open has eluded and frustrated him, success at the British Open arrived in 2013, where he again hunted down Westwood in typical style. The year before, Mickelson had entered the World Golf Hall of Fame—an accolade that seemed long overdue.

He is even more talented than I thought, and I knew he was exceptionally talented.

BUTCH HARMON

Tiger Woods

When he won the 1997 Masters at Augusta (see pp.232–233), Tiger Woods became a cultural and sporting phenomenon. It was not just how he did it, winning by 12 strokes, but who was doing it—the first-ever golfing superstar with an ethnic background. His influence on how the game is perceived has been immense, but he has simply got on with becoming the best golfer ever.

PLAYER STATS

BORN December 30, 1975; Cypress, California
HEIGHT 6ft 1in (1.85m)
TURNED PRO 1996

DEBUT WIN 1996 Las Vegas Invitational
PROFESSIONAL WINS 145
PGA TOUR: 82
OTHER: 25

MAJORS 15
MASTERS: Won 1997, 2001, 2002, 2005, 2019
US OPEN: Won 2000, 2002, 2008
THE OPEN: Won 2000, 2005, 2006
USPGA: Won 1999, 2000, 2006, 2007

HONORS
US Amateur Champion: 1994, 1995, 1996
Rookie of the Year: 1996
PGA Tour Money Winner: 1997, 1999, 2000, 2001, 2002, 2005, 2006, 2007, 2009, 2013
PGA Tour Player of the Year: 1997, 1999, 2000, 2001, 2002, 2003, 2005, 2006, 2007
Vardon Trophy Winner: 1999, 2000, 2001, 2002, 2003, 2005, 2007, 2009, 2013
Ryder Cup Team: 1997, 1999, 2002, 2004, 2006, 2010, 2012, 2018
Presidents Cup Team: 1998, 2000, 2003, 2005, 2007, 2009, 2011, 2013
Presidents Cup Captain: 2019

▶ **TIGER TAKES A MOMENT** to savor victory at the 2006 Open Championship, an emotional time after the death of his father.

◀ **A TYPICAL TIGER WOODS** celebration, at the 1998 Johnnie Walker Classic in Thailand, after a stirring comeback against Ernie Els.

He has this uncanny ability, when someone gets close to him, to turn it up to another level.

CHRIS DIMARCO, RUNNER-UP TO WOODS IN TWO MAJORS

Tiger Woods is a golfer like no other. When he is good, he is so far ahead he cannot be caught. When he is behind, it simply means that he is not on top of his game. Woods's victory at the 2007 USPGA served as a reminder of his dominance—as if one were necessary. The win heralded his fourth triumph at the USPGA, his 13th Major championship title, and the 13th time out of 13 that he has led going into a final round and gone on to win. At the 2008 US Open, he picked up Major number 14 (again leading after 54 holes), and it was only his eventful 15th Major in 2019 where he didn't lead after the opening three rounds.

Woods was still a baby when, having watched his father swinging a club, he decided to have a go himself. At the age of two, he was putting with Bob Hope on *The Mike Douglas Show*. At three, he won a pitch-and-putt competition for 10- and 11-year-olds, and he was playing off scratch by the time he was 13. But it was a little earlier, at the age of five and on the *That's Incredible* television show, that he made this uncannily accurate prophesy: "I want to win all the big tournaments ... and beat all the pros."

IMMEDIATE SUCCESS

First, he had to beat the amateurs. Woods became the first person to win three consecutive US Junior Amateur titles, before going on to win three consecutive US Amateurs. Bobby Jones won five in six years, but Woods became the youngest-ever winner at the age of 18. After winning the third Amateur title, Woods turned professional in 1996. He won his fifth tournament as a professional, beating Davis Love III in a playoff at the Las Vegas Invitational. He won again that year and from only eight starts became the Rookie of the Year.

CHILD PRODIGY

Winning trophies became a habit for Tiger Woods very early in his life. Blessed with natural talent and encouraged by his father, at the age of three, he scored 48 over nine holes at the Navy Golf Club in Cypress. He was soon regularly beating much older children, and it wasn't long before television companies took an interest in his exploits.

 The young cub with his father in January 1989

PROUD PARENTS

Woods once described himself as "cablinasian," an ethnic mix of Caucasian, black, Indian, and Asian. His mother, Kultida, is from Thailand and remains as strong an influence in his life as his father, Earl, was on his golf. Earl Woods was a lieutenant colonel in the Green Berets and served two terms in Vietnam. On the second of them, he became friends with Colonel Vuong Dang Phong, who Earl called Tiger, and they went on to save each other's lives. Kultida named her son Eldrick, a name that she made up, but Earl always used the nickname Tiger. Later, Tiger changed his name by deed poll to include the nickname. Colonel Vuong was captured by the Vietcong, imprisoned, and died in 1976—unaware that his nickname would live on through the planet's most famous sportsman.

Earl Woods oversaw every aspect of his son's golfing education, which included making him the most mentally resilient golfer of his generation. With power to spare, Woods generally outthinks his opponents as well. In 1997, he played his first Major as a professional at the Masters and went to the turn on the first morning in 40, but he came home in 30, with an eagle and four birdies, and after that blew away the field (see pp.232–233). He had simply overpowered the Augusta course, but in the following years, Woods and his coach Butch Harmon reined in his swing so that he had both precision and power. The result was perhaps the most accomplished golf ever seen.

REACHING NEW HEIGHTS

At the 2000 US Open, Woods won by 15 strokes with a record score of 12-under par (see pp.238–239). On the fast greens of Pebble Beach, he never took a three-putt. A month later, on the Old Course at St. Andrews, Woods avoided all the treacherous bunkers. He won by eight strokes with a record score in the Open at St. Andrews. At the USPGA, he beat the relatively unknown American Bob May in a playoff and then went to the 2001 Masters looking for the "Tiger Slam"—his fourth consecutive victory. He held off the challenge of David Duval and Phil Mickelson to make history.

1992
At the age of 16, Woods plays in his first professional tournament— the Nissan Los Angeles Open—and in three other PGA Tour events.

1994
Woods enters Stanford University in California, and in two years, he wins 10 collegiate events. He also wins the US Amateur.

1995
Plays his first Majors, making the 36-hole cuts in the Masters and the Open Championship, but withdraws from the US Open after injuring his wrist.

1996
Turns professional on August 27, bringing to an end an amateur career in which he won six USGA national championships, plus the coveted NCAA title.

1997
Woods wins his first Major, the Masters, and breaks a multitude of records in the process, not least the lowest-ever four-round total.

▲ **WOODS ENJOYED A LONG** and successful partnership with his caddie, Steve Williams, until 2011.

◄ **WITH A FLAIR FOR THE DRAMATIC**, Woods has produced many wondrous shots, including this chip in for eagle at Valderrama in 1999.

CHANGING TIMES

Over 2003 and 2004, Woods did not win a Major. Hank Haney became his new coach, and at Augusta in 2005, Woods won his fourth Masters title. In 2006 at Hoylake, he won the Open for the second year running (and the third time in all), with an awesome display of iron play. It was his first win since the death of his father earlier that year and the most emotional he had ever been on a golf course.

After the 2008 US Open, Woods had to endure 11 tough years without a Major. Well-documented personal and injury problems plagued the superstar, as he came close to leaving the game for good. At Augusta in 2019, Woods somehow found his form and powers of 20-plus years ago to pick up his 15th Major and move to within three of Jack Nicklaus.

1999

Woods's second Ryder Cup appearance, at the Brookline Country Club, ends in a controversial win for the US. Woods contributes two points.

2000

In winning the Open Championship, Woods becomes the youngest player to complete the career Grand Slam of professional Majors and only the fifth player ever to do so.

2001

With his second Masters victory, Woods becomes the first person to hold all four Major championships at the same time.

2005

Woods wins the 2005 Open Championship, making him only the second golfer (after Jack Nicklaus) to have won all four Majors more than once.

2019

Aged 43 and after back fusion surgery in 2017, Woods takes the glory again at Augusta.

2019

PGA Tour win number 82, tying Sam Snead's overall record, at the Zozo Championship in Japan.

Rory McIlroy

One of the most popular players in the game, with fans from both sides of the Atlantic, Rory McIlroy also has the prizes to back up the plaudits. Following in the footsteps of fellow Northern Ireland greats Graeme McDowell and Darren Clarke, his consistency and brilliance has delivered a worthy collection of titles.

PLAYER STATS

BORN May 4, 1989; Holywood, Northern Ireland
HEIGHT 5ft 10in (1.78m)
TURNED PRO 2007

DEBUT WIN 1999 Dubai Desert Classic
TOUR WINS 36
EUROPEAN TOUR: 14
PGA TOUR: 18
OTHER: 4

MAJORS 4
MASTERS: 4th 2015
US OPEN: Won 2011
THE OPEN: Won 2014
USPGA: Won 2012, 2014

HONORS

PGA Tour Money Winner: 2012, 2014
PGA Tour Player of the Year: 2012, 2014
Vardon Trophy Winner: 2012, 2014, 2019
Race to Dubai Winner: 2012, 2014, 2015
Ryder Cup Team: 2010, 2012, 2014, 2016, 2018

Since becoming world champion in the aged 9 to 10 bracket at the Doral Gold Resort in Miami in 1998, Rory McIlroy has been an international golfing star. He became a member of the Holywood Golf Club in County Down, Northern Ireland, at seven years old, and his first hole in one came only three years later. McIlroy's focus on the game did not waiver in his early teens, and he shot a stunning 61 at Royal Portrush just a couple of months after his 16th birthday.

European and PGA Tour wins followed in 2009 and 2010, along with his first victorious Ryder Cup showing at Celtic Manor that year. Despite a memorable collapse at the 2011 Masters, where he led by four going into Sunday but dropped to a remarkable tied-15th after a final round of 80, McIlroy recovered to capture the US Open just two months later. His tournament record of 268 was four better than the previous best, set by Jack Nicklaus, Lee Janzen, Tiger Woods, and Jim Furyk. His first Major at the age of 22 years, one month, and 15 days was younger than players such as Seve Ballesteros and Nicklaus.

That unforgettable Major at Congressional was the beginning of a fantastic few years for McIlroy. He first achieved No. 1 in the rankings in March 2012, when he claimed the Honda Classic title. He also went on to be crowned USPGA champion that summer. Two more Majors came his way in 2014, at The Open and USPGA. McIlroy looked set to achieve double figures at the four big events before the decade was out. However, the rise of talents, including Jordan Speith and Brooks Koepka, combined with McIlroy picking up rib and ankle injuries somewhat slowed his collection of golf's biggest prizes. A switch from using Nike equipment after 2016 should be factored in, too.

McIlroy continues to secure success, registering 15 PGA Tour titles before he turned 30, and has regularly returned to the top of the rankings. He still covets being able to wear the green jacket at Augusta to complete the career Grand Slam. This aim is one he has every chance of achieving and would see him joining legends including Tiger Woods, Jack Nicklaus, Gary Player, and Ben Hogan.

▲ **MCILROY POSES** with the DP World Tour Championship and Race to Dubai trophies in 2015.

▶ **THE NORTHERN IRISHMAN** first reached number one in the rankings in 2012. By the end of 2020, he had spent more than 100 weeks in the top spot.

Brooks Koepka

Before the 2019 USPGA, defending champion Brooks Koepka confidently said he could see himself reaching double figures for Major titles during his career. Even though such a feat has been achieved by only three players in over 150 years, there was a genuine sense that his claim was for real. Nothing should surprise the golf world when it comes to this talented star.

PLAYER STATS

BORN May 3, 1990; West Palm Beach, Florida
HEIGHT 6ft (1.83m)
TURNED PRO 2012

DEBUT WIN Challenge de Catalunya 2012
TOUR WINS 15
EUROPEAN TOUR: 6
PGA TOUR: 7
OTHER: 2

MAJORS 4
MASTERS: T2nd 2019
US OPEN: Won 2017, 2018
THE OPEN: T4th 2019
USPGA: Won 2018, 2019

HONORS
PGA Tour Player of the Year: 2018
PGA Tour Money Winner: 2019
Ryder Cup Team: 2016, 2018
Presidents Cup Team: 2017

Winning a Major is tough enough, but to successfully defend it is an even greater achievement accomplished by greats such as Tiger Woods, Jack Nicklaus, Nick Faldo, and Arnold Palmer. Brooks Koepka added his name to the prestigious list in 2018 before setting his own back-to-back record in 2019. The Palm Beach native is the first player ever to successfully defend both the US Open, in 2018, and the USPGA the following year. Also in 2019, Koepka became only the fifth golfer in PGA Tour history to finish in the top five of all four Majors in the same year. He had already reached No. 1 in the world in October 2018, replacing compatriot Dustin Johnson.

To some, it may be a surprise that Koepka has risen to these heights in the game at all. His father, Bob, played baseball for West Virginia Wesleyan College, and his great-uncle Dick Groat won two World Series with the Pittsburgh Pirates and is also in the basketball Hall of Fame at Duke University.

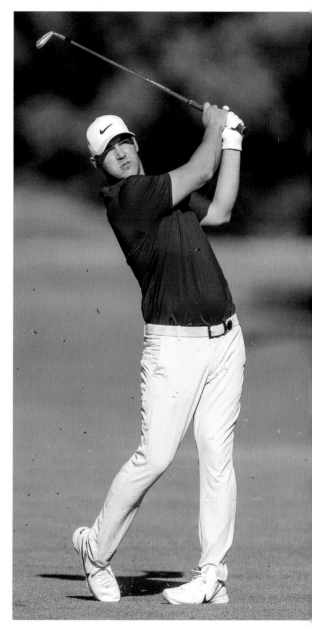

> I think sometimes the Majors are the easiest ones to win. Half the people shoot themselves out of it and mentally I know I can beat most of them.

BROOKS KOEPKA

Koepka was a promising all-arounder, too, but he had to turn his back on baseball, basketball, and hockey as a child after a serious car accident. Instead, the noncontact sport of golf became his driving force, and the rest is history. Fans and experts look forward to seeing how that history shapes up.

◄ **HE PICKED UP THE** Wanamaker Trophy for the first time in 2017. This was the USPGA's 100th championship.

► **KOEPKA HAS FINISHED** in the top four at all four Majors and hopes to add the Masters and the Open to his collection.

Jordan Spieth

In 2015, it seemed like an emerging Jordan Spieth was about to dominate the big tournaments, impressing as he won at the Masters and the US Open. Since bagging the 2017 Open, his game and confidence dipped, but he remains a mighty force capable of capturing the highs again and using his natural talent to play his way back into the world's top 10 rankings.

PLAYER STATS

BORN July 27, 1993; Dallas, Texas
HEIGHT 6ft 1in (1.85m)
TURNED PRO 2012

DEBUT WIN 2013 John Deere Classic
TOUR WINS 17
EUROPEAN TOUR: 3
PGA TOUR: 11
OTHER: 3

MAJORS 3
MASTERS: Won 2015
US OPEN: Won 2015
THE OPEN: Won 2017
USPGA: 2nd 2015

HONORS
PGA Tour Rookie of the Year: 2013
PGA Tour Money Winner: 2015
Vardon Trophy Winner: 2015, 2017
PGA Tour Player of the Year: 2015
Ryder Cup: 2014, 2016, 2018
Presidents Cup Team: 2013, 2015, 2017

▲ **SPIETH WON** his third Major at the Open in 2017 at Royal Birkdale, England.

When Jordan Spieth picked up his second US Junior Amateur title in 2011, he sat proudly alongside Tiger Woods as the only men to win the marque event more than once. Ever since turning pro the following year, he has lived up to his billing as one of the most talented and exciting players in the world. Spieth quickly settled into Tour life, being named 2013 Rookie of the Year and collecting the John Deere Classic, which at 19 years, 11 months, and 18 days old made him the youngest PGA Tour winner since 1931. In many ways, his 2014 was the perfect warm-up for the following campaign, making 24 cuts out of 27, eight top 10 finishes, a tied-second at the Masters behind Bubba Watson, and a Ryder Cup spot. Fast-forward 12 months, and the eye-catching young Texan had two Majors in his pocket following success at Augusta and the US Open at Chambers Bay.

▲ **CAN JORDAN SPIETH** complete the career Grand Slam and win the USPGA, to add to his three other Majors? Time and talent is on his side.

The US Open victory meant he was again in the record books, this time as the youngest double Major winner since 1922. Spieth looked to have the Masters wrapped up again the following year, leading after three rounds before a five-shot margin disappeared on the back nine to concede his title to Danny Willett. He did, however, return to the No. 1 ranking spot that year, giving him the confidence to go on and capture the Open at Royal Birkdale the following summer. That was the third part of his career Grand Slam target, with plenty of time and talent left to rediscover his top form and one day take ownership of the USPGA to complete the set.

Inbee Park

By her mid-20s, Inbee Park was already on her way to becoming a legendary LPGA Tour player after turning pro in 2006. She set a record for scooping the first three Majors in a year before going on to break the $2 million earnings mark for four seasons in a row. With Olympic success, too, she fully warrants the respect she has earned from players and fans.

PLAYER STATS

BORN July 12, 1988; Seoul, South Korea
HEIGHT 5ft 6in (1.68m)
TURNED PRO 2006

DEBUT WIN 2008
TOUR WINS 33
LPGA TOUR: 20
OTHER: 13

MAJORS 7
LPGA CHAMPIONSHIP: Won 2013, 2014, 2015
ANA INSPIRATION: Won 2013
US WOMEN'S OPEN: Won 2008, 2013
BRITISH WOMEN'S OPEN: Won 2015
EVIAN CHAMPIONSHIP: T8 2015, 2018, 2019

HONORS
LPGA Tour Money Winner: 2012, 2013
LPGA Player of the Year: 2013
LPGA Vare Trophy: 2012, 2015
2016 Olympics: Gold

Going into the 2020 season, which would be heavily disrupted by the COVID-19 pandemic, only six women had won more Majors than Inbee Park, the mighty South Korean. She had seven to her name at that stage, with more than $15 million in prize money and making the cut 16 times from 17 events in 2019.

Now residing in Las Vegas, Park has been a big hitter on the LPGA Tour since 2007, and her first win came at the 2008 US Women's Open, where she set a record as the youngest champion at 19 years, 11 months, and 17 days old. Somewhat strangely, Park recorded no wins on the Tour for the following three years, with her best result being the runner-up spot at the 2010 Kia Classic. Still in her early 20s, the South Korean turned a corner in 2012, and the victories soon followed: two on the LPGA Tour and impressive results to take her to the top of the yearly earnings list. The accolades that arrived over the next few years were the results of all Park's hard work on her practice rounds. Six wins came in

2013, including being the first in the modern era to win the first three Majors of the season, plus three more Majors during 2014 and 2015. Throw in the 2016 Olympic gold, and Park can be rightly viewed as a giant of the women's game.

▼ **THE EVIAN CHAMPIONSHIP** is the only Major that Inbee Park has not claimed. She was tied-eighth in 2015, 2018, and 2019.

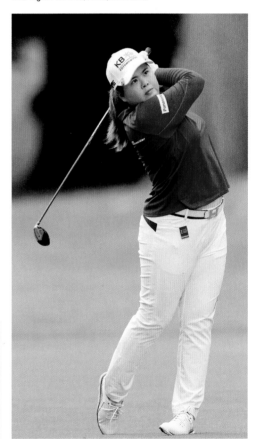

As I have achieved many titles, including the Olympic gold, I want to develop as an individual as well as a professional, with a calm and fearless mind.

INBEE PARK

◄ **INBEE PARK** kisses the Australian Open trophy in February 2020.

Stars of the Men's Tour

At the end of the 2010s and heading into a new decade, one which would ultimately start with the mass disruption caused by a pandemic, fresh names kept appearing on the Major trophies. Brooks Koepka, Gary Woodland, and Shane Lowry had all captured prized silverware, with Collin Morikawa and Bryson DeChambeau to follow for the first time in 2020. Just as players like Rory McIlroy and Jason Day had started to break through 13 or so years earlier, a host of exciting golfers were entertaining the crowds and rubbing shoulders with the more established players.

▲ **COLLIN MORIKAWA** shot a 65 and 64 in the final 36 holes of the 2020 USPGA, which was a tournament record.

Collin Morikawa turned pro in 2019 after impressing in his collegiate career at the University of California, Berkeley. In 2018, he reached the top of the world amateur rankings. As a two-time Arnold Palmer Cup winner, with Walker Cup and Eisenhower Trophy medals to show off, too, Morikawa was always going to have a close eye on him as he joined the Tour. In just his eighth career start at the age of 22, Morikawa's debut PGA Tour win arrived at the Barracuda Championship in California. Tour title number two came at the Workday Charity Open in July 2020, when he beat Justin Thomas in a playoff. This must have helped him get over the disappointment of missing his first PGA Tour cut during the Travelers Championship. Having reached 22 consecutive cuts at the start of his pro career, however, Morikawa is second only to Tiger Woods, whose record of 25 consecutive cuts remains unbeaten. To the wider golfing world, he rose to prominence as the 2020 USPGA champ, in just his second start at a Major. Morikawa's stunning eagle at the 16th during the final round confirmed the 23-year-old as a force to watch over the coming seasons.

WOLFF IS HUNGRY FOR MORE

Matthew Wolff has been eager for success on the course since becoming a professional in 2019 and earning his PGA Tour card at just 20 years old. Prior to that, Wolff was honored with the Haskins Award, given to the top collegiate player—the likes of Tiger Woods, Phil Mickelson, Graeme McDowell, and Justin Thomas all previously held the trophy. Glory came early for the young Californian, collecting the 3M Open in 2019 by one shot over Morikawa and Bryson DeChambeau. Wolff's tied-fourth at the 2020 USPGA was bettered by his solo second-place finish at the

▲ **MATTHEW WOLFF** reached a career-high 12th in the world rankings in 2020. He aims to crack the top 10 consistently.

US Open a month later. Those results and his top form helped carry Wolff into a playoff for the Shriners Hospitals for Children Open, assisted by his three eagles on the third round back nine. Suspect Wolff to hunt eagles and birdies for years to come.

HOT SCOTT

A 2017 Walker Cup winner alongside Collin Morikawa, Scottie Scheffler played the 2016 and 2017 US Open as an amateur before his debut pro season in 2018. He joined the PGA Tour in 2020, following two titles on the Korn Ferry Tour, and swept the Rookie of the Year prize. He matched Xander Schauffele's achievement of three years earlier by securing a top-five standing in the FedExCup. Scheffler's USPGA debut in 2020 produced his best Major result so far, thanks to a tied-fourth finish with Jason Day, Bryson DeChambeau, Tony Finau, and Matthew Wolff. He will grow over the next few years and likely challenge at every Major, perhaps eclipsing his contemporaries like Morikawa and Wolff, as golf fans enjoy a thrilling influx of talented young stars.

This morning I woke up and it felt like it was my time to do it.

COLLIN MORIKAWA REFLECTING A FEW HOURS AFTER WINNING THE 2020 USPGA

▶ **SCOTTIE SCHEFFLER'S** second-round 59 at the Northern Trust in 2020 was only the 12th sub-60 score in PGA Tour history.

Even with the continued debate around whether the PGA Tour is far superior to the European Tour, and with talk of a "World Tour" never far away, there remains no doubt about the talent that keeps impressing on both sides of the Atlantic. The US's crop of hungry younger players through the second decade of this century—the likes of Jordan Spieth, Collin Morikawa, and Patrick Reed—was reminiscent of the group before them that came from all around the world, featuring Rory McIlroy, Jason Day, and Martin Kaymer.

DUSTIN DOES IT

Now seen as one of the older guards after joining the PGA Tour in 2008, America's Dustin Johnson has remained a powerhouse in the game for a long time. Able to mix it with guys in their early 20s, he won the 2020 Masters to add it to his 2016 US Open triumph. His victory at Augusta came with a record-setting 20-under score, and he has been ranked the No. 1 player at stages in every year from 2017 to 2020. In total, Johnson has spent more than 100 weeks at the top of the pile, and it looks like he has many more years of top-class golf ahead of him.

POWER PLAY

Bryson DeChambeau used the enforced break caused by COVID-19 in 2020 to really beef up his game. Adding even more muscle and power to his game, his driving average of 325 yards was enough to sweep the Californian-born Texas resident to the US Open title in September 2020. DeChambeau's brute force approach, combined with his analytical style that has earned him the nickname "The Scientist," has ruffled some feathers among the game. DeChambeau is challenging the norm by changing his body and his way of thinking, with clear results on the course. With seven PGA Tour wins by the end of 2020 and an army of new fans who love his exciting style, DeChambeau will continue to make headlines and collect victories along the way.

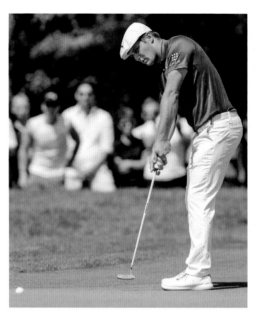

▲ **BRYSON DECHAMBEAU'S** victory at the 2020 US Open came in his 16th appearance at a Major. It will be a surprise if he doesn't add another Major title over the next few years.

▲ **SPAIN'S JON RAHM** recorded top-four finishes at the Masters and USPGA in 2018 and bettered that with tied-third at the US Open in 2019. In 2020, he spent four weeks at No. 1 in the world rankings.

It's a dream come true. As a kid, you always dream about being a Masters champion.

DUSTIN JOHNSON AT AUGUSTA IN 2020

◀ **DUSTIN JOHNSON** slips on the green jacket at Augusta in November 2020, with help from Tiger Woods, the previous champion.

▲ **VIKTOR HOFLAND**, from Norway, turned
pro in 2019 and is a former No. 1 in
the world amateur rankings.

▲ **SOUTH KOREA'S SUNGJAE IM**, born in 1998,
tied second with Cameron Smith on 12-under at
the 2020 Masters. It was his competition debut.

◄ **GARY WOODLAND** became a professional in 2007.
The American finally lifted a Major in 2019, at the
US Open at Pebble Beach.

▲ **RASMUS HOJGAARD**, from Denmark, was the first player born in the 2000s to win on the European Tour. He won the AfrAsia Bank Mauritius Open in 2019, aged 18.

▲ **JUSTIN THOMAS** struggled to make a real impact at the Majors after his surprise win at the 2017 USPGA. The Kentucky-born golfer still has time to rediscover his form from that breakout year.

◄ **JOAQUIN NIEMANN**, from Chile, had six wins in South America as a teenager and wants to make his mark on the PGA Tour.

◀ **XANDER SCHAUFFELE** was the 2017 PGA Rookie of the Year. He enjoyed tied-second finishes at the 2019 Masters and The Open in 2018, as well as tied-third at the 2019 US Open.

▼ **PATRICK REED** won three PGA Tour titles before his 24th birthday, before being crowned the 2018 Masters champion.

▼ **PATRICK CANTLAY** hopes to build on his promise as an eye-catching college and amateur player and push for a Major title.

Stars of the Women's Tour

When Mexico's Lorena Ochoa retired in 2010, aged just 28, it gave other players on the Women's Tour the chance to take the top spot. With Annika Sorenstam also having stepped away from the pro game two years earlier, it was an exciting time as fresh faces competed for glory at the Majors. Ochoa was a tough act to follow, though, having been the top-ranked golfer for a record 158 weeks.

Michelle Wie, who turned 21 only in 2010, was many people's tip to rise quickly in the wake of those retirements. However, she struggled to live up to that early promise and needed another four years to land her first Major. That win was at the 2014 US Women's Open at Pinehurst, North Carolina.

In more recent years, South Korea's Jin Young Ko has gained the spotlight as a player with the potential to stay at the peak of the women's game. Since the age of seven, Ko has been in love with golf and racked up 10 Korean Tour wins by the age of 22. In 2015, having only just celebrated her 20th birthday, she came second at the Women's British Open to compatriot Inbee Park. Four years later, Ko enjoyed her finest season by landing both the 2019 ANA Inspiration and the Evian Championship for her first Major successes. She also carried off the LPGA Player of the Year, Vare Trophy, and Tour money winner prizes that year, as well as being ranked the No. 1 player. Not bad for someone who was awarded LPGA Rookie of the Year in 2018. Ko took a yearlong absence from the LPGA Tour because of the COVID-19 pandemic, and instead continued on the KLPGA scene in her home country. Now back, she is eyeing the big silverware again and increasing her efforts to reach the level of trophy success enjoyed by Inbee Park.

KORDA ON COURSE

Even with both of her parents being former tennis pros, with her father Petr Korda the 1998 Australian Open champion, Nelly Korda turned to golf as her chosen sport. At nearly six feet tall, she probably stood a good chance as a professional on the court; however, she swings a club and not a racket, and a great career lies ahead for her. Korda joined the LPGA Tour in 2017, aged 18, and enjoyed her debut Tour win in October of the following year at the LPGA Taiwan Championship. That victory put her on par with her older sister, Jessica, who also has Tour victories to her name. In 2019, she impressed by getting her best result at that time, registering a tied-third at the Women's USPGA at Hazeltine, Minnesota. Korda then dipped a little at the following British Open, finishing tied-ninth, but worked hard to come second at the 2020 ANA Inspiration. She actually led that tournament at the halfway stage, and it's now surely just a matter of time until she finishes top of the final leaderboard at a Major.

CANADIAN GREAT

As Canada's most successful golfer of all time, including male players, Brooke Henderson had already achieved so much by the age of 22. By that time, she had amassed nine LPGA Tour titles and won nearly $7 million to seal her spot as one of her country's sporting greats. Indeed, she was crowned the Canadian Press Female Athlete of the Year in 2015, 2017, and 2018. In 2015, her world ranking rocketed from the low 200s to inside the top 20, thanks to her first Tour victory at the Cambia Portland Classic. The following summer, aged 18, Henderson took the Women's USPGA trophy, ending third on the Tour money winner list, and making 15 top-10 finishes. In 2019, she claimed her ninth Tour victory at the Meijer Classic.

▲ **BY THE AGE OF 22,** Nelly Korda had already won more than $3.7 million in career earnings.

▲ **SINCE HER ROOKIE YEAR** in 2015, Brooke Henderson has won nine LPGA Tour titles.

▶ **JIN YOUNG KO** has impressed since her rookie year in 2018, winning the ANA Inspiration and Evian Championship in 2019.

▶ **ENGLAND'S GEORGIA HALL** joined the LPGA Tour in 2018, and at Royal Lytham & St. Annes that year, aged 22, she won the Women's British Open.

▶ **CALIFORNIAN-BORN DANIELLE KANG** had five LPGA Tour victories by the end of 2020. Her first, and so far only, Major was the 2017 Women's PGA Championship.

▶▶ **IN 2011, US PRO LEXI THOMPSON** took the Navistar Classic as the youngest LPGA Tour winner at 16 years, 7 months, and 8 days. By 2020, she had 11 wins on the Tour, including the 2014 ANA Inspiration.

▲▲ **SUNG HYUN PARK** had 10 Tour wins on the South Korea Tour, before joining the LPGA Tour in 2017. Her first two Majors were the US Women's Open (2017) and Women's PGA Championship (2018).

▲ **BORN IN 1989** in Hawaii, Michelle Wie West has been a big star since before she was a teenager. She won the US Women's Open in 2014.

▶ **SEI YOUNG KIM** pocketed more than $10 million career earnings since her rookie year in 2015. The South Korean won the 2020 Women's PGA Championship, by five shots ahead of compatriot Inbee Park.

GOLFING LANDMARKS

Willie Park (far left) and assorted professionals in the 1860s.

The earliest origins of the game of golf are, despite the best efforts of generations of historical experts and scholars, sketchy at best. We can say without hesitation, however, that by the middle of the 15th century, golf in Scotland had grown in popularity to such an extent that the powers that be felt it had become an unwelcome distraction. By the mid-18th century, the game had its first set of written rules. A century later, in 1860, it had its first championship—what we now regard as golf's first Major.

Probably the main reason for staging this event was to establish the identity of the "new" best golfer after the recent death of Allan Robertson—the undisputed No. 1 of the time and the first man to break 80 for a round of the Old Course at St. Andrews. The tournament was staged for the leading professionals, although for reasons unknown only eight players took part. And some of the golf was shocking even by the erratic standards of the day—one competitor took 21 strokes on one hole.

However, on Wednesday, October 17, 1860, on the windswept links of Prestwick on the west coast of Scotland, Major championship golf was born. Old Tom Morris, who held the position we would now know as the greenkeeper at Prestwick, was the local favorite and expected to win, but it was Willie Park who won with a three-round aggregate of 174.

Morris atoned for the disappointment of losing the first-ever Open by winning four of the next seven, thus cementing his place in history. His son, young Tom Morris, would go on to emulate that feat and win four Opens himself between 1868 and 1872.

There are three other Majors now—the Masters, the US Open, and the USPGA—but 1860 is still recognized as the year when it all started. The Open will always be the oldest, the greatest, and, by most people's judgment, the most prized championship in the sport.

◄ **OLD TOM MORRIS** (left), Allan Robertson (4th from left), and St. Andrews Captain Hay Wemyss (right).

● Bobby Jones with the US Open trophy in July 1930.

Despite never turning professional, Bobby Jones dominated the game between 1923 and 1930. During that time, he won 13 of the 21 Majors in which he competed. Some consider him to be the greatest golfer who ever lived. Jones achieved much in his short, glittering career, but everything is overshadowed by his achievements in the 1930 season, when he won what was then considered the Grand Slam of championship golf.

One could have gained a measure of Jones's intentions that season from his first-round match in the Amateur Championship at St. Andrews, the first leg of that Grand Slam. Sidney Roper was his opponent that day, and he was in fine form, but Jones started his round on the formidable Old Course with a birdie, then a par, followed by another birdie, an eagle, and another birdie. Jones was five-under par for the first five holes. Poor Roper must have known it was not to be his day!

Jones followed that victory by claiming the Open Championship at Royal Liverpool and later that summer the US Open at Interlachen, Florida, where a sublime third-round 68 gave him a five-shot lead going into the final day. Finally, he completed the Grand Slam in the US Amateur at Merion, Pennsylvania, in September, winning the final by an overwhelming margin of 8 and 7 and confirming his status as a national hero.

No golfer has ever won the modern-day Grand Slam—all four Majors in a single season—but Jones completing the "Impregnable Quadrilateral," as it was dubbed by one New York journalist at the time, is probably the next best thing.

▶ **BOBBY JONES RECEIVES** a hero's welcome in New York after returning from Britain with the Amateur and Open Championship titles.

Master class of Course Design

Come April, and another year's Masters, Augusta is awash with color.

Golf without Augusta National, without the Masters, is as unthinkable as tennis without Wimbledon. We have Bobby Jones to thank that it was created in the first place.

Jones had the golfing world at his feet when he retired at the age of 28, and although his decision was a huge loss to the competitive golfing scene, it would prove to be a shrewd move for him personally. He soon found himself overwhelmed by an avalanche of commercial offers.

Jones had his own agenda, though. In the years since his retirement, he had found it increasingly difficult to venture on to a course without a huge gallery shadowing his every move. He appreciated the support, but at the same time, he yearned to play golf in private with just his friends for company. One such friend was businessman Clifford Roberts, and together they formulated the idea of a private members' golf course. A plot of land, the Fruitlands Nursery in Augusta, Georgia, was earmarked as perfect.

Bobby Jones would later recall his first-ever visit to the site. "When I walked out on the grass terrace under the big trees behind the house and looked down over the property, the experience was unforgettable. It seemed that this land had been lying here for years just waiting for someone to lay a golf course upon it."

To lay this golf course, Jones and Roberts enlisted the services of the great golf course architect Dr. Alister Mackenzie. Together they created Augusta National, a golf course that would be playable for golfers of all standards but at the same time represent the ultimate test of strategic golf.

It is the most beautiful and manicured golf course in the world, and it is home to the Masters Tournament. That was Jones's idea, too. The man was touched by genius, both on and off the golf course.

◄ **AN AERIAL VIEW** of the newly completed Augusta National, taken in January 1933, shortly before its official opening.

Nelson's golfing achievements in 1945 will never be equaled.

Blessed with an elegant swing, Byron Nelson was a sublime ball striker and a great champion.

John Jacobs, top coach and former Ryder Cup player and captain, knew Nelson. He remembers a conversation with the great man, during which they were discussing the swing changes Nelson had made in the winter of 1944. "I could win with my old swing," he said, "but I could also miss the cut. Once I'd changed my swing, though, I knew I would never play badly again." It was an extraordinary statement, and it was also prophetic.

The following year, Nelson won 11 consecutive tournaments on the American Tour and 18 in total. He went five months without losing a golf tournament.

His run started in January at the Phoenix Open; starting with rounds of 68 and 65, he then coasted to a two-shot victory. In his next tournament, the Corpus Christie Open, he shot 66, 63, and 65 to blow the rest of the field apart. He did the same again in the New Orleans Open. Then as the PGA Tour season progressed, Nelson won the Charlotte Open by four shots, the Greensboro Open by eight shots, the Atlanta Open by nine, the Montreal Open by 10, the Chicago Victory Open by seven, the Tam O'Shanter Open by 11, the Knoxville Invitational by 10, the Esmeralda Open by seven, and the Seattle Open by 13!

This was, and still is, the most extraordinary run of dominance in the history of the game. His stroke average that season was 68.33, lower than Tiger Woods manages most years on Tour.

Rather like Bobby Jones before him, Nelson retired when he was at the top of his game, aged 34. However, a handful of years later, he had a brief change of heart. While on vacation with his wife, he decided to enter the 1955 French Open. He won it, of course. This was Byron Nelson. Old habits die hard.

▶ **ED DUDLEY (CENTER)** president of the USPGA, with Sam Byrd (left), present Byron Nelson with the USPGA Championship trophy at Morraine Country Club in Dayton, Ohio, on July 15, 1945.

"Lord" Byron Sets the Standard

Hagen wins his third USPGA Championship in September 1925.

Walter Hagen was an extraordinary character—a man's man; a ladies' man; a man about town; a showman. He once proclaimed that he did not want to be a millionaire, rather just live like one. He achieved both.

But there was more to Hagen than showy gestures and a champagne lifestyle. Above all, he was a champion golfer with a rare and exquisite array of skills. He was known to walk on the 1st tee and say, "Who's going to finish second, then?"

For a while, Hagen's bold pronouncement was prescient. In the 1920s, when the USPGA Championship was a matchplay event, Hagen made it to the final six times in seven years, winning five, including four in succession from 1924 to 1927. The man was virtually unbeatable, as four fine challengers would testify. Jim Barnes pushed Hagen to the limit at French Lick in 1924 but ultimately went down by two holes. Will Mehlhorn took a 6 and 4 hammering at Olympia Fields in the following year's final, and Leo Diegel was trounced 4 and 3 at Salisbury in 1926. J. Turnesa stood in the way of Hagen's fourth consecutive win at Dallas in 1927 and, despite putting up a good fight, lost on the last hole.

During that period, Hagen also managed to win four Open Championships. Bizarre, then, that he seems remembered now not so much for his golfing prowess but more for his witty turn of phrase, his flamboyant lifestyle, and the unbridled "joie de vivre" that characterized everything he did. In so doing, we risk overlooking what an incredible golfer he was. The man won 11 Major championships at a time when there were only three Majors to play for, not four as there are today. Hagen was a legend for all the right reasons.

◄ **WALTER HAGEN PRACTICING HIS** swing on the roof of the Savoy Hotel, London, in June 1922, prior to that year's Ryder Cup matches.

Hogan being transferred home after his car crash, on April 7, 1949.

Ben Hogan's car crash in February 1949 is the stuff of legend. Hogan crashed head-on into a Greyhound bus that was overtaking a truck and suffered horrific multiple injuries.

Few dared entertain the thought that he might be able to play golf again—a local newspaper even published his obituary—but they had not reckoned with Hogan's steely resolve. This was a man who was known to practice until his hands bled. Just 18 months after the accident, he won his second US Open.

In 1953, he played golf of a standard that may never again be equaled. He entered six tournaments that year and won five of them. Three were Majors.

At the Masters, he smashed the tournament record by five strokes, closing with rounds of 69, 66, and 69 to win by a handful of shots.

The US Open was played at Oakmont in Pennsylvania, a golf course with a fearsome reputation. But Hogan brought it to its knees. After the first round, Skip Alexander, a fellow competitor playing in the group behind Hogan, pronounced that he knew how to shoot 67 on this golf course. "You hit every goddamn fairway and every green about 10 feet from the hole, just like Hogan did." Hogan's round contained 13 pars, five birdies, and no bogeys. It set the standard, and he went on to win by six shots.

The Open Championship at Carnoustie was next. Hogan had never played in the Open; he hated the traveling. He arrived two weeks early to get accustomed to the smaller British golf ball and to study the course and formulate his strategy. No one stood a chance. Hogan broke the course record on the last day and won by four shots.

He never played in the Open again.

▶ **HOGAN SHOWS OFF** his signature driver after another scorching shot straight down the middle.

● Tiger Woods seals the Grand Slam with victory at St. Andrews in 2000.

The Grand Slam winners' club is the most exclusive clique that exists in the game of golf. Gaining membership requires the player to win all four Majors, a feat that only five players—Gene Sarazen, Ben Hogan, Gary Player, Jack Nicklaus, and Tiger Woods—have achieved.

Others have come close. Sam Snead won more tournaments on the PGA Tour than any other player in history, but the US Open escaped him; for Arnold Palmer and Tom Watson, it was the USPGA.

The founding member, Sarazen, had already won three legs of the Grand Slam when he turned up at Augusta National to play in his first US Masters in 1935. He did not just win the tournament; he also hit probably the most famous golf shot in history—holing a 5-wood on the 15th for an albatross-two.

Ben Hogan was next to win the Grand Slam, sealing it with his one and only visit to the Open at Carnoustie in 1953.

Gary Player beat his great rival Jack Nicklaus to the Slam by almost a full calendar year. Player won his first Major championship in the 1959 Open at Muirfield and completed the quadruple six years later at the US Open. Jack Nicklaus followed Player into the Grand Slam Winners club in 1966 when he won the Open Championship. Nicklaus would go on to win more Major championships than any other golfer—18 in all. By most people's reckoning, it was a record that would stand forever … but then along came Tiger Woods.

Woods won his first Major, the 1997 Masters, by a remarkable 12 strokes—just nine months after turning professional. Three years later, he had the full set of Majors to his name. He was in the club. By 2019, Woods had reached 15 Majors.

▶ **FOUR OF GOLF'S** famous five pictured in July 1970. From left to right, Sarazen, Hogan, Player, and Nicklaus.

McCormack and IMG changed the face of sports marketing.

Mark McCormack was a visionary. He opened the door for riches that were beyond anything any sportsperson could have dreamed of and, in so doing, became the king of sports marketing. Today's mega-rich golf stars should tip their visors to the great man.

McCormack's first smart move was signing up Arnold Palmer as his first client in 1960. Palmer was like no other golfer. He had extraordinary charisma, raw appeal, and a crash-bang-wallop style of play that transformed the world of professional golf.

McCormack saw the commercial value in someone like Palmer. His energy and entrepreneurial skills enabled him to become the architect of a burgeoning new industry. It was not long before McCormack had also signed up a talented young South African named Gary Player and a chubby young American with a crew cut named Jack Nicklaus.

McCormack had golf's undisputed "Big Three" on his books. Between 1958 and 1975, the three of them shared the spoils in 29 of the 72 Major championships played in that period, a 40 percent strike rate over the rest of the world's top golfers.

McCormack's relationship with the "Big Three" was the foundation of his International Management Group (IMG) company. He became immensely rich, but then so did his clients. Over the years, IMG managed other top people in the world of sports, including Rod Laver, Bjorn Borg, Martina Navratilova, Nick Faldo, Greg Norman, Colin Montgomerie, and Tiger Woods.

McCormack created an extraordinary empire. He deserved all the plaudits he received before he passed away in 2003, aged 73.

◀ **LEGENDS IN THE MAKING** Player, Palmer, and Nicklaus during the World Series of Golf in Akron, Ohio, in September 1962.

Seve with the Claret Jug in 1979—the first of his five Majors.

European golf was in the doldrums in the early to mid 1970s. Then along came a dashing, handsome young Spaniard named Severiano Ballesteros. Aged just 19, Seve almost won the Open at Royal Birkdale in 1976, thwarted on the last day by Johnny Miller. But by finishing tied-2nd with Jack Nicklaus, Seve had signaled his intentions to the world. Here was a Major champion in waiting.

Seve was Europe's No. 1 money winner three years in a row following his emergence at Birkdale. He arrived at Royal Lytham & St. Annes for the 1979 Open as one of the pretournament favorites, with a win and a second-place finish in his previous two tournaments. He was still only 22.

A brilliant second-round 65 thrust him to the head of the field, and he never looked back. His last round was a roller-coaster affair. Seve used his driver nine times and hit just one fairway. Some critics subsequently labeled him the "Car Park Champion" on account of him driving his ball into a temporary parking lot on the 16th hole.

But he had a strategy that day that is largely overlooked. It was windy and the fairways were baked hard. Seve figured that by hitting driver, he could at least take some of the dangerous fairway bunkers out of play. He could then also use his power and length off the tee to his advantage, a premeditated strategy that yielded relatively straightforward-approach shots into the greens. It was a great win that owed nothing to luck.

The following year, Seve won his first Masters and would go on to win 70 tournaments all over the world, on all types of golf courses. It all started that day at Lytham on July 21, 1979.

▶ **BALLESTEROS** acknowledges the crowd's applause on the 18th fairway at Lytham. He enjoyed a great rapport with the British public throughout his career.

Nicklaus and Watson show mutual respect at Turnberry in 1977.

The intense rivalry between Jack Nicklaus and Tom Watson started at the 1977 Open Championship at Turnberry. The pair had shot identical scores in the first three rounds—68, 70, 65—and in the final round, in blazing hot sunshine, the pair continued to play sublime golf. As they strode toward the 18th tee, Nicklaus was trailing Watson by one shot, 10-under par plays 11-under par.

After a solid 1-iron, Watson hit a towering 7-iron to 30in (75cm). Nicklaus tried to go for the green but pushed it right into the fringes of a gorse bush, from where he muscled a shot to the edge of the green, some 30ft (9m) from the hole. Before Watson could hole his putt, Nicklaus rolled in his. The crowd was ecstatic. Watson's expression did not change at all. He calmly placed his ball back down on its spot and rapped in the putt to win by one shot. As they walked off the green, Nicklaus said to Watson, "I gave you my best shot, and it just wasn't good enough. You were better." The greatest winner who ever lived was also the best loser.

Just as well, because Nicklaus suffered again in the 1982 US Open at Pebble Beach. Big Jack started the final round three strokes in arrears, but a run of five straight birdies helped his cause. As Watson came to the tough par-3 17th (with Nicklaus in the clubhouse), they were tied for the lead on 4-under par.

Watson missed the green to the left where his ball buried itself in ankle-deep rough. It looked like an impossible situation, but he produced an outrageous stroke of genius, holing his chip for a birdie-two and a one-shot lead. Victory was effectively his.

Always the gentleman, Nicklaus was there on the 18th green to congratulate the winner.

▶ **TOM WATSON SINKS** his birdie putt on the 15th to move into a tie with Jack Nicklaus during a dramatic final day at Pebble Beach.

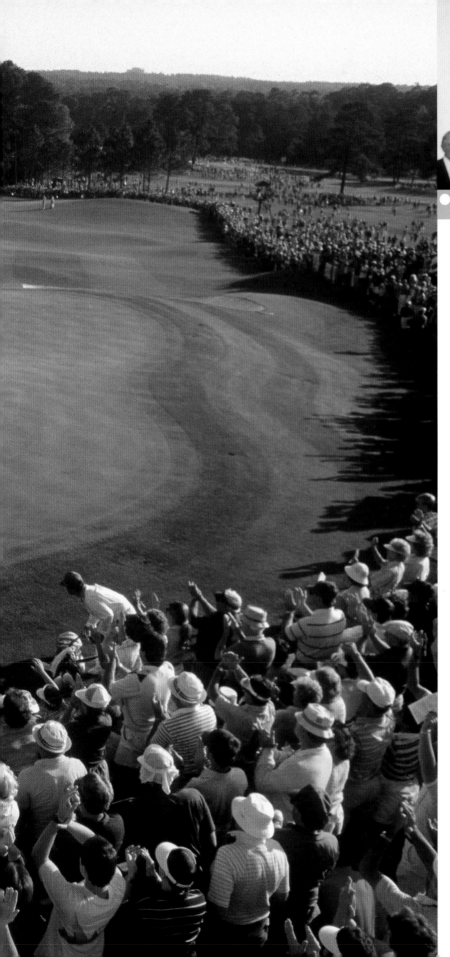

Nicklaus is helped into his sixth Green Jacket by Bernhard Langer.

Jack Nicklaus winning his sixth Green Jacket, and the last of his 18 Major championships, is one of the greatest days in the history of the sport.

By 1986, everyone thought Jack was past it. He was 46, he had not won a golf tournament in more than two years, and his last Major win was six years earlier in the US Open. A local newspaper even ran an article during the buildup to that week's Masters saying that Jack was "done, through, washed-up and finished."

It was all the motivation he needed.

After fairly modest rounds of 74, 71, and 69, Jack was not even on the radar as far as most commentators were concerned. They were all expecting Greg Norman to win; he had a four-shot lead. Should he stumble, there were others—Seve Ballesteros, Tom Watson, Nick Price, and Tom Kite—ready to pounce. The young lions were circling, but a golden bear muscled in on the party with one of the greatest charges in the history of the game.

After a methodical first eight holes, Jack birdied the 9th, 10th, and 11th. He stumbled at the 12th with a bogey but recovered to birdie the par-5 13th and then eagled the 15th after a majestic 4-iron to 10ft (3m). At the 16th, he struck an imperious 6-iron and, as the ball was in the air, turned to his son Jackie who was caddying, and winked. The ball came down 3ft (1m) from the hole. He holed that, too. He sunk a snaking 10ft (3m) putt on the 17th for another birdie; then, just as Jack always had done throughout his heyday, he secured a safe par on the 18th ... when he really needed it.

Jack had played the last 10 holes at Augusta in just 33 strokes to shoot 65. It was like the old days—Jack playing his own game to the end, rivals crumbling around him. "It was the most gratifying win of my career," said Jack.

He remains the tournament's oldest winner.

◀ **NICKLAUS HOLES OUT** on the 18th green to rapturous applause. His four-round total of 279 proved good enough for victory.

Tiger with his proud parents, Kutilda and Earl, in 1996.

Tiger Woods was famous long before he turned professional at the end of August 1996. He had won three consecutive US Junior Amateur titles—no other golfer had ever won it more than once. Then he won three consecutive US Amateur titles from 1994—not even the greatest amateur of them all, Bobby Jones, had achieved that astonishing feat.

After making the cut in his first tournament as a pro, the Greater Milwaukee Open, Tiger then finished 11th, tied-5th, and tied-3rd in his next three events. He won his next tournament, the Las Vegas Invitational, finished second the week after that, and then won again the week after. Despite starting his season effectively eight months after everyone else, he won more than $700,000 in prize money and finished 24th on the year-end money list.

The following season, he got ready to tee up in the 1997 Masters, his first Major championship as a professional. Things started badly. Playing in the company of the previous year's champion Nick Faldo, Tiger was four-over par for his first nine holes.

Things then started to go a lot better. He played the remaining 63 holes in a mind-boggling 22-under par and won the tournament by 12 shots. Records fell like ninepins. He was the youngest-ever winner; it was the lowest-ever winning score and the biggest-ever winning margin; he was the most shots under par for Augusta's back nine (16-under); he had the lowest middle 36 holes (131); he had the lowest first 54 holes and the largest 54-hole lead; and he had more threes than anyone had ever had at Augusta.

Tiger has continued to break records ever since. He is the only player of the last 30 years who has looked to even have a remote chance of approaching Jack Nicklaus's tally of 18 Major victories.

▶ **TIGER SINKS THE FINAL PUTT** on the 18th green at Augusta to win the Masters with a then-record low score of 18-under par and signal his arrival as the new force in Major championship golf.

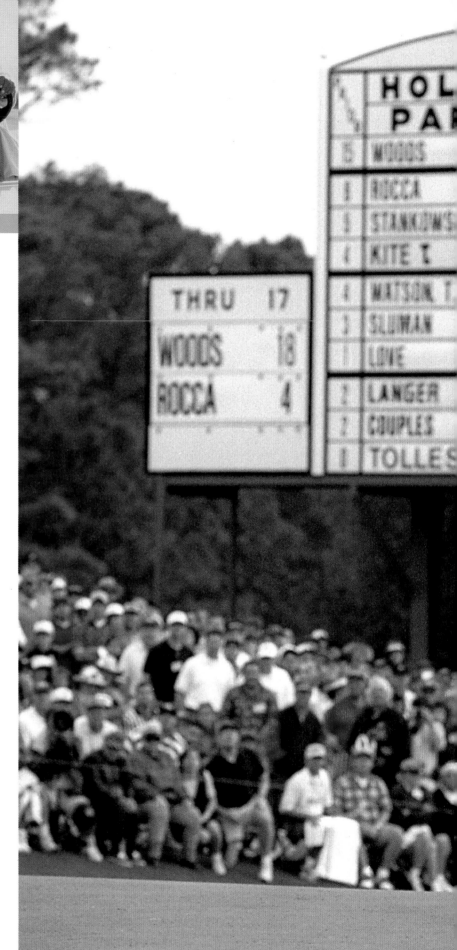

Tiger Roars to Major Victory

An elated Bernhard Langer holes a chip shot on Day One.

Up until the 1980s, Ryder Cup matches on US soil were very one-sided affairs—the Great Britain & Ireland team were always heavily beaten. In 1983, the US came close to losing for the first time on home turf. After a resounding victory at The Belfry, England, in 1985, the European team traveled to Muirfield Village in Ohio two years later with hopes higher than ever of an overseas win.

This was Europe's dream team, captained by Tony Jacklin but led in many ways by Seve Ballesteros, at that time a winner of four Major championships and a Ryder Cup colossus. Nick Faldo had just won his first Open Championship; Sandy Lyle had won it two years earlier and would go on to win the Masters; Bernhard Langer had won his first Masters already. This was a team with serious talent, and even more serious intent.

Honors were even after the morning foursomes on Day One, but in the afternoon four-balls, Europe produced a clean sweep. By the end of Day Two, Europe had a five-point advantage.

The Americans came out with guns blazing in the final day singles, claiming five victories and a half in the first seven matches, but the Europeans countered strongly. Eamonn Darcy ensured Europe could not lose by holing a slippery-quick 6ft (2m) putt on the 18th green to defeat Ben Crenshaw.

Fittingly, it was Seve, the talisman and inspiration of the team—the man who in many ways revitalized European golf—who delivered the knockout blow minutes later, beating Curtis Strange on the 17th green. It was the first time the US had lost on home soil, and it would prove to be the first in a run of eight epic, close contests between the two teams.

▶ **EUROPE'S HEROES** with Tony Jacklin center stage, dance with joy after winning the Ryder Cup for the first time on US soil.

The Battle of Brookline

A tearful Sergio García (center) finds defeat hard to take.

It was the greatest comeback in the history of team golf. Ben Crenshaw's US team had taken quite a pounding on the first two days of the 1999 Ryder Cup at Brookline Country Club, Boston, and were trailing Europe by a hefty margin of 6 points to 10 going into the last day's singles matches.

The US put its big guns in the top half of the draw, and the results were truly explosive. They quickly built big leads and won the first six matches, and their momentum was unstoppable. On an afternoon of high drama and quite deafening crowd noise, this Ryder Cup contest would hinge on the result of American Justin Leonard's match against José Maria Olazábal.

Leonard had been four down with just seven holes to play, but he won four holes in quick succession and arrived at the 17th all-square and with everything—not just his match but the Cup itself—to play for. Both players found the green in regulation and faced birdie putts, Leonard from 50ft (15m) away; Olazábal from about half of that distance.

Leonard to putt first, then. He hit it sweetly, if a little hard, and the line looked perfect. Then, bang, the ball hit the back of the hole, and in it went. Leonard went bananas. The US team then invaded the green to congratulate him but in the process stampeded over the line of José Maria Olazábal's putt. Such exuberance was understandable, but it gave Olazábal little chance of composing himself for his now vital putt. He missed it, inevitably, and the US was guaranteed the half-point they needed.

In 2012, the "Miracle at Medinah" edition matched Brookline, with Olazábal, now captaining Europe, seeing his team battle back in extraordinary scenes. Red dominated the board on Day One, and the Europeans trailed 10 to 6 as the final day's play began. The visitors took eight and a half points to seal a dramatic 14½ to 13½ victory. Martin Kaymer's 5ft (1.5m) putt on the 18th took Olazábal's men to the magical 14 points needed to retain it, with Francesco Molinari's halved point with Tiger giving Europe the trophy outright.

◄ **JUSTIN LEONARD'S** birdie on the 17th green sparks scenes of unbridled celebration in the US camp.

Woods in a Class of His Own

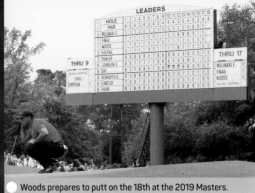

Woods prepares to putt on the 18th at the 2019 Masters.

For most of his career, Tiger Woods has been in a class of his own. His most stunning victory, when he finished 15 shots ahead of second place, was in the 2000 US Open at Pebble Beach, but his most emotional triumph came much later.

Woods opened the 2000 US Open with a blistering round of 65 to lead by one shot. After two rounds, he led by six shots; after three rounds, he had increased his lead to 10 shots; and at the end, the margin was an incredible 15 shots. He was the only player under par—12-under par, to be precise. Tied for second, on three-over, were Miguel Ángel Jiménez and two-time US Open champion Ernie Els.

"If you want to watch a guy win the US Open playing perfectly, you've just seen it," said Els, graciously. It was true. Every other competitor that week averaged five bogeys a round; Tiger had only six bogeys in total. Moreover, he did not three-putt once, an astonishing feat in any Major, let alone a US Open.

Tiger made it look easy in 2000, unlike his tough and emotional win 19 years later. Ahead of the 2019 Masters, Woods had not won a Major since the 2008 US Open. Many called his Augusta redemption the greatest comeback story in sports, not just in golf, coming as it did after high-profile personal problems and years of near career-ending injuries.

At the age of 43, and 14 years after he last slipped on the green jacket, Tiger took the title. This time, he secured only a one-shot finish over Dustin Johnson, Xander Schauffele, and Brooks Koepka, but that figure mattered little to him, the thousands on course, or the millions watching around the world.

The fans admired the way he battled that April weekend to take the lead—this was the first time he lifted a Major when trailing after 54 holes. "It will be up there with one of the hardest I've had to win because of what has transpired in the last couple of years," he admitted. His heartfelt words reinforce the significance of the win and a return to form many could not have foreseen.

◀ **TEEING OFF AT THE 12TH,** Woods makes a charge for his 15th Major at Augusta.

Sorenstam Reigns Supreme

○ Sorenstam wins the ANZ Masters, one of 13 victories in 2002.

In the early 2000s, one could endlessly debate who was the most dominant player on their respective tour, Tiger Woods or Annika Sorenstam. That the answer was even in question, given the standard of play achieved by Tiger in that period, says everything about Sorenstam's talent.

Annika drove the ball long and straight, her judgment of distance on approach shots was sublime, and she could putt like an angel. She was blessed with an ice-cool temperament and a fierce will to win.

Her 2001 season was special enough. She won eight tournaments, became the only female golfer in history to shoot 59, and was the first LPGA golfer to top $2 million in prize money in a season. Her great rival Karrie Webb remarked in an interview at the end of that year that she would "eat her hat" if Annika won eight times again in 2002.

Yet she did more than that—much more. In 2002, she played a season's golf to almost rival that of Byron Nelson's epic streak in 1945. She won 11 LPGA tournaments in a single season, beating all records. Annika won her fourth Major at the Kraft Nabisco and set a scoring record at the Kellogg-Keebler Classic where she won by 11 shots. During the course of the season, she also became the first female golfer to pass the $9 million, $10 million, and $11 million in LPGA career earnings.

Not content with trouncing the opposition in the US, Annika traveled abroad to conquer other territories, too. She won the ANZ Ladies Masters in Australia and the Compaq Open in Sweden. All in all, she competed in 26 events and won 13 of them. She had 20 top-10 finishes, and by the end of the season, her stroke average was an incredible 68.70, another new record, and secured her place in the LPGA Hall of Fame. She also pocketed $2.8 million in prize money, smashing her own record that she had set the previous year.

◄ **ANNIKA SORENSTAM (LEFT) REACTS** as she nearly holes in one at the 2005 Solheim Cup, watched by Suzann Pettersen (right).

Ely Callaway in January 2001 with the clubs that made his name.

The game of golf was destined to change forever when millionaire businessman Ely Callaway walked into a pro shop in Palm Springs in 1982. So impressed was Ely with a particular pitching wedge that he saw for sale that he bought not only the club but, with it, half of the company.

Pitching wedges are not what made the Callaway company what it is, of course. It was drivers, metal drivers. And it was not that long before Callaway was the club of choice. By the end of the 20th century, Ely's company had become a giant in the world of golf clubs, utterly dominating the driver market.

Ely Callaway was typical of that rare breed of super-entrepreneurs with a vision to do things differently. Like all successful people, he had the courage of his convictions. When he launched the company's iconic Big Bertha, the world's first oversize steel-headed driver, he was so confident of its success that he preordered 300,000 heads and charged top dollar for it, too.

It was a massive hit. For many golfers, the transition from persimmon-headed drivers to metal-headed drivers was not without its difficulties—the metal clubs looked, felt, and sounded different. But no one could deny the effectiveness of this new technology in terms of game improvement.

The company continues to make great golf clubs that pioneered a new era in the game of golf and genuinely made the game more enjoyable for the average golfer. "Until we came along the driver was the most feared club in the bag," Ely told *Golf World* magazine in an interview in 2001, not long before his death. "Today it is probably the most popular."

He was right. That is Ely Callaway's legacy.

◀ **CALLAWAY'S OVERSIZE** steel-headed drivers enabled players of all levels to hit the ball straighter and farther than ever before.

Golfers' Grand Designs

Nick Faldo (left) studies plans for a new course, in 2004.

There was a time when the demarcation was clear: players played golf courses; designers designed golf courses. Gone are those days of seminal golf course architects like Dr. Alister Mackenzie, Donald Ross, and Harry Colt.

Nowadays, developers know that if they want immediate credibility and recognition for their new golf course, the best way to do it is to enlist the services of one of the world's best players. Most of the top players are in on the act: Jack Nicklaus, Gary Player, Greg Norman, Phil Mickelson, Ernie Els, Ben Crenshaw, Annika Sorenstam, Sergio García, Vijay Singh, José Maria Olazábal, Davis Love III, Colin Montgomerie, and even Tiger Woods—they have all embraced the world of golf course design.

Arnold Palmer was in many ways the trailblazer. "When I started building golf courses," he remembers, "there were only a few golfers who were architects. Today just about everybody who plays or plays well has become an architect."

One can see the attraction. Although golfers enjoy longer playing careers than any other sportsperson, they are at their peak for only so long. This is a way of seamlessly stepping into a new career, a way of staying involved with the game of golf when their best playing days are behind them.

"I wanted to be young enough to just flip over (to full-time course design) when I'm done playing; I didn't want to start doing this at age 50," says Ernie Els, whose design company is building many golf courses in the Far East, Middle East, and India.

There is big money in this business, too. Golfers can make seven-figure sums for designing a single golf course. It has changed everything, and one of the benefits is that it has brought to the fore the art of golf course design, whereas 75 years ago, it was a mystery. That has to be a good thing.

◄ **JOSÉ MARIA OLAZÁBAL** plays what will become the par-5 15th hole of his eponymous course at Mission Hills, China, in March 2003 .

THE GREATEST COURSES

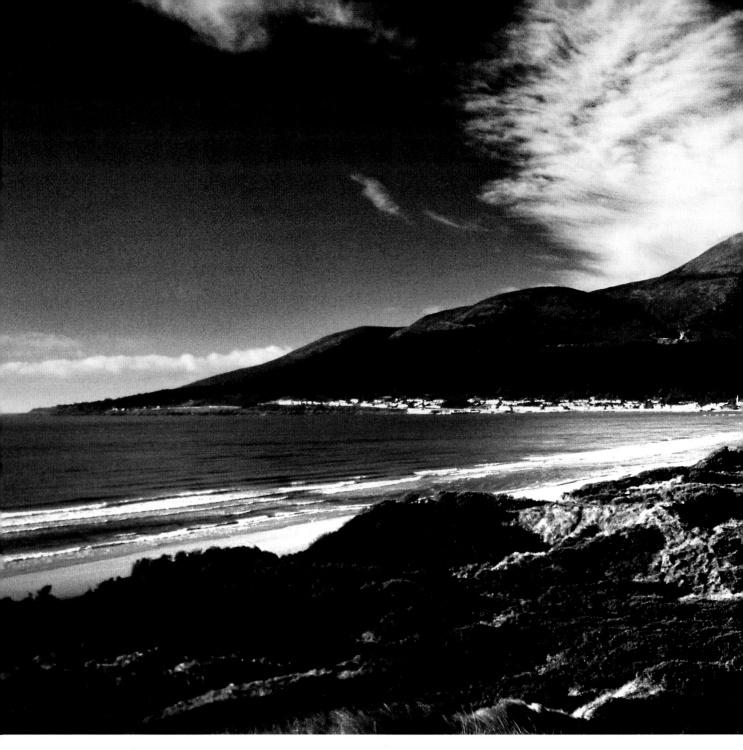

Links Courses

While the true origins of golf are muddled in the mists of time, one fact is not in dispute—the sport evolved on the sandy coastal wastes of Scotland and England. For centuries, links golf dominated the game. The creased landscapes and changeable weather make for the ultimate and most original golfing test.

▲ **THE LINKS COURSE** at Royal
County Down stands beside
the sweep of Dundrum Bay
in Northern Ireland.
◄ ◄ **WATERVILLE GOLF** in Ireland
faces the Atlantic Ocean and is
the most westerly great links
in Europe.
◄ **THE LINKS** of the Ailsa Course
at Turnberry in Scotland enjoys
one of the most beautiful settings
in the world of golf.

Unpredictability is the watchword, both in the weather conditions and in the fate of your ball, which trusts to fortune as it lands and bounces on the hard, hummocked ground—but purists would not have it any other way.

It seemed natural to the early intrepid golfers to practice their pastime on the land between the sea and more fertile fields inland, as its crumpled and grassy features were not much good for anything apart from kiteflying and walking. Hence, the name "links" was coined—the land connecting pasture and sea. The challenges of a links course are unique, and a golfer who has been schooled purely on the modern high ball game will struggle at first with the features and the methods needed to conquer them. The inevitable winds that can whip across a links have not only created the dunescape you play on but also test your shotmaking skills. A links asks for special shots to be played—often ones to punch low through the breeze as well as delicate running pitches that use the natural contours of the ground.

NATURAL COURSE

Fairways tend to find their natural route through the valleys between the humps and hollows, and they are punctured by signature pot bunkers that have been gradually groomed and shaped from age-old pits of sand into what we know today. Traditionally, links were left to fend for themselves against the elements, so although the fairways, tees, and greens were tended to, they have

◀ **INLAND SISTERS** mimic the characteristics of a true links, except for the sea! Two of the best in Europe are The Montgomerie at Carton House near Dublin and The Faldo Course in Berlin. They were designed by the golfers who bear their name along with architect Stan Eby.

▲ **DOONBEG ON THE WEST COAST** of Ireland is one of the few links to have been built in recent times. Designed by Greg Norman, the holes weave through massive dunes that are synonymous with linksland on the west—but not the east—of the British Isles.

always been firm and fast. In long, hot summers, it is no surprise to see the dry turf turn a light shade of brown. The fine blend of seaside grasses is kept alive only by the combination of nature's sea frets— damp, drizzly sea fogs—and by a greenkeeper's careful hand. Water is used sparingly to avoid bringing on rogue grasses and to preserve the unique characteristics of the links.

Many old links also follow a similar layout because of the narrow nature of the linksland they sit on. The holes move away from the clubhouse until they reach a point when they need to turn around and make their way back to the sanctuary of the clubhouse. It is not uncommon to find yourself working with the wind on the way out, only to return into the teeth of it on your way back.

There are times, however, when an unlucky golfer battles the wind going out, only to find that the turning tide has caused the breeze to swing around so that they have to fight the elements coming home, too. That is the beauty of a links course. Unpredictability is the watchword, both in the weather conditions and in the fate of your ball, which trusts to fortune as it lands and bounces on the hard, hummocked ground—but purists would not have it any other way.

INLAND LINKS

Despite its historic significance and continuing fame, links golf is a rarity today. Fewer than 250 true links exist, with the vast majority flirting with the cool seas around

▲ **FANCOURT GOLF COURSE** in South Africa was designed by Gary Player and is one of the new breeds of inland links courses.

the British Isles. Forever it will remain so, too, with coastal strips around the world now protected and getting a permit to create new links becoming increasingly difficult.

Luckily for links enthusiasts, the foibles of this particular style of golf course will continue through the building of so-called "inland links." Although the fickle sea breezes are not there to test a golfer's skills, clever designers are creating the same kind of challenges as a true links course, often not even within a whiff of the ocean. These courses will never be like the real thing, but when so few can now be added to the brilliant pedigree of our most historic courses, the new breed of "links" are a welcome alternative.

BUNKER HELL

Links bunkers are deep and shell-like by default, so the sand in their depths is not as easily gouged out by the winds. Yet wind erosion is a problem for the faces of these dastardly traps and, therefore, a special way of building them has evolved over the years. Revetting, as it is known, is the practice of making firm, stable, and imposingly steep faces by layering slices of turf on top of each other. In effect, it builds a wall of turf. Not only does it maintain the bunker shape, but it also poses difficult question for the golfer who finds the sand. A turf nursery helps provide the thousands of strips of grass needed to revet all St. Andrews's bunkers, including the infamous "Road Hole" bunker and "Hell" bunker, a massive cross trap up to 10 ft (3 m) deep.

The massive "Hell" bunker on the 14th at St. Andrews

Waterville, IRELAND

A big, powerful, mean, and magnificent challenge, Waterville is located in a wonderfully remote and inspiring setting on the Ring of Kerry. Waterville is Europe's most westerly great links and, because of that, has a unique transatlantic bond. According to Henry Cotton, this is "one of the greatest courses ever built. If it were located in Britain, it would undoubtedly be a venue for the British Open".

Stewart's statue and his wife, Tracey

Waterville is known for its unforgiving links—the 1st is called "Last Easy"—but its reputation is not based solely on the bravado needed to tackle it. The course is much more than that. First, Waterville rambles over a sensational corner of duneland, flanked on one side by the breaking Atlantic waters of Ballinskelligs Bay and on another by the estuary of the River Inny. A glance at the panorama away from the waters reveals the dark, brooding hills of the Macgillycuddy's Reeks. Second, it is a charming, romantic links course despite its brutality and deserves praise for its wonderfully creative design.

DRAMA AT EVERY HOLE

The roots of the course go back to the late 1800s when the curious village was transformed by a cable station that linked it to the United States of America via an undersea communications line. Golf found a home nearby, providing recreation for the workers.

Over time, the links fell into disrepair until an Irish American named John A. Mulcahy rekindled its fire and in the early 1970s set about creating a benchmark modern links course fit to test the best. It was a roaring success, attracting and wooing visitors from all over the world, but it has been made even greater since 2003.

Tom Fazio, responsible for many superb new courses and renovations of some of the world's greatest, was asked to put drama into every hole. Waterville has always been known for its stupendous back nine and a few stunners on the front, but Fazio made every hole memorable. He included two new holes and even improved on the most renowned ones. All holes are edged with tumbling dunes and dotted with grassy-banked, shell-like bunkers. Each tee shot needs to be thought out and committed to, because big numbers await a wayward golfer. Some holes are scary, others gripping and thrilling in their beauty.

Stand on any of the par-3 holes here and you will be struck by how sensational they look. Then reality sets in and you see the difficulty. The 4th is played off a windy elevated tee by the estuary to a long green flanked by encroaching banks. At the 6th, a downhill tee shot must find the green. Miss it right and a burn lurks; miss left or long and your ball rolls away down a slippery slope.

At the 12th, you must play over an ancient dell where Mass once took place. Finally, the 17th is pure exhilaration. Mulcahy's Peak, as it is known, is the largest dune on the course, and sitting atop its wilderness is an isolated tee from where you can spy the whole course. The ocean is on the right, and almost 200 yards (183 m) away, lies a green surrounded by trouble. One solitary deep bunker and grassy swales guard the front left. Around the back, snagging mounds wait for a miss-club, and tantalizingly close to the right is the drop-off to the beach.

Heart-in-the-mouth shots are not just limited to the short holes. Both greens at the par-4 2nd and 3rd holes are startlingly close to the river. A snaking burn down the right of 7th swallows many drives. Massive dunes line the par-5 11th, once described by a writer as "like walking through Manhattan," so enclosing are the sand hills. The drives on the 15th and 16th are awesome in the wind.

The course is equal to any famous British links, yet its remoteness excludes it from attracting a top-class tournament. Still, the world's finest test their mettle here, particularly before the Open—Tiger Woods, Mark O'Meara, Jim Furyk, and Payne Stewart have been regular visitors. They love the solitude as well as the no-nonsense, demanding, and ultimately thrilling course.

▶ **KNOWN AS LIAM'S ACE,** the 16th is prone to offshore winds as it follows the curve of the dunes where the estuary of the River Inny meets the sea.

Waterville possesses the best par-3 holes I have ever encountered on the same golf course.

TOM WATSON

THE COURSE

Brushed by stiff Atlantic winds, this awesome links in an idyllic setting is demanding from the off and never lets up. Tumultuous dunes, wispy rough, and scooped-out bunkers make every shot an adventure. To beat it, nothing but nerveless and pure striking will do.

The green is awkwardly angled and contoured

The fairway is hard to find between the sands on the right and bunkers on the left

The 4th is a testing par-3 that starts the sequence of dune holes

The 2nd green is close to the river, with great views

The 18th fairway runs parallel to the nearby sands

The 1st plays away from the sea and is called "Last Easy"

HOLE 18 "O'GRADY'S BEACH"

Terrifying but brilliant, the home hole is a colossal par-5. The fairway looks impossibly hard to find from the tee set close to the drop to the beach. To the right, the hole is flanked along its entirety by the sand, while to the left lie serious bunkers. The fairway weaves its way down the hole and through wild mounding for almost 600 yards (550 m). At the end sits a tricky green—one of the greatest finishing holes in golf.

The colossal 18th

WATERVILLE

Waterville golf links, Waterville, Co. Kerry, Ireland
www.watervillegolflinks.ie

THE COURSE

FOUNDED 1889
LENGTH 7,378 yards (6,746 m)
PAR 72
DESIGNERS John A. Mulcahy, Eddie Hackett, Claude Harmon, Tom Fazio

SELECTED CHAMPIONS

KERRYGOLD INTERNATIONAL CLASSIC
George Burns (1975); Tony Jacklin (1976); Liam Higgins (1977)

CARD OF THE COURSE

THE FRONT NINE			THE BACK NINE		
HOLE	YARDS	PAR	HOLE	YARDS	PAR
1	445	4	10	475	4
2	464	4	11	506	5
3	433	4	12	200	3
4	199	3	13	504	5
5	595	5	14	456	4
6	194	3	15	428	4
7	424	4	16	386	4
8	436	4	17	194	3
9	445	4	18	594	5
OUT	**3,635**	**35**	**IN**	**3,743**	**37**

Ballybunion, IRELAND

As eye-popping links go, the Old Course at Ballybunion is right up there with the best. A swooping course that rides over and around some vast hairy dunes beside the dramatic waters of the Atlantic Ocean, it also boasts, arguably, the greatest par-4 hole on a links course—the terraced yet bunkerless 11th. Rather like St. Andrews, it has been seen as a mecca for golfers searching for the ultimate links experience.

▲ **THE GREEN ON THE PAR-3** 15th hole nestles among the extensive dunes on the Old Course at Ballybunion Golf Club.

Ballybunion leaves no one undecided about its merits. Set hard by the River Shannon Estuary on the west coast of Ireland, most golfers who walk the fairways fall in love with its quirkiness and demanding nature. A few are exasperated by its reliance on "Lady Luck" and its raised greens and snagging rough—usually, those who have had a bad day.

Even in its infancy, back in the late 19th century, Ballybunion courted controversy and golfers were divided. A report in *The Irish Times* of 1897 laid into its peculiarities and described it as "a rabbit warren below the village, where a golfer requires limitless patience and an inexhaustible supply of golf balls." A harsh verdict on a brilliant course, although it is still true today that a cool nerve is needed to not lose your head and a stack of balls among the dunes.

Walking onto the 1st tee for your maiden outing is an exciting moment, yet the anticipation can turn into intrigue as you stare down the fairway and catch sight of the town's cemetery over a stone wall just to the right. Even with the morbid start, the opener is a relatively gentle introduction to a course that gets

Without question, it [Ballybunion] is the most exhilarating golf venue in the British Isles.

MARK BROWN

THE COURSE

Sharp contours on both the fairways and the greens are distinctive features of the Old Course, where there are no trees to negotiate but play is forever at the mercy of the offshore winds and breezes. There are few blind shots, and the course demands that you play accurate shots onto the green.

The 11th hole is famous for its great ocean views and challenging shots

The green at the 16th is particularly exposed to the elements

The green is guarded by bunkers, left and right

A central bunker awaits a less-than-perfect drive

The fairway looks frighteningly narrow from the tee and tongues of rough eat into it from all sides

A series of stepped "terraces" lead you down to a plateau green nestled among sand hills and perilously close to the drop into the Atlantic

BALLYBUNION

Sandhill Road, Ballybunion,
Co. Kerry, Ireland
www.ballybuniongolfclub.com

THE OLD COURSE

FOUNDED 1893
LENGTH 6,739 yards (6,162 m)
PAR 71
DESIGNERS James McKenna, Tom Simpson, Tom Watson

SELECTED CHAMPIONS

IRISH PROFESSIONAL CHAMPIONSHIP
Harry Bradshaw (1957)
MURPHY'S IRISH OPEN Patrick Sjoland (2000)
PALMER CUP (UNIVERSITIES CUP)
Europe (2004)

CARD OF THE COURSE

THE FRONT NINE			THE BACK NINE		
HOLE	YARDS	PAR	HOLE	YARDS	PAR
1	405	4	10	356	4
2	439	4	11	471	4
3	218	3	12	209	3
4	527	5	13	498	5
5	554	5	14	130	3
6	383	4	15	209	3
7	425	4	16	513	5
8	157	3	17	399	4
9	462	4	18	383	4
OUT	3,570	36	IN	3,169	35

The dramatic 11th

HOLE 11 A MAJESTIC MONSTER

As dramatic as any par-4 in golf, the 11th is known the world over as one of the greatest links holes on the planet. The setting is majestic. All the way down the right of this 471-yard (431 m) bunkerless monster, the ocean crashes onto the beach some 30 to 40 ft (9 to 12 m) below. This mixture of "on-the-edge" shotmaking and the incredible vistas make this a hole every golfer should play.

---

tougher and tougher. The roller-coaster nature of the fairways can take its toll on a game, as rarely would you play off a truly flat lie. Approach shots are often played from these hanging lies into greens that perch on a raised area of ground with drop-offs into grassy swales. Exact striking is always needed at Ballybunion.

A TRULY ENJOYABLE RIDE

The Old Course is best known for its 11th hole (see above), its five par-3s, and the last three holes that all skirt right to left around large dunes and flirt with the sea. The short holes are truly spectacular, and, quirkily, three of them are found within a 4-hole stretch on the back nine. Probably the pick of the par-3s is the 15th, which plays downhill toward the ocean. Its green is long and two-tiered, set down in the dunes and studded with four bunkers. With the wind in your face off the ocean, it can be a hellish shot in.

With a decent score, going the last three holes can make or break a round. A birdie is definitely on at the 16th, but the tee-shot fired from the beachside will cause trouble. It is semi-blind, and you have to decide how much of the dogleg to bite off before striking up a dune-lined valley to the green, which is particularly exposed to the elements.

The 17th is another severe dogleg, this time played back down toward the beach and then around to the left along the shoreline. Finally, the home hole is a brute of an uphill par-4. Its fairway is split in two by a yawning bunker, and the green is surrounded by steep, grassy banks and three pot bunkers.

Ballybunion's Old Course is a truly enjoyable ride over a dramatic landscape. It is also very challenging, especially in a hard breeze, and in parts alarmingly idiosyncratic, but its holes stand alone as memorable and fun despite their difficulty.

CLINTON PLAYS A ROUND

In 1998, President Bill Clinton played on the Old Course at the end of his official visit to Ireland. A life-size bronze statue of the president, ready to tee off, stands in the center of town in commemoration of the visit.

Distinguished visitor

Royal County Down, NORTHERN IRELAND

An exhilarating ride over untamed country, Royal County Down is many golfers' idea of heaven and hell together—a marriage best described as a brutal beauty. With many fairways framed by thick gorse and boasting 130 distinctive bunkers, the course has many quirks and idiosyncrasies that are both enthralling and punishing. Yet despite these ultra-traditional nuances, this unique links has become a favorite the world over.

THE COURSE

Backed by the imposing fells of the Mountains of Mourne and skirting close to the Irish Sea, this rugged and uncompromising links is both delightful and exasperating in its traditional style. Blind shots and fortuitous bounces play with the head as well as the game.

The 15th has a wide fairway and its green is like an upturned saucer

The 16th green is guarded by large bunkers

High dunes with gorse and heather border the 13th

The long, narrow 8th green slopes from front to back

The 1st fairway is contoured, with well-placed bunkers

The hole plays over a sea of gorse and several deep greenside bunkers

The green is narrow and long, with sharp fall-offs on both sides and at the back

HOLE 4 A CARD WRECKER

This par-3 has one of the finest views and is much photographed. The back tee perches high among the dunes, and a sea of gorse stands between you and the green. There are 10 bunkers in play (seven are short of the green). Nothing but a well-struck straight shot will do to hold the putting surface.

ROYAL COUNTY DOWN

36 Golf Links Road, Newcastle,
Co Down, Northern Ireland, BT33 0AN
www.royalcountydown.org

THE LINKS COURSE

FOUNDED 1900
LENGTH 7,186 yards (6,571 m)
PAR 71
DESIGNER George Combe

SELECTED CHAMPIONS

AMATEUR CHAMPIONSHIP Michael Bonallack (1970); Graeme Storm (1999)
SENIORS BRITISH OPEN Christy O'Connor Jr. (2000); Ian Stanley (2001); Noburo Sugai (2002)
WALKER CUP US (2007)

CARD OF THE COURSE

THE FRONT NINE			THE BACK NINE		
HOLE	YARDS	PAR	HOLE	YARDS	PAR
1	539	5	10	196	3
2	444	4	11	442	4
3	475	4	12	525	5
4	229	3	13	446	4
5	440	4	14	212	3
6	396	4	15	468	4
7	144	3	16	337	4
8	429	4	17	433	4
9	483	4	18	548	5
OUT	3,579	35	IN	3,607	36

● The fantastic 4th

Golf never has been fair, even when its early pioneers took to the links. Over the years, we have tried to iron out the traditional idiosyncrasies many modern players find infuriating, but that fortune still always plays a part in golf has never been truer than at Royal County Down. Of all the finest links, this has to be the one that most combines the need for great skill and good fortune.

A SENSE OF THE UNKNOWN

Old Tom Morris was originally credited with the design of the course, but little of his layout remains. Member George Combe shifted the holes from the flatter part of the coastal strip into the wilder, more crumpled dunes nearby. In 1900, he had no earthmovers, only men and horses, so the holes took on the sand hills headfirst. His trademark blind holes remain in abundance.

A golfer stands on many a tee with a marker post or white stone on the horizon as a guide for caressing a drive. Not knowing what is over the top can cause timid players to sweat, but the sense of the unknown can also be a joy. Sometimes there is nothing finer than to nail one over the marker, walk to the brow of the hill, and spot your ball smack bang in the middle of the fairway. It is more important for that to happen here than anywhere, as the trouble you can find otherwise is nasty indeed.

▲ **ACROSS THE WHOLE LINKS,** a tumble of dunes erupts boldly, covered in gnarled grasses and vast tracts of gorse and heather.

The bunkers are deep and thoughtfully placed, with an almost disheveled look, where neat faces are replaced by grasping fronds of grass and patches of heather. This deliberately natural state adds to the mystique of the place, especially compared with the beautifully kept fairways and emerald greens.

As opening holes go, the 1st has just about everything. A potential two-shot par-5 makes you think of a birdie, but it is fraught with danger. The waters of Dundrum Bay hug the right side just over the top of the dunes while snagging banks line the left. Anything pitching short of the slightly sunken green is liable to bound away, but at least you can see where you are going.

This cannot be said of several of the subsequent holes. At the 5th, for example, the hole swings from left to right, and a bright-white rock gleams at you on the rise in an attempt to show you the way. Long hitters may want to hit over it with a fade or fire just right of it as the hole bends that way. However, overdo it and gorse will snaffle your drive. You will have a shorter shot to the green if you take the bolder route, but perhaps the cagey way is to take less club and go down the left. The dangers around this green are typical of the course: fringed bunkers, run-offs, and banks at the back with heather and rough. The safe miss is short and straight, as with nearly all the greens here. Overclubbing brings nothing but trouble.

The 8th green has big drops into trouble around it (which you cannot see from the fairway). The long par-4 9th has a disconcerting blind drive and, if it was not for some work Harry Colt did in the 1920s, the second shot would still be blind, too. This is County Down's most famous hole, along with the Colt-inspired 4th.

THE RUN FOR HOME

Although the front nine is the more heralded—Tom Watson called it "as fine a nine holes as I have ever played"—the run for home also has much to admire. It has two cracking par-3s, some monstrous two-shotters, with the 13th particularly acclaimed, and a guts-or-glory par-5 home hole that features 24 devilish bunkers. It all adds up to a rare, formidable, heart-in-the-mouth challenge in the most superb of surroundings.

▲ **THE 10TH IS FULL OF CHARACTER,** with the tee beside the clubhouse window and a large green guarded by bunkers.

OPEN FOR BUSINESS

Technically, Royal County Down could host the Open as it is part of the UK and it certainly has the pedigree. The main reason it has never been granted the honor is politics, as the area was considered too great a security risk. The Open has only twice been played in Northern Ireland—at Royal Portrush in 1951 and 2019. In recent times, however, the Royal & Ancient Golf Club of St. Andrews, the game's governing body and organizer of British championships, has taken the Seniors British Open to County Down, meaning the names so synonymous with the Open, such as Jack Nicklaus and Tom Watson, have been able to enjoy her delights.

Turnberry, SCOTLAND

Classy, elegant and enjoyable, the Ailsa Course at Turnberry in Ayrshire boasts one of the most beautiful settings in golf. Overlooking the Irish Sea, with the Isle of Arran and the granite dome of Ailsa Craig dominating the seaward horizon and an old lighthouse hovering on the headland, its remarkable holes provide a dramatic challenge that has always produced great champions.

Scenery this good can overshadow a mediocre course. At Turnberry, however, the gentle fall of the land taking the holes all the way down to the craggy rocks enhances an already dazzling links.

Golf has been played on this coastline stretch since the turn of the 20th century, but the sport took a back seat during the World Wars, when the fairways were flattened and tarmac was laid to create an airfield. Golf was almost abandoned until Frank Hole, owner of the nearby opulent whitewashed hotel, insisted the course should be resurrected. It was left to Mackenzie Ross to make the place look natural again and in 1951, after intensive work, it reopened—and what a course it became. In 2014, it was bought by the Trump Organization and rebranded as "Trump Turnberry."

TURNING UP THE HEAT

The 1st hole is a short four that breaks you in gently, but then the heat is immediately turned up on your game. After two tough two-shotters, the course runs north and close to the shoreline for five holes that test your driving in particular. Golf can often be into and across the wind, making this string of holes one to tough out rather than burn up.

The 8th green is only a few feet from the rocky oblivion on the left, but the walk to the 9th—named Bruce's Castle and Turnberry's most famous hole (see left)—will capture your attention the most. The 10th hugs the beach and is high in shot values. Its new tee in front of the lighthouse requires a carry of 220 yards (200 m) over water and rocks to reach the fairway and from there you often need a piercing long iron to find the green.

After the pretty 11th, played from a tee close to the sea, the course turns inland and tacks back over the gorse-spattered and heavily grassed dunes. On every hole coming home, there is at least one heart-stopping shot: the pick of the knee-knockers are probably the drive-dangerous 13th, the tee shot at the hit-and-hope par-3

◀ **THE CHAMPIONSHIP TEE FOR THE 9TH** teeters on a rocky promontory, with the lighthouse on the left, a rugged inlet in front and a distant cairn indicating the fairway.

15th, the approach over the burn on the 16th and the drive between dunes at the 17th.

The Open Championship returned for its fourth visit in 2009, and much work was done to toughen up the course. Even though the Ailsa Course could always be a challenge in a wind, on a calm day, it lacked a true fear factor. Many of the fairway bunkers were becoming too easy to miss; others were not a stern enough test. Today, thanks to the work done in conjunction with the Royal & Ancient, the course has been lengthened and tightened, bringing far more pressure shots than before. Seventeen new fairway bunkers were added and four more on approaches. In 2016, further improvements were made to this world-class course.

In 2009, Stewart Cink mastered the course to capture the Open in a round of 278. Tom Watson was up with the best when he outlasted Jack Nicklaus in 1977; Greg Norman shot a 63 in 1986 as the rest of the field floundered; in 1994, Nick Price came home in only 31 shots on Sunday, including a monster eagle at the 17th.

A WONDERFUL CHALLENGE

Turnberry's fairness and variety means a golfer needs all the shots and a great brain to conquer it. You need to shape drives, hit bump-and-runs, and be imaginative around the greens, which are generous in size and vary greatly in their shaping. It is no surprise that all three Open winners here were fantastic putters, too.

It is very rare indeed to find a golfer who has visited Turnberry and not wanted to return, because the Ailsa Course checks all the boxes. It is simply a wonderful challenge in the most glorious of surroundings.

DUEL IN THE SUN

A celebrated head-to-head between Jack Nicklaus and Tom Watson (see pp.228–229) was played out at Turnberry in 1977. As Tom led by one going down the last, he stroked a 7-iron toward the pin. Jack gouged a 7-iron out of thick grass, found the green, then grabbed a birdie, but Tom kept his nerve to win and the hole was named "Duel in the Sun."

Tom Watson and Jack Nicklaus go head-to-head

THE COURSE

A breathtaking beauty set hard to the crashing waves of the Irish Sea. It is a demure, tranquil links where bunkers are used sparingly but cleverly, and its subtle lines and constant change of pace mean finesse and power have to be used hand in hand.

The 9th green has nasty grassy humps but no bunkers

After the 11th green, the course turns inland

An awkward bank protects the front of the 13th green

The 16th green is guarded by a burn with sloping banks

Anything short of the 6th green may find sand or roll back down the hill

Missing the 4th green on the left spells disaster

HOLE 16 "WEE BURN"

The name of the hole "Wee Burn" undersells the 16th. Yes, the channel of water meandering across the front and right of the green is small, but the banks that slope down to it are not. Virtually any ball-pitching short or right of the putting surface will struggle to keep dry as a huge rounded bank dips steeply down to Wilson's Burn, dragging underhit shots into trouble. Yet a bolder shot designed to take the burn out of play can struggle to hold the green, too—especially downwind—often leaving either a delicate chip or a deft putt from the back. The hole is 50 yards (46 m) longer than it was in 1994 and doglegs left to right, making the approach even more difficult.

TURNBERRY

The Westin Turnberry Resort, Turnberry, Ayrshire, Scotland, KA26 9LT
www.turnberry.co.uk

THE AILSA COURSE

FOUNDED 1946
LENGTH 7,489 yards (6,848 m)
PAR 71
COURSE RECORD 63 Greg Norman (1986)
DESIGNER Mackenzie Ross

SELECTED CHAMPIONS

OPEN CHAMPIONSHIP Tom Watson (1977); Greg Norman (1986); Nick Price (1994); Stewart Cink (2009)
WOMEN'S BRITISH OPEN Karrie Webb (2002)
SENIORS BRITISH OPEN Tom Watson (2003); Loren Roberts (2006)

CARD OF THE COURSE

THE FRONT NINE			THE BACK NINE		
HOLE	YARDS	PAR	HOLE	YARDS	PAR
1	441	4	10	565	5
2	425	4	11	215	3
3	496	4	12	468	4
4	194	3	13	409	4
5	531	5	14	568	5
6	171	3	15	234	3
7	575	5	16	479	4
8	476	4	17	509	4
9	248	3	18	485	4
OUT	**3,557**	**35**	**IN**	**3,932**	**36**

The bridge at the 16th

The new doglegged fairway makes the approach even more dangerous

Anything short or right will be sucked into the burn by steep, smooth sides

Kingsbarns, SCOTLAND

One of the few links to have been built in modern times, Kingsbarns is as much a feat of civil engineering as it is a brilliant piece of course design. While many of the holes unashamedly pay homage to other links courses, such as St. Andrews, Turnberry, and Carnoustie, Kingsbarns is a spectacular addition to links culture and robustly holds its own against the more vaunted links several miles away at the "Home of Golf."

Kingsbarns has a remarkable tale to tell. This hamlet, a few miles southeast of St. Andrews, has had a fluctuating love affair with golf since the late 1700s. The original links was plowed over in 1850 by the tenant farmer, and golf did not return to the sweep of linksland above Kingsbarns Bay until 1922, when famous St. Andrews professional Willie Auchterlonie laid out nine new holes. With the onset of war in 1939, it suffered again and was mined for coastal defenses.

It took another five decades for the rather flat pasture to see golf again—and what a transformation. Before the earthmovers rolled in to craft this genius of a links, the land simply fell gradually toward the sea, split only by a natural terrace. There were no dunes to speak of, just easy pasture that farm machinery could run smoothly over.

Then Americans Mark Parsinen and Kyle Phillips got hold of the prime piece of seaside above the dark, crusty rocks of the North Sea and turned their dreams into a links wonder. After thousands of hours of manipulating the land to build natural-looking dunes, a course rose from the levels, and now no one can tell that this higgledy-piggledy land has not been like this for centuries.

STRATEGY AND GUILE

Parsinen and Phillips's team formed the features that the holes would weave into. They thought of every detail and their inspiration was drawn from all the great links courses. They are unabashed when they say a little piece of St. Andrews is there, along with strategic influences from Carnoustie and others, right down to the sympathetic mimicking of Turnberry's ball-gobbling burn at the 16th, which appears at Kingsbarns's home hole. These are not copies but rather a homage to the great links, for Kingsbarns stands alone in its own right.

Every hole is fun as well as distinctive. No two holes are alike, yet the course comes together as a group

▶ **QUICK AND CHALLENGING GREENS,** such as the 5th, lie in wait amid the evening shadows cast across the low-lying artificial dunes beside Kingsbarns Bay.

wonderfully well. The par-3s are a varied test—the 15th is the star, with its green delightfully placed over a rocky inlet. Most courses have a few humdrum slogs of par-4s, but at Kingsbarns, they go in for strategy and guile rather than out-and-out length. All par-5s are risk-and-reward chances, reachable for some but with trouble lurking for the brave.

Every hole gives you a choice—either safety first or the brave line. The bolder the drive, the easier the approach tends to be, and for every pin position, there is a preferred line to take off the tee.

A BREATHTAKING GAMBLE

There is no letup on the greens either, as most are quick and heavily contoured. Again, it would have been easy to lay down mundane putting surfaces, but instead the designers were bold and looked for inspiration from some of the more ancient links, such as Prestwick. A few greens border on the unfair, but that, in its way, is what is so distinctive about Kingsbarns, and there is no denying you will remember them. Kingsbarns was a breathtaking gamble, but the bold features mean it has come off superbly and will stand the test of time.

INFAMOUS GREEN

Kingsbarns is notorious for its green designs, and none are more infamous than the 9th. After just one year of play, it was recontoured and had 1 ft (30 cm) shaved off the height of the middle shelf. It remains a very difficult target with a raised and shallow plateau running across the green, and with many wicked potential pin positions.

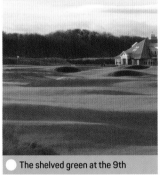

● The shelved green at the 9th

THE COURSE

This modern great is brilliant in its variety and is a very fair test despite some vast rolling greens. It has been made to look so natural and the gnarled dunes have been cleverly groomed and the bunkers placed to create a strategic gem.

● The sloping 12th green

KINGSBARNS

Kingsbarns, St .Andrews,
Fife, Scotland, KY16 8QD
www.kingsbarns.com

THE COURSE

FOUNDED 2000
LENGTH 7,126 yards (6,516 m)
PAR 70
COURSE RECORD 62 Lee Westwood (2003)
DESIGNERS Mark Parsinen, Kyle Phillips

SELECTED CHAMPIONS

DUNHILL LINKS CHAMPIONSHIP (WITH ST. ANDREWS AND CARNOUSTIE)
Paul Lawrie (2001); Pádraig Harrington (2002, 2006); Lee Westwood (2003); Stephen Gallacher (2004); Colin Montgomerie (2005); Nick Dougherty (2007)

Loosely based on the 18th at Pebble Beach, the hole curves gracefully from right to left around the rocks

The sloping green is narrow and about 70 yards (64 m) long

A bold drive over the bunker on the 4th leaves the easiest approach

The best tee shot is down the left of the 5th fairway

A burn protects the 18th green

Right-to-left contours dominate the 7th fairway

The 15th green is located over a rocky inlet

The large bunker guards the 12th green

HOLE 12 STAGGERING SCENERY

Scenically, this is the stand-out hole at Kingsbarns. If you can tear your eyes off the staggering view of the crashing waters on the arc of rocks, you will see a master hole to go with the beauty. A big drive down the left side will leave a tempting second to the long sloping green. The safe route is to lay the second up to the right of the fairway, then pitch down the length of the green. Birdies and double bogies galore.

CARD OF THE COURSE

THE FRONT NINE			THE BACK NINE		
HOLE	YARDS	PAR	HOLE	YARDS	PAR
1	414	4	10	387	4
2	200	3	11	455	4
3	516	5	12	606	5
4	408	4	13	148	3
5	398	4	14	366	4
6	337	4	15	212	3
7	470	4	16	565	5
8	168	3	17	474	4
9	558	5	18	444	4
OUT	3,469	36	IN	3,657	36

Royal Birkdale, ENGLAND

Etched into the large sand dunes overlooking the Irish Sea, Royal Birkdale is a rough-and-tumble challenge with a fantastic array of varied holes. With a reputation for being hard but fair, it is often ranked as the best course in England. Located on the west coast of Lancashire, it sits on the greatest stretch of linksland in the country, which gives it the "wow" factor that all golfers love.

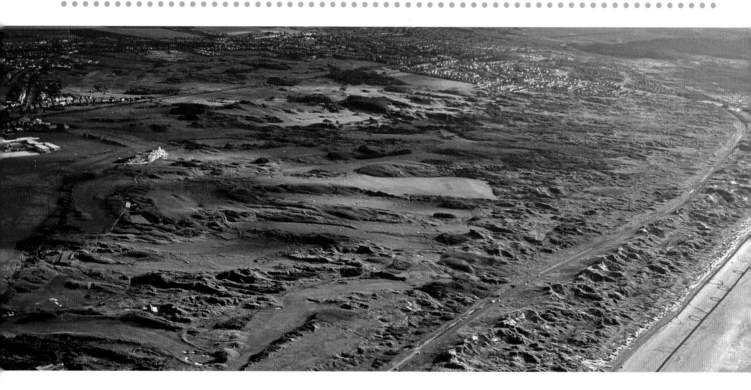

4TH TIME LUCKY

At the age of 24, Peter Thomson of Australia won the Open Championship at Royal Birkdale in 1954 with a final round of 71. Thomson had made three previous attempts to win the Open but went on to win it four more times—in 1955, 1956, 1958, and 1965. This last victory was also at Royal Birkdale.

Thomson and the trophy

The big west-coast dunescape piled up by the prevailing westerly wind over thousands of years was the perfect place to create a "stadium-style" links, where fairways and greens are watched over by huge piles of sand swaying with wild grasses. Over the fence to the south lie two more golf clubs—Hillside and Southport & Ainsdale—which are both magnificent tests sharing the same terrain, but Royal Birkdale stands out for its boldness and escapism.

AN EVOLVING COURSE

Modern course builders can only dream of having such a brilliant piece of land to work with, but it still needs a clever eye to get the best out of it and lay out a truly spectacular golf course. Despite the club being formed in 1889, it was not until the 1930s that a pair of talented designers were commissioned to update the course and get the best out of the linksland. Five-time Open champion J. H. Taylor and his architect partner Fredrick Hawtree routed the fairways through natural valleys between the dunes and sited the greens superbly—many nestled in the sand hills, creating mini amphitheaters. Because they used the valley floors, instead of riding the mounds, the fairways were not excessively contoured, and Birkdale's reputation for fairness was born.

After Arnold Palmer's slaying of the course in the 1961 Open, it was thought crucial to update the links, both in terms of difficulty and spectator viewing. Hawtree's son Fred was asked to add bite, and among his changes was a brand-new hole in the farthest reach of the course. One of the most celebrated short holes in golf, the par-3 12th cannot be improved on. It is beautiful to the eye, and the green perches above a shaved apron across a wasteland of scrub surrounded on three sides by tall, fearful dunes.

The Art Deco clubhouse

The front corners are studded with pot bunkers, and it takes an extremely well-struck long iron to hit it.

In preparation for the 2008 Open, Martin Hawtree, son of Fred Jr., removed 12 fairway bunkers and added 16 new ones. Six new championship tees not only add length but have changed the lines of play on many holes, making the course a tougher test but still wonderfully honest.

THE MANLY FIGHT

The world's best golfers have always contended with long carries over wild space from small, secluded tees, but now the fairways are harder to find and need long, shaped shots, not just big, straight blasts. When you reach the greens here, you face subtly undulating surfaces rather than ridiculously severe slopes.

The art of green-reading is such an important factor at Birkdale. One famous example saw the emergence of a modern genius. In the dry and dusty 1976 Open, the shot that Severiano Ballesteros played on the final hole to secure his runner-up spot has gone down in folklore. He had missed the 18th green then produced a piece of magic to thread a running chip from the rough between two bunkers and down to the hole to save his par.

If you survive the manly fight, especially the run-in from the 15th, you are greeted by the landmark white Art Deco clubhouse, reminiscent of an ocean liner. Whatever a golfer scores here, they will know that they have been on a beautiful walk on the wild side.

◄ **FEW GOLFERS** are privileged to have a plaque on any course for a historic feat, yet Arnold Palmer has one at Royal Birkdale on the 16th. It marks a spot just off the right edge of the fairway among the willow scrub from where, in the 1961 Open, he smashed a 6-iron onto the green in the second round. It astounded onlookers, and the fearsome blow had to be commemorated.

THE COURSE

In a huge dunescape, the holes weave down the valleys between the sand hills. Big carries over crumpled ground, angled fairways, devious bunkering and subtle greens make this a fair but bruising encounter in a wind.

An awkward bunker guards the front left of the 11th green

A small channel runs along the left of the 6th fairway

Two bunkers lie in wait on the right of the 17th fairway

The 1st hole has the narrowest fairway, with dune grass on the left

The hole plays as a slight dogleg, more so from the back tee

The pear-shaped green is guarded by two front bunkers

ROYAL BIRKDALE
Royal Birkdale Golf Club, Waterloo Road, Southport, England, PR8 2LX
www.royalbirkdale.com

THE COURSE
FOUNDED 1889
LENGTH 7,156 yards (6,543 m)
PAR 70
DESIGNERS J. H. Taylor, Fred Hawtree Sr., Fred Hawtree Jr., Martin Hawtree
COURSE RECORD 65
Tiger Woods (1998), John Huston (1998)

SELECTED CHAMPIONS
OPEN CHAMPIONSHIP Peter Thomson (1954, 1965); Arnold Palmer (1961); Lee Trevino (1971); Johnny Miller (1976); Tom Watson (1983); Ian Baker-Finch (1991); Mark O'Meara (1998); Jordan Spieth (2017)
RYDER CUP US (1965); GB&I tied with US

CARD OF THE COURSE

THE FRONT NINE			THE BACK NINE		
HOLE	YARDS	PAR	HOLE	YARDS	PAR
1	448	4	10	402	4
2	422	4	11	436	4
3	451	4	12	183	3
4	199	3	13	499	4
5	346	4	14	200	3
6	499	4	15	542	5
7	177	3	16	438	4
8	458	4	17	576	5
9	416	4	18	473	4
OUT	3,416	34	IN	3,740	36

HOLE 18 MOMENTOUS HOLE
The scene of many great shots and moments, the home hole is very demanding. There is a bunker in the middle of the split fairway at about 230 yards (210 m) from the tee, which should pose problems only in the wind. Instead, the thick rough and gorse on the right are more of a threat. Once on the fairway, a long iron will be needed to thread between two front bunkers to find the pear-shaped green. In the 1965 Ryder Cup, Arnold Palmer issued the coup de grâce to the Great Britain and Ireland team by cracking a 3-wood to 4 ft (1.2 m). Tom Watson also hit a mind-blowing shot here in the 1983 Open, firing a 2-iron from 213 yards (195 m) out through the narrow 15-yard (14 m) entrance to 18 ft (5.5 m). He calmly took two putts and won by one shot from Hale Irwin and Andy Bean.

The pear-shaped 18th green

Muirfield, SCOTLAND

Home to the oldest golf club in the world—The Honourable Company of Edinburgh Golfers— this links overlooks the Firth of Forth near Edinburgh. It is often rated the finest course in the British Isles and among the top-10 in the world. In 1744, members of the golf club drew up the game's first official rules, the "Articles & Laws in Playing at Golf," to be followed during that year's inaugural golf competition, which was won by Gordon Rattray.

It is hard to argue with the experts who rate this course so highly. Muirfield is a stupendous design, not because it is the most dramatic course, or even the toughest, but because it is clever and ultimately the fairest of all the great links. In the scheme of links history, this demure course is not all that old, coming into existence in 1891, almost 150 years after the club was formed in 1744. Since that day, it has been at the forefront of golf, wooing all who are lucky enough to have walked its fairways.

In 1836, The Honourable Company moved, because of overcrowding, from the Leith Links, where they played on only five holes, to the nine holes of the Old Course at Musselburgh. Then they moved again to the present location to the east of Edinburgh and laid out their course on the far-from-wild open fields just a few hundred yards from the sea.

Not blessed with tumultuous dunes, the course design team, led by Old Tom Morris, relied more on the particular placing of the deep bunkers to test both strategy and ball-striking, but more than that, they brilliantly devised a way of constantly changing the directions of the holes. The outward nine runs in a clockwise direction and hugs the perimeter of the site. Then, cunningly, the holes reverse and run counterclockwise within the outer nine.

A CEREBRAL TEST

A golfer must contend with 13 changes of direction— only the 3rd, 4th, and 5th can be called a stretch of holes running the same way. On every tee, the wind has to be thought about, and it is these subtle changes, combined with the brilliant bunkering, that makes Muirfield a cerebral test. So good was the original layout that the great Harry Colt was able to keep it roughly the same when he added some bite in 1922. If you glance down the list of Open Championship winners, it seems the cream always rises to the top.

▶ **THE GREEN AT THE PAR-3 13TH** is narrow, slopes from back to front, and is protected by three bunkers on the right and two on the left.

KEY MOMENTS ....

◄ **NICK FALDO FINALLY** fulfilled his promise and won his first Major title at Muirfield in 1987 with a perfect 18, but he had to do it the hard way. Starting the final round level with David Frost and one behind Paul Azinger, Faldo strung together a remarkable 18 pars in a row. His mix of pure striking, thoughtful play, and scrambling culminated in a nervy 4 ft (1.2 m) putt at the last.

◄ **ERNIE ELS'S SHOT OF THE YEAR** came at the tough par-3 13th, where severe bunkers eat into the putting surface like trenches. He found a bunker on the left of the green on the final round of the 2002 Open. Els recalls, "The ball was tight against the face of the bunker and just getting it out—never mind close—would be a reasonable result, I thought. I pulled out my 59-degree sand wedge and I said to my caddie, 'I'm going to hit this as hard as I can.' I was amazed. I got it out and almost holed it! It was a really, really good save and helped me win the Open." It was voted European Tour Shot of the Year.

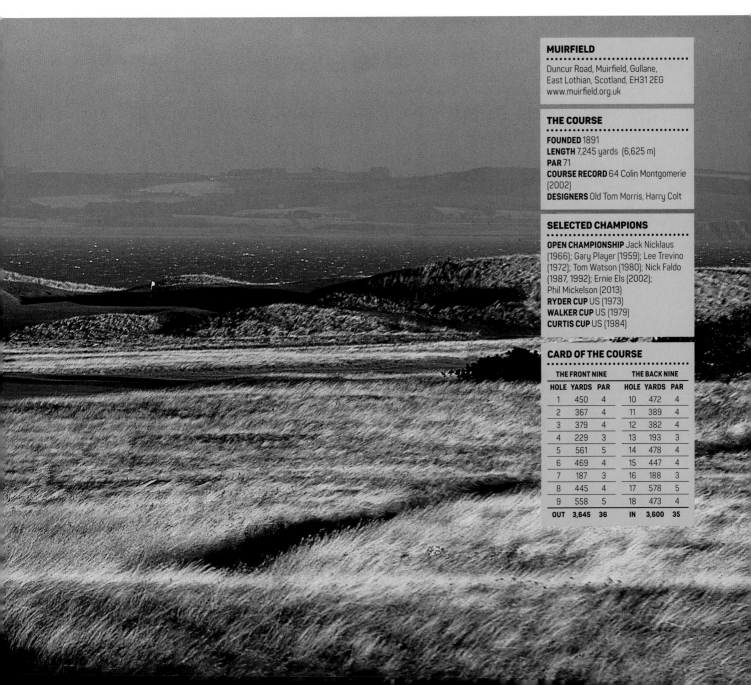

MUIRFIELD
Duncur Road, Muirfield, Gullane, East Lothian, Scotland, EH31 2EG
www.muirfield.org.uk

THE COURSE
FOUNDED 1891
LENGTH 7,245 yards (6,625 m)
PAR 71
COURSE RECORD 64 Colin Montgomerie (2002)
DESIGNERS Old Tom Morris, Harry Colt

SELECTED CHAMPIONS
OPEN CHAMPIONSHIP Jack Nicklaus (1966); Gary Player (1959); Lee Trevino (1972); Tom Watson (1980); Nick Faldo (1987, 1992); Ernie Els (2002); Phil Mickelson (2013)
RYDER CUP US (1973)
WALKER CUP US (1979)
CURTIS CUP US (1984)

CARD OF THE COURSE

THE FRONT NINE			THE BACK NINE		
HOLE	YARDS	PAR	HOLE	YARDS	PAR
1	450	4	10	472	4
2	367	4	11	389	4
3	379	4	12	382	4
4	229	3	13	193	3
5	561	5	14	478	4
6	469	4	15	447	4
7	187	3	16	188	3
8	445	4	17	578	5
9	558	5	18	473	4
OUT	**3,645**	**36**	**IN**	**3,600**	**35**

● The raised green at the 3rd

● The comfortable locker room

● The expansive 10th hole

THE COURSE

Known as the fairest links of them all, Muirfield is an honest but tough examination on a gently sloping "meadow." Deep bunkering, subtle changes of direction, and cambered greens make it a strategic beauty.

THE FRONT NINE ❶ A tough start with a C-shaped trap down the left and thick rough on both sides. ❷ Straightforward par-4, but a tricky green guarded front right by a nest of traps. ❸ Two large sand hills pinch the fairway and can obstruct the view to the green beyond. ❹ Although bunkers patrol the front the green has run-offs all around. ❺ Drive over the fairway traps on the right for the best line in. ❻ Four traps in the lee of the dogleg have to be avoided for any chance at par. ❼ Difficult to judge the club as the green sits level with your eyeline and with nothing beyond. ❽ A nasty collection of sand sits in the corner of the dogleg on the right. ❾ A great par-5 that needs careful plotting.

THE BACK NINE ❿ A semi-blind approach thanks to two large cross bunkers. ⓫ The only true blind shot with a drive over a large saddle. ⓬ The best line to the green is from the left side toward the bunker. ⓭ A raised and angled green deviously bunkered on both sides. ⓮ Three traps on the left and a solo bunker on the right patrol the drive. ⓯ Thirteen bunkers taunt you for the entire length of the hole. Precision is key. ⓰ Classy three with several deep traps and a steep drop off the left side. ⓱ Reachable in two, and the green sits in a natural amphitheater. ⓲ Exacting finish needing a great strike to find the green and avoid the ring bunker on the right.

The flat, moundless green sits only yards from the boundary wall

The fairway has a large bunker on the left at 260 yards (238 m) out and a diagonal string of five bunkers

HOLE 9 **FEARSOME AND HAZARDOUS**
Though not long for a modern par-5, the 9th is dangerous. The tee shot can be fearsome, especially into the wind, with an Out of Bounds stone wall all along the left of the hole and thick rough on the right. After avoiding these hazards and the large fairway bunker, it is decision time—a layup or a go at the green. The long approach is trickily angled, and the more you go right to avoid the wall, the more the string of bunkers comes into play. Many feel this is a birdie hole, but it has entrapped the best, too.

The tee shot at the 16th must avoid the bunkers around the green

The long approach to the 9th green must avoid a string of bunkers

Approach shots can fall prey to the bunkers around the 11th green

Bunkers congregate where tee shots land on the 5th fairway

A crosswind often makes the tee shot even more demanding

The green drops off sharply to the left and has five bunkers at the front corners, with two more on the right

HOLE 16 **ABSOLUTE PRECISION**
A brilliant one-shotter that requires absolute precision with a mid to long iron depending on the wind. Going long may seem preferable, but the green tilts slightly from the back and to the front right, making putting quite tricky from beyond the hole.

The banks around the green can act as a ball gatherer

A cluster of bunkers cross the hole at around 110 yards (100 m) short of the green

HOLE 17 **STRATEGIC THINKING**
This hole can turn fortunes as it is reachable in two par-5s, given a favorable wind. However, such is the severity of the bunkers up the left and also short of the green that a par has to be earned with a good strategy and precise striking. The banks around the green make for an awkward chip if the ball stays up in the grass.

○ The angled and well-protected 13th green

○ TV crew above the 16th green in 2007

Harold Hilton won the first of Muirfield's Opens in 1892, and from then on, the list of winners includes many of the greatest names in golf—Harry Vardon, James Braid, Walter Hagen, Henry Cotton, Gary Player, Lee Trevino, Tom Watson, Jack Nicklaus, Nick Faldo, Ernie Els, and Phil Mickelson. The course also holds the distinction of being the only course to have held the Open and the Amateur as well as all three of the transatlantic team contests—the Ryder, Walker, and Curtis Cups.

A REPUTATION FOR HONESTY

Those golfers fortunate to have played in these various championships are always impressed by Muirfield's honesty. Holes glide through golden knee-high rough and very few have an up-and-down nature. There is only one truly blind shot—the drive at the 11th—but generally what you see is what you get.

Fairways are predominantly straight, but several of them dogleg almost imperceptibly and nests of traps patrol the corners. Because it lies on quite flat land, the fairways, along with Royal Birkdale's, are probably the least contoured of all on the Open course list. It means that the best ball strikers are not compromised by fortune so much and can get the best out of their game. All a golfer needs to do is avoid the devilish bunkers—easier said than done since there are more than 150 eager to devour even a slightly off-line shot.

They are particularly gruesome on the short holes, where missing the green is not a savory option. Seven deep traps are entrenched around the 16th, and coming in the home stretch as it does, its 186 uphill yards become a potential card wrecker. Even if you avoid the numerous traps on any of Muirfield's holes and find the greens, the work is not done—far from it. Although not lightning fast, the greens are almost always firm and sloping and tend to filter off shots that land close to the edges. Putting is an art here.

Muirfield is hard to fault golf-wise as it tests the all-around quality of a game like few others. The only slight quibble from some who like to be truly wowed is the lack of real drama in its landscape. Unassuming and reserved rather than eye-popping and spectacular, to walk Muirfield's holes is a more serene experience than at other more rough-and-tumble links. It is a special place to play because of that. It is a thinking man's course, not necessarily for cavaliers—and pure and simple, it is a cracking challenge.

▼ **THE DISTINCTIVE RING BUNKER** to the right of the 18th green, and in front of the clubhouse, presents players with a demanding challenge at the end of their round.

St. Andrews, SCOTLAND

The Old Course is known as "The Home of Golf," and for centuries, every champion who has ever played the game has done so here. The game of golf was nurtured on this strange links—with its multitude of bunkers and double greens—and for that reason alone, there is no place like it. As Jack Nicklaus declared, "I fell in love with it the first day I played it. There's just no other golf course that is even remotely close."

The St. Andrews story is an extraordinary one. No one knows whether this is the oldest golf course in the world, but it is said that the sport has been played on the town's links since around 1400. The earliest written proof was when King James IV bought clubs in the town in 1502. Whenever it was first played, it is true to say that it is the most famous course in the world, and one that every golfer must aspire to play.

The Old Course (there are six other courses) started out as 22 holes—11 out and 11 back. In 1764, when some of the holes were deemed too short, they amalgamated a few to become 18 holes, and that is why we have that standard number today.

The Royal and Ancient Golf Club of St. Andrews is the governing body of world golf (except for US) and runs the national championships of the UK as well as being responsible for the Rules of Golf. However, despite its prominent position on the course, it does not own the links but is just one of many golf clubs that are allowed to play on the town's courses. The links are public and run by a trust. No play is allowed on Sundays on the Old Course except for major tournaments.

DOUBLE GREENS AND SINGULAR NAMES

Until the late 1890s, when Old Tom Morris tinkered with the course, a golfer played out and back to the same holes. Old Tom widened the fairways through the gorse and made the greens bigger so they could hold two flags. That is why St. Andrews has seven huge double greens, and why only the 1st, 9th, 17th, and 18th holes have their own green. This configuration is also responsible for the way the bunkers come into play, as they were designed to be a hazard whether you were going out or coming back. Many are hidden to the eye, and it comes as a shock to the first-timer to find their ball in sand from a seemingly perfect drive. Even an experienced campaigner will do well to avoid a fairway bunker in a round, so cunning are their placement.

▶ **THE SUN SETS OVER** the 18th, the most famous finishing hole in golf. Old Tom Morris considered it to be his finest work.

KEY MOMENTS

THE FIRST OF JACK NICKLAUS'S two Opens at St. Andrews in 1970 was the most memorable but probably for the wrong reason. American Doug Sanders needed two putts at the 72nd hole to win. His first stopped 3 ft (1 m) shy of the hole. Nervously and famously, he pushed his second wide to put him in an 18-hole playoff with Nicklaus. One ahead on the last, the Golden Bear (see p.137) drove to the back of the green, chipped down from the rough, and holed out for a winning birdie.

TIGER WOODS HAS PLAYED four Opens at the Old Course, winning two of them. His first, at the 2000 championship, saw him demolish the field by eight strokes and establish a record score of 269 (19-under par). It also meant that, at the age of 24, he became the youngest player to win the career Grand Slam (win all four Majors)—only the fifth golfer to do so. In 2005 (left), he won by a mere five strokes from Colin Montgomerie and registered the 10th Major of his career.

ST. ANDREWS

Pilmour House, St. Andrews, Fife, Scotland, KY16 9SF
www.standrews.com

PLAYER STATS

FOUNDED 1764 (when it was 18 holes)
LENGTH 6,721 yards (6,146 m)
PAR 72
COURSE RECORD 64 Bradley Dredge (2006)
DESIGNERS Unknown, Old Tom Morris (1890s), Alister Mackenzie (1920s)

SELECTED CHAMPIONS

OPEN CHAMPIONSHIP Jack Nicklaus (1970, 1978); Seve Ballesteros (1984); Nick Faldo (1990); John Daly (1995); Tiger Woods (2000, 2005); Louis Oosthuizen (2010); Zach Johnson (2015)
WOMEN'S BRITISH OPEN Lorena Ochoa (2007); Stacy Lewis (2013)

CARD OF THE COURSE

THE FRONT NINE			THE BACK NINE		
HOLE	YARDS	PAR	HOLE	YARDS	PAR
1	376	4	10	340	4
2	411	4	11	174	3
3	370	4	12	316	4
4	419	4	13	418	4
5	514	5	14	530	5
6	374	4	15	414	4
7	359	4	16	381	4
8	166	3	17	455	4
9	347	4	18	357	4
OUT	3,336	36	IN	3,385	36

▲ **"HELL" BUNKER IS** the largest bunker on the Old Course. This monster trap lies around 100 yards (91 m) from the green on the par-5 14th and should be avoided at all costs.

photographed feature in golf. Everyone who is anyone has strode across it and felt pride, in the same way that every newcomer feels nervous excitement on the 1st tee.

Despite the historic fame of this quirky course, the actual game of golf still has to live up to the billing. Fairways, often hidden from full view off the tee by banks of gorse and scrub, are almost ludicrously rippled and seamlessly run into many of the greens, which are also tantalizingly cambered. The art is to weigh up the wind then know which line to take off the tee for the best chance of maneuvering the ball toward the flag.

It takes many rounds to know how the ball will skip in and be affected by the slopes, and where to miss if you are

Many of these deep pits of sand, some way over head high, have acquired singularly appropriate names, such as the ominous "Hell," "Principal's Nose," "Pulpit," "The Beardies," "Coffins," "Lion's Mouth," and "Cat's Trap."

The titles of other features are also recognizable the world over—"Miss Grainger's Bosoms" appear as mounds on either side of the 15th; "The Elysian Fields" are the flat part of the 14th fairway; the "Valley of Sin" is the deep-shaved swale below the 18th green. Probably the two most notable in golf are the "Swilcan Bridge" and the "Road Hole." The ancient stone bridge over the burn that runs in front of the 1st green is the most

going to. Once on the greens, you could be faced with a very long putt. Most have huge putting surfaces—the 5th and 13th joint green is 100 yards (91 m) long, with an area of 1½ acres (0.6 hectares). The Open has been held here 27 times since 1873; you will find that most champions are those who avoid the bunkers the most and three-putt the least.

The Old Course is not to everyone's liking, simply because it is so hard to read. Even if you have done your homework, Lady Luck can turn against you. Yet it is for the very fact that nature built this unparalleled course that St. Andrews will always be cherished.

There is no other golf course in the world that can say that every great player who has ever played the game has played that golf course.

TIGER WOODS

● St. Andrews and the Eden Estuary

● The world-renowned "Swilcan Bridge"

● The infamous "Road Hole" bunker on the 17th

THE COURSE

This is a bizarre links, with its naturally rippled ground, quirky layout with shared fairways and greens, and its devious bunkering. It takes a long time to get to know, but it is the "must-play" experience in world golf. There is nothing like it on Earth.

THE FRONT NINE ① Possibly the widest fairway in golf but still a nerve-wracking experience due to the weight of history. **②** Semi-blind drive over gorse. Anything landing short of the green is prone to a bad bounce. **③** The safer line down the left leaves an approach that flirts with a large bunker. **④** There is plenty of room down the left side, but a large mound defends the front of the green. **⑤** Reachable in two downwind, but the green is 100 yards (91 m) long, often needing monstrous putts. **⑥** A dip at the front of the green dictates your strategy. Go aerial or run it through. **⑦** Difficult ridges run through the green, making putting tricky. **⑧** One of only two short holes. Avoid the two front pots. **⑨** Drivable for the longest hitters, but gorse left and two small traps await.

THE BACK NINE ⑩ A cut drive can find one of three bunkers, from which par is tough. **⑪** The dastardly "Strath" bunker is a card wrecker and guards a wickedly sloping green. **⑫** Difficult to plot through the bunkers on the drive, and a running approach may be needed to this shelf green. **⑬** Finding the "Coffins" bunkers down the left will leave you dead. **⑭** A real birdie chance if you can avoid Out of Bounds on the right and "Hell" bunker on the second. **⑮** Aim at the steeple in the distance for the best line. **⑯** The safe line is down the left but leaves a tougher approach. A steep bank crosses the front. **⑰** The safe play is to aim for the front right of the green to avoid the "Road Hole" bunker. **⑱** Best to aim for the clubhouse clock left, then pitch in over the "Valley of Sin."

The green at the 7th has a view of the Eden Estuary

"Hell" bunker is a gargantuan pit waiting to trap you

An Out of Bounds wall runs down the right side

The 11th features the nasty "Strath" bunker

The 5th fairway has a pair of bunkers called the "Spectacles"

"Hell" bunker lurks on the 14th

Aim your drive over a green shed and avoid the stone wall

"Cartgate" bunker guards the joint 3rd and 15th green

The most severe and most famous bunker in golf awaits on the left

The large green slopes quite sharply from back to front

A burn crosses in front of the 1st green

A road crosses the fairway between "Swilcan Bridge" and the green

HOLE 14 "LONG" One of only two par-5s on the course and a brief respite before the rigors of the home stretch. The landing area from the drive is generous. Into the wind, a player has to decide how to take on "Hell" bunker. Downwind many can reach the green, but a steep bank at the front can play havoc even with seemingly perfect shots.

HOLE 17 "ROAD HOLE" As strange a hole as you will find on a championship course, the Road Hole has peculiarities at every turn. If you have found the fairway, you must run a long shot up onto the green, avoiding the bunker on the left but not overcooking the approach as it will fall off the back and either end up on a tarmac road or worse against the stone wall beyond.

HOLE 18 "TOM MORRIS" Aim for the clock on the R&A clubhouse and give the ball a good crack so that it clears the road. A deep crease eats into the front left edge of the green. You can either hit a low running shot through it and up onto the green or fly it and hope for some spin. Most people finish beyond the hole (having avoided the "Valley of Sin"), leaving a slippery putt to the hole.

● An aerial view of the double green shared by the 2nd and 16th

● The Royal & Ancient clubhouse

Royal St. George's, ENGLAND

Often known as Sandwich, named after the quaint town nearby, Royal St. George's is a powerhouse of variety set over a vast 400 acres (160 hectares) of wonderful linksland on the Kent coast in southeast England. It was the first English club to host the Open Championship back in 1894. A massive area of duneland boasts examples of rare flora as well as a mind-blowing, precocious links that offers a complete golfing examination.

THE COURSE

A massive piece of wild ground houses a course of tremendous variety and power. Large dunes at one end of the course gradually level out to a gently undulating test at the other. Many fairways are humpbacked and rolling, while the greens have awkward run-offs and are studded with bunkers. Fortune plays a big part at St. George's.

The 12th is a dogleg with five traps around the green

The 11th green has a wickedly steep bank across the front half

The 16th is surrounded by eight bunkers

Beside the 18th green is a tricky dip called "Duncan's Hollow"

At the tee, the player's choice of club will be heavily influenced by the state of the wind

The green has two tiers and is surrounded by four bunkers

The 5th has a big sand ridge that makes the approach blind

ROYAL ST. GEORGE'S

Sandwich, Kent, England, CT13 9PB
www.royalstgeorges.com

THE COURSE

FOUNDED 1887
LENGTH 7,204 yards (6,587 m)
PAR 70
DESIGNER Laidlaw Purves
COURSE RECORD 63
Payne Stewart & Nick Faldo (1993)

SELECTED CHAMPIONS

OPEN CHAMPIONSHIP Bill Rogers (1981); Sandy Lyle (1985); Greg Norman (1993); Ben Curtis (2003); Darren Clarke (2011)
CURTIS CUP GB&I (1988)
AMATEUR CHAMPIONSHIP CRAIG Watson (1997); Julien Guerrier (2006); Harry Ellis (2017)

CARD OF THE COURSE

THE FRONT NINE			THE BACK NINE		
HOLE	YARDS	PAR	HOLE	YARDS	PAR
1	442	4	10	412	4
2	426	4	11	242	3
3	239	3	12	379	4
4	496	4	13	457	4
5	416	4	14	545	5
6	176	3	15	493	4
7	573	5	16	161	3
8	457	4	17	424	4
9	410	4	18	456	4
OUT	3,635	35	IN	3,569	35

HOLE 6 "MAIDEN"

Simply one of the great short holes in golf. Known as "Maiden," it is named after the massive dune that towers above the green on the left, and it sets the heart beating fast. It is a semi-blind shot (if the flag is on the front half), and four venomous bunkers surround it. Two patrol the front right corner, which means you have to take enough club to clear them, but have to have enough control to stop it from skipping through or, worse, turning left into another trap. A ridge running across the angled green adds problems. Missing this green is almost always a bogey or worse.

The well-bunkered 6th green

The genius responsible for this course, way back in 1887, was Laidlaw Purves. He was lucky to have so much elbow room to give the golfer a feeling of seclusion and lucky to be able to cherry-pick the best parts of the land overlooking Pegwell Bay. Nonetheless, he did a splendid job.

Play changes direction on virtually every tee. Given the mix of holes, it is no wonder that all your skills are needed. There is an 80-yard (73 m) range between the four brilliant short holes. Depending on the wind, some par-4s are unreachable in 2, yet a couple are on the edge of being drivable. The only two par-5s play in opposite directions, meaning one usually plays a good deal harder than the other. Rarely will someone put the flag back in the hole on the difficult 18th and not have used nearly all the clubs in their bag—a true mark of a legendary test.

LUCK PLAYS A PART

The course starts with a bang, as Tiger Woods knows only too well. On his opening hole of the 2003 Open, he cut his driver right into the rough and lost a ball for the first time in his professional career. Tiger also found out how luck plays a part at Sandwich—something that some professionals do not like about the course. Many of the fairways are humpbacked and kick balls off even if you have hit one straight down the middle—the 17th is probably the hardest to hit.

The greens can do similar things, too. The 4th green, which sits at the end of an extreme par-4, is monstrously shaped. A huge upslope rises from the front left, and it also dips away severely off on the right. Likewise, the 10th, which in a wind is just about the hardest to hit and hold, even with a wedge in your hand. The putting surface is a tilting plateau a good 15 ft (4.5 m) above the level of your approach shot and consequently has huge drop-offs, either into very deep traps or down into the rough.

Unfavorable bounces, frustratingly awkward bunkers, and vile rough are not the only obstacles a golfer has to contend with. There are upward of 10 totally or semi-blind shots on the course, although none are truly perplexing. Generally, the line you consider to be the right one usually is, although the drive at the 4th should really take on the huge bunker rather than go left of it to find the heart of the fairway. Incidentally, it is the second highest bunker in golf (behind the Himalaya bunker at St. Enodoc) and does prey on your drive.

THE FAMOUS FIVE

If Royal St. George's is famous for one stretch of holes it is the final five, although the par-3s as a set are as good as anywhere. From the 14th in, you are faced with some palpitating shots. Standing on the par-5 14th tee is very nerve-racking—a noticeable out-of-bounds fence just yards away from you runs all the

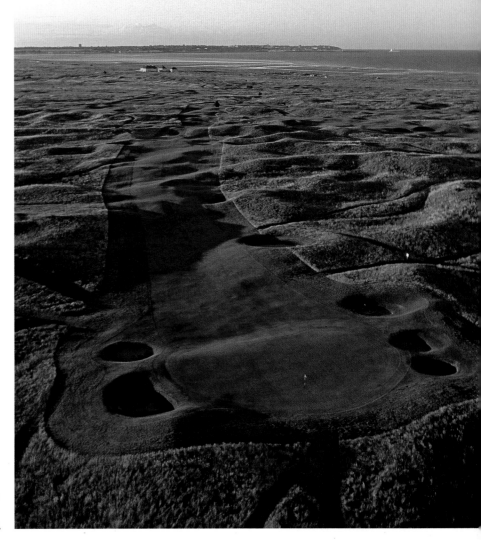

▲ **THE UNDULATING CARPET OF THE 17TH** fairway has every player praying for a favorable bounce, particularly if they drive too far. The raised green is well guarded on both sides.

way down the hole on the right. The hole is also dissected by a wide ditch called "Suez" that, depending on the breeze, can trouble the drive or the 2nd. The 15th is a slog, with a green that is guarded across the front by bunkers and should not be missed left. The 16th is a magnificent short hole, scene of the first televised hole in one and the collapse of Thomas Bjørn in 2003 when he took three to get out of the right greenside bunker and lost the Open by one.

Cross your fingers for a favorable bounce at the 17th, and even the best find it hard to hit the green at the 18th in two. If the wind stays away, the course is supremely serene. If it does not, then you can be thankful that after your inevitable fight, you can find sanctuary in one of the most convivial clubhouses in Britain.

A KNEE-TREMBLER

Sandy Lyle famously sunk to his knees and thumped his club into the ground after a chip on his final hole at the 1985 Open came back to his feet. Luckily, he composed himself and went on to win by one from Payne Stewart.

○ Sandy Lyle wins the Open

Fancourt, SOUTH AFRICA

Designed by one of the game's greats and hometown favorite Gary Player, The Links at Fancourt is one of the new breeds of inland courses built to resemble a seaside masterpiece. Located near the town of George on South Africa's scenic Garden Route, it is one of four courses at Fancourt. Although the dunes are artificially created and water comes into play, this demanding and surreal test boasts many true links characteristics.

▲ **BUNKERS SET INTO LARGE HUMPS** and a nasty water hazard left of the green make the 12th the hardest hole on the course.

Mother Nature did most to build our greatest links courses, with original landscapes merely tinkered with by a golf architect. Yet here in deepest South Africa, bulldozers rather than wind and waves have shaped the course. Fancourt was already an established golf venue, with two excellent and beautifully lush courses, when in 2000, they added a third 18 holes that quickly became the star of Africa. It is called The Links for a reason.

A flat airfield site and adjoining farmland were taken over and transformed into a gnarled artificial dunescape, where holes rock and roll over gently rippled ground and are flanked by shaped sand hills. Most characteristics of a links course are in evidence—isolated tees, creased fairways, deep and strategic bunkers, fast and firm greens with swales and roll-offs, and tangly hummocks of grass. It may be a little greener than some of the best-known links, but it still plays like one. The only giveaways to its pretender status are the network of lakes that come into play on several holes, including the 15th, which has a peninsula green, and the impressive Outeniqua Mountains that rise majestically behind the course. Otherwise, you could easily be beside the sea.

Gary Player, an expert links exponent having won the Open Championship three times, used his

Links golf is how the game originated and at The Links we take golfers back to the roots of golf—and they can play a "British Open" all of their own!

GARY PLAYER, COURSE DESIGNER

THE COURSE

Completely man-made but shaped to look like natural rippled linksland, it is a big, strong course that true links experts thrive on. Because of its design, it needs to be tackled with an imaginative mind and a shotmaker's skill. The bunkers can be evil (deep and cleverly placed), but the wild grasses flanking the fairways are equally tough.

The gnarled landscape at Fancourt is unforgiving, and wayward shots are severely punished

Four fairway bunkers make an accurate drive essential on the par-4 3rd

The 16th fairway narrows toward the green where bunkers await

The large bunker on the left of the 13th fairway can cause problems

A humpbacked fairway makes controlling the approaches difficult to this shallow, well-guarded green

The tee shot is blind and the landing area tight. A good drive still requires a mid to long iron approach

N

HOLE 3 "CALAMITY"

This hole, called "Calamity," is ranked the second-hardest hole on the course and for good reason. A marker post on the undulating fairway shows the way on this faint dogleg left, but beware the huge bunker on the left and the small pot on the right. The approach needs to clear a stonewalled burn that cuts right across the front of the green and then to pull up before it risks scampering into large grassy mounds or two pots on the left.

The undulating 3rd

FANCOURT

Montagu Street, Blanco, P.O. Box 2266, George 6530, South Africa
www.fancourt.co.za

THE LINKS COURSE

FOUNDED 1991
LENGTH 7,579 yards (6,930 m)
PAR 73
DESIGNER Gary Player
COURSE RECORD 68
Shared by six players

SELECTED CHAMPIONS

PRESIDENTS CUP US/Rest of World tied (2003)
WOMEN'S WORLD CUP OF GOLF Japan (2005)
SOUTH AFRICAN OPEN Retief Goosen (2005)

CARD OF THE COURSE

THE FRONT NINE			THE BACK NINE		
HOLE	YARDS	PAR	HOLE	YARDS	PAR
1	396	4	10	408	4
2	236	3	11	161	3
3	469	4	12	481	4
4	494	4	13	533	5
5	549	5	14	361	4
6	341	4	15	477	4
7	476	4	16	584	5
8	202	3	17	186	3
9	609	5	18	616	5
OUT	3,773	36	IN	3,806	37

knowledge of the great courses of the world to manufacture a natural-looking landscape of windswept hillocks. An incredible 500,000 cubic yards (382,278 cu m) of earth were dug, moved, pushed and scraped to form the many contours, and 25 acres (10 hectares) of wetlands also sprang to life.

Then, painstakingly, the mounds were hand-planted with links grasses. Instead of the wispier European fescue grasses, the unkempt rough here consists of the more robust savanna types, able to withstand the fierce southern African climate. The wild amber-tinged rough grasses, so reminiscent of true links courses, frame wonderfully the immaculately kept fairways, but also are a punishing hazard.

AN AWESOME CHALLENGE

As in real links fashion, the fairways are far from flat. Player created a wavy effect, and even if you strike a perfect drive, luck does play its part in keeping the ball on the short grass. Although it is possible to get an awkward lie on the fairways because of the slopes, usually a ball trickles off the slopes into the hollows, making life a little easier for the next shot.

Throw the bunkers into the mix (many are scooped out of the man-made hills), and the fact that it is a modern links stretching out to almost 7,655 yards (7,000 m) off the championship tees, and you have an awesome challenge to contend with. A glance down the scorecard reveals holes called "Calamity," "Sheer Murrrder," "Wee Wrecker," and "Prayer"—clearly an indication of its brutality.

It may be long and extremely testing, but it is fair and tamable—the best ball strikers tend to come out on top. Retief Goosen birdied the last two holes to defeat fellow South African and Fancourt homeowner Ernie Els in 2005 to win his country's Open Championship with a score of 10-under par 282—a case of a classy striker winning on a classy golf course.

ALL THE PRESIDENT'S MEN

In the 2003 Presidents Cup, a biennial team event between the US and the Rest of the World, the teams tied at 17 all. Captains Jack Nicklaus and Gary Player chose Tiger Woods and Ernie Els for the playoff. They parred three extra holes, but darkness intervened so the captains agreed to share the cup.

Thabo Mbeki presents the cup

Kiawah Island, US

Remembered for one of the most pulsating Ryder Cups in history, Kiawah Island's Ocean Course is brutal and unforgiving but also a beautiful place to play golf. The waves of the Atlantic Ocean are in view from every hole. A "target golf" element and a sign that says "Caution: Alligators Are Dangerous" suggest that this is not a typical links course, yet the closeness of the ocean and the sandy wastes provide a unique links experience.

WATER HAZARD

The waterways threading through the holes of the Ocean Course are a natural habitat for dozens of alligators. They rarely attack humans but can be very dangerous if provoked. Stay clear.

● An alligator lurks in the water

Set in the low country of South Carolina, the Ocean Course has no towering dunes, so holes skip over the scrubland and skirt the marshes rather than follow natural valleys. Instead of creating large dunes, architect Pete Dye, famed for his bruising designs, relied on building up the tees, fairways, and greens to raise them slightly off the scrubland that butts up to the ocean.

The raised fairways drop off into sandy waste areas where the line between the deliberately unkempt and the more shaped bunkering is blurred. So that no one is left in any doubt where the real hazards begin, players are allowed to ground their clubs in the sand. Water comes into play on many holes, either as a marsh or an inland seawater channel.

DANGERS AND DIFFICULTIES

When Pete Dye and his wife, Alice, came to develop the site, the course had already been chosen to host the 1991 Ryder Cup, so the pressure was on. An unpredictable wind blew quite consistently from both east and west. Dye's solution was ingenious—to build two loops of nine, one designed to play with an easterly and the other would be friendlier in a westerly. Great in theory, but sometimes it blows so hard that neither nine offers any respite.

Kiawah's style creates dangers and difficulties for a golfer. Tees and fairways are like small islands surrounded by sand and marsh. Grasses can be chest high, and squat trees edge in tight. The greens are often incredibly hard to hit and hold; balls are tossed off down wicked slopes, leaving tough chip shots. Ideally, golfers would like to play links-like shots—like a low runner to combat the wind—and skip the ball up to the green, but they cannot. Bermuda grass (totally alien to a true links) is the only strain that can thrive. Its coarse grain snags a ball like velcro, and pitch-and-runs are virtually ruled out. Just about every tee shot on the Ocean Course is a heart-pounding affair. Even the par-3s can put the

> ## Each Kiawah course tells its own story, in its purest form, and makes contact with the soul of the game.
>
> **JUSTIN LEONARD**, 1997 OPEN CHAMPION

▲ **PLAYERS AND THE CROWD** celebrate a US victory in the 1991 Ryder Cup at Kiawah Island, after an intense cliffhanger on a tough course that became known as the "War on the Shore."

frighteners on. The humpbacked green of the 14th sits way over head height above the surrounding wastes. If you miss the green, the only safe place is short right on the closely mown run-off. Even from here, a par is difficult.

The 17th is fronted by a lake, and the angled green looks intimidatingly hard to find. Anywhere short or right will be wet, and going left will find sand or worse. Even the best can fall foul of this course. There is no doubting its beauty and its clever design, but it is certainly one of the toughest courses in the world.

▼ **AT KIAWAH ISLAND'S OCEAN COURSE,** the holes are raised slightly above the marsh and scrubland, and the South Carolina climate is both hot and humid.

THE COURSE

Stunning yet brutal, the holes saunter over sandy scrub and are buffeted by the Atlantic winds that sometimes scream in from the ocean. Most of its trouble comes in the form of the haphazard natural bunkering and the channels of seawater and marsh. It takes power and bravery to combat Kiawah's daunting challenge.

The 6th fairway has sand on both sides and is only 120 ft (36.5 m) wide

Natural dunes impinge on the left of the 7th fairway

The 1st has the narrowest fairway, with a bunker on the right and dune grass on the left

At the 11th, bunkers guard the inside of each turn on an S-shaped fairway

The 10th tee sits on a sand dune from where you can spy the whole of the back nine

The 14th has a great view of the Atlantic Ocean, as players turn back to the east

HOLE 18 STRONG PAR-4

The tee sits up and plays across a waste area to a fairway that features a saddle that takes the ball away to the right. A large waste bunker patrols the right side. From the crest, the green sits slightly below you. For the best line into the angled green, aim for the right of the fairway if you dare. A nasty complex of bunkers eats into the front left and grassy scrub flanks the right.

KIAWAH ISLAND

One Sanctuary Beach Drive, Kiawah Island, South Carolina 29455
www.kiawahresort.com

THE OCEAN COURSE

FOUNDED 1991
LENGTH 7,356 yards (6,726 m)
PAR 72
DESIGNER Pete Dye
COURSE RECORD 67
Tom Kite (2006)

SELECTED CHAMPIONS

RYDER CUP US (1991)
USPGA Rory McIlroy (2012)
WORLD CUP OF GOLF Ireland—Pádraig Harrington and Paul McGinley (1997); South Africa—Trevor Immelman and Rory Sabbatini (2003)
SENIORS PGA Denis Watson (2007)

CARD OF THE COURSE

THE FRONT NINE			THE BACK NINE		
HOLE	YARDS	PAR	HOLE	YARDS	PAR
1	395	4	10	439	4
2	543	5	11	562	5
3	390	4	12	466	4
4	453	4	13	404	4
5	207	3	14	194	3
6	455	4	15	421	4
7	527	5	16	579	5
8	197	3	17	221	3
9	464	4	18	439	4
OUT	3,631	36	IN	3,725	36

● The angled 18th green

The green is guarded by bunkers in the front and grassy scrub on the right

Sand lines the fairway, and the dunes can be very severe

Shinnecock Hills, US

If we are happy to categorize Shinnecock Hills as a links, then there is probably no finer outside of Great Britain and Ireland. Sweeping over 260 acres (105 hectares) of old Native American Reservation land near Peconic Bay on Long Island, it is a tranquil gem. One of America's founding fathers in golf terms, Shinnecock belonged to the group of five clubs that formed the United States Golf Association back in 1894.

There is a real sense of freedom at Shinnecock Hills. Stand in the middle of this vast space, and the meandering course delivers a 360-degree panorama of nothing but gently swaying sandy pasture and the odd stand of trees, watched over from on high by the oldest clubhouse in America. A privileged air washes over you.

The original links has melted away with time and has been replaced by the masterful creation of Messrs Toomey and Flynn, which came into play in 1931. Only a few holes remain from an earlier course, including the tricky par-3 7th, a "Redan" hole based on the original type of raised tilting green seen at North Berwick in Scotland.

All the other holes are superbly routed around it, and nine of the par-4s dogleg, leaving a golfer to think about the wind twice on each hole. The holes were crafted by a 150-strong contingent of local Native Americans, the Shinnecock Indians, who were part of the Algonquin tribe that still reside close by today.

Although the site, not far from the Atlantic Ocean, does not feature piles of dunes like many seaside courses, it does pitch and roll, especially on the back nine, making it a slightly unusual area for a links. It is more Muirfield than Royal Birkdale, meaning it is more demure and strategic than big and bold. Flirting with wild dunes, it has plenty of bunkers, many in clusters, that patrol the corners of the

> It is probably the best course in the world. It naturally changes tack continually—that is the genius of the layout. It's a special place.
>
> **RAY FLOYD**, WINNER OF 1986 US OPEN AT SHINNECOCK

SHOT OF THE YEAR

The diminutive American Corey Pavin came to the awkward 18th on the final day of the 1995 US Open thinking a par might be good enough to see off the chasing pack. He hit a great tee shot to the right edge of the dogleg left uphill hole. He knew if he hit his next shot onto the green and two-putted for par that he would probably win. As it was a little uphill and the wind was blowing right to left, he took a 4-wood and knew it was going to be good the second he hit it. It finished 4 ft (1.2 m) away from the pin, and although he missed his birdie chance, his solid par sealed the victory.

● Corey Pavin with the trophy

doglegs. They are shallower than their transatlantic counterparts and have few extremely steep faces. They give you a chance, unlike the rough, which can get knee-high and sways with the customary golden hues.

FAST-RUNNING SURFACE

As modern greens go, these are small. Today, you have to cope with their size from farther out off the championship tees, where there are six par-4s over 440 yards (400 m) long. Most of the surfaces are quick, contoured, and have smooth run-offs. If you do not hit the heart of them, you can slide away down a nasty bank. The problem deepens when the course is allowed to become fast-running. It became a controversy in the 2004 US Open when the course was borderline playable in a strong wind. Out of 66 players in the final round, 28 failed to break 80. Retief Goosen won with an amazing 71, but to do that, he had to single putt 12 times (24 putts in total) because he hit only six greens in regulation. That is Shinnecock's defense.

Shinnecock Hills thrills the best with its ever-changing paths, firm, thoughtfully angled fairways and heart-wrenching greens. It is a cracker and neighbor to two other fine links—The National Links of America and Southampton Golf Club—making this part of Long Island a golfer's paradise.

◄ **THE PAR-4 18TH HOLE** exemplifies the wide-open spaces of Shinnecock Hills, seen here during the third round of the 104th US Open.

THE COURSE

This links swoops over Long Island's gently tilting landscape and is fringed with wavy, straw-colored rough. Over 2 miles (4 km) from the ocean, Shinnecock Hills is extremely well defended by an abundance of bowl-shaped bunkers and small greens that have shaved run-offs into the rough. When the conditions are hard and fast-running, it is a devil of a course to conquer.

The sharply tilting green at the 7th makes the approach difficult

Tee shots aim for the flat part of the 15th fairway

A nest of bunkers must be carried at the end of the 16th fairway

The rolling 12th fairway leads to a green without bunkers

Approaches to the 9th green are overlooked by the clubhouse

The undulating 10th fairway creates indecision for the tee shot

The green has a slippery putting surface and a drop-off at the back

The slightly uphill fairway snakes between 20 bunkers

HOLE 16 BUNKERS RULE
A stunner played slightly back uphill, directly toward the clubhouse, and where bunkers rule. On every shot, you are confronted by a choice—do you fly the bunkers to find the next bit of fairway, or do you tack your way up the hole avoiding them? The shot into the green is all carry as 10 bunkers patrol the front and short left with no route to run a ball up.

● The remarkable 16th

SHINNECOCK HILLS

200 Tuckahoe Road
Southampton, New York 11968
Tel no: 631-283-3525
www.shinnecockhillsgolfclub.org

THE COURSE

FOUNDED 1891
LENGTH 6,996 yards (6,397 m)
PAR 70
COURSE RECORD 65
Neal Lancaster (1995)
DESIGNERS Willie Dunn (original), Charles Macdonald and Seth Raynor, Howard Toomey and William Flynn

SELECTED CHAMPIONS

WALKER CUP US (1977)
US OPEN CHAMPIONSHIP Ray Floyd (1986); Corey Pavin (1995); Retief Goosen (2004); Brooks Koepka (2018)

CARD OF THE COURSE

THE FRONT NINE			THE BACK NINE		
HOLE	YARDS	PAR	HOLE	YARDS	PAR
1	393	4	10	412	4
2	226	3	11	158	3
3	478	4	12	468	4
4	435	4	13	370	4
5	537	5	14	443	4
6	474	4	15	403	4
7	189	3	16	540	5
8	398	4	17	179	3
9	443	4	18	450	4
OUT	3,573	35	IN	3,423	35

Parkland Courses

Golf continues to take over the world. Due to its sustained growth in popularity, there are now more than 35,000 courses. The vast majority of these are parkland courses. Parkland is a vague term covering similar styles—including forest layouts—that depend on components such as topography, types of trees, the use of bunkers and water, and the prevailing winds.

◄ ◄ ◄ **PARIS INTERNATIONAL** to the north of Paris was designed by Jack Nicklaus and opened in 1991.
◄ ◄ **THE BRABAZON COURSE** at The Belfry in England has hosted the Ryder Cup four times.
◄ **MERION GOLF CLUB** is located in Ardmore, Pennsylvania.
▼ **LES BORDES,** surrounded by ancient forest in the Loire Valley in France, has been described as a "floating golf course."

Why are parkland courses so prevalent around the world? To answer this, you have to consider the pure geography of our planet. Centers of population have usually grown and multiplied near an area of fresh water—whether a lake or a river—and tend to avoid inhospitable places wherever and whenever possible. Except for the rare links courses that sit on the sandy coastal strips and the few hundred desert and out-and-out mountain courses, we tend to build most of our courses among the pastures, fields, forests, and woodlands that are easily accessible to the majority of golfers.

Parkland courses tend to be lusher than any other style, as often they are not exposed to the coastal winds

▼ **THE TWO COURSES AT WINGED FOOT** were created in pastures and woodland near Mamaroneck, north of New York City.

experienced by a links or the searing temperatures that a desert course has to bear. Trees play a vital role, too, giving shade and protection from the elements. The soil is also more fertile than a sandy heath or links, and, therefore, even grass coverage is easier to cultivate.

TOPOGRAPHY AND TREES

Trouble usually comes in various forms. Fairways are tree-lined, and so they often lead to doglegging. Bunkering becomes strategic rather than deep and menacing, as they are called upon to protect landing areas and greensides. The rough beside the fairways is often verdant, thick, and ankle-deep. Parkland courses vary greatly in their topography. Some, such as Augusta National, swoop and climb, while others simply wend their way around large specimen trees on a flat pasture.

The variety of trees is also endless. Broadleaf deciduous trees are much more abundant in the mid-European nations and Northeastern America, while the forest layouts of Canada and Scandinavia tend to be lined with softwood coniferous species, such as pines and firs. Go further south in Europe to warmer climes, such as the Mediterranean conditions you find in Spain, and umbrella pines, eucalyptus, and cork oaks may provide the woodland canopy.

Each style makes for different challenges. Often, a course threaded through pine forest gives a golfer a chance to escape the trees with a low accurate punch, as the canopy tends to be higher and the trunks more slender than a wood of broad-trunked oaks and beech, for example. In the latter case, a golfer must be able to shape the ball around trouble, as going through it is less of an option.

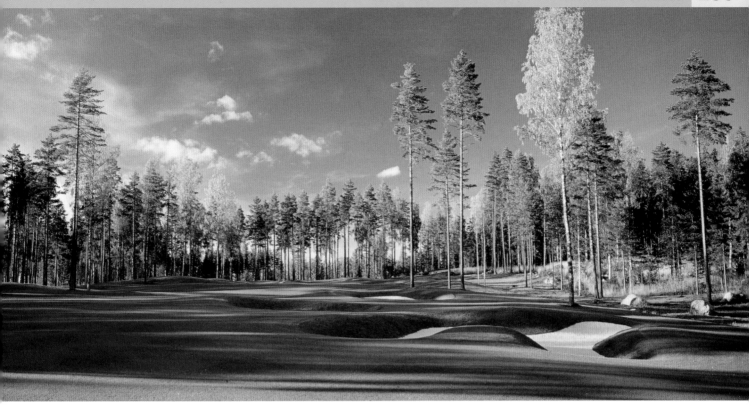

COPING WITH WIND

Wind plays a big part on parkland courses. While on a links the wind tends to blow, sometimes quite hard admittedly, from the same direction, on a parkland course, it can swirl and be dragged into the holes by the tall canopies of trees. Sometimes you can look at the skitting clouds moving serenely one way and the flag on the green blowing the other. Club selection then can become taxing. As a general rule, you should trust more to the direction in which the clouds are moving, or how the treetops are behaving, than the flag.

FLYING HIGH

As the parkland fairways tend to be slower running, and bunkers often patrol the fronts of greens, the high ball game is needed more than on a heathland or links course, when you can bounce the ball short and let it run

▶ OAK HILL GOLF COURSE, designed by Donald Ross, was created out of farmland near Rochester in Upstate New York.

onto the green. From the parkland tee, you cannot rely on getting a huge amount of run, so golfers tend to favor long, bombing carries, especially on the US-style parklands, where the ground staff are likely to water the courses more freely.

Firing into greens, too, can mean going the aerial route to fly over the trouble rather than skip past it on the floor. However, it is also wise to think about the wind. Because you can be

protected from the full force of it on a blustery day, it can be best to try and hit lower shots to avoid flying above the canopy.

On most parklands, the bunkers are relatively shallow, because there is no wind erosion to worry about, and so the art of the long bunker shot, especially from a fairway trap, needs to be in the golfer's armory. Splashing out sideways is rare on the majority of parklands. A wooded course can be a

▲ LINNA GOLF COURSE is set among the tall, spindly evergreen pines and deciduous birch trees north of Helsinki in the heart of Finland. The undulating course, which opened in 2005, features rocky outcrops and the chance to play by natural light at midnight in the summer.

stunning place to play, especially as the seasons change. Playing over a green rolling landscape as the leaves turn a fall brown, yellow, and orange can be a magical experience.

Merion, US

The proverb "the best things come in small packages" is true of Merion. Squeezed into only 126 acres (50 hectares) of woodland, its clever design makes the most of a leafy suburban site in Pennsylvania. The course is simply a classic, and Merion's history adds to the atmosphere. Every great player has walked the hallowed turf, and the stories that come from its numerous national championships are written in golfing folklore.

Around the turn of the 19th century, cricket and tennis were all the rage in smart neighborhoods of Philadelphia, and Merion Cricket Club, founded in 1865, was at the heart of sporting affairs. As golf was also coming into the mainstream, these sports' clubs realized that a golf course would make a fine and popular addition to their facilities. The Philadelphia Cricket Club took the lead and even hosted the US Open in 1907 and 1910. Merion, which had had a short course (The West Course) since 1896, wanted something grander so that it, too, could hold such illustrious championships.

The members met together and chose one of their own—a 32-year-old golfing Scottish expat named Hugh Wilson—to design a course. In 1910, he traveled back to his native lands for seven months to take inspiration from the great links and heaths, returning with vigor to set about designing Merion Cricket Club's East Course.

Wilson was given a small but wonderfully wooded site in the Main Line suburbs of the city, and what he produced was a compact but magnificent gem in the shape of an L. Eleven of the holes (from the 2nd to the 12th) are located across Ardmore Avenue in one half of the L, while holes 1 and 13 to 18 are on the clubhouse side. Because the course was short, its defenses had to be strong, and that is still true today, although in the last few years 400 yards (366 m) have been added to bring it into the modern day.

WHITE FACES

Wilson may have been an amateur architect, but his routing and bunkering were exquisite. The course he devised uses natural gifts well. Mature trees dot the entire landscape, and stony creeks snake through it. Areas of rocky, broken ground and enough gentle elevation changes make life interesting. The bunkering is superb and yawning. Many of the 120 bunkers are jagged edged, and their steep faces are fringed with grasses—someone described them as having eyebrows. Their look led Chick Evans, the winner here of the 1916 US Amateur, to call them the "White Faces of Merion."

▲ **RED WICKER BASKETS** instead of flags sit on top of Merion's pins. They give no clue as to which way the wind is blowing.

HOGAN'S WONDER SHOT

After a horrific car crash in 1949, Ben Hogan, the preeminent golfer of his time, fought back to semifitness and came to Merion a year later to take a tilt at the US Open once more. During 36 demanding holes on the final day, he tired and his lead dwindled. He stood on the 18th fairway with a 1-iron in hand, needing a par to get himself in a playoff. He raked a long-iron wonder shot into the heart of the green and secured his playoff place, going on to win it the next day.

○ Ben Hogan on the 18th at Merion in 1950

The greens need to do their defensive job, too. Precision rather than power is the name of the game at Merion, as the greens are cunningly cambered and small. Some have quite distinct levels, and if golfers are to score well, their approaches must be controlled and distancde perfectly.

A course's short holes are often a telltale sign of its quality, and Merion has four to savor. The 3rd is uphill and dotted with half a dozen traps. At the 9th, you play downhill to a kidney-shaped green fronted by a stream and pond. Over the road at the pretty 13th, the green is tiny and surrounded by sand. The 17th is a brute over an old quarry and measures 246 yards (225 m) off the back—and it is all carry. Lee Trevino once described it as "the shortest par-4 in Open history."

GREAT PLAYERS

The legendary Bobby Jones is inextricably linked with Merion. He first played the US Amateur here in 1916 at the age of 14 and got through to the quarterfinals. He won it here in 1924 and then again in 1930. What made this feat so remarkable was he had already won the US Open, British Amateur, and Open in the same year, and so his quartet of titles became known as the Grand Slam (see pp.212–213). He won his 36-hole final on the 11th green, and a plaque stands there today to commemorate his feat. He gave up competitive golf a few months later.

Merion is a true classic and, now that its compact charms have been updated, it can welcome great players once again. It hosted the US Open for the fifth time in 2013.

◀ **SUNSET OVER THE 4TH GREEN** highlights the putting surface that slopes from back left to front right. Five grass-fringed bunkers lie in wait for any wayward shots.

THE COURSE

Compact but intricate, this historic parkland features small sloping greens and gaping deep bunkers that draw the eye and mercilessly gobble up balls. Strategy, imagination, and control, rather than power and bravery, are needed to conquer Merion's superb variety of holes.

The green at the 7th is narrow and deep

The 16th has been ranked in the top-18 holes in the world

The dogleg 14th hole plays uphill toward a long green

The 1st green slopes right to left and back to front

The 10th green is small and narrow with a ridge in the center

The tee shot at the 18th is blind, and the fairway is undulating

The 11th green is guarded by Cobb's Creek and a deep bunker on the left

The 13th green has a huge bunker in front

The fairway bypasses a dell to the right

The green has a small front portion before a steep slope up to the top

HOLE 16 **THE "QUARRY"**

The 16th is known as the "quarry" hole for obvious reasons. The bold player must first find the fairway then decide whether to take on the sunken rock and sand waste area right in front of the green. From the end of the fairway, it is 100 yards (91 m) to the front of the green, but many players come from much farther back.

○ The quarry at the 16th hole

MERION

450 Ardmore Avenue
Ardmore, Pennsylvania 19003
www.meriongolfclub.com

THE EAST COURSE

FOUNDED 1912
LENGTH 6,846 yards (6,260 m)
PAR 70
DESIGNER Hugh Wilson

SELECTED CHAMPIONS

US AMATEUR Bobby Jones (1924, 1930); Eduardo Molinari (2005)
US OPEN Ben Hogan (1950); Lee Trevino (1971); David Graham (1981); Justin Rose (2013)
CURTIS CUP US (1954)

CARD OF THE COURSE

THE FRONT NINE			THE BACK NINE		
HOLE	YARDS	PAR	HOLE	YARDS	PAR
1	350	4	10	303	4
2	556	5	11	367	4
3	219	3	12	403	4
4	597	5	13	120	3
5	504	4	14	438	4
6	487	4	15	411	4
7	345	4	16	430	4
8	359	4	17	246	4
9	206	3	18	505	5
OUT	3,623	36	IN	3,223	34

Les Bordes, FRANCE

Secluded, refined, and brilliantly bold, Les Bordes is a tranquil haven in a wondrously natural woodland setting. Deep in the heart of the Sologne, a lake-strewn forest area in the Loire Valley, it is a mammoth but beautiful challenge where there are so many thrilling shots to be played. Although no championships have been played here, many good players have tasted her charms, but none have conquered her.

AGONY OF A MISSED PUTT

A gigantic putting green—the largest in Europe—doubles as a sculpture garden. On a small island of grass sits a sculpture by Rodin of a naked man clasping his forehead. Baron Bich thought it perfect for the spot as he saw it depicting the agony of a missed 3 ft (1 m) putt.

○ Rodin's sculpture of a naked man

Rarely can you describe a course as eclectic, but Les Bordes is exactly that. Predominantly forested, it has smatterings of heath and a US-style watercourse. Opened in 1986, it was originally a private course for two rich families. Baron Marcel Bich—of Bic biro and razor fame—and his Japanese business partner Yoshiaki Sakurai enlisted the expertise of American Robert Von Hagge to turn Bich's hunting estate into a world-class golf course.

Design-wise, it has everything. Frightening carries, doglegs, plenty of risk-and-reward shots to contemplate, mounds instead of bunkers, sleepered greens next to water, snaking white fairway bunkers, some sadistic greens, open-your-shoulder drives, and even an island green. Quite a mix, but they work perfectly.

There are only 44 bunkers on the course, and a few of these are nastily deep, but that does not tell the full story. Hole 1 is a dead-straight par-4 with only one bunker, but it almost entirely circles the green. More monster traps flank the 6th, 12th, and 15th fairways. In any case, the fairways dart through such dense forest in places that no bunkers are needed to make a golfer feel claustrophobic and jittery on their drive. Only five traps feature in the last four holes, but it is undoubtedly as tough a finishing stretch as you will find anywhere.

Von Hagge does not seem to do simple, gentle doglegs. Nearly all of the six swinging holes are seriously curved. The pulsating 7th is a full 90 degrees, and the second shot must fire over a huge pond to reach the green. He has created three par-3s that are absolute crackers over water and one difficult uphill hole. Of the three over ponds, the 4th green is buttressed with wood sleepers and the 13th is perhaps the toughest. From the back tee, it is a carry of 174 yards (158 m) to the front edge of the green. In a wind, the strike had better be pure.

Then, just when you think you might be over the worst, the 14th confronts you. Water is everywhere. You must carry it from the tee and avoid it on the right and left with your second, before hitting over some more to an island green reminiscent of the 17th at Sawgrass (see pp.364–367). A five here is treasured.

Yet for all Les Bordes's challenges through the most picturesque countryside, it is fair. If a golfer is humble and chooses the right tee for his or her ability, then this graceful yet powerful course will charm all comers.

▼ **SURROUNDED BY MISTY WATER,** the extraordinary island green at the 14th hole is reached by a footbridge where you can see Koi carp swimming beneath you.

THE COURSE

Full of on-the-edge shots, Les Bordes meanders through mature forest, and its fairways and greens flirt with several graceful lakes. Sand is used sparingly, but, where it does come into play, it is both confrontational and bold. Because of its power and dangers, Les Bordes is a very tough proposition, even for the best golfers.

The final approach on the 18th is to a seriously ridged green

One bunker almost surrounds the 1st green

HOLE 6 NATURAL AND CLEVER

The 6th looks very natural despite its two massive bunkers—one hugs the driving area on the right, while the other starts just a few more yards on and patrols the front and right of the green. The fairway is cleverly raised so that the fall-offs into the traps are quite deep but not jarring to the eyes, and wild grassy banks frame the hole, too. A big swale midright means your approach must be precise and thereafter your putting, too.

A huge oak stands serenely by the green on the left

A bunker almost 120 yards (110 m) long waits beside the fairway

Only a well-struck shot will make the carry over water to the 13th green

An island green at the 14th hole makes for some nervous approaches, even with a wedge

The 7th hole turns through a full 90 degrees

A huge stretch of sand protects the right side of the fairway

LES BORDES

41220 Saint-Laurant-Nouan, France
www.lesbordesgolfclub.com

THE COURSE

FOUNDED 1986
LENGTH 7,009 yards (6,409 m)
PAR 72
DESIGNER Robert von Hagge
COURSE RECORD 71
Jean Van de Velde

CARD OF THE COURSE

THE FRONT NINE			THE BACK NINE		
HOLE	YARDS	PAR	HOLE	YARDS	PAR
1	439	4	10	512	5
2	522	5	11	399	4
3	388	4	12	413	4
4	165	3	13	185	3
5	435	4	14	558	5
6	385	4	15	437	4
7	507	5	16	215	3
8	156	3	17	454	4
9	390	4	18	447	4
OUT	**3,388**	**36**	**IN**	**3,402**	**36**

The genteel-looking 6th

Valderrama, SPAIN

Consistently ranked the No. 1 course in Continental Europe, Valderrama in southern Spain is not for the fainthearted. Home to the European Tour's flagship event, the Volvo Masters, for many years, this is no easy challenge, and even the greats have been humiliated at times. It is brilliant but has so many almost frightening shots that it is a test for the spirit as much as for the game. There is so much drama in Valderrama.

Love has been poured onto Valderrama in the pursuit of perfection. Creating uncompromising but graceful holes through the forest of bent cork oaks and olives has been the passion of Valderrama's owner ever since he bought the original Los Aves course in 1984. Jaime Ortiz-Patino took an average course and, with the talents of architect Robert Trent Jones, masterminded a rebuild of epic proportions. It went from little known to highly acclaimed in a few short years, thanks to countless millions thrown at it, a mind-boggling amount of earth moved, and thousands of trees planted, moved, and chopped. Even to this day, Patino's quest for the best did not idle, and he constantly tried to improve on the already outstanding golf course.

An abundance of drives, approaches, even chips and putts are on the edge. At every turn, you must take a deep breath and trust your game to pull you through. The terrain and design make it tough. Trees hem in the fairways; dazzling white bunkers, banks of wiry rough and yet more trees defend the greens. Two greens—the 4th and 17th—are notoriously guarded by water, and all have super-slick putting surfaces that tilt steeply in places.

ACCURACY AND CONTROL

Accuracy off the tees is the No. 1 priority, simply because the trees encroach on the landing areas and their canopies kill even a slight mishit. Advancing a ball from the squat and gnarled trees is possible but tricky—you have to fire out low to escape. Often, a bended recovery is needed. With bunkers guarding green entrances and the fairways not rolling fast, it is hard to run an escape shot up onto the green.

Even if fairways are found, control is still vital on approaches as missing greens causes severe problems. Anyone going long at, say, the brilliant par-3 12th will have a nightmare bunker shot back onto a green that slopes viciously away from them. The crux of the matter is, whether you hit or miss a green, make sure you are in the

▶ **THE LEAST PARKLAND IN NATURE,** the 17th is definitely Valderrama's most notorious hole, with a lake and a trio of bunkers guarding its green.

KEY MOMENTS ....

◀ **THE 17TH HOLE** produces dramatic moments like no other. Tiger Woods found water here in the last round of the 1999 American Express Championship with a seemingly perfect pitch and took a triple-bogey eight but still went on to win in a playoff. However, Woods was one of only three players to finish under par.

◀ **IN 1997, VALDERRAMA** hosted the first Ryder Cup on mainland Europe, and Seve Ballesteros was nonplaying captain. On the final afternoon, Europe led by five points going into the singles. Only three Europeans won their matches, including Colin Montgomerie, whose stonewall par-4 on the nasty 18th sealed the victory.

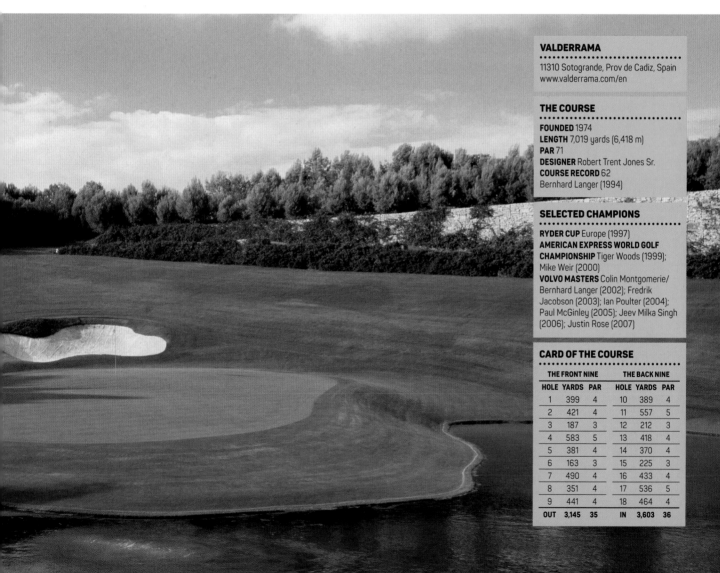

VALDERRAMA
....
11310 Sotogrande, Prov de Cadiz, Spain
www.valderrama.com/en

THE COURSE
....
FOUNDED 1974
LENGTH 7,019 yards (6,418 m)
PAR 71
DESIGNER Robert Trent Jones Sr.
COURSE RECORD 62
Bernhard Langer (1994)

SELECTED CHAMPIONS
....
RYDER CUP Europe (1997)
AMERICAN EXPRESS WORLD GOLF CHAMPIONSHIP Tiger Woods (1999); Mike Weir (2000)
VOLVO MASTERS Colin Montgomerie/ Bernhard Langer (2002); Fredrik Jacobson (2003); Ian Poulter (2004); Paul McGinley (2005); Jeev Milka Singh (2006); Justin Rose (2007)

CARD OF THE COURSE
....

THE FRONT NINE			THE BACK NINE		
HOLE	YARDS	PAR	HOLE	YARDS	PAR
1	399	4	10	389	4
2	421	4	11	557	5
3	187	3	12	212	3
4	583	5	13	418	4
5	381	4	14	370	4
6	163	3	15	225	3
7	490	4	16	433	4
8	351	4	17	536	5
9	441	4	18	464	4
OUT	**3,145**	**35**	**IN**	**3,603**	**36**

THE COURSE

Ancient cork oaks and olives crowd the emerald fairways and shadow some of the tabletop greens. Blindingly white bunkers filled with crushed, locally sourced marble hug the fringes, and the odd water hazard puts a premium on accuracy.

HOLE 8 "EL BUNKER"

Short but dangerous, this slight dogleg left is dominated by trees on either side of the fairway and a large bunker that arcs its way all around the front of the green. If you miss the fairway, you cannot fire out low under the branches and expect to skip it through the sand on to the green.

A large semicircular bunker guards the green

The tight fairway is hemmed in by distinctive cork trees

THE FRONT NINE ❶ The left side of the fairway leaves the best line into the shady green. **❷** A huge oak sits in the middle of the fairway. If you are long, you may get past it. **❸** Better to be short than long or left as violent slopes can take the ball into trouble. **❹** Best to play it as a genuine three-shotter, as the lake by the green shows no mercy. **❺** No need for a driver off the tee, better to play for position on this dogleg left. **❻** Great downhill short hole. Try to be short right of the flag to leave an uphill putt. **❼** Needs two big smacks to get home but well guarded by huge bunkers. **❽** Must find the fairway as there is no chance of chasing one on to the green from the trees. **❾** Dead straight and flat, making judging the approach tricky.

THE BACK NINE ❿ Shaping left to right around a pond, the green is a sloping devil. **⓫** Although approach is semi-blind up a hill, it is a birdie chance. **⓬** Amazing par-3 over a small valley to a back-to-front tilting green. **⓭** No bunkers but very narrow as flanked by trees down both sides. **⓮** Very hard to judge approach as the green sits way above the fairway. **⓯** Daunting par-3 over valley of scrub. Aim for left side of green. **⓰** Let tilting fairway feed your drive left as it leaves the best line into green. **⓱** It takes guts to go for this in two. Anything short will be swallowed by a lake. **⓲** A kink in fairway means you being creative to keep out of trouble.

The well-guarded green sits into the sidehill but slopes quite sharply

The fairway tilts from right to left but doglegs to the right

After boldly hitting over the trees, you are left with a shorter approach to the green

The green is slightly crowned and well protected by several bunkers

HOLE 16 "MUY DIFICIL"

The perfect line flirts with the trees down the right, and the ball should feed down to the left, leaving a clear sight of the green that sits downhill of the landing area. Left is best. An awkward driving hole plus putting is a trial. No wonder this hole is called "Muy Dificil" (Very Difficult).

HOLE 18 "CASA CLUB"

A finishing hole where anything can happen, there are two ways to play the 18th. Play safe and hit straight into the corner, leaving a long raking shot that may need to bend around some trees. Play boldly and hit blindly over the trees on the left, hoping to find the narrow fairway, which doglegs left.

The lake at the 4th

The huge bunker at the 8th

Bunkers guarding the 7th green

The richness of the landscape and wildlife ... means that each player completes his round challenged by the layout and enriched by the beauty of nature.

JAIME ORTIZ-PATINO, FOUNDING OWNER AND PRESIDENT

right place. Being beyond a pin at Valderrama makes putting so much harder. Always aim to leave your ball below the cup. As Christy O'Connor Jr. says, "You will sweat tears if you miss the greens here."

The wind does not make it any easier. Close to the sea but set up in the hills, Valderrama is prone to fickle winds. The Poniente wind blows hot air from the inland north; the Levante is a cooler breeze sweeping in off the sea to the south. Depending on which is blowing and how hard, the course can be a different animal from one day to the next.

NO EASY HOLES
Valderrama tests a golfer's skills and patience from the off. At the 1st, you can find the fairway and still not see the green clearly. A shaped shot around or a strike over tall trees is needed if the drive finishes up the right side. At the 2nd, there is a huge cork oak in the middle of the fairway, 284 yards (260 m) from the back tee. It forces a decision for both the drive and approach, and so it goes on. Not one hole can be seen as a pushover.

Perhaps the 11th, an elevated par-5, is one of the few genuine birdie chances. Another par-5, the 4th, features an astonishing green complex. Tucked away behind a lake and waterfall in the shadow of a large oak, it may look stunning, but there is a real danger. The tiny green is at the end of a long hole. It has two distinct levels and the top plateau, although flat, is extremely hard to get at.

Many golfers do find the water there, but more will sink at the infamous 17th. For a chance of reaching the green in two, you must avoid the gaping fairway bunker on the left and then make a decision. If you are in range,

do you go for it over the water to the small sloping green or simply lay up and trust your short game? Because the banks of the green are shaved tightly, only the most precise shots will hold the surface.

The world's touring professionals have a love-hate relationship with Valderrama. While they sometimes find that luck plays a big part, they also know that great golf brings rewards. What they love most is the sensational conditioning of the course—fairways are like carpets, the bunkers of crushed white marble are firm and just the consistency they like for control, and the greens are unbelievably smooth and true. It might be as taxing a course as there is in Europe, but it is a supreme venue and a wondrous test for the best.

▲ **VALDERRAMA'S BUNKERS** are a trademark feature and are filled with crushed white marble instead of sand. Not only do the coarse grains have a bright sparkling appearance, but they also make for a great surface to play from. It compacts well, and so the ball lies superbly and means a skillful golfer can spin the ball for better control.

The 15th and the Serrania de Ronda in background

The beautiful setting of the 16th green

Hirono, JAPAN

Ever since Hirono opened in 1932, it has been acclaimed as the best course in Japan, which is no mean feat considering almost 2,500 courses are crammed into the islands. Ranked among the top 50 in the world and part of a private members' club, Hirono is located in a pine-lined parkland but has a character more associated with the great heathland courses of the Surrey sand belt in England.

THE COURSE

The best-ranked course in Japan has a heathland feel to add to its pine-flanked holes, but rocky ravines and winding lakes and streams also add to its intrigue and bite. Hirono may be a traditional test, but it has lost none of its early vigor over the years.

To reach the 14th fairway, the tee shot carries over water and scrub

The 15th fairway has a long, right-to-left dogleg

The tee shot at the 6th is through woodland until it finds the fairway

The tee shot at the par-3 17th is all carryover scrub, water, and sand

HIRONO

Shijimi, Hyogo, Kinki, Honshu, Japan
Tel no: 794-85-0123

THE COURSE

FOUNDED 1932
LENGTH 7,169 yards (6,555 m)
PAR 72
DESIGNER Charles H. Alison

SELECTED CHAMPIONS

JAPAN OPEN Shingo Katayama (2005)

CARD OF THE COURSE

THE FRONT NINE			THE BACK NINE		
HOLE	YARDS	PAR	HOLE	YARDS	PAR
1	502	5	10	351	4
2	453	4	11	458	4
3	461	4	12	596	5
4	451	4	13	167	3
5	152	3	14	388	4
6	425	4	15	568	5
7	211	3	16	401	4
8	353	4	17	231	3
9	542	5	18	459	4
OUT	3,550	36	IN	3,619	36

HOLE 5 ALL OR NOTHING

As with all par-3s at Hirono, the 5th is played over a no-go area, in this case, a corner of a large lake some 25 ft (8 m) below. The green sits behind a wide and gleaming bunker, with three others guarding right, left, and back. It is also backed by trees, and so this hole is all or nothing. Luckily, it is only 150 yards (137 m) or so, but hit the green you must.

Trees surround the elevated tee

The green sits above an unkempt bank

Viscount Kuki was a feudal warlord and expert golfer who wanted a course built on his estate. He asked Charles Alison, one-half of the famous Colt and Alison partnership, to design him a course while he was touring Japan in the early 1930s.

When he arrived at the site 12 miles (19 km) northwest of Kobe, Alison was impressed with the range of natural gifts he was given. The land over which he would design Hirono was gently undulating and featured a great number of pines as well as thick, junglelike undergrowth and several lakes, streams, valleys, and rough ravines. He spent some days walking the site and sketching holes before checking into a suite in the Oriental Hotel near the train station in Kobe. A week later, he emerged with his brilliant routing and many special holes and was paid a handsome fee of $1,920.

WONDERFUL EFFECT

While in England, Alison had been involved in creating many great heathland courses. He used his experience of them and their visual tricks to wonderful effect at Hirono. The fairway bunkers he built are large expanses set into mounding, which makes them a big target for off-line drives. Those beside the greens are set into raised plateaus, effectively making them deeper and more menacing than otherwise. The greens have fall-offs into dips or the surrounding bunkers, and their putting surfaces are tilting and tricky to hold. A handful of greens are almost completely encircled by sand traps, but all have narrow entrances.

In 1932, when the course opened, Alison remarked, "In America Pine Valley is more tightly bunkered and definitely more brutal, but Hirono comes up well to the first-class standard of the United States, and will afford much pleasant excitement, and perhaps a little pain, to players from that country."

Alison used the natural terrain superbly, and several tee shots have to fire over wastelands or water. Three of the four par-3s are played over lakes to greens guarded by bunkers. They include the 17th, which is 231 yards (211 m) in length and can ruin a good

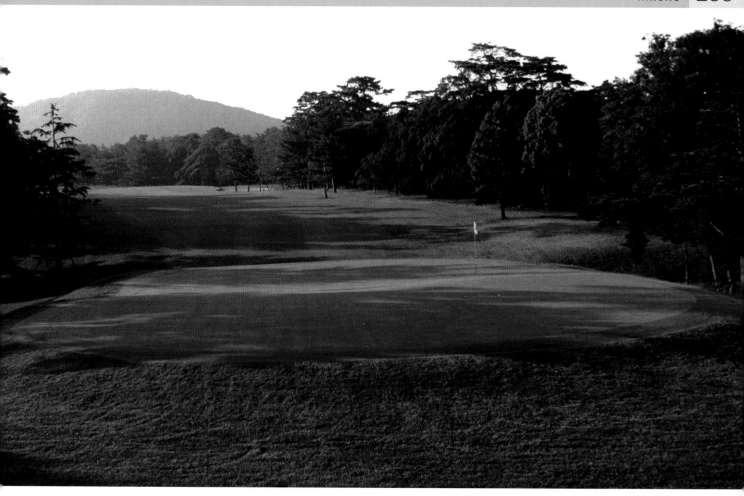

▲ **THE GRAND PARKLAND DESIGN** and intensely private nature of the course at Hirono is epitomized by the lush woodland and glorious fairway of the long 9th hole.

scorecard in a heartbeat. Some carries are long on the par-4s, too. Off the championship tee on the 14th, you must fire first over an inlet of water and then over more scrub to reach the fairway just over 200 yards (183 m) away. Next comes the most notable hole on the course—the par-5 15th, which has been ranked among the world's top-500 golf holes. It is famous for a huge, very old Kuromatsu (black) pine that sits in the crook of the long, right-to-left dogleg. Without it, the hole would be much shorter and, therefore, easier. In fact, the pine is

so important to the hole that the club has insured it for 5 million yen. Sadly, netting now protects it from the battering it gets from those who either try to cut the corner or fail to bend around it. This hole is also famous for a shot Jack Nicklaus hit in an exhibition match of 1963 (see right).

Hirono is old school, including the wood-paneled clubhouse adorned with the kind of gold-lettered honors boards that are featured in traditional golf clubs the world over. It is a very private club, so the mysticism of the course is heightened by its exclusivity. Nonetheless, Alison did a fine job in bringing a little bit of classic golf design to this once secluded corner of Japan and created a temptress of a course for the privileged few.

JACK'S PURE POWER

During an exhibition match in 1963, Jack Nicklaus stood on the 15th fairway after hitting a big drive and with 250 yards (229 m) to go. The club captain told him that no one had ever reached the green in two. Nicklaus smiled and said, "I'll try." With his persimmon 3-wood, he smacked it with pure power. It rose high over the pine, pitching over the bunker at the front of the green and rolling up to the flag on the back right.

● The power of Jack Nicklaus

Whether for a blood match from the back tee or a gamble among the portly ... I can name no superior among British inland courses.

CHARLES ALISON, ARCHITECT

Muirfield Village, US

Known as "The Course that Jack Built"—Nicklaus that is—Muirfield Village is an immaculate parkland in Ohio, close to where the Golden Bear grew up. A lush, rolling setting intersected by streams, this course oozes class. Each year, between the Masters and the US Open, Muirfield Village hosts the Memorial Tournament, an invitation-only event where the golfing elite come to enjoy this majestic test.

Until Tiger Woods burst on to the scene and started winning Majors hand over fist, it was always assumed that Jack Nicklaus was the greatest player the world has ever seen. Many people think it should stay that way, at least until Tiger passes the 18-Major mark that Jack reached. Whatever the outcome of the argument, when Jack Nicklaus sets out to create himself a golf course, you can be sure that it will be a special place and as brilliant as the man himself.

Muirfield Village is unashamedly Augusta-esque (see pp.296–299). It was while sitting in the Augusta National clubhouse back in 1966 that Nicklaus had the idea to build

▼ **MEANDERING CREEKS AND STREAMS,** many of them hugging the side of a fairway, are an important feature of the hazardous nature of the golf at Muirfield Village.

a course near his hometown that would be fit to host an annual PGA Tour championship. Ivor Young, a real estate friend, was sitting with him at the time, and he went back to Columbus, Ohio, and identified 10 sites that could potentially be suitable. Nicklaus plumped for the first he saw—a neat 160-acre (65-hectare) undulating woodland site that was filled with an array of trees and winding streams.

A THRILLING EXAMINATION

Nicklaus intended to give it the feel of exclusivity, prepare it faultlessly, and make it into a course where the cream would rise to the top. He and Desmond Muirhead designed a thrilling examination, one that would see the best shots rewarded and poor ones cruelly dealt with. It looked superb, too. As Nicklaus commented later, "I set out to build not only an outstanding golf course for every level of player, but a magnificent course for watching a tournament ... I thought the Masters was a great thing for golf and that I'd like to do the same thing in Columbus."

The course opened in 1974 and was named in honor of Jack's victory in the Open Championship at the original Muirfield in Scotland in 1966, the year this project was conceived. Apart from the name, the two courses share only one trait, whether deliberate or not. The Muirfield links runs in two loops of nine—the front nine loop runs clockwise while the back nine loop runs counterclockwise. Muirfield Village has a rough configuration of two loops, but both run counterclockwise. Nicklaus was not afraid to be brutal in parts and design on-the-edge holes where a slight mishit would surely be punished. Water comes into play on 11 of the holes. Lakes or a widened creek sit dauntingly in front of a few greens—namely, the 3rd, 6th, 9th, and 12th—but the snaking streams pose just as many problems on several more holes.

UNIQUE CREEKS

Almost uniquely in world golf, the creeks hug one side of the fairway. Some cut across them, dangerously splitting the landing areas in two. The stream then plays havoc with wayward shots near the green. The split fairway holes are the 5th, 11th, and 14th, and your strategy is tested just as much as your ball-striking.

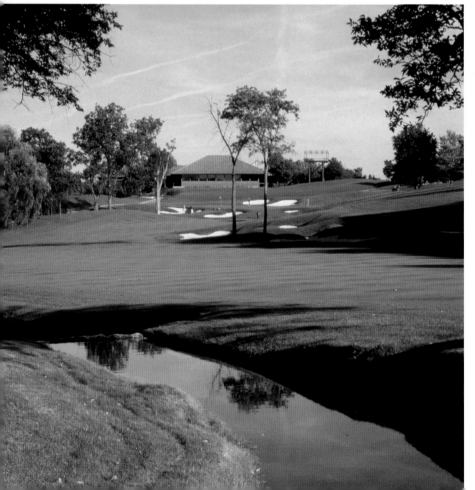

MUIRFIELD VILLAGE

5750 Memorial Drive, Dublin,
Ohio 43017
Tel no: 614-889-6740
www.mvgc.org

THE COURSE

FOUNDED 1974
LENGTH 7,366 yards (6,735 m)
PAR 72
DESIGNERS Jack Nicklaus,
Desmond Muirhead

SELECTED CHAMPIONS

RYDER CUP Europe (1987) **US AMATEUR**
Justin Leonard (1992) **SOLHEIM CUP** US
(1998) **MEMORIAL TOURNAMENT** Tiger
Woods (1999, 2000, 2001, 2009, 2012);
Matt Kuchar (2013); Hideki Matsuyama
(2014); David Lingmerth (2015); William
McGirt (2016); Jason Dufner (2017);
Bryson DeChambeau (2018); Patrick
Cantlay (2019); Jon Rahm (2020)
PRESIDENTS CUP US (2013)

CARD OF THE COURSE

THE FRONT NINE			THE BACK NINE		
HOLE	YARDS	PAR	HOLE	YARDS	PAR
1	470	4	10	471	4
2	455	4	11	567	5
3	401	4	12	184	3
4	200	3	13	455	4
5	527	5	14	363	4
6	447	4	15	529	5
7	563	5	16	215	3
8	185	3	17	478	4
9	412	4	18	444	4
OUT	3,660	36	IN	3,706	36

THE COURSE

Holes swoop down wooded hillsides and many fairways are intersected cleverly by snaking streams that can play havoc with a wayward golfer. Its style and conditioning are deliberately reminiscent of Augusta National.

The approach from the 3rd fairway must carry over water

The 8th green sits a few feet above a mass of sand

The fairway on the 11th is split in two

A creek on the left of the dogleg 18th fairway can cause problems

HOLE 12 · JUST LIKE AUGUSTA

Jack Nicklaus has often said he thinks the 12th hole at Augusta National is the greatest short hole in golf. It is no surprise, then, that he pays homage to it here. The 184-yard (168 m) 12th at Muirfield Village plays at a similar angle with a shallow green sitting behind water, this time not a creek but a lake. The front bunker is bigger than Augusta's but similarly mops up short shots. Going into the bunker behind the green leaves a nervy recovery back toward the water, just as at Augusta.

Standing on the tee, you could easily imagine you were at Augusta

The shallow green is guarded by one bunker in front and another behind

The lake at the 12th

The most unusual of these holes is the par-5 5th, which is 527 yards (482 m) long. The drive fires downhill into a secluded wooded valley and, at around the 300-yard (274 m) mark, the creek appears from the left edge to cut into the fairway. It then meanders down the middle of the hole all the way to the green before swinging left and hugging the green edge. The layup shot into the split fairway is a tricky one as you can on go either side of the water. Cunning and beautiful at the same time.

DO OR DIE

The course uses the elevation changes wonderfully well, too, with fairways diving down hills and rumbling over humps and through valleys. Probably one hole epitomizes the course's nature and spirit more than any other, and that is the do-or-die par-5 15th. It is dead straight and flanked on both sides by gorgeous mature oaks, pines, and beeches. A rocky stream runs down the left side before swerving across the hole in a deep channel some 40 yards (37 m) shy of the green. The fairway is cut across by a grassy dell at about halfway. It is a perfect risk-and-reward hole. The big boys can reach it in two but danger lurks.

The hole sums up Muirfield Village, where the best golfers in the world come to play each year for the Memorial Tournament hosted by Jack Nicklaus. The setting is eye-catching and the golf is clever, rewarding the bold but punishing mistakes.

EUROPE'S DAY

In 1987, the European Ryder Cup team came to Muirfield Village as holders of the trophy, but no team from across the Atlantic had ever won on American soil. As Jack Nicklaus was US captain on his home course, the unthinkable could not happen—but it did (see pp.234–235). Europe were inspired for the first two days and withstood the US fightback in the Sunday singles. Seve Ballesteros, the master of the Ryder Cup, holed the winning putt and ruined Jack's day. The score finished Europe 15, US 13.

Augusta National, US

If there is one course in the world that every golfer aspires to play, it is Augusta National. The thirst stems from watching the world's elite golfers testing themselves every April in the Masters Tournament. It is a course that cannot be beaten for beauty and drama. A sacred place on the golfing map, it is an exclusive, even mysterious club that has an exquisitely prepared and remarkable golf course to swoon over.

Augusta was a late starter in the annals of golfing history, even though today the course is woven inextricably into them. In 1930, when the late great amateur Bobby Jones had the idea to build a course that could host an annual tournament for the prominent players of the day, Augusta was still a tree and flower nursery. Jones and designer Alister Mackenzie set about turning the swooping site—then known as Fruitlands—into the most recognizable golf course in the world.

ELEVATION CHANGES

The setting was already blessed with many trees, most notably 80-year-old pines that now tower above the areas around the 10th. Many more were planted along with 30 species of azalea and dogwoods. Despite its natural potential, it was not an easy site to work with, largely because of the massive elevation changes. The old clubhouse, built as a plantation home in the 1850s, overlooks the course from on high. In front, the course drops some 200 ft (61 m) beyond the trees and away to the furthest point of the course by Rae's Creek. The slope is most noticeable on the 10th and 18th, which arc together side by side. From the 10th tee, the fairway is blind, falling away and around a corner until it reaches a green 120 ft (37 m) below. The rise from the 18th tee is equally severe, although the hole starts farther up the slope. At the end of a tiring day, the uphill battle tests stamina as well as technique.

ATTENTION TO DETAIL

Today, the condition of the course is unsurpassed; the attention to detail by the army of greenkeepers is second to none. Barely a blade of grass is out of place—come Masters time, the edges of the bunkers may even be trimmed with a pair of scissors. It was not always so from the beginning, when Bermuda grass was sown on the fairway to combat the sticky heat of the

▶ **THE IMMACULATE GREEN** of the 12th hole, known as "Golden Bell," lies among the flowers and trees of Augusta National's trademark parkland setting.

KEY MOMENTS

◄ **A BRIGHT GREEN JACKET** is awarded to the winner of the Masters and is presented by the previous year's champion. Here, Phil Mickelson presents the jacket to Zach Johnson in 2007. Sam Snead received one first, in 1949. All champions and members keep their jackets in the clubhouse. Only the current champion can take it off-site but cannot display it in public.

◄ **AT THE FINAL HOLE** in the 1988 Masters, Sandy Lyle drove into a gaping fairway bunker on the left, leaving a 160-yard (146 m) uphill shot. With a 7-iron he muscled the ball up and out, pitching it 20 ft (6 m) behind the pin. The ball wobbled slightly, then slowly fed back down the slope to within 10 ft (3 m), from where he calmly holed for a birdie and the title.

AUGUSTA NATIONAL

2604 Washington Road,
Augusta, Georgia 30904
www.masters.org   www.augusta.com

THE MASTERS COURSE

FOUNDED 1933
LENGTH 7,445 yards (6,808 m)
PAR 72
DESIGNER Alister Mackenzie
COURSE RECORD 63
Nick Price (1986)
Greg Norman (1996)

SELECTED MASTERS CHAMPIONS

Nick Faldo (1996); Tiger Woods (1997, 2001, 2002, 2005, 2019); Mark O'Meara (1998); José Maria Olazábal (1999); Vijay Singh (2000); Mike Weir (2003); Phil Mickelson (2004, 2006, 2017); Zach Johnson (2007); Charl Schwartzel (2011); Bubba Watson (2012, 2014); Adam Scott (2013); Jordan Spieth (2015); Danny Willett (2016); Sergio García (2017); Patrick Reed (2018); Dustin Johnson (2020)

CARD OF THE COURSE

THE FRONT NINE			THE BACK NINE		
HOLE	YARDS	PAR	HOLE	YARDS	PAR
1	455	4	10	495	4
2	575	5	11	505	4
3	350	4	12	155	3
4	240	3	13	510	5
5	495	4	14	440	4
6	180	3	15	530	5
7	450	4	16	170	3
8	570	5	17	440	4
9	460	4	18	465	4
OUT	3,735	36	IN	3,710	36

Flowers adorn the path on the 6th, 1981

The well-guarded 12th green

Caddies wait in the "Caddie Shack," 1989

THE CHAMPIONS DINNER

On the eve of the Masters, all former winners gather for dinner in the clubhouse and the current champion chooses the menu. Previous featured dishes include haggis, neeps and tatties (Sandy Lyle); Texas BBQ (Ben Crenshaw); fish and chips (Nick Faldo); cheeseburger and fries (Tiger Woods); chicken Panang curry (Vijay Singh).

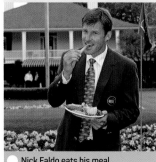

Nick Faldo eats his meal

Deep South. Yet today the course is closed for the summer and then resown with finer grasses for winter play. Historically, there was no rough, just vast areas of immaculate lawns that seamlessly joined up with the fairways. The only trouble if you hit the ball wide were the trees and shrubs (and the manicured bark below), and the water on holes 11 to 16 (except for the 14th). Rough is now a feature after Tiger Woods's record 12-shot win in 1997 (see pp.232–233). Some called the toughening of the course "Tiger proofing," with the aim to curb the monster hitting of the top pros. Since then, tees have been pushed back and a semi-rough grown, which affects ball control.

SLIPPERY GREENS

Ultimately, the skill needed most at Augusta is the ability to hit controlled approaches. As driving has been made harder, firing into the greens and what happens after is now the crunch.

Augusta's putting surfaces are notoriously contoured and extremely quick. A slight error of judgment on the approach can see a ball swept away to another part of the green—or worse, taken off the green to find sand, water, or simply a resting place in an awkward spot down a bank from where chipping is painfully tough. Few courses have such a fine line between success and failure.

Even if a ball finds the green quite close to the hole, severe slopes mean that putting is loaded with danger, especially if the ball finishes above the hole leaving a downhill putt. For Masters week, the greens run at 13 plus on the Stimpmeter (a device that measures the speed of greens; see p.301), which is frighteningly slippery.

UNMISSABLE THEATRE

Such an "on-the-edge" setup means the course throws up spellbinding drama. Watchers know the course inside out because the Masters is always played here. No wonder then that the greatest names in golf have blessed the honors boards since the first tournament in 1934. Ben Hogan, Sam Snead, Arnold Palmer, Gary Player, Jack Nicklaus, Seve Ballesteros, Nick Faldo, Tiger Woods ,and Phil Mickelson are all multiple winners. They have all dealt with the pressure the course brings to bear when other lesser players have crumbled.

The back nine is filled with do-or-die holes, where eagles, birdies, and double bogies are commonplace. The two par-5s at 13 and 15 are brilliantly conceived, offering the brave a chance of something special but also serving up potential for disaster. The same is true for the short holes at 12 and 16. Probably the most famed par-3 in golf, the 12th is a devilish test, with its angled and slender green perched above Rae's Creek and backed by sand and colorful shrubs. Anything goes here, as clubbing in the swirling wind is bewildering even to the best.

Yet at every turn, golfers need to strike the ball purely and precisely to avoid a scramble for par, and one's sanity. Augusta National is not afraid to change to cope with today's masterful players, but it will always be an incredibly evocative and dazzling place and the one course on the planet that all golfers would love to play.

AUGUSTA NATIONAL GOLF CLUB 3109

AUGUSTA NATIONAL INVITATION TOURNAMENT

Fourth Round Tournament

SUNDAY, APRIL 4th

PRICE $2.00—TAX 20c

TOTAL

$2.20

I love going to that golf course. I fell in love with it watching it on TV. It's one of the greatest places we can ever play.

TIGER WOODS

"Gang mowers" trim the 15th

Ticket collection of a Masters' fan

Augusta's famous clubhouse

THE COURSE

Immaculately prepared and enticing in its beauty and danger, Augusta swoops through lofty pines and skirts banks of shrubs and encroaching water. Every facet of the game is tested to the limit, as a golfer faces extreme challenges at every corner. Its greens are legendary for their speed and slope.

AMEN CORNER

The 11th, 12th, and 13th holes have become known as Amen Corner. Writer Herb Warren Wind coined the phrase after the 1958 Masters. He thought it described the stretch of the course that was critical to the outcome of the tournament. It stuck, as these three holes are demanding, stunning and risk-ridden.

The wide 4th green gives plenty of opportunities for long putts

The 8th green sits in an amphitheater of grassy mounds

Bunkers await on the left of the steeply rising 18th fairway

A steep ridge on the 5th green makes putting from front to back very tough

Successfully negotiating the dogleg is the key to success on the 13th

The tee shot on the 11th is through a long corridor to an open fairway

The green is guarded by Rae's Creek, a bunker in front and two at the rear

THE FRONT NINE

1 A gaping bunker on the dogleg confronts you. It can be carried, but it takes a mighty strike. **2** Reachable in two for the longest hitters but bunkers virtually surround the green. **3** A plateau green with sharp run-offs teases even the best. **4** A monster par-3 where three-putts are common as the green is severe. **5** Another green where it is difficult to get the ball close. It is huge and sloping. **6** The hole drops down over a bank of shrubs to a back-to-front tilting green. **7** The fairway is hemmed in by pines, and you need a very precise approach to find the shallow green. **8** Uphill and turning left, a birdie is definitely on if you avoid the yawning fairway trap. **9** Danger looms on the approach. Too short and the ball will run back down the hill. Too long and putting is a nightmare.

THE BACK NINE

10 A downhill sweeping hole from right to left shadowed by staggering pines. **11** A heart-in-the-mouth second shot with water guarding the left. A bale out right still spells danger. **12** Nothing but a pure strike will do, as water awaits at the front and banked traps at the back. **13** An arcing dogleg to a green defended by a rocky stream. Anything is possible—eagles and doubles. **14** Bunkerless, but a humpbacked green awaits. Miss it and chipping close is almost impossible. **15** Find the right side of the fairway, and you can go for the green in two. Anything short, though, gets wet. **16** A ridge in the green can be your friend as it might feed the ball to the hole, but it can also make putting tough. **17** "Eisenhower's tree" looms large on your drive. Avoid it for any chance at par. **18** Judging distance up to the flag is tricky as the hole plays incredibly steeply uphill.

A rocky creek guards the green across the front and right

Slopes and a bunker guard the right of the green

The approach is dangerous, with a lake to the left and Rae's Creek flowing behind

The bridge spanning Rae's Creek is named after Ben Hogan, who won the Masters in 1951 and 1953

The bend in the dogleg is many players' target off the tee

HOLE 11 "WHITE DOGWOOD"

This is the first par-4 at Augusta to be longer than 500 yards (457 m) and the first of the water holes. Accuracy off the tee is important.

HOLE 12 "GOLDEN BELL"

The 12th is a mid iron over water, and the legendary Jack Nicklaus was so respectful of its dangers that he used to aim for the middle of the green wherever the flag was.

HOLE 13 "AZALEA"

You need a big draw around the corner. Then, if going for it in two, a long iron or wood off a hanging lie to the green.

Oakmont, US

One of America's most historic courses, Oakmont is revered the world over for its uncompromising design and immaculate conditioning. It has hosted more US Open Championships than any other course, nine times so far and most recently in 2016. Only a few hundred yards from the Allegheny River that flows through the city of Pittsburgh, Oakmont is a beautifully lush, rolling wonder that packs a real punch.

Oakmont is a difficult course to categorize. Is it a parkland or an inland links? Certainly, when it was founded in 1903, there was a distinct lack of trees on the pastureland, and it was said that 17 of the 18 flags could be seen from the clubhouse porch. A huge tree-planting program in the 1950s altered the look and feel of the course, and many of the fairways became tree-lined like a classic parkland test.

Over the last few years, however, almost 5,000 trees have been removed, and the original open feel has returned. What has not changed, though, is its unique and demanding nature. The course is neatly packed into 170 acres (69 hectares) and split into two by the Pennsylvania turnpike road. All those who drive through her gates enter with trepidation, as Oakmont has a reputation for being one of the toughest classic tests in the US. Perhaps it is the classic test.

PENAL BUNKERS AND SPECIAL GREENS

Founder and architect Henry Fownes knew exactly what philosophy would be applied to his creation, as he was famously quoted as saying, "a poor shot should be a shot irrevocably lost." His thinking applies to every part of the course, from tee to green. Tightly mown fairways that swoop and pitch are hemmed in by strings of very deep bunkers—there are 210 in all. The sand traps come in strange formations—some are in rows of five or six, while others are grouped in clusters. A couple appear as long strips, such as the aptly named Sahara bunker on the 8th, which is 100 yards (91 m) long.

The "Church Pews" bunker is a massive area of sand between the 3rd and 4th holes. It is split into sections by strips of grassy banks some 3 ft (1 m) high and covered in hairy grass. The bunker originally had seven "pews," but for the 2007 US Open, it was extended and now has 12. More than 130 yards (119 m) long, it is not just for show, as it catches many golfers' drives on both holes, and they find it very hard to advance the ball far from it.

▶ **MIST HANGS OVER THE COURSE AT OAKMONT,** where the greens are fast and challenging, and nearly all the bunkers are cut very tightly to the edges of the fairways and greens.

KEY MOMENTS

◄ **FLAMBOYANT AMERICAN** Johnny Miller put together a blistering round of 63 in the 1973 US Open. Many experts consider it the finest round of golf ever. It broke the Major scoring record, enabling him to win the first of his two Majors. He came from behind to beat Arnold Palmer and Jack Nicklaus through the purity of his striking.

◄ **THE ROUND OF THE YEAR** in 2007 came from Paul Casey on Day Two of the US Open. On a day when only three players out of 156 shot par or better, and the scoring average soared to 76.9, Paul Casey's round of 66 was truly remarkable. With only one bogey, despite the buffeting wind, it catapulted him from 104th to inside the top 15.

◄ **THE SPEED OF A GREEN** can be measured by a Stimpmeter, invented by Edward Stimpson after he watched the 1935 US Open at Oakmont. A track like a yardstick is held at an angle until a ball is released from a notch. The distance traveled by the ball in feet is the speed of the green. For example, 10 ft equals a green speed of 10 on the Stimpmeter.

OAKMONT

1233 Hulton Rd, Oakmont, Pennsylvania 15139-1199
www.oakmont-countryclub.org

THE COURSE

FOUNDED 1903
LENGTH 7,230 yards (6,611 m)
PAR 70
DESIGNER Henry Fownes
COURSE RECORD 66
Paul Casey (2007)

SELECTED CHAMPIONS

US PGA CHAMPIONSHIP Sam Snead (1951); John Mahaffey (1978)
US OPEN Ben Hogan (1953); Jack Nicklaus (1962); Johnny Miller (1973); Larry Nelson (1983); Ernie Els (1994); Angel Cabrera (2007); Dustin Johnson (2016)
US WOMEN'S OPEN Patty Sheehan (1992); Paula Creamer (2010)

CARD OF THE COURSE

THE FRONT NINE			THE BACK NINE		
HOLE	YARDS	PAR	HOLE	YARDS	PAR
1	482	4	10	435	4
2	341	4	11	379	4
3	428	4	12	667	5
4	609	5	13	183	3
5	382	4	14	358	4
6	194	3	15	500	4
7	479	4	16	231	3
8	288	3	17	313	4
9	477	4	18	484	4
OUT	3,680	35	IN	3,550	35

THE COURSE

Incredibly tough but a pleasant beauty nonetheless, Oakmont is famed for its diving fairways, diabolical bunkering, and wicked greens that sweep and dip like a sea swell. An awesome test for even the best golfers.

THE FRONT NINE ❶ A beast of a start

where the approach is semi-blind to a green that tilts away. ❷ Landing area is tight with six bunkers right and a ditch on the left. ❸ First encounter with the massive "Church Pews" bunker on the left. ❹ A big swinging par-5, where the "Church Pews" and five deep traps right must be avoided. ❺ A hole needing precision, crucially on the approach to this rolling green. ❻ Tightly guarded par-3 with a right-to-left sloping green. Missing right is trouble. ❼ Tough par-4. A narrow entrance and tilting green make it hard to get the ball close. ❽ The ideal shot is a draw into this huge par-3, but the long Sahara bunker awaits. ❾ A well-bunkered fairway leads to an almost rectangular and awkwardly rippled green.

THE BACK NINE ❿ Downhill but testing

because the green slopes away and to the back left. ⓫ Aim to reach the plateau portion of the fairway from where a short iron is left. ⓬ Unreachable for most, it is one to plot carefully to miss the 20 bunkers. ⓭ A long, narrow, well-guarded green puts a premium on accuracy. Try to stay below the hole. ⓮ Luckily, it is a short par-4, as 10 deep bunkers patrol the landing area, so an iron from the tee will do. ⓯ Pray you hit the fairway and avoid the nasty bunker ruts left, as it is a monster par-4. ⓰ Big short-hole where left-to-right shot may be needed to get at the flag. ⓱ Drivable semi-blind par-4 but fraught with danger. A nest of bunkers have to be carried, and the greenside traps are deep. ⓲ Awesome finish, whose crowning glory is the wickedly undulating green, where a three-putt can ruin the day.

A cluster of bunkers lies about 90 yards (82 m) shy of the green

The notorious "Church Pews" bunker is on the left of the fairway

HOLE 4 — TOUGH PROPOSITION

The "Church Pews" bunker hugs the right-turning hole for 100 yards (91 m) or so. A cluster of deep traps is tucked into the corner opposite. If a drive finds any of these bunkers, reaching the par-5 green in three is a very tough proposition. As the fairway kinks further right around some more traps, it is hard to get at the hole wherever you are coming in from.

The "Sahara" bunker to the left of the green is around 100 yards (91 m) long

The green at the end of this monster par-3 is fairly large

HOLE 8 — HUGE ONE-SHOTTER

From the tee, the view to the green is dominated by the massive strip of sand called "Sahara." From the back tee, it is a carry of 200 yards (182 m) to clear the corner of it, preferably with a right-to-left shape so the ball can run up the length of the green. Anyone erring to the right or hitting too straight will find one of the four other traps.

A large bunker sits on the right of the fairway

The green is very undulating, which makes putting difficult

HOLE 18 — NOT FOR THE FAINT OF HEART

Although the tee shot is slightly downhill, the massive bunker on the right and two pairs of traps on either side farther up will catch anything not perfectly struck. The approach is uphill to an almost ludicrously rolling green. Many balls finish short of the putting surface and roll down a slope from where an up-and-down is extremely difficult.

The 17th has penal bunkers around 50 yards (45 m) short of the green

At the 15th, the other "Church Pews" bunker is on the left, with ditches and bunkers on the right

At the 3rd hole, the "Church Pews" bunker is on the left, with several severe traps on the right

N

○ The sloping 6th green

○ The 1st tee beside the clubhouse

○ The rolling 18th green

The putting surfaces mark Oakmont out as somewhere special. Today, many run-of-the-mill designers build standard back-to-front sloping greens where the golfers' choices are far too predictable. Not so at Oakmont. Many defy design logic and feature terrifying slopes, terraces, and dips. Some also very definitely slope from front to back, like the 10th, which makes getting near a flag here incredibly difficult. Because the fairways are firm and fast, a ball sometimes has to land well short of the green, then be allowed to trickle out down the slope onto the putting surface, trusting as much to luck than to judgment.

All greens feature something out of the ordinary. The 9th is almost rectangular, and the 18th resembles a sea swell, with the slopes rolling down the green like waves. To make the course even tougher, the speed of the greens can measure up to 14 on the Stimpmeter (see p.301), which is searingly fast for such sloping surfaces.

THE 2007 US OPEN

As if this is not penal enough, the course for the 2007 US Open Championship was pushed up to 7,230 yards (6,611 m)—the second longest in US Open history—and the rough was like wire. The course featured the longest hole in Major history—the 667-yard (610 m) par-5 12th—plus four par-3s that averaged 224 yards (205 m) in length, including the monster 8th, which was 288 yards (263 m) long. No wonder, then, that less than 60 sub-par rounds have ever been achieved in the nine US Opens that Oakmont has held. Remarkably, two of these were claimed by Argentine Angel Cabrera, who was the eventual winner in 2007.

Oakmont thrives on its individuality and, although highly demanding, it is thought by the best to be as much a true test of patience as of skill—a place where it is best to go in with a safety-first game plan.

▲ **THE CHURCH PEWS BUNKER** between the 3rd and 4th holes has strips of grass and is one of the most famous sand traps in world golf.

The clubhouse clock

The undulating 5th green

The bunker at the 2nd green

Heathland Courses

Rather like a links course, a true heathland course is quite a rarity. As with their seaside cousins, the greatest heaths are mainly found in the British Isles, although there are less-celebrated pockets elsewhere in northern France, Belgium, Denmark, and Holland, as well as some in northeastern America, Asia, and South Africa.

▲ **GLENEAGLES** boasts three championship courses located among the sweeping landscapes of Perthshire, Scotland.

◄◄ **ALWOODLEY,** set in natural moorland in Yorkshire, England, was the first course that Dr. Alister Mackenzie designed.

◄ **BOAT OF GARTEN** golf course was fashioned from a birch forest and set in the Cairngorms National Park, south of Inverness, Scotland.

A true heath has to have—and be able to sustain—the growth of heather. This is a low, ground-covering, evergreen shrub that has small, usually pink or purple, bell-shaped flowers at certain times of the year. Heathers thrive on sandy, acidic soils and are often found on moorlands and in pine forests.

▼ **EYE-CATCHING BUNKERING** is a feature of heathland courses. Many bunkers have faces covered with either heather or thick grass. Often, they are just short of the greens, which tests distance perception and accuracy.

A heathland's characteristics are very similar to the great sand belt courses of southern Australia, and a few astonishing venues in North America that have no heather to speak of. Because of that, all have been put under one banner here.

BRITISH HEATHS

The finest true heathland courses are found in what is known as the Surrey Berkshire sand belt—a wide corridor of sandy, wooded land running southwest of London in England. Household names such

as Walton Heath, Sunningdale, The Berkshire, Swinley Forest, and Wentworth all share the soil in this sand belt with less-heralded gems such as St. George's Hill, Woking, and Hankley Common. Many cracking heaths are also found in the heartland of England, such as the courses at Alwoodley near Leeds, Notts Golf Club, Ganton, and the amazing Woodhall Spa. Others can be found on the south coast. The middle of Scotland, in Perthshire and Moray, is also home to a smattering of terrific heaths

and moorlands—courses include the Boat of Garten, Blairgowrie, Ladybank, and Gleneagles.

AUSTRALIA AND THE US

Farther afield from this British nucleus is the Melbourne sand belt in Australia. The most famous of its several incredible courses is the Royal Melbourne, while others include Kingston Heath, Huntingdale, and Metropolitan Golf Club. In the US, the No. 1 ranked course in the world rests in a heathlike setting at Pine Valley.

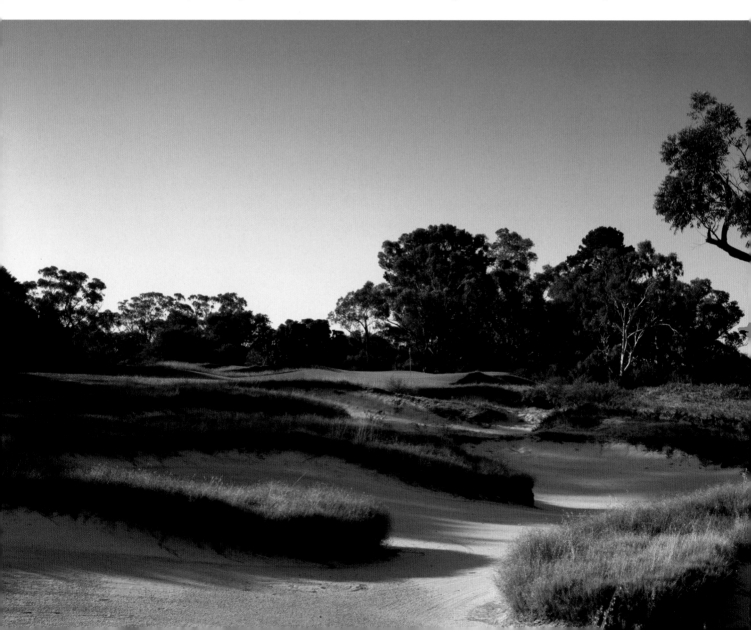

SOIL AND BUNKERING

What do these heathland courses share? Soil is the answer. Their sand-based land does two jobs. First, it can create very attractive, natural-looking settings in which heather, pines, birch, broom, gorse, grasses, and, in some case, flowering shrubs thrive. Second, it is naturally well-draining land, which makes for firm, fast-running courses reminiscent of a links.

As you might suspect with sand-based courses, bunkering is key in their design. The master architects of heathland courses were Harry Colt, Herbert Fowler, James Braid, Tom Dunn, Willie Park, and Alister Mackenzie. They all put great store in the bunkers being real hazards and strategically placed.

Many of the bunkers are deep and fringed with heather or thick grass and appear in thought-provoking places. Although traps do guard the greenside as you would expect, some are deliberately short of the green by some 10 to 30 yards (9 to 27 m). It gives the golfer the chance to clear them or land beside them and still be able to run the ball up onto the green if the course is playing fast. A little mistake on judgment, however, and you can find the next shot being a midrange bunker shot, one that even the pros are not keen on. These bunkers also provide a visual trick and make distance perception deceptive.

Cross-wastes feature on many holes, too, eating into the fairway or splitting them in two. They are a main feature of Pine Valley, although its bunkers are less formal than those of the British Isles.

Australia's sand belt courses have slightly different bunkers, although they are designed by some of the renowned heathland architects. Their traps tend to be shallower, bigger, and more free-form in shape, and tend to come in clusters rather than singles, but all these courses, apart from some holes at Pine Valley, feature a route through the hazards up by the green so that a golfer can play the running ball onto the putting surfaces, which tend to be fast and contoured.

HEATHER TROUBLE

A heathland's troubles are made worse by the heather itself—in fact, sand belt–style courses tend to rely on tall grass and sandy wastes as the main source of trouble. Some people consider a sprig of white heather to be a lucky charm, but golfers do not feel fortunate at all if they find it.

Heather is a nightmare to play from and is more punishing than even the thickest rough. Its wiry, woody stems grab your club as you try to strike the ball. Normally, you would use a wedge or a short iron and attack the ball steeply to ensure as little contact as possible with the heather. It is worth remembering that the clubface almost always closes through impact as it snags on the woody stems.

As a general rule, you should take your medicine and play out with a lofted club back to the safety of the fairway rather than try a miraculous shot.

▲ **WHEN THE HEATHER IS IN BLOOM** and the sun is shining, a heath can be one of the most alluring settings in the world of golf. Many courses feature heather as a hazard and, even though it is colorful and beautiful, it can also be a troublesome experience if you stray from the straight and narrow.

AIRING THE HEATHS

Some heaths are trying to return to their real roots by "opening up" the landscape again. Hankley Common, to the southwest of London, undertook a massive tree clearance program to give the heath some "air" and bring it back to how it would have looked in 1895 when it was first laid out. The wind now has more effect on the golf and the heather grows more virulent than ever.

○ Hankley Common

A heathland's troubles are made worse by the heather itself.... Some people consider a sprig of white heather to be a lucky charm, but golfers do not feel fortunate at all if they find it.

Sunningdale, ENGLAND

The archetypal heathland course, Sunningdale mixes old-world charm and grace with demanding golf in a delightful corner of England. Hemmed in by mature woodland, the Old Course is also a pleasure to walk around, and it is hard to believe that it is only 25 miles (40 km) from central London. Each year, Sunningdale plays host to many professional and amateur tournaments.

Sunningdale's potential was recognized in 1900 by two golfing brothers who asked Willie Park Jr. to design a course for the club's 100 or so members, who each put up a £100 bond. What Park saw over a century ago is somewhat different to today's landscape, but what he laid out is essentially the same course, although Harry Colt added to its prowess in the 1920s.

Heather is abundant and noticeable, especially on the carries from the sheltered tees and alongside the fairways. It also cuts across in front of the 6th and 7th greens but is not so brutal around the fringes of the excellent bunkering as it is at, say, Walton Heath. The Old Course is less taxing than other heaths and is short by modern standards, yet it has a wonderful subtlety to its predominantly straight holes. Any doglegs that do occur are only gently offset, but just that simple change of direction can make the angles for attacking the greens cleverly cunning.

CRITICAL LINES OF PLAY

Strategy plays a huge part in defeating Sunningdale. It is typically firm and bouncy and must be plotted around rather than bludgeoned. The bunkering is thoughtful and hampers every shot on the course, except for drives at the 1st, 2nd, and 6th. Archetypal heathland tricks are used, with traps set close to the line of play but some yards shy of the greens to catch a slightly misdirected approach intended to be run in. On the 12th, 16th, and 18th, a string of traps runs across the entire width of the fairway—very much a Willie Park trademark and a wonderfully provocative feature.

Lines of play are critical to counteract the influence of the traps hovering near and next to the subtle greens, but the perfect line often has to flirt with other hazards. A superb example of thinking golf comes at the 7th, where placement of the tee shot is vital to have the best line into the green. There are plenty of birdie chances, which adds to the feel-good factor of this divine heath. Nothing makes a golfer feel better than starting with a birdie—a definite possibility as the opener is a short par-5 at 492 yards (450 m). However, with trees right and heather down the left, it is a confident strike that finds the fairway.

▲ **THE TEE OF THE LONG,** swooping, par-4 10th hole lies close to the back of the 9th green and invites a big, booming drive down the hill.

STUNNING START

It was the most dramatic beginning to any round in Major championship history. At the 2004 Weetabix Women's British Open, England's Karen Stupples was one shot behind leaders Heather Bowie and Rachel Teske with a round to go. Stupples grabbed an eagle-three at the 1st, then holed a 5-iron from 205 yards (187 m) for an albatross-two at the 2nd. She added five more birdies to finish on 64 and win by five shots. Finland's Minea Blomqvist fired a 62 to set a record score for a Major championship, for both men and women, in the third round. Branden Grace equaled the record at the 2017 Open.

● Karen Stupples waves to the crowd

Sunningdale's finish is a classic challenge, and the last quartet is the toughest stretch on the course. At the 15th, you fire out from trees over a daunting expanse of purple heather to a green patrolled by four bunkers. The 16th has a bunker smack bang in the middle of the fairway to taunt the drive, then your approach is cracked over a necklace of deep traps up to a raised green, which makes distance hard to judge.

The last two are pure golf holes that need precise drives and perfectly struck approaches—downhill to the 17th, uphill to the 18th. Once you have walked off the final hole and repaired to the elegant and traditional clubhouse, you can reflect on what is a graceful, shrewd, and timeless test in lovely, soothing surroundings. Sunningdale is the quintessential heathland experience.

▶ **THE GREENS AND FAIRWAYS AT SUNNINGDALE** are shaded by an eruption of pines, oaks, and birch as they rise and fall over the sweeping sandy ground owned by St .John's College, Cambridge.

THE COURSE

Short by modern standards, the Old Course relies on its subtle design, strategic bunkering, fast firm ground, and the brutality of its clinging heather for its defenses. Its beauty is enhanced by the stands of pine, oaks, and birches that flank all holes in some way. A classic test.

HOLE 18 THE HOME HOLE

The 18th has been the scene for many fine victories from some of the game's great players—James Braid, Harry Vardon, Bobby Jones, Bob Charles, Gary Player, Nick Faldo, and Greg Norman, as well as one of the greatest lady golfers of all time, Nancy Lopez. After your uphill tee shot has avoided bunkers right and left, your approach is again uphill over a diagonal run of bunkers to the green and beneath Sunningdale's massive famed oak tree, which doubles as the club's emblem. If a flag is cut back right, as it often is on championship days, a player can use the left-to-right slope to feed the ball around to the cup.

The 3rd fairway is littered with bunkers

The 12th fairway has a string of traps

The best line into the 7th green comes from a drive down the right

At the 14th, a diagonal line of bunkers cuts across the fairway

Heather-fringed bunkers cross the 18th fairway

The tee shot on the 18th is slightly uphill to an angled fairway

The 18th green is exceptionally well guarded

SUNNINGDALE

Ridgemount Road, Sunningdale, Berkshire SL5 9RR, England
www.sunningdalegolfclub.co.uk

THE OLD COURSE

FOUNDED 1901
LENGTH 6,320 yards (5,779 m)
PAR 70
DESIGNER Willie Park Jnr

SELECTED CHAMPIONS

EUROPEAN OPEN Bernhard Langer (1985); Greg Norman (1986); Ian Woosnam (1988); Peter Senior (1990); Nick Faldo (1992)
WOMEN'S BRITISH OPEN Karrie Webb (1997); Se Ri Pak (2001); Karen Stupples (2004)
WALKER CUP US (1987) US 16, GB&I 7
SEVE TROPHY Continental Europe (2000)

CARD OF THE COURSE

THE FRONT NINE			THE BACK NINE		
HOLE	YARDS	PAR	HOLE	YARDS	PAR
1	492	5	10	467	4
2	470	4	11	289	4
3	292	4	12	416	4
4	157	3	13	173	3
5	400	4	14	477	5
6	386	4	15	222	3
7	393	4	16	423	4
8	168	3	17	417	4
9	267	4	18	411	4
OUT	3,025	35	IN	3,295	35

Woodhall Spa, ENGLAND

Intimidating carries, dishearteningly deep bunkers, and riots of gorse and heather make the Hotchkin Course at Woodhall Spa the most daunting pure heathland test in the world. Set in a remote, wooded haven in rural England, it is worth the journey just to sample her alluring menace. A thoroughbred heath in every way, Woodhall displays a pedigree that often has it ranked as the finest inland course in the British Isles.

Approaching the environs of this quaint, slightly time-warped town in middle England does not prepare you for the oasis of Woodhall Spa. Here, open farmland quickly turns to woodland and the sandy soil under the canopies of the pines, oaks, and birch is heaven for prolific heather, bracken, gorse, and broom. By any yardstick, the Hotchkin Course is an extraordinary golf links. Its endless variety of holes can charm and humiliate in equal measure.

Golfers played on a 9-hole course in the town as early as 1890, but it was not until 1905 that a proper 18 was hewn from the heath by Harry Vardon. It was tinkered with soon after by J. H. Taylor and later modified over a period of years by Harry Colt. Then the landowner Colonel Stafford Hotchkin added his style to the masterpiece. The course has remained very much the same for 70 or so years, except for adding new tees to combat ongoing technological advances.

NOTORIOUS BUNKERS

Four influences, one unique course, playing Woodhall for the first time is an enlightening experience. Golfers may have heard stories about the notorious bunkering, but nothing quite prepares you for the reality. Some say the course once had a bunker for every day of the year, although now a mere 110 remain—but what bunkers they are. Anyone tugging their drive at the difficult 2nd can find the cavernous bunker dug deep into the heath sand shaded by a heavy stand of birch and gorse. Any hope of reaching the green is long gone, and it takes some skill to splash out—but that is just a fairway bunker. Compared to some of the greenside traps, it is a baby.

Most golfers give up trying to knock the ball close out of the greenside bunkers at the 4th and 5th. Just getting the ball onto the green is a feat. The short 5th is a prime example of the punishment fitting the crime, though, as the green should be hit from the tee.

HOME OF THE ENGLISH GAME

In 1995, Colonel Hotchkin's son Neil sold Woodhall Spa to the English Golf Union (EGU) to provide it with a thriving home, while safeguarding the future of this magnificent heath. The EGU, now known as England Golf, has since built another course, The Bracken, and a state-of-the-art academy to help develop homegrown talent.

The 16th on The Bracken course

▲ **THE YAWNING BUNKER** beside the 5th green on the Hotchkin Course is head-high deep and provides plenty of peril for those tee shots that do not make the green.

For unparalleled theater, you must go deeper into the course and admire the midlength 12th, where five ludicrously deep traps surround a green only 18 yards (16 m) across at its widest. The trap front right and the simply gargantuan pit on the left could lay claim to being the toughest bunkers to get out of in world golf. Such traps ruin perfectly good rounds, with golfers merrily hacking away for several shots before emerging.

DEMANDING BUT FAIR

The pressure the bunkering puts golfers under can turn a normally reliable and solid swing into a nervy heave. This has never been truer than from the tees, when you also have to contend with long carries over heather and gorse, with more heather and trees hugging the fairways. In all honesty, the tee shots are demanding but fair. Good striking will be rewarded with a good look at the green, and there are very few tricky angles to deal with.

The 2nd to the 10th holes are in more open heath, but from the 11th onward, the holes enter a dense tree-lined section, and the golf becomes increasingly claustrophobic. Yet every hole is distinct, and you finish with one of the most intimidating drives in England. Two sets of tees are available. One is set back by the 17th green, and from the back tee a drive must carry 210 yards (192 m) to reach the bony fairway. The other, set deep in the forest, gives you a more direct line to the fairway, but it is down the narrowest of channels between the walls of trees, which go on for more than 150 yards (137 m).

Yet that is Woodhall in a nutshell. It will ask ultra-challenging questions at every turn, but, like at the reachable par-5 home hole, it gives you opportunities to score if you can hold your nerve and game together. It is inspired but dangerous golf.

◀ **THE REMARKABLE 12TH GREEN** on the Hotchkin Course is a small gem, but it is guarded by particularly deep bunkers that drive golfers to distraction as they try to escape.

WOODHALL SPA
••••••••••••••••••••••••
The Broadway, Woodhall Spa,
Lincolnshire LN10 6PU, England
www.woodhallspagolf.com

THE HOTCHKIN COURSE
••••••••••••••••••••••••
FOUNDED 1905
LENGTH 6,921 yards (6,328 m)
DESIGNERS Harry Colt, Harry Vardon,
J. H. Taylor, Col. Hotchkin

SELECTED CHAMPIONS
••••••••••••••••••••••••
ENGLISH AMATEUR David Gilford (1984);
Ian Garbutt (1990); Mark Sanders
(1998); Todd Adcock (2008);
Jack Cope (2020)
**BRABAZON TROPHY (ENGLISH
STROKEPLAY)** Jochen Lupprian (2000);
Kyle McClatchie (2017)
HOME INTERNATIONALS (MEN) England
(2001)

CARD OF THE COURSE
••••••••••••••••••••••••

THE FRONT NINE			THE BACK NINE		
HOLE	YARDS	PAR	HOLE	YARDS	PAR
1	361	4	10	338	4
2	411	4	11	437	4
3	415	4	12	172	3
4	414	4	13	451	4
5	148	3	14	488	4
6	510	5	15	321	4
7	437	4	16	395	4
8	192	3	17	336	4
9	555	5	18	540	4
OUT	3,443	36	IN	3,478	37

⬤ The cross bunker and heather on the 11th

HOLE 11 NERVE-RACKING BRUTE

Often chosen as the pick of the par-4s, the 11th is a brute, especially into a prevailing westerly wind. Standing on the back tee is nerve-racking, even though the fairway framed by tall pines is generous enough. In the distance, you can just spy the green beyond a gently rising fairway. Your second shot is slightly downhill over a wide stretch of rough grass, heather, and a large cross bunker to a green backed by tall trees. The real dilemma occurs if you have found rough off the tee or are a long way back, as it takes a brave man to go for the carry over the waste. If you do not make it, a big score beckons.

THE COURSE

This is probably the most ruthless pure heathland in the world, where the cavernous bunkers, banks of gorse and broom, and claustrophobic fairways hemmed in by pines and birch are extremely intimidating to all. Woodhall's variety is legendary, and it is not for the fainthearted.

The 11th fairway is cambered and flanked on both sides by dense trees

Serious cross bunkering splits the 9th fairway

An intimidating carry faces you as you try to find the 16th fairway

The 17th is a short dogleg left that needs two precise strikes

A long drive that finds the 18th fairway puts the green in range for two

From the tee, the carry over the heather is 185 yards (169 m)

The green has no bunkers to defend it—it is tough enough without one

Royal Melbourne, AUSTRALIA

The famed sand belt around Australia's second city houses several amazing courses, but Royal Melbourne stands out from the crowd. Set in gently rolling landscape, the terrain could be described as a blend of heathland and linksland. The Composite Course is ranked the best course in the Southern Hemisphere and has been host to prestigious championships, such as the World Cup, the Presidents Cup, the Heineken Classic, and many Australian Opens.

If there was ever an area so perfect for golf, the Melbourne sand belt is it. Gracefully undulating sandy ground covered in native bush scrub and shadowed by eucalyptus and acacia trees, it is an ideal setting for one of the world's great courses.

Melbourne's club was founded in 1891 and given its royal moniker in 1895 by Queen Victoria. It was not until 1931, after two moves from other sites, that its famous West Course was opened, designed by Dr. Alister Mackenzie. The East Course soon followed, and today the two courses are mixed come tournament time to create a wonderful test of golf.

Twelve holes from the more heralded West Course and six from the East make up what is known as the Composite Course. The two courses were melded together for two reasons: first, to keep all the holes on one side of the property and not split into two by a road, easing the flow of spectators; second, to give the course extra length and bite. The Composite is just over 7,000 yards (6,400 m), whereas the West and East are only 6,589 and 6,566 yards (6,025 and 6,004 m), respectively.

A PUSSYCAT ON PAPER

Royal Melbourne's sandy soil makes for fast-rolling playing surfaces, and, coupled with generous-looking fairways, it appears a bit of a pussycat on paper. Yet being on top of your game is essential if you are to score well, because the course has so many subtleties that you can be caught out very easily.

Mackenzie liked to give the player options, and that is why the fairways are wide in parts. There is always the choice for a player to play safe, but rarely will they beat their handicap unless they take on the tighter lines. The difference between the two routes can mean someone playing a 4-iron in or an 8-iron. Given the way the greens and their encroaching bunkering is designed, there is a big

▶ **PROTECTED BY CLUSTERS OF BUNKERS,** the large and inviting green on the long 18th offers birdie chances in a welcome finish, especially to accurate hitters who have safely negotiated the fairway bunkers.

KEY MOMENTS

◄ **IN THE 2004** Heineken Classic, Ernie Els came within a whisker of shooting the magic number of 59—only rarely achieved in competitions. In his first round, he was 12-under with four holes to play, then caught a flier at the 15th and bogeyed. Two birdies put him back on track. Needing a birdie at the last, his putt slipped by and he had to settle for a course record of 60. The next day, he scored 66 to be 18-under and then went on to win by a stroke.

◄ **DR. ALISTER MACKENZIE'S** 12-week visit to Australia in 1926 led him to have a hand in designing 18 golf courses, many of which bear his trademark wavy-edged sweeps of sand. The shapes of his bunkers mean that every player can glimpse the sand, which helps them with their perception and strategy but also puts pressure on their game. Mackenzie never saw his finished work at Royal Melbourne and instead entrusted the final shaping of the course to his partner Alex Russell.

ROYAL MELBOURNE

Cheltenham Road, Black Rock, Victoria, Australia 3193
www.royalmelbourne.com.au

THE COMPOSITE COURSE

FOUNDED 1891
LENGTH 7,007 yards (6,407 m)
PAR 72
DESIGNERS Alister Mackenzie, Alex Russell
COURSE RECORD 60
Ernie Els (2004)

SELECTED CHAMPIONS

WORLD CUP US—Ben Crenshaw and Mark McCumber (1988)
PRESIDENTS' CUP International Team (1998)
HEINEKEN CLASSIC Ernie Els (2002, 2003, 2004); Craig Parry (2005)

CARD OF THE COURSE

THE FRONT NINE			THE BACK NINE		
HOLE	YARDS	PAR	HOLE	YARDS	PAR
1	429	4	10	476	4
2	491	5	11	439	4
3	333	4	12	433	4
4	440	4	13	354	4
5	176	3	14	504	5
6	428	4	15	383	4
7	148	3	16	201	3
8	317	4	17	568	5
9	455	4	18	432	4
OUT	3,217	35	IN	3,790	37

Royal Melbourne is Mackenzie's masterpiece. By any judgment, it must have strong claim to equal anything on Earth.

PETER THOMSON, FIVE-TIME OPEN WINNER

▲ **LOCAL BOY PETER THOMSON** hits a screamer during the Canada Cup (which later became the World Cup) at Royal Melbourne in 1959, when the Composite Course was used for the first time. Thomson, who had won four Open Championships, teamed up with Kel Nagle, and they destroyed the field by 10 shots.

advantage going in with less club. Standing on any tee, what you see before you is obvious. There are no hidden tricks. Eyes are drawn to the large spreading bunkers with white sand and tongues of grass. You must take some of them on and fly, and you must be carefully skirt others. Fearless, skillful drivers are rewarded with better positions than those more timid or slightly less precise.

Booming driving has to be backed up by exacting and imaginative iron play—you either have to bounce a shot through narrow entrances or shape it to get at tightly cut pin positions on the enormous and rippled greens. The putting surfaces are famously smooth rolling and lightning fast, with slopes that can intimidate the less confident. Putting becomes like a game within the game. Top players can hit the greens relatively easily, but, because the course is fast-running, an approach can finish many yards away, from where keeping a three-putt off the card is an art in itself.

DECEPTIVE BUNKERS

If a green is missed, the shot is likely to find sand or run away into a scrubby lie. Often, the bunkering comes in clusters. The bunkers are shaped like deformed clover leaves, and their sweeping sand faces tend to feed the ball down into the center of the trap. Many are cut sharply next to the putting surface. They are not the most fearsome depth-wise, and getting spin from them is easy; however, they are deceptive when combined with the sloping and speedy greens, and splashing out close to a flag is often difficult. Some days you seem to always face tricky six-footers for par, even if you have hit the green.

RISKS, REWARDS, AND PUNISHMENTS

Mackenzie and his sidekick Alex Russell, who designed the East, built a very fair test nonetheless. You can score well despite its difficulties. The par-5s are reachable with two exacting shots, and brave golfers can thrive on the few short par-4s. The 8th (the 10th on the West Course) is a terrific do-or-die hole at only 317 yards (290 m). You have to take on a gaping bunker in the lee of the slight dogleg left if you are to go for the green, but tug the drive left, and it will find bushes. Hit it too straight, and it might run across the fairway into more bunkers or worse into thick undergrowth on the far side. An easy birdie chance can quickly become a double bogey.

That is a testament to the designers. The routing and shaping of the holes are brilliant and tempt a golfer into taking risks, but the punishments can be great, too. The risk-and-reward element is evident at the three short holes on the Composite Course. A skillful golfer can go for the flags, using slopes and a shaped shot to get the ball close to a pin. The trouble, should you miss the target, is severe because of the large spreads of sand or rough grass and bushes.

Both courses are marvelous tests of ball-striking in a wonderfully natural setting where the wind can also play havoc. Put together as the Composite Course, they lose little in charm and style but gain in pure golfing terms. Little wonder it is the greatest course south of the equator.

● The Royal Melbourne clubhouse

● The tricky 5th green on the West Course

THE COURSE

Royal Melbourne's Composite Championship Course is an amalgam of the best holes from its two world-beating 18s. Holes weave gracefully over sandy terrain and flit past vast sweeping bunkers and native scrub, and the course plays firm and fast. Such is the strategic nature of the course that it nearly always identifies the best golfers.

THE FRONT NINE ❶ A gentle opener that features just one bunker up by the green. **❷** Once the vast fairway bunker is flown, a birdie is a definite possibility. **❸** A short par-4 but an awkward sloping green tests wedge play. **❹** The raised green tests club selection as much as ball-striking. **❺** Benchmark short hole, with dangers on all sides, and a very sloping green. **❻** Long dogleg right. Take on the carry over the traps to leave shorter shot in. **❼** An uphill beauty where most of the trouble is right of the green. **❽** Great risk-and-reward hole—big hitters can take the corner bunker on. **❾** A dogleg left where a drive that flirts with the fairway traps leaves the best line in.

THE BACK NINE ❿ A very tough, long par-4, where a bunker just short of the green catches many. **⓫** A nest of bunkers to the right of the green toy with the eyeline from the right side of the fairway. **⓬** Taking on the massive cluster of sand in the dogleg makes for a much shorter shot in. **⓭** A well-placed long iron to the corner will leave a good birdie chance. **⓮** Fly the traps and the ball bounds down a hill. A reachable par-5. **⓯** The green is brilliantly guarded at the front by sand. **⓰** A cracking long par-3, where a right-to-left shot is best to get at the flag. **⓱** A line of traps short of the green dictate your strategy—go for it or lay up. **⓲** Generous off the tee but a mass of sand surrounds the green. A top finish.

HOLE 12 · A CLEVER DESIGN

This hole typifies Melbourne's clever design. First, you have to decide how much of the dogleg you want to cut off. Big hitters can take a direct line over the bunkers on the right and get a kick down the hill, leaving a much shorter shot than someone who has played safe will face. Swathes of sand focus your attention on the approach, which can be flown high or run in through a narrow entrance.

The 12th has a dogleg and a green well protected by bunkers

Bunkers cluster to the right of the 11th green and make the approach tricky

The 8th has a huge bunker that causes trouble on the left of the fairway

The 6th has a swinging, left-to-right dogleg and a sloping green

Anything to the left or right of the green will find sand

The fairway has no bunkers on the drive, but a string of traps awaits the second shot

HOLE 5 · A TERRIFYING GREEN

Only a straight and distance-perfect shot will find the slick and steeply sloping back-to-front green on this par-3. Go long and a grassy hollow or bushes await. Pitch short and the ball could run back down the hill. Any ball finding the green beyond the flag is in danger of being three-putted as the slope makes it terrifyingly fast.

Bunkers lie on the right of the dogleg on the fairway

Swathes of sand focus the golfer's attention on the approach

HOLE 17 · A TRICKY DILEMMA

If the drive is long and straight, a golfer faces a dilemma—either go for the green in two by taking on the sand or lay up to leave a short pitch in. The left side of the green is the place to miss, as going right spells real danger, with bunkers, bushes, and Out of Bounds guarding that side.

● Aerial view of Royal Melbourne

● The 7th hole on the West Course

Pinehurst, US

Rambling over the forested sand hills of North Carolina, the No. 2 Course at Pinehurst is a design benchmark. Both fun and exasperating, it tests the short game like few other courses in the world. Pinehurst Resort boasts eight terrific 18 holers, but the No. 2 Course wins all the plaudits. Sam Snead once said, "No. 2 has always been number one with me." It is a classic and one from which golf course designers the world over take inspiration.

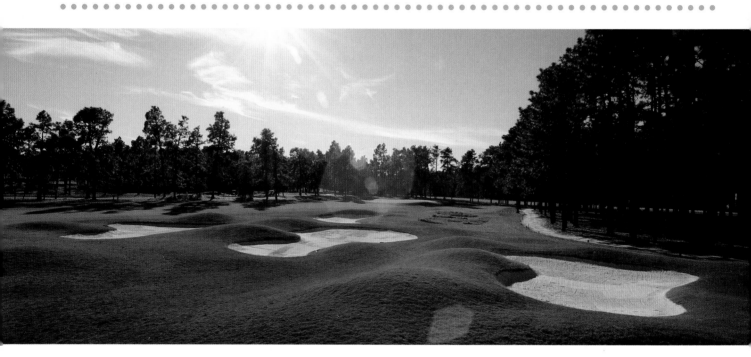

▲ **THE GREEN COMPLEXES** at the celebrated No. 2 Course at Pinehurst are a constant source of frustration and a persistent challenge to the imagination.

The No. 2 Course is the handiwork of Donald Ross, a Scotsman who came to live among the tall shady trees of Pinehurst in 1900. By 1907, he had redesigned the fledgling course that was there already, built the No. 2 Course, and was on his way to creating the imaginatively named No. 3 and No. 4 courses. For Ross, his "baby" would always be the No. 2, and it became a labor of love.

ROSS'S GIFT TO GOLF

This course has no gimmicky par-3s, no manicured flower beds as backdrops, no waterfalls or man-made streams—simply a collection of excellent and cohesively designed holes that come together to provide golfers with a thorough test. When it finally got grass greens in 1935, in readiness for the 1936 PGA Championship, the course was already up to 6,879 yards (6,290 m) long, way ahead of its time in length terms. Players could cope with that length because it was fast running. Little

has changed today, except for adding another few hundred yards, because its defenses are as good and as relevant as ever.

Trouble comes in the form of sandy waste areas, thick Bermuda rough, pine straw on the ground under the lofty pines, and the odd, more formal bunker edged with native wire grass. Fairways are generous, however, allowing a bit of leeway from the tee. Yet if a golfer is to conquer this course, drives must find the correct side of the fairway so they can attack the flags from the right place. Coming in from the wrong angle makes life hard, as the green complexes can make grown men weep.

The greens and their surrounds are Ross's gift to the world of golf. Most of the greens are raised with mounds and dips all around. They are also studded with bunkers. The greens invite both a low running ball and a high stopping shot, but if the approach is not well executed, shots are tossed away down a shaved bank or fed to a different part of the green.

THE COURSE

Many golf course architects come and study No. 2's intricacies, and players think of it as a mecca, too, thanks to its shady nature, gently turning holes, and amazing green complexes that tease all-comers. No one can come to Pinehurst and expect to score well without their "A" short game, such is the severity of the slopes on and around the greens.

The 5th hole was ranked hardest hole on the course at the 1999 US Open. Only 24% of players who hit the fairway put their next shot onto the green

Like many of the putting surfaces on No. 2, the 18th green is raised

Tee shots on the 4th need to avoid the bunker to the left of the fairway

The dogleg at the 7th makes the hole a difficult challenge

The generous fairway doglegs from right to left as it approaches the green

The green is small with slopes that channel wayward shots into a bunker or down a bank

● The small green at the 5th

HOLE 5 A TYPICAL CHALLENGE

This hole typifies the challenges of Pinehurst. The fairway is generous but the right side should be favoured to have the best line into the angled green. The target is small and trademark slopes sweep away anything slightly off track, either into a deep greenside bunker or down a steep bank. At this length (476 yards/435 metres), it takes a pure strike with a mid-to-long iron to hold the green.

PINEHURST

1 Carolina Vista Drive, Village of Pinehurst, North Carolina 28374
www.pinehurst.com

THE NO. 2 COURSE

FOUNDED 1907
LENGTH 7,588 yards (6,938 m)
PAR 72
DESIGNER Donald Ross
COURSE RECORD 66
PETER HEDBLOM (2005)

SELECTED CHAMPIONS

USPGA CHAMPIONSHIP Densmore Shute (1936)
RYDER CUP US (1951)
TOUR CHAMPIONSHIP Craig Stadler (1991); Paul Azinger (1992)
US OPEN Payne Stewart (1999); Michael Campbell (2005); Martin Kaymer (2014)

CARD OF THE COURSE

THE FRONT NINE			THE BACK NINE		
HOLE	YARDS	PAR	HOLE	YARDS	PAR
1	402	4	10	617	5
2	507	4	11	483	4
3	387	4	12	484	4
4	529	4	13	385	4
5	576	5	14	473	4
6	242	3	15	202	3
7	424	4	16	528	5
8	502	5	17	205	3
9	191	3	18	451	4
OUT	3,760	36	IN	3,828	36

▶ **PIN BADGES** were worn by members of the Silver Foils, an exclusive club formed by women golfers at Pinehurst in 1909 to fight for equal treatment with the men.

Donald Ross's philosophy is made clear by his 1935 quote after he had just rebuilt the greens: "This mounding makes possible an infinite variety of nasty short shots that no other form of hazard can call for. Competitors whose second shots have wandered a bit will be disturbed by these innocent appearing slopes and by the shot they will have to invent to recover."

AN ALL-AROUND GAME

As Ross had hoped, the arts of pitching, chipping, and putting are never more challenged than on No. 2. If you have missed one of these "upturned saucer" greens and rolled away down a slippery slope, there are usually three ways to play the next. The high-tariff shot is the lob, but get it wrong, and you could be way past the hole or down the other side. You can try the bump and run, which skips up the bank, or you can take the putter, as the slopes around the greens are so closely mown.

Pinehurst's No. 2 Course favors great iron players who have the skill to hit the precise shot into the green, but they must also be great chippers and putters. If you look down the honors boards, a list of legends leaps out at you. Walter Hagen, Ben Hogan, Sam Snead, Byron Nelson, and Jack Nicklaus have all won here.

The best players in the world love No. 2's balance and the fact that for once the premium is on an all-around game, not just on power and keeping the ball out of the rough. Despite the advance in technology, this brilliant sand belt course will go on teasing all-comers for years to come. No. 2 is a masterpiece.

KIWI BEATS TIGER

Michael Campbell won the 2005 US Open at Pinehurst by two strokes over Tiger Woods. He used his heath knowledge brilliantly to hold the world's best at bay. He became the second New Zealander, after Bob Charles, to win a Major.

● Campbell holds the US Open trophy

Pine Valley, US

An oasis of calm and beauty just 15 miles (24 km) southeast of downtown Philadelphia, Pine Valley is rightly rated the best golf course in the world—an amazing fact when you consider it was the designer's one and only golf course. A punishing mixture of sand, scrub, and pine forest, the course has little room to host Major championships and is home to a private club, so few golfers are able to sample its delights.

A staggering course in every way, Pine Valley came into existence in 1914 thanks to a group of golf-mad businessmen from Philadelphia, one of whom was hotelier George Crump. They chose a wondrous 184-acre (75-hectare) wilderness site in pine-scented sand hills for its natural beauty and obvious golf course potential. Crump was the main mover behind it, and he even sold his hotel to help build his dream.

Crump had a noble design philosophy—if at all possible, no consecutive holes should run parallel to each other or play in the same direction. Nor should another hole be seen from the one that was being played. It works brilliantly here. Although Crump died in 1918 before holes 12 to 15 were complete, he had laid down a course of unspeakable splendor and, without a doubt, a monumental challenge.

BEAUTY AND THE BEAST

The heaving landscape of unkempt sandy scrub houses holes that sweep majestically through the wasteland. There is no margin for error, as the scrub acts as rough that both flanks the fairways and often cuts spectacularly across them, so dividing the holes into islands of green. From the back tees, there is a carry of at least 120 yards (110 m) to reach safety on every hole, either over the wastes or a shimmering lake. The cross wastes in the fairways are intimidating, too—for example, at the 7th, called "Hell's Half-Acre," the fiendish scrub stretches for more than 100 yards (91 m) and makes reaching this monster par-5 in two a virtual impossibility, given that there is another tranche of waste shy of the green.

Pine Valley's trademark, the waste areas are stunning in their natural devilish state but are also a huge psychological barrier. Three-time British Walker Cup player Edward Storey summed up the beauty and beast element of the course when he saw the gorgeous and

▶ **EVERY HOLE AT PINE VALLEY** seems to be cut off from every other by quite impenetrable trees, wasteland, or water. Conquering the greens at some holes is like unlocking the code of a closely guarded secret.

KEY MOMENTS

◀ **THE WALKER CUP OF 1936** saw Francis Ouimet, one of America's finest amateurs and the 1913 US Open champion, as nonplaying captain. He had played in the first eight encounters and led his US side to a record ninth victory in a row against Great Britain and Ireland, winning 10½ to 1½. The second-day singles was a mauling, with GB&I gaining a solitary half point out of the eight matches.

◀ **THE 1985 WALKER CUP** was a tight affair until the young American Davis Love III beat Peter McEvoy in the singles, winning by 5 and 4 to put daylight between the two teams. Love III did not carry a wood, and hit his 1-iron everywhere, proving that Pine Valley can be plotted around, not just overpowered. Team US won 13–11.

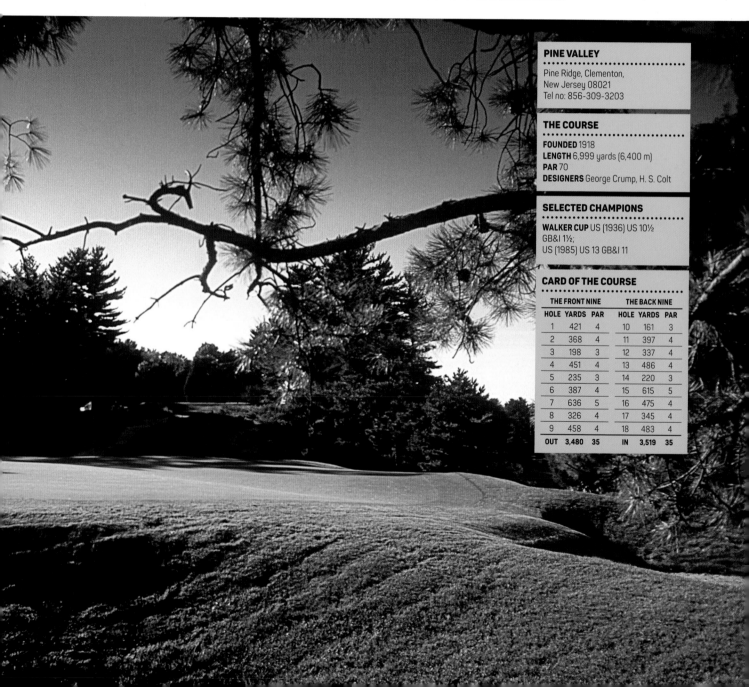

PINE VALLEY

Pine Ridge, Clementon,
New Jersey 08021
Tel no: 856-309-3203

THE COURSE

FOUNDED 1918
LENGTH 6,999 yards (6,400 m)
PAR 70
DESIGNERS George Crump, H. S. Colt

SELECTED CHAMPIONS

WALKER CUP US (1936) US 10½ GB&I 1½;
US (1985) US 13 GB&I 11

CARD OF THE COURSE

THE FRONT NINE			THE BACK NINE		
HOLE	YARDS	PAR	HOLE	YARDS	PAR
1	421	4	10	161	3
2	368	4	11	397	4
3	198	3	12	337	4
4	451	4	13	486	4
5	235	3	14	220	3
6	387	4	15	615	5
7	636	5	16	475	4
8	326	4	17	345	4
9	458	4	18	483	4
OUT	3,480	35	IN	3,519	35

The lake at the 14th

The view to the 17th green

The tree-lined 13th green

THE COURSE

Once open scrubland but now shrouded by a dense forest of pines, Pine Valley is an immense challenge, with its tees, fairways, and greens virtual islands amid sandy wastes. A few serene lakes add to its ambiance and bite.

N

The 10th green is small and heavily contoured

The 18th green is large and sloping

The 12th is a pitch-and-run hole with a sharp left turn

The 8th fairway is sloping and leads to a tiny green

The 6th fairway doglegs to the right

The 3rd green is high on the right

An unusual series of sandy ruts line both sides of the fairway

A huge rippled green ensures the terror is not over even if you find it

HOLE 2 · TYPICALLY DANGEROUS

A short but demanding par-4 that typifies Pine Valley's dangers. If you miss the fairway, you cannot reach the green in two as a 50-yard (46 m) stretch of sandy waste sits in front; therefore, the approach is all carry. If you find the green, three- or even four-putts are common.

The 14th green is just about the flattest on the course

The elevated tees are set back in the trees

HOLE 14 · FEARSOME PAR-3

This hole is as difficult as it looks. Anything short will find the lake or, if you are lucky, the sandy "beach" beyond. A strong pull might bound to the back left into the reappearing lake or get tangled in the pines. It is simply a case of finding the green or potentially racking up a big score.

The green's putting surface is 42 yards (38 m) long and 34 yards (31 m) wide

The tee shot demands a carry over scrubland

HOLE 18 · A SPIRITED FINISH

A finishing hole epitomizing Pine Valley's dangers and spirit. The tee shot is generous but potentially horrible if you stray off the short grass as trees, bunkers, and wastes await. The approach is long over a wide stream and a nest of bunkers to a raised and sloping green. The putting surface is large and so finishing with a three-putt is always on the cards.

THE FRONT NINE ❶ A dogleg right with huge traps that hug the inside line. **❷** Dead straight par4, with a long row of rutlike bunkers on both sides. **❸** A sea of sand makes the green of this par-3 into an island in the wilderness. **❹** Fairway cross bunkers force everyone to have at least 150 yards (137 m) in. **❺** Terrifying one-shotter over a lake to a green flanked by trouble. **❻** Great dogleg right, which rewards a bold drive over the waste. **❼** "Hell's Half-Acre" bunker splitting the fairway in two makes this a genuine three-shot hole. **❽** Short but awkward hole, as the wedge approach needs to be played from a hanging lie. **❾** Looks intimidating from the tee, but this hole has the widest fairway on the course, and the dual green only adds to the intrigue.

THE BACK NINE ❿ Features a nasty small pot bunker at the front and more sand nearly all the way around. **⓫** The fairway twists and narrows up by the elevated green. **⓬** A sharp dogleg left. The farther you drive down the hole, the more the green opens up. **⓭** Often a swinging right-to-left approach is needed to find the green tucked around a corner. **⓮** Another scary par-3, with water at the front and back left, trees and sand everywhere else. **⓯** A gradually narrowing long uphill par-5 flanked by trees. **⓰** Bolder drives down the right leave the more direct route to the wicked green by a lake. **⓱** A 60-yard (55 m) sandy waste stretches back from the green so finding the fairway is vital. **⓲** Magnificent finish, with an approach over waste, water, and bunkers.

Water hazard along the fairway at the 15th

The elevated green at the one-shot 5th

The small, well-protected 10th green

daunting 2nd for the first time: "Tell me, do you chaps play this hole, or do we just photograph it?"

Although the holes are scary to look at and the trouble is extremely penal, the fairways are generally spacious from the tee—up to 60 yards (55 m) wide. This does not tell the full story, though. To play the holes properly, a golfer always has to decide the best side for approaching the green.

RISKS AND DANGERS

The par-4 6th brilliantly illustrates another decision about how much of a dogleg to chew off. The hole bends right, and a waste area hugs the corner. Play the safe drive into the heart of the fairway and the approach is longer than if a bolder line had been taken over the scrub. Risk-and-reward golf at its best. The perfect line nearly always sails closer to the trouble than the safe way.

Danger envelops the holes all the way up to and around the greens. Nine of the holes feature scrub or bunkers directly in front of the putting surfaces, and a handful are almost completely surrounded by fiendish sand. Those that are not have more formal bunkers around their fringes or, like the 1st, have very steep slopes dropping off into impenetrable trees and shrubs. The only saving grace is that the putting surfaces are huge, but they are deviously contoured making three-putting a definite possibility.

A FINE MIX OF HOLES

Short, tricky par-4s (although none drivable); long sweeping doglegs; a set of par-3s that will need anything from a 9-iron to a driver to conquer; and two stunning par-5s—Pine Valley has a fine mix of holes, none of which is even remotely weak.

Possibly the only drawback of this mix is that neither of the par-5s are reachable in two. The 7th is 636 yards

(582 m) long and is split by the "Hell's Half-Acre" waste area, while the 15th hole at 615 yards (562 m) features a carry over water and a gradually narrowing uphill fairway to a green that sits over 30 ft (9 m) higher than the tee box.

The course possesses perhaps the most brilliant set of short holes in the world, both scenically and from a players perspective. Sandy wastes surround the 198-yard (181 m) 3rd, and the 5th hole is daunting in the extreme, playing a mammoth 235 yards (215 m) over a pond and scrub to a green that has no safety net.

The 10th hole requires only a short to mid iron, but the green is small and heavily contoured, with nasty bunkers to protect it. One tiny pot right at the front is so punishing it is called the "Devil's Ass-hole." The 14th is another long par-3 over water and scrub where a carry of about 200 yards (183 m) is needed to find the front edge of the green.

ONLY THE BEST SURVIVE

It has been said that Pine Valley is an easy course for players to make bogies, because many holes are endowed with a safety-first route. Pars and better are much harder to come by because of the risks of a more attacking game. For many years, the members bet all newcomers they could not break 80 at their first attempt. They made good money, as nearly everyone failed. One notable exception was a fresh-faced Arnold Palmer, who visited after winning the 1954 US Amateur. He took on more bets than he could afford, but that spurred him on to shoot a dazzling 68.

Only the best survive the torment, mental anguish, and the pressure placed on the golf game. Great store has been put on the strategic element of the game as well as on the ball-striking, and it is all played out in one of the most glorious but dangerous settings in golf.

SNAPPER SOUP

Several lakes are featured at Pine Valley—for example, at the 5th, 15th, 16th, and 18th holes. At the 14th, the water is as much of an obstacle as sand. Pine Valley's network of lakes not only provides golfers with a challenge on a few holes, but they also teem with turtles. Locals go "snappering," a term for collecting them, to make the famous Snapper Soup, served in the clubhouse.

A turtle in the water

We build them [bunkers] so high that dub golfers would all break their necks. This is a course for champions and they never get into trouble.

GEORGE CRUMP, FOUNDER AND DESIGNER

Ocean Courses

Dramatic, exhilarating, and often challenging, ocean courses are a departure from the conventional and excite the senses like almost no other style of course. The sight and sound of crashing waves, the smell of the salty sea, and an emerald fairway leading to a green perched above the foaming waters is a winning combination for every golfer.

◄◄ **PEBBLE BEACH,** which overlooks the Pacific Ocean on the Monterey Peninsula in California, has hosted many dramatic tournaments.
◄◄ **THE 16TH AND 17TH HOLES** at Cypress Point, also on the Monterey Peninsula, are perched above the foaming waters of the Pacific Ocean.
▼ **THE 11TH HOLE** on the Shore Course at Monterey Peninsula Country Club is exposed to Pacific Ocean winds.

The featured courses in this chapter are categorized as ocean layouts because they are not strictly links courses, even though they are located close to the sea—sometimes perilously so. Apart from Cypress Point on the Monterey Peninsula in California, whose inland holes wind through a sandy waste, these coastal courses feature holes that teeter on the very ocean's edge, most sitting atop rocky cliffs rather than playing through dunes and tall grass. Their playing surfaces, too, are unlike a pure links. Bone-hard fairways are less common, and instead, fairways are usually lusher and more suited to the high ball game.

Because of their proximity to the open seas, however, they share one thing with a true links, and that is their susceptibility to the raging ocean winds. When the offshore winds play havoc with the air above the course, the links-style game can come in handy as golfers attempt to keep the ball under the breeze and stop it from careering away.

A STEADY MIND

It is not just the swing that has to be under control to play these cliffside treats. A golfer's mind must be tuned in to the job at hand to prevent it from succumbing to the waves. Imagine standing beside a rocky precipice with a driver at the ready, a craggy inlet of spuming water directly before you, and a fairway beyond that runs tight to the cliff edge. It might look stunning, but it can be intimidating, too, and a wary golfer is not necessarily the best golfer. Negative thoughts can creep into your game and destroy even the best swing.

Ocean holes must be treated with respect, especially if a wind is blowing, but they must be tackled with a positive frame of mind. A golfer should, by all means, admire the view—as, ultimately, enjoyment of the surroundings is one of the major reasons why we play—but, come action time, the scenery should be put firmly toward the back of the mind. Concentration is key.

GREAT HOLES

Of course, top designers cannot just rely on the landscape to do all the talking. They still have to produce great golf holes to back up the drama, but get it right and some holes on ocean courses become the most spectacular and sought-after experiences in golf.

The courses featured in this chapter—from Cape Kidnappers in New Zealand and Casa de Campo in the Dominican Republic to Pebble Beach and Cypress Point in California—are all brilliant examples of golfing design. There are world-

Imagine standing beside a rocky precipice with a driver at the ready and a craggy inlet of spuming water directly before you. It might look stunning, but it can be intimidating, too.

A CLIFFTOP SPECTACULAR

The Challenge Course at Manele is exactly that—a clifftop spectacular on the tiny island of Lanai in Hawaii, which was once known solely for its vast pineapple fields. Manele's diving fairways were designed by Jack Nicklaus and opened for play in 1993. Bill Gates of Microsoft fame was married on the 12th green. Three holes use the Pacific Ocean as a hazard, and the rest of the course cascades over lava outcroppings. The course is raw, wild and without a single sand dune.

○ Clifftop holes at Manele

◀ **VALE DO LOBO** golf course has undulating fairways with eucalyptus and pine trees and stands beside the waters of the Atlantic Ocean in the central Algarve region of Portugal.

famous challenges throughout their holes, not just on the ones—such as the classic 16th at Cypress Point— that grapple with the ocean's edge.

VARIETY OF STYLE

Stylistically, virtually anything goes, unlike a heathland or a links course. Bunkering does not follow set patterns, the type of rough depends entirely on the native surroundings, and the more inland holes interact with many different types of flora. The soil is not necessarily sandy and, therefore, not hard running, so the holes can be designed to be more target-style. This rich variety of style, mixed in with the undoubted charm of a seaside setting, makes ocean golf a spine-tingling and uplifting test.

▶ **CRAGGY FINGERS OF ROCK** above the ocean at Cape Kidnappers in New Zealand provide a weather-beaten location for some of the most dramatic holes in golf.

Cape Kidnappers, NEW ZEALAND

It is rare that a modern course built within the last decade makes such an impact, but Cape Kidnappers has made so many waves that it has already crashed into the top-30 courses in the world. The course is located on seven craggy, weather-beaten fingers of rock that jut out over Hawkes Bay on the east of New Zealand's North Island, and the holes rock and roll along the spines between the ravines.

▲ **SEVERAL HOLES** at Cape Kidnappers sit on top of long fingers of land where the cliffs play host to an enormous gannet colony.

"Heady" and "intoxicating" describe the golf on the Cape Kidnappers course, and not just because some of the holes teeter heroically on the edge of precipitous cliffs or because a 400 ft (122 m) drop into the Southern Ocean awaits a wayward shot.

The course is brilliant from start to finish, and while the landscape speaks for itself, the design also does some serious talking. It was the brainchild of Julian Robertson, an American hedge fund manager who also owns New Zealand's other star course, Kauri Cliffs in the north. While he was playing golf at Pacific Dunes in Oregon, he was so taken with the course's use of the natural terrain that he enlisted its architect, Tom Doak, to create Cape Kidnappers on his behalf.

OCEANSIDE DRAMA

While some might think that you could not go wrong with a property like this, Doak drew the best out of the gnarled terrain and created a variety of holes that not only challenge and excite but also draw wide smiles from all who play them. It opened to wild acclaim in 2003.

It cannot be said that the course starts gently, as a dipping 440-yard (400 m) par-4 opens up the journey. In terms of pure oceanside drama, the course starts to thrill only at the 4th, where you play down a winding fairway toward the sea. The excellently strategic 5th takes you closer still, and then you hit the dangerous 6th, a breathtaking par-3 over a deep gully. To your left is a drop down to the beach way below. A

▲ **THE 13TH IS THE SHORTEST HOLE** on the course, but its small green right next to the cliffs makes it a little devil. For once, the bunkers on the left are not a bad place to be, considering the alternative.

bridge takes you to the other side and to a green you will have done well to find some 225 yards (206 m) away.

While the superb and varied front nine only toys with the ocean, the back nine confronts the clifftops sensationally. The 12th hole is aptly named "Infinity." Although the cliffs are not directly in play, the green seemingly sits on the very edge of the Earth, as all you can see is the putting surface framed by the glistening waters of the sea and distant hills on the horizon beyond.

A HIGH-CLASS EXAMINATION

Next comes a little beauty, but a stomach-churner, too. At only 130 yards (119 m), the 13th looks like a pushover on paper until you stand on the tee and look left and down to the surf way below. The wind is a major factor at Cape Kidnappers, and playing a precise short iron here in a stiff breeze is awkward. Just hope that if the shot is heading left, it gets down quickly enough to catch one of the four pot bunkers rather than floating away to join the whales.

After a deliciously devious short four, the 15th, called "Pirate's Plank," comes at you to test nerve and skill to the limit. A long sliver of fairway tiptoes along a flat ridge toward a perilous green 650 yards (594 m) away. On the right, a ravine 60 ft (18 m) deep awaits a slice. On the left is oblivion. Doak reckons that if a ball disappears over the fence up by the green, it will hit water some 10 seconds later, so precipitous is the drop. Unless you walk to the edge, which is not recommended for those of a nervous disposition, you cannot really get a sense of the precarious nature of your position.

Throughout this amazing walk, a golfer encounters all manners of shots, a testament to the designer's skills. Booming drives, long raking irons, knockdown pitches, and imaginative chips that use the significant contours on the greens to filter the ball close—these are all part and parcel of the game here. Some bunkers are dastardly, so strategy plays its part, too. It all adds up to a high-class examination of the game, in possibly the world's most spectacular golf setting.

THE COURSE

Laid out on one of golf's most glorious sites and teetering 400 ft (122 m) above the South Pacific Ocean on rocky promontories, this is escapist golf at its finest. It is as much a sensual journey as it is an exacting modern test that encompasses many unique challenges.

CAPE KIDNAPPERS

446 Clifton Road, Te Awanga, Hawke's Bay 4180, New Zealand
www.capekidnappers.com

THE COURSE

FOUNDED 2003
LENGTH 7,137 yards (6,526 m)
PAR 71
DESIGNER Tom Doak

CARD OF THE COURSE

THE FRONT NINE			THE BACK NINE		
HOLE	YARDS	PAR	HOLE	YARDS	PAR
1	440	4	10	470	4
2	540	5	11	224	3
3	205	3	12	460	4
4	544	5	13	130	3
5	420	4	14	348	4
6	225	3	15	650	5
7	453	4	16	500	5
8	182	3	17	463	4
9	403	4	18	480	4
OUT	3,412	35	IN	3,725	36

Approach shots to the 1st are played from a rolling fairway

The 12th fairway is the widest on the course and plays out to the ocean

The 17th green has a nasty set of bunkers on the front left

A massive drop flanks the entire left side of the 15th fairway

The 16th tee perches precariously way above the ocean

● The 7th green on a crest

HOLE 7 "14 FLAGS"

From the elevated tee with the ocean behind, you can spy 14 greens (the name of the hole is "14 Flags"), but not one of them is the 7th! A heart-in-the-mouth drive over a deep, wooded crease to a humpbacked fairway needs all your concentration. A really big drive can reach the summit and tumble down the fairway, making the approach much shorter. The green sits on a crest below the level of the fairway and over a manicured gully. A ball going right or long will bound away into trouble.

Your tee shot needs a carry of nearly 260 yards (238 m)

The green slopes viciously, and bunkers eat in from the left

Cypress Point, US

Carved out of sparse woodlands and dunes, Cypress Point on California's Monterey Peninsula has been called the "Sistine Chapel of Golf." The course has a certain mystique—before you step onto the springy turf for the first time, adrenalin surges around your body in anticipation of the meeting with golfing heaven. If a faint sea mist veils the crooked cypress trees, the eerie calm just adds to the expectancy.

Cypress Point offers otherworldly golf on a majestic piece of land jutting out into the Pacific. Many holes tack through stands of cypress trees and dunes that bear whiter-than-white sand. Two holes, the 13th and 14th, sniff the seaside before leading you down to the three most celebrated ocean holes on the planet, played over impossibly beautiful rock-strewn inlets.

Dr. Alister Mackenzie, aided by Marian Hollins, the 1921 US Amateur champion, created the drama and laid out a course that became an emotional journey and a fantastic challenge. Their masterpiece was finished in 1928. Away from the sea, Mackenzie routed the holes superbly using natural sand heaps to funnel the fairways and provide backdrops for his greens, with wavy-edged and white sandy bunkers seemingly climbing up their faces. The bunkering is brilliant—always in the eyeline and making a golfer think on every shot.

There is a rugged natural beauty to the inner holes, many ambling over a wooded hillside. Mackenzie's use of sandy waste areas eating into and narrowing fairways is clever and pleasing to the eye. That tactics always play a part with Mackenzie holes is perfectly illustrated at Cypress Point. Perhaps the only exception here is the first of the amazing oceanside holes.

Strategy does not really come into play at the stunning par-3 15th. You must hit the green or struggle. You need only think of the club, the wind, and the shape of your shot. There is no safe way to play it. The tee balances on a barren neck of land above the turbulent sea; the green nestles over a spiteful, foaming cove, with squiggles of sand all around. Beyond to the right lurk dark, brooding rocks; to the left and beyond, banks of ice plant and twisted cypress taunt you. Both are no-go areas.

▼ **THE 15TH HOLE,** the first of the famous clifftop sequence, offers a taste of what is to come. Sitting beyond a narrow cove, the green is protected by bunkers on each side.

CYPRESS POINT

17 Mile Drive, Pebble Beach,
California 93953
Tel no: 831-624-6444
www.cypresspointcc.com

THE COURSE

FOUNDED 1928
LENGTH 6,541 yards (5,981 m)
PAR 72
DESIGNER Alister Mackenzie
COURSE RECORD 62
Gay Brewer (1963)

SELECTED CHAMPIONS

AT&T NATIONAL PRO-AM (WITH SPYGLASS HILL AND PEBBLE BEACH)
Fuzzy Zoeller (1986); Johnny Miller (1987); Steve Jones (1988); Mark O'Meara (1989, 1990)

CARD OF THE COURSE

THE FRONT NINE			THE BACK NINE		
HOLE	YARDS	PAR	HOLE	YARDS	PAR
1	331	4	10	428	4
2	536	5	11	198	3
3	149	3	12	413	4
4	530	5	13	333	4
5	168	3	14	537	5
6	438	4	15	384	4
7	437	4	16	317	4
8	508	5	17	157	3
9	161	3	18	516	5
OUT	3,258	36	IN	3,283	36

The 15th tee balances on a barren neck of land above the sea

The doglegged 17th fairway leads to a green on a precipice

The clubhouse stands amid the incomparable landscape

The 9th is downhill and drivable, making it a good short par-4

A windy, watery chasm beckons the golfer who chooses to go direct for the green

The green is perched on a promontory and surrounded by dazzling white bunkers, with rocky pitfalls nearby

The tantalizing 16th green

THE COURSE

Cypress Point is a wondrous mix of holes, where a golfer must contend with rolling sandy wastes and trees on the inland stretch and "on-the-edge" shots on its spectacular ocean trio. The course is short by modern standards but tests both nerve and skill in equal amount.

HOLE 16 THE TOUGHEST PAR-3

The chances of successfully striking a ball more than 200 yards (183 m) across a windy, watery chasm and making the green are small. The alternative is to aim well left and go for the patch of fairway about 140 yards (128 m) from the tee.

What follows is even more frightening. Mackenzie wanted to play the 16th as a two-shotter because of the carry over the cove, but it became a scintillating and dangerous par-3 at Hollins's insistence. Many holes of irrepressible fame are often followed by one that lets you down emotionally. Not so here. Another hole of unspeakable beauty hits you between the eyes.

GNARLED LIMBS AND BUSHY CANOPIES

Among its rocky and sea-swirling charms, the 17th is a wonderfully thought-out hole. The tee perches high on a cliff above the waves, and the fairway gently arcs around Pacific boulders to a green on a natural promontory. Yet the 17th is dominated by a huddle of gaunt cypresses. Standing proud on the right edge of the fairway some 250 yards (229 m) from the tee, their gnarled limbs and bushy canopies dictate how the hole is played.

The shortest route to the precarious green is to flirt with the water's edge down the right, but it is dangerous, so most golfers go left to the heart of the fairway. Depending on exactly what line you take and how far the ball has rolled, you are faced with a variety of shots to a green edged with a stone wall and sand. Too safe a line and you face a long shot over the trees, but if the ball runs closer to the trees, blocking the view and line, you must either hit a high one over or shape a shot around the leafy obstacle. Thinking golf at its finest.

After this exhilaration, the 18th is something of an anticlimax. It turns inland and doglegs almost tamely up to the understated wooden clubhouse. It is a minor blip on an outstanding and unforgettable course.

▲ **A LONE WINDSWEPT CYPRESS** stands on a cliff overlooking the waters of Monterey Bay. Cypress trees feature throughout most of the holes on the course.

I do not suppose anywhere is there such a glorious combination of rocky coast, sand dunes, pine woods, and cypress trees.

ALISTER MACKENZIE, COURSE DESIGNER

Pebble Beach, US

Less than a mile away from Cypress Point, as the crow flies, Pebble Beach careers along the equally impressive cliffs of the Monterey Peninsula and features nine spellbinding holes that meet head-on the influences of the Pacific. Scene of many heroic tournaments—Jack Nicklaus triumphed here in the club's first US Open in 1972, and Tiger Woods took the 2000 US Open by storm (see pp.238–239)—it holds a special place in the hearts of many golfers.

Anyone with a handicap and a large wallet can play at Pebble Beach, as it is the greatest public course in the world. It was laid out in 1919 by two well-known local amateurs, Jack Neville and Douglas Grant, as part of a major resort complex owned by the Del Monte fruit company. Neville was always modest in his assessment of the course and downplayed his achievement by saying, "It was all there in plain sight. Very little clearing was necessary. The big thing, naturally, was to get as many holes as possible along the bay. It took a little imagination, but not much. Years before it was built, I could see this place as a golf links. Nature had intended it to be nothing else. All we did was cut away a few trees, install a few sprinklers, and sow a little seed."

THE SEASIDE SEQUENCE

It is a testament to how great a job they did that the course remains very much the same to this day. The only major change was a new 5th hole designed by Jack Nicklaus in 1998. For almost 70 years, the owners of a beachfront property had declined to sell, so the hole was always played inland. Finally, in 1995, the company managed to acquire the precious land, and another superb hole was borne. It meant the seaside sequence was now unbroken from the 4th to the 10th—and what a journey those holes are.

The 4th is a short but tricky par-4 with a typically small and sloping green just a few yards from the beach. Nicklaus's 5th hole is a splendid one-shot hole with the beach on the right and pines on the left. It often needs a shaped left-to-right shot to avoid a front bunker and to get a clear run up the length of the green. Then you hit the 6th, where the old ocean sequence used to start. Lee Trevino once quipped to the gallery on the tee, "If you're five-over when you hit this tee, it's the best place in the world to commit suicide." He knew that he was about to begin probably the hardest five-hole run in golf. Even without a wind, the tee shot and second at the

▶ **SITTING ON A SMALL ROCKY PROMONTORY** just above the waters of the Pacific Ocean, the spectacular green at the famous par-3 7th is surrounded by a ring of bunkers.

KEY MOMENTS

◀ **THE GREATEST CHIP EVER** came from Tom Watson in the 1982 US Open as he stood just left of the 17th green in ankle-deep rough. He whispered to his caddie, "I'm going to make it," and dropped the clubhead softly in behind the ball. It popped out and rolled gently into the cup for a birdie two. He leapt in the air and ran around the fringe pointing to his caddie mouthing, "I told you." Watson also birdied the last, winning the championship by two. His incredible chip became known as "The shot that was heard around the world."

◀ **TIGER WOODS** provided irrefutable evidence at the 2000 US Open that he is one of the best-ever players. His opening 65 was a record for a Pebble Beach US Open. He backed it up with a 69 and a 71, despite a triple bogey, and led after three rounds by 9. Tiger's bogey-free 67 on Sunday blew away the field, and he finished at 16-under par and an unbelievable 15 strokes clear—both records for the championship.

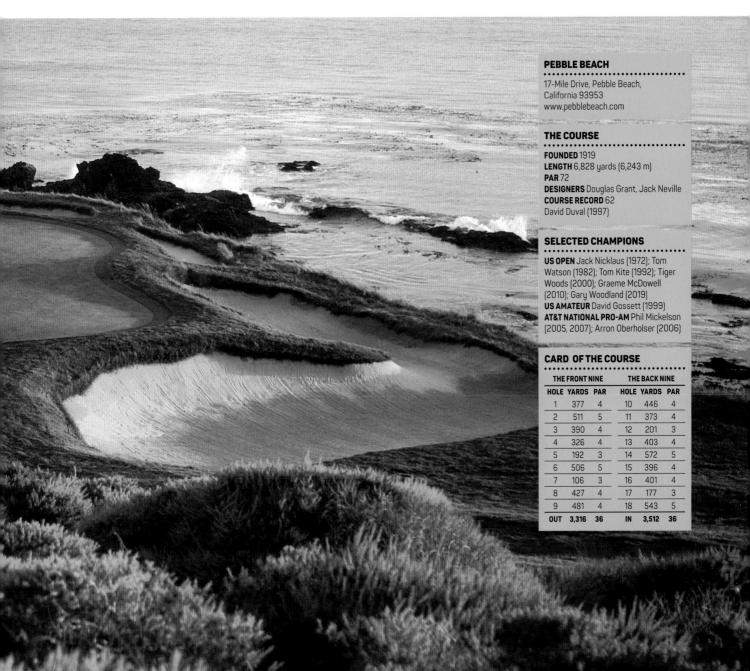

PEBBLE BEACH

17-Mile Drive, Pebble Beach, California 93953
www.pebblebeach.com

THE COURSE

FOUNDED 1919
LENGTH 6,828 yards (6,243 m)
PAR 72
DESIGNERS Douglas Grant, Jack Neville
COURSE RECORD 62
David Duval (1997)

SELECTED CHAMPIONS

US OPEN Jack Nicklaus (1972); Tom Watson (1982); Tom Kite (1992); Tiger Woods (2000); Graeme McDowell (2010); Gary Woodland (2019)
US AMATEUR David Gossett (1999)
AT&T NATIONAL PRO-AM Phil Mickelson (2005, 2007); Arron Oberholser (2006)

CARD OF THE COURSE

THE FRONT NINE			THE BACK NINE		
HOLE	YARDS	PAR	HOLE	YARDS	PAR
1	377	4	10	446	4
2	511	5	11	373	4
3	390	4	12	201	3
4	326	4	13	403	4
5	192	3	14	572	5
6	506	5	15	396	4
7	106	3	16	401	4
8	427	4	17	177	3
9	481	4	18	543	5
OUT	3,316	36	IN	3,512	36

The AT&T Pebble Beach National Pro-Am is an annual 72-hole tournament in which 180 professionals pair up with 180 amateurs. Bing Crosby hosted the original event in 1937 at Rancho Santa Fe Golf Club, which is why it is known affectionately as "The Crosby Clambake," or simply "The Crosby." Professionals who have played include Tiger Woods and Phil Mickelson (who won it in 2007), and celebrities include Clint Eastwood and Bill Murray.

Clint Eastwood

uphill, semi-blind and exposed par-5 6th are tough. Any shot veering right will probably disappear over a cliff and sail down to the gushing waters of the Pacific. The hole does offer birdie chances, but big numbers can be racked up, too. Many would be forgiven for thinking that the tiny par-3 7th is a respite from the rigors of the course, but it has optical properties that make it both dangerous and spectacular (see opposite).

FROM EVIL TO SAVING GRACE
The 8th features a preposterous approach (see panel), and the 9th is equally terrifying and demanding, with a steep cliff down the right side. Anything short or left will probably find the deep gully, but these are safer options than the ball missing right, which is dead. It is Pebble Beach's most evil hole, made harder by the fact that quite often it must be approached with a long iron or wood off a hanging lie.

Just when you think it is going to get easier, however, the 10th confronts you. Again with ocean cliffs on the right, this time the sloping fairway is patrolled by a large bunker complex on the left at driving distance. There are only 35 yards (32 m) to play with on the drive and then, from another sidehill lie that wants to push your shots toward the sea, an approach must avoid the ravine that eats into the front right of the green. The only saving grace is that, if you do go long, a bunker waits at the back to stop the shot from disappearing into a creek.

▲ BUNKERS LIE BETWEEN THE 17TH GREEN and the cliff above the ocean waves. The green is shaped like a figure eight and is a devil to reach when the wind is heading in toward you.

THE JOURNEY HOME
From then on, the lush fairways meander through pines and cypress, and it feels a little tame after the thrill of playing above the coastal bluffs. The course reappears by the sea at the quirky-shaped 17th, a par-3 that plays out to the cliffside and the ocean beyond. The angled green is like a narrow figure eight that is protected by seven bunkers, including a huge antler-shaped trap across the front. By far and away, the most teasing pin position is back left as the cliff awaits a pull just yards away. In 1972, Jack Nicklaus sealed his US Open win with a crunched 1-iron that hit the flagstick and finished inches away. The risk-and-reward 18th is a great finishing hole (see opposite). Perhaps the most amazing moment it has seen is the miraculous birdie four Hale Irwin made in 1984. He stood one behind leader Jim Nelford at the Bing Crosby Tournament, only to yank his drive left toward the ocean, where it hit some rocks and pinged back into play. He reached the playoff, which he duly won.

This is a perfect example of how Pebble Beach toys with emotions. It mixes bravado and brains and taunts you to play the shots of your life.

> If I had one last round to play, I would likely choose Pebble Beach. I've loved this course from the first time I saw it. It's possibly the best in the world.
>
> **JACK NICKLAUS**

The 6th, 7th, and 8th holes on a peninsula

The shoreside 10th hole

The demanding 9th hole

THE COURSE

Away from the ocean, fairways sweep through pines and cypress trees and are splashed with white sand, but it is the amazing Pacific stretch that draws golfers to its cliffs. Even on a calm day, the seaside holes are tough, but given a stiff ocean wind, they can tear you apart.

THE FRONT NINE ❶ A gentle dogleg right. Aim to drive short of the fairway trap on the left. **❷** Deep gorge 75 yards (68 m) short of the green dictates strategy. **❸** Right-to-left shot from the tee to hug the contours of this dogleg. **❹** Precise short-iron approach to find the small, sand-surrounded green. **❺** To get at a back flag position, a left-to-right shot is best, even though it shapes toward the cliff. **❻** The semi-blind 2nd onto the fairway needs total confidence as the ocean awaits right. **❼** Great one-shotter where wind and concentration are key. **❽** Very dramatic approach shot high over an ocean inlet. **❾** Best to aim just inside of the fairway bunker left and let the natural fall of the land move your drive into the center.

THE BACK NINE ❿ Bold approach to carry the ravine eating into the front right of the green. **⓫** Difficult to judge approach on this uphill hole going back inland. **⓬** All carry to a shallow green as a huge bunker front left leaves little room for a run-up shot. **⓭** Very difficult to get approach close as it plays uphill to a seriously sloping and fast green. **⓮** Tempting to carry bunker in the corner of the dogleg right, but best to play it as a three-shotter. **⓯** A decent carry is needed, then a pinpoint approach to green sloping right-to-left. **⓰** Aim directly over the bunker in midfairway. Hit approaches right of the flag as the green is sloping. **⓱** Pray it is not into the wind, as it becomes a monster three with a very shallow angled green. **⓲** The best line is just to the left of a tree in the fairway. Play as a three-shotter, as trouble lurks all down the left.

The 5th green sits just a few yards away from the rocks

A huge bunker at the front protects the 12th green

Anything left of the 18th fairway spells trouble

The wide but shallow angled green makes the 17th hard to hit

A ball short right of the 10th green is swallowed by a ravine

The tee shot plays downhill over a large sand trap

The green sits on a rocky promontory just above the waves

The tee shot is a blind drive up a steep hill

The green has an awkward putting surface that sits 60 ft (18 m) above the waves

HOLE 7 — A LITTLE DEVIL

This downhill par-3 is a photographer's dream. It is the shortest hole in Major championship golf but still a little devil. You are wary of hitting too far, as all you can see behind the green is the ocean, so you may underhit your tee shot. Optical effects can play with the brain and the swing, especially when a wind is blowing. If it is breezy, it is best to take more club than you think and swing within yourself to keep the ball lower and under control.

HOLE 18 — A CRACKING DRIVE

It is not time to be greedy on the drive, as the ocean hugs the entire left side of the arcing dogleg, but do not be tempted to bail out right either, as Out of Bounds awaits. Aim at the tree in the fairway, and a good crack should see the drive past the obstacle. It is often best to lay quite well back from the green and take your chances with the 3rd. It will also lessen the risk of the huge tree short right of the green coming into play.

HOLE 8 — A THRILLING PROSPECT

The adrenalin rush you experience as you walk up the hill after your drive is extraordinary, as the sight that greets you is eye-popping. A few yards ahead the fairway ends, then the hole swings sharply right and swoops downward across a steepling cliff to a small green hemmed in by sand. You have to hit the green with a long iron or fairway wood, as you can easily face a shot of more than 200 yards (183 m) from the top fairway.

The fairway narrows up toward the green

The green slopes steeply toward the ocean

● The dangerous 7th hole

● The eye-popping 8th hole

● The ocean-hugging 18th hole

Casa De Campo, DOMINICAN REPUBLIC

The locals call the serrated coral reefs that sprout from the sea the Dientes del Perro (Teeth of the Dog) because of their jagged and menacing nature. It was the perfect name for this oceanside course that has serious bite and where the golf is heavily influenced by the sea. The Teeth of the Dog is the jewel in the crown of a vast playground in the Dominican Republic and is ranked as the best course in the Caribbean.

A MAMMOTH COURSE

There are two other courses designed by Pete Dye on the site of the Casa de Campo resort, which is set over 7,000 acres (2,833 hectares). These are the Links Course and the Dye Fore Course, which is the latest creation—it measures a mammoth 7,770 yards (7,105 m) long and follows the Chavon River to where it flows out into the ocean.

● Course designer Pete Dye

Pete Dye's treacherous Teeth of the Dog Course boasts an astonishing seven holes along the jagged water's edge. On each of them, golfers are so close to the sea and barely above the waves that they can feel the sea spray brushing over them as they play.

It might look like this southern Dominican coastline was born for golf, but when the architect first clapped eyes on this land from the air, he was filled with doubt. It was a barren strip of ground, and the sea's edge was just a jumble of encrusted coral. It was not until Dye got his feet on terra firma and strode along the shore that he found ready-made inlets and small bays that would be the perfect length for some stunning golf holes. He still maintains to this day that he created 11 holes and "the man upstairs laid out the other seven."

That was in 1969. It took two years to build, mostly by hand. A few tractors trailing heavy metal bars smoothed the jagged coral after it had been pickaxed. Then cartload upon cartload of topsoil was brought down from the mountains and painstakingly spread by hand. Three hundred local workers maneuvered the soil to form Dye's trademark mounds and pot bunkers. Tees were built on rocky outcrops, and small rippled greens were pushed as close to the sea as they dare. Even the seed was scattered by hand and palms were planted in strategic positions.

OCEAN HOLES

The inland holes sneak through stands of palm and long patches of sandy waste bunkers flank the fairway. They are great holes in their own right, but it is the ocean holes everyone remembers and craves to play. After four holes to whet the appetite, you arrive at the seaside nervous but excited. The 5th is the first of three staggering par-3s by the ocean. It may be only 157

yards (143 m), but an inlet cuts in between the tee and green, and there is nowhere to go apart from the green. If the wind is whistling in from the ocean on the left, it is a confident golfer who can aim out to sea and hope for the breeze to bring their ball back toward the green.

The same goes for the 6th and the very demanding 7th. At 229 yards (210 m) from the back tee, the 7th is just about the scariest proposition on the whole course, although an arc of sand rings the left side of the green and catches the slightly wayward shot. Just to add variety, the short 16th plays back along the shore the other way so that the ocean is on the right. Dye was clever here, too, placing four magnetic bunkers on the left of the green to catch those players erring too much on the side of caution.

INDIVIDUAL AND MEMORABLE

That is the theme with the ocean holes. All tee shots are intimidating and require a pure strike, but they are not impossible. A properly thought-out and well-executed shot will find the short grass, but a wayward shot will find trouble. If you miss the fairways or greens, then the landside of the holes is the lesser of the two evils, but Dye has put in enough danger so that if you land safe but wide of the target, you will have some tricky escape shots.

It would have been easy for Dye to be repetitive, as the ocean terrain is so similar, but he has varied the lengths of the holes and the subtleties of the green complexes and hazards so well that each feels individual and memorable. Then again, no one ever forgets the Teeth of the Dog—it would be impossible. Nowhere in world golf have so many holes been directly influenced by the ocean, which is so close to play as to be disturbing yet inspiring.

This course will come out of nowhere, and it will throw you down and stomp on your head.

GARY KOCH, AT THE 1974 WORLD TEAM CHAMPIONSHIPS, WHICH HIS TEAM WON!

▶ **THE WATERS OF THE CARIBBEAN** break on an encrusted coral shoreline from which seven holes on the remarkable Teeth of the Dog Course have been fashioned.

CASA DE CAMPO

La Romana, Dominican Republic
www.casadecampo.com.do

TEETH OF THE DOG COURSE

FOUNDED 1969
LENGTH 7,471 yards (6,831 m)
PAR 72
DESIGNER Pete Dye

SELECTED CHAMPIONS

1974 EISENHOWER TROPHY (WORLD AMATEUR TEAM CHAMPIONSHIPS) US (George Burns, Gary Koch, Jerry Pate, Curtis Strange)
1974 ESPIRITO SANTO TROPHY (WOMEN'S WORLD TEAM CHAMPIONSHIPS) US (Cynthia Hill, Debbie Massey, Carol Semple-Thompson)

CARD OF THE COURSE

THE FRONT NINE			THE BACK NINE		
HOLE	YARDS	PAR	HOLE	YARDS	PAR
1	404	4	10	405	4
2	390	4	11	604	5
3	551	5	12	483	4
4	489	4	13	201	3
5	176	3	14	497	5
6	501	4	15	374	4
7	229	3	16	204	3
8	414	4	17	463	4
9	602	5	18	484	4
OUT	**3,756**	**36**	**IN**	**3,715**	**36**

Bunkers are scattered beside the 11th fairway

An enormous bunker patrols the left of the doglegged 10th

Sand and water provide the hazards on the right of the 14th

The short 16th has no bail-out areas

A deep grassy swale is dug in behind the green to catch anything overhit

The rocky shoreline of the Caribbean is the hazard on the left

The 5th is tiny yet thrilling

The splendid 8th green

THE COURSE

The holes cannot get any closer to the ocean without actually having waves breaking on the fairways. The Teeth of the Dog Course features seven holes on the water's edge, and each one, while varied, is intimidating but beautiful in its exhilarating nature.

HOLE 8 SKILL AND COURAGE

The 8th hole feels like the 18th at the TPC at Sawgrass (another Dye creation), as it hugs a curving waterline. You are tempted to fire safely right, but sandy humps and hollows await. The approach shot really tests your skill and courage. A patch of grassy knolls guards against a bailout right, and a massive bunker cuts in across the front. Anything left pings around on the coral and will most probably go swimming.

Mountain Courses

Mountain golf is invigorating and breathtaking—quite literally at times, depending on the altitude. Yet golfing in the world's highest places is not what it seems. It is impossible to craft a course on steep, uncompromising slopes, yet through valleys, between peaks, or over lofty plateaus is possible and makes for fabulous golf in staggering surroundings.

▲ **KANANASKIS COUNTRY** Golf Course is located in boreal forest high up in the spectacular Rocky Mountains of Canada.

◄ ◄ **THE LLAO LLAO** course is overlooked by mountains and framed between two lakes in the Nahuel Huapi National Park in Argentina.

◄ **THE MÉRIBEL** Golf Course is set in a glorious alpine landscape of the Trois Vallées region in France.

What virtually all "mountain" courses have in common is the beauty or ruggedness of their backdrops. Smacking a drive off an elevated tee that arcs gracefully against the distant pinnacles is a never-to-be-forgotten experience.

The most famous mountain regions for golf include the Alps, with courses such as Seefeld Wildmoos and Eichenheim in Austria, Chamonix in France, and Crans Sur Sierre in Switzerland. They all provide incredible scenery to go with their courses, as they wind through pines and birch and are crisscrossed with streams.

The Rocky Mountains of Canada and the US hold many superb examples of mountain golf, too— from Whistler in British Columbia through Jasper, Kananaskis, and

Banff in Alberta, and all the way down to Colorado, where you will find internationally acclaimed courses such as Redlands Mesa and Castle Pines.

Further off the beaten track, mountain golf excites both locals and intrepid visitors. In Argentine Patagonia, tourists delight in the lakeside Llao Llao resort near Bariloche, with the steepling Andes behind. Royal Thimpu in Bhutan, at 2,570 yards (2,350 m) above sea level, entertains royalty and Buddhist monks alike among the barren Himalayas.

MOUNTAIN CONDITIONS

While these are just a few examples of where mountain golf is played, the terrains are very different. The alpine and Canadian Rockies'

courses disappear under a blanket of snow for six months, not just limiting game time but also giving the greenkeepers headaches. Their playing surfaces tend to be green and lush and will rarely get dry and fast, even in the warmest of summers. At other courses further south in the Rockies, however, the air tends to be thin and dry, making the courses run faster. Their conditions are more desertlike, which means the fairways are watered regularly and can provide a stark contrast to the craggy barren surroundings.

Yet wherever you play mountain golf, you will find two unique aspects. First, because of the sheer size of the backdrops, judging distance is extremely difficult. Even though many holes are framed by

pines and birch, they are dwarfed by the mountain peaks and a sense of scale is hard to achieve. Add to that the fact that some holes change elevation quite dramatically at times, so you are playing downhill or off a sidehill lie, and clubbing becomes even trickier.

ALTITUDE EFFECTS

The single most unique aspect of playing mountain golf, however, is the altitude and the remarkable effect it has on the ball. The air is thin, making the ball travel farther—and at high altitudes, much farther. As a general rule, you should add 10 percent to the distances you would usually hit each club. For example, if you usually strike a 5-iron 160 yards (146 m), it will travel more like 176 yards (161 m) at altitude. The difference becomes more marked the longer club you take. For example, a normal 270-yard (247 m) driver will probably go almost 300 yards (275 metres) at altitude with a similar strike. That can be quite flattering, but it does not necessarily mean you will play better. Hitting it farther into

trouble is not what you want. In any case, course designers are well aware of the effect altitude has on shots and build golf holes accordingly. While the par-3s are not made much longer (in relative terms, shorter clubs do not go as far), some par-5s are stretched massively to

stop them from being overpowered. At Castle Pines in Colorado, once the home of The International tournament on the PGA Tour, the 1st is 644 yards (590 m) long on a course measuring a whopping 7,619 yards (6,967 m) from the professional tees.

As far as hazards go, they can be just about anything, although water tends to feature on many mountain courses. Because valleys are easier than mountainsides to build courses on, you will often encounter snaking rivers and babbling streams as well as lakes. This is particularly true in

◄ AMID SNOWCAPPED PEAKS, majestic conifers, and mountain lakes ,Arnold Palmer designed the distinctive Whistler Course in British Columbia, Canada, and made it into a unique golfing experience.

▲ THE GLACIER-FED WATERS of the Kananaskis River flow beside the 4th hole on the Mount Kidd Course at Kananaskis Country Golf Club near Calgary, Canada. The spectacular mountain course was designed by Robert Trent Jones. One of the limestone peaks in the stunning mountain backdrop to the course is known appropriately as The Wedge.

the glacial regions, where seasonal snow- and icemelt contribute to the flow. The presence of an icy and rocky river winding through a course only adds to the beauty of the scene, and holes can interplay with the waters wonderfully well. Mountain golf is a treat. The air is clean and fresh and the scenery undeniably gorgeous. For once, it is gratifying to be able to drive as far as Tiger Woods.

Banff Springs, CANADA

Golf courses are often criticized for not harmonizing with the landscape and being an artificial setting—by nongolfers, obviously. Here at Banff Springs in the mind-blowing Rocky Mountains, you would have to be hard of heart to disapprove of the golf course and its wondrous setting, where elk are allowed to wander the plains and golfers must sometimes wait for a stag and his entourage to pass by before driving.

Banff Springs owes its existence to the Canadian Pacific Railway. In 1929, the railroad company asked Stanley Thompson to design a golf course fit for the best players in the world. He had already built one for a rival company at Jasper, 150 miles (240 km) away.

Thompson went to extravagant lengths to create this gem at Banff, with the railroad bringing in vast amounts of topsoil to help with the shaping and grooming. It cost the princely sum of $1 million—at the time the most expensive course ever built, but it was worth every cent.

Apart from changing the hole sequences around in the late 1980s to accommodate a new clubhouse, a relaying of the greens, and some bunker work, the course has remained much as it was for almost 80 years.

A STRATEGIC BEAUTY

Since the panorama is so spectacular and the river so captivating, what players should see from the tee looking down each golf hole needs to be eye-catching as well. Thompson did that perfectly. His bunkering style is legendary and similar to Alister Mackenzie's. His free-form wavy-edged traps dominate a player's thinking. Long, lazy sweeps of sand are tucked in at the corner of doglegs, and nests of traps need to be carried to get the best line into the greens. On the par-5s, the odd bunker toys with a layup shot, and every green is well guarded, many heavily so. All the trouble is visible. Thompson left nothing to chance, and Banff is a strategic beauty.

The front nine gets its name, Rundle, from the mountain overshadowing it (while the back nine is named after Mt. Sulphur). Thompson's men blasted out rock at

▼ **THE GRANDIOSE** Scottish baronial style of the Banff Springs Hotel, which was built in 1887-1888, set the tone for the golf course.

▲ **A LOCAL RULE** reads: "Any shot striking an elk may be replayed with no penalty." The advice for players facing a bear looking for food is "do not run, but retreat slowly."

the base of it so the holes could play as close as possible to the towering face. The superb one-shot 2nd and the fabulous arcing par-5 3rd play toward the mountainside. So dominating is its sheer presence that correct clubbing is virtually impossible by eye alone. You have to trust the yardage and take the altitude into account.

A CHARMING VARIETY OF HOLES

The holes then move farther away from the face of Mt. Rundle until they gracefully reach the river at the 8th. Standing just yards away from the impossibly blue waters of Bow River, you must take your eyes off the scene and concentrate on finding the green over a small lake. The next six holes, separated from the river's edge by stands of pine and spruce, are charming in their variety—a reachable par-5 with a green 15 yards (14 m) from the stream; two juicy par-3s; and three very testing par-4s.

The 14th is one of Thompson's finest. The perfect line is to fly the nest of sand on the left, a hit of 255 yards (233 m) that leaves a clear sight of the green. Going right of the bunkers means a long approach over an imposing set of traps until just shy of the green. A strategic masterpiece, it is a wonderful sight, too, as you play directly toward the grand old hotel 43 yards (40 m) above, framed by the pines of Mt. Sulphur.

Banff's finishing stretch befits a course so at one with nature. The holes all play toward the distant snow-dappled range, and the course climaxes with a roaring dogleg par-5. Even if a birdie proves elusive, the scenery and the quality of the course leaves everyone thirsting for more.

◀ **BANFF SPRINGS NESTLES** at the bottom of Bow River valley and is overshadowed by majestic peaks, including Mt. Rundle and Mt. Sulphur.

THE COURSE

The wondrous Rocky Mountains may dominate the skyline, but the course is a star in itself. Flirting with the Bow River and snaking through pines and past clever curving bunkers, Banff Springs is a fabulous walk as well as a fine strategic test of golf. Its many optical illusions are cunning and it is the benchmark mountain course.

The Bow River runs all the way along the northern fringe of the golf course

The par-5 3rd hole has a long undulating green, with a lower tier at the back

The par-5 18th is a roaring climax to the course

Along the riverside, the 12th hole is a testing par-4

Surrounded by pines, the 14th is a strategic masterpiece

BANFF SPRINGS

405 Spray Avenue, Banff, Alberta, T1L 1B5, Canada
www.banffspringsgolfclub.com

THE STANLEY THOMPSON COURSE

FOUNDED 1929
LENGTH 6,938 yards (6,344 m)
PAR 71
DESIGNER Stanley Thompson
COURSE RECORD 65 Moe Norman

CARD OF THE COURSE

THE FRONT NINE			THE BACK NINE		
HOLE	YARDS	PAR	HOLE	YARDS	PAR
1	414	4	10	218	3
2	171	3	11	417	4
3	528	5	12	442	4
4	192	3	13	225	3
5	424	4	14	440	4
6	373	4	15	475	4
7	602	5	16	414	4
8	150	3	17	374	4
9	501	5	18	578	5
OUT	3,355	36	IN	3,583	35

● "Devil's Cauldron"

HOLE 4 "DEVIL'S CAULDRON"
Unquestionably in the top-10 most recognizable par-3s in golf, the 4th defies words. The almost sheer face of Mt. Rundle seemingly crashes into the pines directly behind the punchbowl green, which sits behind a glacial lake. The water's eerie mottled look is down to the boulders that litter the bottom of the pond. From the elevated tee, it is a wondrous sight, if not a little disturbing, because the deep dell is enclosed by trees and often shadowed by the massive mountain above. It takes an exacting strike with a mid to long iron to find the green, and a par should be cherished.

The well-bunkered green lies in the shadow of Mt. Rundle

From a spectacular high tee, golfers strike across a glacial lake to the green

Desert Courses

As a rule, desert golf is some of the most imaginative on the planet, simply because the courses run over a vast nothingness and the designers can run riot with their designs. Some of the scenery is spellbinding, and the golf, although inevitably target-style due to the lush manicured surfaces, can be of the highest order.

◀ ◀ ◀ **THE GOLF CLUB** Scottsdale lies in the Sonoran Desert in Arizona. ◀ ◀ **AN EYE-CATCHING** water feature dominates the 18th hole of the Raptor Course at Grayhawk at Scottsdale, Arizona. ◀ **THE COURSE AT** Desert Forest at Carefree, Arizona, was one of the first desert designs. ▼ **GRAND SAGUARO** cacti stand guard over the holes at Troon North in the Sonoran Desert in Arizona.

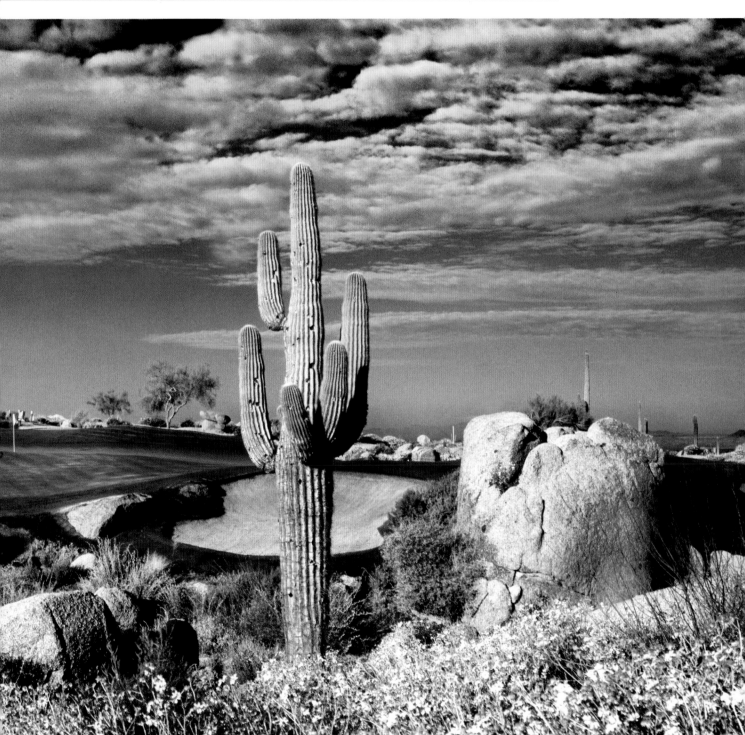

The first desert courses, mostly in the Middle East, were rough-and-ready affairs where grass was nowhere to be seen. The greens, or browns as they are known, were leveled-out patches of oiled sand that were brushed after a group had been through. A player would either tee up all over the course or carry a small mat to play from, but as water management became increasingly clever, grass courses started to spring up like oases.

Today, there are fantastically lush and beautiful desert golf courses, particularly in California, Nevada, Utah, New Mexico, and Arizona, with a few in Qatar, Bahrain, Egypt, the United Arab Emirates, and Oman. The courses of the Middle East are carved out of shifting sand dunes, but the hundreds of desert courses in the US are laid out over rocky landscapes dotted with native cacti and scrub. All are artificial, as soil was brought in, and the grass is constantly watered.

No desert golf course is allowed more than 90 acres (36 hectares) of grass. This creates dramatic scenery,

▼ THE WATERBOUND GREEN of the 17th, called "Devil's Drink," is a feature of the Talon Course at Grayhawk Golf Club in Scottsdale, Arizona.

▶ HEAVILY CONTOURED sand traps around the 7th hole threaten golfers from all directions on the Faldo Course at the JW Desert Ridge Resort near Phoenix, Arizona.

where thin ribbons of green are in stark contrast to the inhospitable environment they meander through. Boulders, cacti, and thorny scrub make up the rough, and within the wilderness lurk "critters" such as coyote, scorpions, and rattlesnakes.

THE WATER ISSUE

Water is a complex issue in the main desert course areas of the US. In the Greater Phoenix/Scottsdale area of Arizona, probably the most famous desert golf region of the world, there are more than 3 million people and over 150 golf courses.

The average yearly rainfall is 8.3 in (210 mm), so most of the water comes via pipelines and canals from the mountains north of the valley, siphoned from the Salt and Verde rivers that carry snowmelt out to the Gulf of California. Golf courses also have reservoirs, and many pump treated used water onto the courses, but there are strict regulations to minimize the amount of water needed.

AMERICAN LAYOUTS

The Scottsdale courses ramble through the Sonoran Desert, which is famous for its saguaro cacti. These spiny, fluted, columnlike growths can reach over 25 ft (7.5 m) tall, and some are 200 years old. They make a bizarre backdrop and hazard for the golfer. The courses at Troon and Desert Mountain are brilliant examples

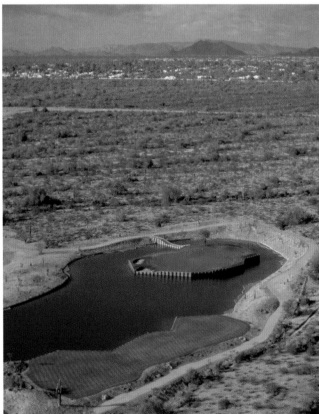

of Sonoran Desert layouts, punctuated by a mass of eerie saguaro and using the rocky and undulating topography superbly.

Elsewhere in the US, where the deserts are far less contoured and have no iconic vegetation, the recent trend has been to build courses like oases. From flat, featureless land, designers create lush and exotically landscaped environments.

The two best examples are Shadow Creek and Cascata Golf

This creates dramatic scenery. Boulders, cacti, and thorny scrub make up the rough, and within the wilderness lurk "critters" such as coyote, scorpions, and rattlesnakes.

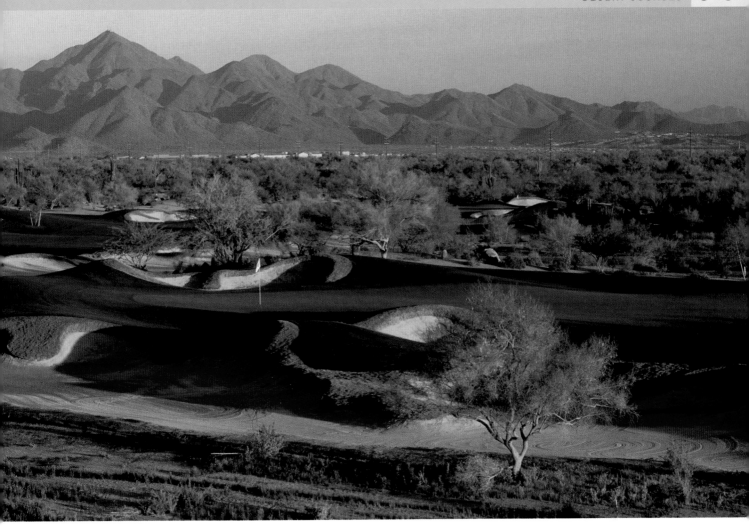

Clubs outside Las Vegas, Nevada. Both were built by casino groups, and no expense was spared. Masses of earth were moved and shaped, allowing the designers to let their imaginations run wild.

The Cascata course cost around $60 million and features a 420 ft (128 m) long cataract that cascades down the artificial hillside and even runs through the middle of the clubhouse. This is opulence in true Las Vegas–style.

▶ **GOLFERS ON THIS** desert course in Namibia can play on grass but only on the tees and greens; otherwise, they have to tee up on the composite clay fairways.

Emirates, DUBAI

Home of the Dubai Desert Classic on the European Tour, this desert wonder set the standard for grass courses in the Persian Gulf when it sprang to life in 1988. Known locally as the "Desert Miracle," it winds its way over sand dunes and through palm trees and spiky grass. Named after the Arabic word for meeting place, the Majlis Course rose from the desert thanks to His Highness General Sheikh Mohammed bin Rashid Al Maktoum.

COURSE SPECIALIST

Ernie Els first played on the Emirates Course in the Dubai Desert Classic of 1993. In 40 competitive rounds here, he never signed for an over par score. A staggering 157-under par, he has a stroke average of 68.05. Out of 10 starts, his worst finish is 8th in 1993. He has eight top-three finishes, including three wins, to his name.

Ernie Els's 2nd shot to the 13th

When all around is an endless, scorching desert of wind-whipped sand dunes, and the only water is the saltiness of the Persian Gulf, it is no mean feat to build a world-class golf course. Despite the natural problems surrounding the Emirates Golf Club, they managed to fashion an emerald stunner from the uncompromising landscape. The Sheikh, who is Crown Prince of Dubai and the Minister of Defense of the UAE, realized there was a niche for a grass golf course and one that his nation would be proud to offer the world. So he asked American architect Karl Litten to build him a pedigree course, the first grass layout in the Gulf.

At first, it was a problem finding suitable land, not because there was a dearth of desert to build on—there were miles and miles of emptiness—but because each time a particular site was chosen, local Bedouin tribesmen complained that they would be encroaching on ancient camel-grazing routes.

Eventually, the Sheikh himself donated a rectangular parcel of his own land 13 miles (21 km) southwest of the Old City and only 2 miles (3.2 km) from the sea. Its 190 acres (77 hectares) had a solitary tree and large undulating dunes. Back then, it lay in isolation, although it has since been engulfed by the rapid expansion of the city.

A MILLION GALLONS A DAY

Litten immediately encountered problems. Although given a blank canvas, it seemed as though every time his team marked out the holes with poles over the dunes, they had all but disappeared the next day under the shifting sands. So he decided to water them in the hope that they would stabilize. They did exactly that, but there was also a welcome by-product of the irrigation. Suddenly, as if waiting for centuries to come to life, camel grass, date palms, coconut palms, flame trees, and petunias erupted from the desert floor. With some extra planting, the course took on a magical oasis feel. The designers used the excess desalinated water from an aluminum plant, and even now more than a million

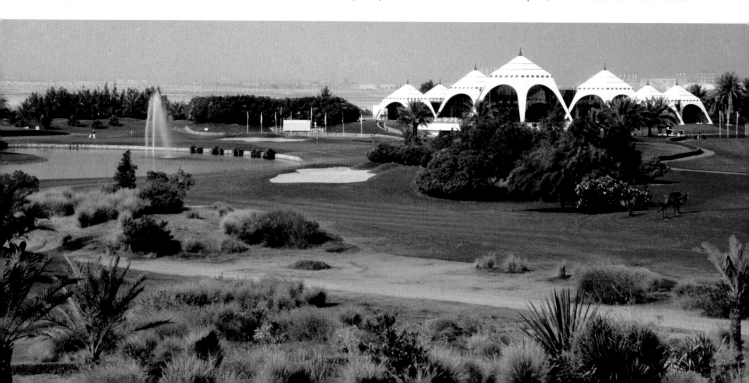

gallons a day is pumped on to the course to keep it in the pristine condition for which it is known.

The conditioning is incredible given its geography, but the design is also fabulous, with an excellent mix of gently rolling holes. There seems to be a natural balance to the holes that ask different questions at every turn, and no two similar holes follow each other. Water plays a big part on the course, as a network of lakes means that 10 holes feature a shot that contends with a pond. Some holes, however, are more affected than others. Water eats into the right side of the short 4th and makes a real nuisance of itself at the long par-4 9th. Those two, along with the 18th, are probably the most affected.

The pick of the holes on the front nine are the 8th and 9th. The 8th is a desert classic. It swings right and uphill to an elevated green in front of the unusual halfway house. Flanking the fairway is a nasty scrub—if a golfer tries for the perfect line up the right side, it takes only a slight miscue to find the camel grass and palms. The desert floor is hard-packed, but escaping the scrub from anywhere on the course can be a problem.

PLENTY OF BIRDIE OPPORTUNITIES

The iconic holes on the back nine are the 10th and 18th. Both reachable par-5s, they can define a round. Although the 10th is in range with two huge hits, the green is almost completely ringed by a wiggly-edged bunker so that the ball has to be flown all the way.

Emirates ends with a risk-and-reward par-5. A long 90-degree dogleg from right to left means that anyone aiming for the green in two has to take the corner on and hope they skip the clinging Bermuda rough onto the fairway. The players then face a long shot in over a glistening lake to a wide but shallow green. There is a fine line between winning and losing the tournament on this hole. In 1996, Colin Montgomerie played the European Tour's Shot of the Year on the 72nd hole with a driver off the fairway over the lake to win the championship. A year later, needing only a par to win, Ian Woosnam dunked his third-shot wedge into the water and blew his chance.

There is no denying the Majlis is a benchmark desert dune course, and the professionals love it. It is eminently fair and always in immaculate condition, and of course there seems to be plenty of birdie opportunities to excite both the players and spectators. Thomas Bjørn holds the tournament record of 22-under par for four rounds, but every year Europe's best go low on this bizarre but absorbing course. It truly is a "Desert Miracle."

◄ **BESIDE THE PRACTICE GREEN** stands the unusual and striking clubhouse, which has been built to resemble a cluster of welcoming Bedouin tents.

THE COURSE

As much a feat of engineering as golf course design, the Majlis was a daring project but one that worked brilliantly. The pristine fairways wend their way through desert scrub and past palms and sparkling lakes, and the greens are simply immaculate.

Behind the 4th green lies a deep bunker, with water on the right

The par-4 8th goes uphill and is bordered by desert scrub on both sides

The 3rd fairway is bounded by desert grass on the right

The 10th green is almost completely surrounded by sand

The tee shot on the 18th passes over the lake

The 9th fairway lies next to the largest of the four lakes

The 2nd fairway lies between water and trees

EMIRATES
....
PO Box 24040, Dubai
www.dubaigolf.com

THE MAJLIS COURSE
....
FOUNDED 1988
LENGTH 7,301 yards (6,676 m)
PAR 72
DESIGNER Karl Litten
COURSE RECORD 61 Ernie Els (1994)

DUBAI DESERT CLASSIC WINNERS
....
José Maria Olazábal (1998); Thomas Bjørn (2001); Ernie Els (2002, 2005); Robert-Jan Derksen (2003); Mark O'Meara (2004); Tiger Woods (2006); Henrik Stenson (2007)

CARD OF THE COURSE
....

THE FRONT NINE			THE BACK NINE		
HOLE	YARDS	PAR	HOLE	YARDS	PAR
1	458	4	10	549	5
2	351	4	11	169	3
3	568	5	12	467	4
4	188	3	13	550	5
5	436	4	14	434	4
6	485	4	15	190	3
7	186	3	16	425	4
8	459	4	17	350	4
9	463	4	18	564	5
OUT	**3,594**	**35**	**IN**	**3,707**	**37**

The green sits tight to the water

The fairway snakes right then back to the left

HOLE 9 DANGEROUS WATER
Playing this hole conservatively means a par is hard to come by, but attacking can be dangerous. The drive is downhill toward a lake, and the best line is up the right, which makes the approach more direct. However, a large bunker awaits down that side. A drive safely down the left will make the approach much tougher as it has to be taken over the corner of the water.

● The lakeside 9th

Shadow Creek, US

Created a few miles north of the world's most renowned gambling city, casual passersby might think they have stumbled across a mirage in the Mojave Desert, such is the lush, artificial nature of this amazing course. From the moment it opened, Shadow Creek was hailed as one of the best new courses in the US. Its reputation has brought it recognition as one of the top-100 courses in the world.

THE COURSE

Opulent and extravagant, the course is a totally artificial, man-made theater of golf where fairways burst through lush flora and skirt creeks and lakes. A great design tops off the experience.

A lake borders the 4th hole, and the fairway narrows as it approaches the green

SHADOW CREEK

3 Shadow Creek Drive, North Las Vegas, Nevada 89081
www.shadowcreek.com

THE COURSE

FOUNDED 1989
LENGTH 7,560 yards (6,913 m)
PAR 72
DESIGNER Tom Fazio
COURSE RECORD 60 Tiger Woods (2004), Fred Couples (2007)

CARD OF THE COURSE

THE FRONT NINE			THE BACK NINE		
HOLE	YARDS	PAR	HOLE	YARDS	PAR
1	415	4	10	437	4
2	435	4	11	324	4
3	486	4	12	405	4
4	581	5	13	257	3
5	202	3	14	493	4
6	507	4	15	482	4
7	571	5	16	622	5
8	200	3	17	154	3
9	460	4	18	529	5
OUT	3,857	36	IN	3,703	36

The 18th fairway is accompanied by a lake until it reaches the green

HOLE 17 HEAD-SHAKINGLY PRETTY

All the high rollers lucky enough to play the course coo over this most head-shakingly pretty and testing of holes. It is a dazzling par-3 that would not look out of place on a movie set. The carry from the back tee is around 155 yards (142 m) to reach the green over a shimmering pond fed by a babbling creek on the left. A 15 ft (4.5 m) waterfall spills out from the bank of ornamental trees behind the green, creating a very surreal scene. Because the green is so small and the dangers encroach from all sides, a par here is one to treasure.

The tiny green is surrounded by bunkers, rocks, and water

From tees secluded in the trees, the shot to the green is slightly downhill

Las Vegas is no stranger to the weird and wonderful. To a city that has recreated the Pyramids, the Eiffel Tower, and the canals of Venice, and where people gamble away millions each day, nothing seems a surprise. Back in 1988, however, when casino magnate Steve Wynn embarked on creating Shadow Creek, thousands of eyebrows were raised.

Wynn set about building one of the most ambitious golf course projects ever seen. On a plain, completely flat desert site 9 miles (14.5 km) north of Las Vegas's famous "Strip," an area of 320 acres (130 hectares) was marked out, and the spectacular transformation began under the gaze of the highly respected Tom Fazio. He was given free rein and an astronomical budget. Wynn is a rich man, and legend has it that no expense was spared, with rumors abounding that it cost anywhere between $40 and $60 million. Someone in the know once said about the course, "Steve had an unlimited budget for Shadow Creek and he exceeded it. Whatever it took to make the place special, they did it." Wynn hit the jackpot, for it is a startling landscape.

What Fazio fashioned was not so much a desert golf course but a golf course in the desert. If someone were to be dropped blindfold in the middle of the course, they would open their eyes and not have a clue that they were standing in the middle of the Mojave Desert. The only giveaways would be the searing heat and the barren backdrop of the Spring Mountains.

A GAMBLER'S DELIGHT

Shadow Creek resembles a tropical parkland despite lying in an area with an annual rainfall of only 4.5 inches (115 mm). Fazio imported more than 200 plant species and built lakes, rocky creeks, and waterfalls to complement the piles of earth that gave the whole site definition and unexpected elevation changes. It could be described as an ornamental garden setting with a golf course seamlessly

▶ **THE SPLENDID SETTING** of the 9th hole epitomizes the emerald course that Tom Fazio fashioned from the desert at Shadow Creek—an immaculate fairway beside a sparkling creek with fabulous mountains in the background.

woven in. All holes are isolated from each other and shaded by the mass of foliage, and they flow beautifully. There are no ridiculously sharp doglegs, but a few of the holes do arc majestically, most notably at the 1st, 4th, 10th, and 16th. The pick of these sweeping holes is the 553-yard (505 m) 4th, which bends from right-to-left around a twinkling, curvaceous lake edged with strips of sand. As befits a golf course in Las Vegas, it is a gambler's delight, goading a player to risk taking it on.

RISKS AND REWARDS

As a rule, all the par-5s are exceptional risk-and-reward holes, with the finest saved until last. Fazio summed up the design here, bringing all the elements found around the course together into one spectacular hole. At the 18th, tees are elevated and set at different angles to the fairway. Stands of trees and bunkers patrol the left, and a series of lakes linked by three waterfalls flow down the right from the green. The final rocky drop cuts across the front of the green, which is reachable in two by the long and brave. Most, however, will face a charming but tricky pitch in over the stream to a shallow green framed by weeping willows, pines, and shrubs.

Other holes of note are two par-3s—the 5th and 13th. The former is a midlength one-shotter that woos the eye as it drops down over a stunning valley of shrubs. The 13th is a beast of a hole, needing a long iron or fairway wood downhill to an angled green, which is tightly guarded on the right by a small pond and a large bunker. A direct line takes you straight over the corner of the trouble, so it is often best to fade a left-to-right shot in, especially if you have to get at a flag in the back right portion. It is a blow of approximately 230 yards (210 m) that frays the nerves, rather like a gambler watching a roulette wheel spinning.

After it opened, Shadow Creek became the preserve of the rich and famous, and A-list celebrities have always had strong connections. Basketball legend Michael Jordan and actor George Clooney were regulars. Despite the fact that no championships are held here, Shadow Creek has an impressive course record holder—one Tiger Woods, who shot a game 60.

Strokeplay will never be a main feature of Shadow Creek—it does not have an official USGA rating. Fazio designed it to be the ultimate matchplay course, where golfers face each other with their poker faces and play for their hard-earned dollars. Unless you have lost a mint against a bandit, its impossible to go away from this stunner disappointed. It is surreal golf and a magnificent experience, fitting for a town that is sometimes beyond belief.

PRIVILEGED FEW

Technically, Shadow Creek is a daily fee public course, but it is owned by MGM Mirage, and to have any chance of playing, you must register at one of its properties in Las Vegas. After that, you must pay $500 for the privilege. The fee includes limousine transfers from the city, your own personal caddie who meets your carat at the clubhouse, practice balls, drinks, and snacks.

The MGM Grand Hotel in Las Vegas

> The golf course exists for one single reason ... to bring pleasure to my guests.

STEVE WYNN, COURSE FOUNDER AND FORMER OWNER

Troon North, US

Desert golf does not come any better than this. Its combination of vibrant green fairways diving over the boulders and scrub of the Sonoran Desert is a treat for the eyes as much as for tacticians of the game. The original Monument Course at Troon North, watched over by the rubble-clad Pinnacle Peak, is a stunning piece of architecture that uses the dramatic prehistoric landscape to perfection.

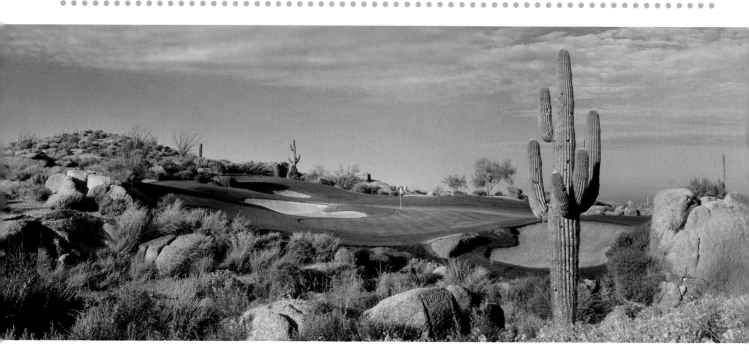

A COURSE WITH BITE

The desert floor at Troon North hides two menaces. Rattlesnakes are native to the rock-strewn landscape but are rarely seen—and it s against Arizona law to kill one. More hazardous is the Jumping Cholla, a magnetic plant that is drawn to humans walking past by the magnesium in their bodies. It has nasty barbs like fish hooks.

A rattlesnake on the sand

When asked to picture pure desert golf, most players will conjure images of arid, brown scrub and rocks dotted with tall, spiky "cowboy" cacti surrounding neatly striped lush islands of green. Troon North may well be the perfect pure desert golf course based on those archetypal thoughts.

The Monument Course, so named after the gigantic boulder in the middle of the 3rd fairway, was created by Tom Weiskopf and Jay Morrish. This "stone" was seen as such an important piece of the desert that the local planning authorities asked specifically for it to stay. While the design team was worried about having such a vast boulder in play for safety reasons, the city of Scottsdale waived any legal responsibility to the course.

A DISTINCTIVE COURSE

The original course was arranged in two distinct loops of nine holes. The front nine circled counterclockwise on lower ground, and the back nine (now part of its sister course, The Pinnacle, as of November 2007) turned

▲ **A SAGUARO CACTUS STANDS TALL** beside the 10th hole on the "New" Monument Course at Troon North, adding a calming influence to the travails of playing golf in such a rugged landscape.

clockwise on higher, more sculpted land. New houses have taken away some of the wilderness feel, but they do not detract much from the very enjoyable challenge.

Whenever fairways are edged with sandy, thorny scrub and rough boulders, as they are here, the potential for trouble is great, but the playing areas are generous in size. While they look intimidating—especially when the desert floor creeps across as it does on five holes, most notably on the wonderful 10th—the fairways are wide and rippled, and the greens are large and not hemmed in by the bush. For such a lush, green course, it is surprising to see the ball bound nicely from the tees—this is probably down to the pristine, close-cropped nature of the playing surfaces. With the greens being reasonably firm and

▲ FROM THE TEE AT THE PAR-5 11TH HOLE on the original Monument Course, the vibrant green of the cambered fairway leads gradually uphill, then swings to the right around rocky terrain.

quick, it is a delight to be able to use the contours to filter approaches close to tricky flag positions.

There are plenty of holes where you can open your shoulders, including all the par-5s. Standing on the 11th tee, staring at the cambered and funneled fairway in the distance, entices you to smack a drive away, hopefully with a touch of left-to-right to mimic the shape. It is one of five holes that do not have any fairway bunkers in the landing area, but you do not miss them because of the clever contouring of the fairways. When fairway traps do come into play, they are a mixture of styles—you must fly some, skip past others, and sensibly lay up short of a few.

One superb hole—a short drivable par-4 that Tom Weiskopf always tries to put into each of his courses—gives a player two of these options. The 6th is 306 yards (280 m) long and has three bunkers that split the hole in two. One big sweep of trap patrols the right, and two pots cut off the direct route. If you can carry the drive around 250 yards (228 m) and avoid another small pot farther up, you can find the green or get mighty close. The sensible choice is to play short of the trouble and take your chances with a wedge into the small sloping green.

TANTALIZING THE EYE

The real gift of the course is the way it uses the land and tantalizes the eye. Isolated among the wilderness, the tees are often stepped gradually so you can see all in front of you. The humps and hollows of the undulating land seduce the visual senses and challenge the golfer with an awkward stance on the fairways or a merciless kick to your ball by the green. Troon North is full of smooth lines and understated contours, and, despite the harsh surroundings, it is as fair as you could wish a course to be.

Just to add to the pleasure of playing both courses here, thousands of saguaro cacti stand defiantly in the undergrowth and somehow have a calming influence on the place. As the sun goes down and an orange blanket of light is thrown over the desert, their ghostly silhouettes are a wondrous sight. Troon North is a treat.

THE COURSE

Ribbons of green cascade over the rocky scrub of the desert floor and invite a golfer to turn on the power and style. The clever routing and strategic design is watched over by the ancient missilelike cacti that sprout from the earth. A benchmark desert course.

TROON NORTH
....
10320 E Dynamite Blvd, Scottsdale, Arizona 85262
www.troonnorthgolf.com

THE ORIGINAL MONUMENT COURSE
....
FOUNDED 1990
LENGTH 7,039 yards (6,436 m)
PAR 72
DESIGNERS Tom Weiskopf, Jay Morrish

CARD OF THE COURSE
....

THE FRONT NINE			THE BACK NINE		
HOLE	YARDS	PAR	HOLE	YARDS	PAR
1	444	4	10	396	4
2	172	3	11	512	5
3	556	5	12	426	4
4	420	4	13	222	3
5	464	4	14	570	5
6	306	4	15	299	4
7	205	3	16	244	3
8	408	4	17	495	4
9	530	5	18	370	4
OUT	**3,505**	**36**	**IN**	**3,534**	**36**

● The dogleg 3rd

HOLE 3 A TRICKY DOGLEG

An obelisk-like boulder in the middle of the fairway is the signature of this hole and dictates how it is played. The safest route is to go left of it, but, because the hole swings right, going this way means the green is out of range even for the big hitters. The bolder drive right of it, and flirting with a corner of the encroaching desert, gives decent golfers a chance of getting home, but it still takes a great strike slightly downhill to reach the green. One solitary bunker pinches the fairway in about 40 yards (36 m) short of the green.

The 16th green is protected by a lake front right

A rocky waste cuts the 12th fairway in two

The tee shot on the 11th is best shaped left to right

The desert creeps across the 10th in front of the green

A boulder shaped like an obelisk stands in the dogleg of the 3rd fairway

The 6th is drivable, but cross bunkers await mishits

The monument boulder stands in the middle of the fairway as it swings right

A bunker near the green can cause problems for those laying up

Unique Courses

With thousands of golf courses the world over laid out on all sorts of terrain, it is very difficult to categorize them all into certain styles. Many are an amalgam of styles or played in such unique surroundings that you cannot neatly pigeon-hole them. This chapter features some of the most singular examples of such courses.

▲ **THE DRAMATIC 15TH** hole is at the Quarry Course at Black Diamond Ranch near Tampa, Florida. ◄ ◄ ◄ **PRINCEVILLE GOLF COURSE** is magnificently placed on the island of Kauai, Hawaii. ◄ ◄ **THE GOLF COURSE** at Elephant Hills, Zimbabwe, lies beside the Zambezi River and is within earshot of the Victoria Falls. ◄ **THE LOST CITY** course has unique water hazards and belongs to the Sun City complex in South Africa.

When does a parkland become a jungle? What determines an ocean course as opposed to a links? The classification of golf courses inevitably has some fuzzy edges, because golf is played in such diverse landscapes. When you add various architectural oddities, such as island greens, many courses simply do not fit into a category.

As a general rule, heathland must have heather, but how much does it need so that it does not become known as, say, an inland links or simply a parkland?

WHISTLING STRAITS

The category problem is exemplified by Whistling Straits, situated on the shores of Lake Michigan. It is a staggering piece of design by Pete Dye, where there are few trees, tumbling dunes on otherwise flat land and a ludicrous number of bunkers—albeit in a haphazard style. The lake is so vast that it looks like a sea, and the soil is sandy.

Is Whistling Straits a links or an ocean course? Many of its holes have design features that are not necessarily found on a links—for example, some forced carries into greens and much lusher turf than a real links. This means that it does not play like a true links, although it looks like one.

FROM SWAMP TO BIG GAME

The courses of some of the more traditional areas for golf tend to find themselves within a category, but there are still many examples that do not fit perfectly. For example, in the low country of The Carolinas and Georgia, marshland is ubiquitous, and holes weave over wetlands and

swamp. Even though they may feature trees, the classic styles cannot be applied.

The problem is exacerbated in other more tropical parts of the world, too. In the Far East, where the vegetation is unique to the hot and wet climate, golf courses are built through almost pure jungle. Monkeys swing from the trees, and there is little or no roll on the coarse grass fairways. Can they be called parkland? Perhaps, but it would be pushing the boundaries.

In Africa, some courses are built in the dry savanna lands, where the fairways are roamed by wild animals. At Victoria Falls, Zimbabwe, the local golf course is named after the noble beast that trudges over the fairways of Elephant Hills. At the parkland course at Hans Merensky, on the

edge of the Kruger National Park in South Africa, golfers can spot the "Big Five" (lions, rhinos, elephants, buffaloes, and leopards).

RAINFOREST AND LAVA

Golf course developers know no bounds when trying to create a unique golfing experience and turn to ever more bizarre land for building courses. Golf usually goes hand-in-hand with the tourist dollar, and no more so than in the Hawaiian Islands.

The most northerly island of Kauai is a rainforest paradise, with steep-sided valleys shrouded in exotic flora cutting through the isle. It is almost insulting to label somewhere so dramatic as, say, Princeville as a parkland course, despite it being flanked by trees. Even more confusing, and less able

to be categorized, are the courses on the lava fields of the Big Island. The shores of the actively volcanic island are encrusted with razor-sharp black lava that has erupted from the massive volcanoes of Mauna Loa and Mauna Kea, or been forced up from the waters of the deep.

The lava is extremely difficult to walk over, and so golf courses seem a very strange partner, but a lava-munching machine that shreds the rock and spits it out to form smooth surfaces has made golf a surreal reality. Perfectly manicured strips of fairways using imported soil sweep across the black rock that acts as the rough. These courses are as far away from a links as possible, despite many being right next to the coast.

▶ **WHISTLING STRAITS** has characteristics of both a links and an ocean course. It lies on a two-mile stretch of the Lake Michigan shoreline north of Sheboygan in Wisconsin.

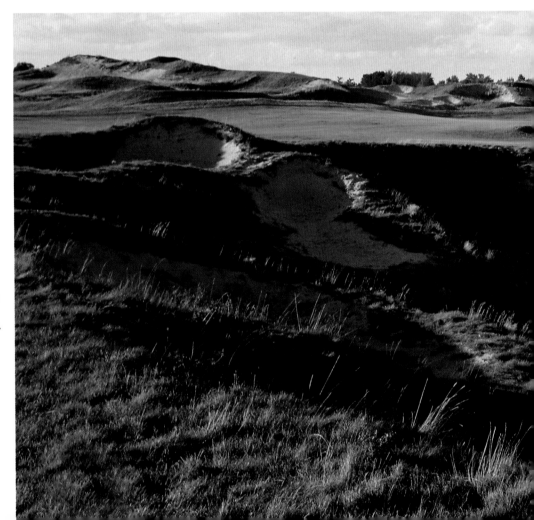

BEWARE THE 13TH HOLE!

Sun City in South Africa has two magnificent courses, and its Lost City Course has a distinctive style. With a background of the Pilansberg Mountains, Lost City runs through high rough and past boulder-strewn lakes. Closest to a desert style, it has an inland links-like feel, too. On the 13th, a vast walled pit between tee and green is home to two dozen Nile crocodiles that laze around in the reeds and water.

○ Crocodile pit on the 13th hole

▲ **CARVED FROM BLACK LAVA,** the Beach Course at Waikoloa is located along the Kohala coastline on the Big Island of Hawaii. Designed by Robert Trent Jones Jr., the scenic course has many challenging water features and sand bunkers as well as views of humpback whales in the waters of Anaeho'omalu Bay.

Loch Lomond, SCOTLAND

A design classic in poetic surroundings, Loch Lomond appeals to all the senses. Just north of gritty Glasgow, on the "bonnie banks" of a graceful lake, it is an out-and-out feel-good golf course. Considering it opened for play only in 1994 and is an upstart in the "birthplace of golf," it has enjoyed staggering accolades. It is constantly voted one of the best golf courses in the British Isles, along with Muirfield and Royal County Down, and ranks in the top 100 of the world.

Undeniably, Loch Lomond is predominantly a parkland course, but its variety and setting make this moniker too simplistic. Yes, the fairways weave through mature woods of oak, pine, Douglas fir, larch, beech, limes, and the odd chestnut, with a few rhododendrons to add color, but there is much more to it than that.

Several holes flirt with marshland edged with untidy areas of broom, heather, reeds, bracken, marram grass, thistles, and bramble. Six holes are directly influenced by the lapping waters of Loch Lomond—the 3rd, 5th, 6th, 7th, 17th, and 18th—while others are crisscrossed with streams and edged by natural ponds. As you gaze at the panorama, both the loch and the bracken-shrouded highland fells of the Trossachs leave you wide-eyed in appreciation of their natural charms.

EXCEPTIONALLY FAIR AND VARIED

Rating a golf course is mostly a subjective process. Yet to find the real greats, sometimes objective criteria have to be applied, because judgment can be clouded by the surroundings. At Loch Lomond, even if you look away from the sumptuous landscape, you would still be left with a completely awesome course.

In the late 1980s, the expert design team of Tom Weiskopf and Jay Morrish were invited to lay their artistic hands on the land that has been for centuries the ancestral home of the Clan Colquhoun. At its heart was the impressive Rossdhu House overlooking the loch, and the pair of architects would have to fulfill the faith shown in them if they were to match the estate's class and grandeur. While Morrish was most certainly an influence, a heart attack limited his involvement and Weiskopf, the Open Championship winner of 1973 at Troon, became the main player behind the brilliance of the course's design.

What the course delivers is exceptionally fair and varied holes that have outstanding memorability. All the fairways have "elbow room" but also awkward or nasty

▶ **FEW GOLFERS PLAYING THE COURSE** at Loch Lomond can fail to be inspired by the awesome setting of the water and the wonderful panorama of the mountains beyond.

KEY MOMENTS ....

◀ **EUROPE'S WOMEN** won back the Solheim Cup from the US at Loch Lomond in 2000. Half of the team of 12 were Swedish. After the clean sweep of the first morning's foursomes, 3½ points of the 5 Europe won on the final day came from Carin Koch, Helen Alfredsson, Liselotte Neumann and Catrin Nilsmark. Europe won 14½ to 11½.

◀ **FRENCHMAN THOMAS LEVET** came from a distant 14th place and 7 behind in the final round to win the Barclays Scottish Open in 2004. His blistering 63 shot him through the field to pip Michael Campbell by one. He came home in just 29 strokes and was 6-under for his last eight holes, finishing with a birdie three for victory and a total of 15-under par.

LOCH LOMOND
. . . .
Rossdhu House, Luss,
Dunbartonshire G83 8NT, Scotland
www.lochlomond.com

THE COURSE
. . . .
FOUNDED 1994
LENGTH 7,139 yards (6,528 m)
PAR 71
DESIGNERS Tom Weiskopf,
Jay Morrish
COURSE RECORD 62
Retief Goosen (1997)

SELECTED CHAMPIONS
. . . .
STANDARD LIFE Lee Westwood (1998);
Colin Montgomerie (1999); Ernie Els
(2000)
SOLHEIM CUP Europe (2000)
SCOTTISH OPEN Retief Goosen (2001);
Eduardo Romero (2002); Ernie Els
(2003); Thomas Levet (2004); Tim Clark
(2005); Johan Edfors (2006); Gregory
Havret (2007); Graeme McDowell
(2008); Martin Kaymer (2009);
Edoardo Molinari (2010)

CARD OF THE COURSE
. . . .

THE FRONT NINE			THE BACK NINE		
HOLE	YARDS	PAR	HOLE	YARDS	PAR
1	425	4	10	455	4
2	455	4	11	235	3
3	518	5	12	415	4
4	385	4	13	560	5
5	190	3	14	371	4
6	625	5	15	415	4
7	440	4	16	490	4
8	160	3	17	205	3
9	340	4	18	455	4
Out	3,538	36	In	3,601	35

The picturesque 17th green

The brilliant par-3 17th overlooking Loch Lomond

This is probably the best course in Europe; it is a really good layout and the condition is very pure. It is beautiful.

ERNIE ELS, WINNER OF THE 2000 AND 2003 SCOTTISH OPENS AT LOCH LOMOND

hazards to protect them. The forever-changing direction and pace enthrall all. The holes change tack no less than 15 times, and the four incredible one-shotters range from 160 to 235 yards (146 to 215 m), and all play on different bearings.

Two of the short holes are world-beaters. At the 5th, the tees aim you over a pretty, natural waste area toward a green backed by the mirrored lake and framed by huge oaks. Although the loch looks as though it is just over the back, there is room to maneuver, but an undulating green and four bunkers keep you on your toes. Of the many ridiculously picturesque holes on the course, the 5th is just about the best.

The 5th is, however, rivaled by another par-3. The 17th is a heart-stopping 205 yards (187 m) over a marsh, with the loch only a few paces to the left. Getting to a back left pin placement takes courage as well as a cultured draw. It was the scene of a great European triumph in the 2000 Solheim Cup, when Sweden's Carin Koch rolled in a 10 ft (3 m) putt to beat Michelle Redman 2 and 1 and clinch victory over the US.

HELPFUL BUNKERS

Every hole has its own identity and challenges. Bunkers are used sparingly, and not one is wasted. Weiskopf has always believed that sand should present different tests, and he was at pains to get it right here. Only one bunker—a small pot on the 8th—is hidden. On every other, you get a glimpse of sand, helping with depth perception and visualization of the shot you need to play. On fairways, they are reasonably shallow, letting players escape with an exacting shot. They are not only put in troublesome spots; they help focus a player's tactics, too.

The greenside traps are deeper and settle delightfully into the banks of the trademark slopes and humps. Just as the sand catches the eye, so too do the wild and ingenious patches of waste and the majestic specimen trees, which in themselves are hazards. On the long and winding par-5 6th that skirts the shore of the loch, magnificent single oaks make their presence felt on both sides of the fairway and definitely fashion your strategy, just as much as the bunkers.

GUILE, GRACE, AND POWER

While this course tends to suit great mid to long iron players, being a top putter will always help, too. The greens are generous in size but are cambered and swift, providing options for some devious pin positions. This is exemplified by the 18th, an elegant but dangerous par-4 curving left around an inlet of the loch toward the ruins of Rossdhu Castle. A good drive should leave a mid iron into a steep two-tiered green, which has a small shelf at its back-right portion. It may not be so much of a problem to hit the green, but to get your ball in the right spot for the most straightforward putt takes a skillful shot. That is the way of Loch Lomond. It is very fair to all, but to score well, approaches must be pinpoint-accurate.

Loch Lomond has become the home of the Scottish Open, and the professionals who come from all over the world to play it cannot get enough of the place. Nick Faldo once said, "It's just absolutely fabulous. It is by far and away the best golf course in Great Britain by miles." Colin Montgomerie called it "faultless," and Ernie Els, twice winner here, remarked, "It's in the top five of my worldwide golf venues." High praise indeed, but they are on the mark.

Loch Lomond is an astonishing course enhanced by the splendor of the landscape. It has guile, grace, power, and a soothing quality, too, making it one of the most pleasurable rounds of golf you can find anywhere.

BRUSH WITH DEATH

Tom Weiskopf was a hands-on designer who lived in the gardener's cottage on-site for 18 months during construction. Early one morning, he went for a walk down to the marshy part of the course, near what is the 14th hole, to see whether his thoughts could be brought to reality. When Tom tried to jump a burn, he slipped into the marsh, sinking slowly in the mire. He hung on to a grass tuft on the bank but could not pull himself clear. He held on desperately for some hours until he was rescued.

Weiskopf at Loch Lomond

The breathtaking 5th hole

The two-tiered 18th green

THE COURSE

Beguiling in its elegance, Loch Lomond is an architectural masterpiece where holes gracefully saunter through marshlands and mature parkland. Generous off the tee but still a strategic genius, its main dangers lie in the tracts of wild grass, well-placed sand, stands of trees and large undulating putting surfaces.

The 7th green sits close to the waters of the loch

The 5th green is framed by huge oaks and backed by the loch

Bunkers present danger up the right of the 18th fairway

THE FRONT NINE ❶ A wide-open

fairway, with tricky lone oak on the right. ❷ A wall stretching across the fairway catches the eye on this strong par-4. ❸ Reachable in two, but a lake short right and the loch long left punish the wayward. ❹ Seems simple, but the double green (shared with the 2nd) is awkward. ❺ A stunning and dangerous par-3 with a carry over a wild marsh. ❻ Massive par-5 with the loch down the right and huge trees to snake through. ❼ Green sits close to the loch. Long-iron approaches must be pinpoint-accurate. ❽ Missing the green leaves a difficult up and down for par. ❾ Just drivable for the longest, but sand can catch the overbold.

THE BACK NINE ❿ Beautiful swooping

par-4. A lake edges across the front and left of the green. ⓫ Toughest short hole on the course. Slightly uphill and very long, often needing a wood. ⓬ Anything short right of green is drawn back down a steep slope. ⓭ Avoid bunkers on fairway for a good chance of birdie. ⓮ A devious short four. Anything can happen. ⓯ A wicked ridge splits green in two. It can be friend or foe. ⓰ Very difficult par-4 in terms of length and the burn just short of green. ⓱ Awesome par-3 by the loch. Green looks like an oasis across the marsh. ⓲ A dangerous tee shot with the loch down the left and bunkers up the right.

A burn runs across the front of the 16th green

A marsh and towering oak dictate your risk-and-reward strategy

A pond threatens the approach to the 10th green

The green is drivable, but the safe route is up the left

HOLE 9 DECEPTIVELY SIMPLE
It may be the shortest par-4 on the course and in range downwind for the biggest hitters, but the 9th can also jump up and grab you. The perfect strategy is to lay up short of the traps up on the right. Traps around the green put pressure on your wedge play. Seems simple, but silly mistakes are common.

A huge nest of traps lies in wait up on the right of the fairway, and more still hem in the green

A bunker down the left of the fairway keeps golfers on their toes

Gargantuan oak trees can create visibility problems and may block the view of the green

The green is small and has a few mounds that make putting tricky

HOLE 14 DO OR DIE
This risky hole gives golfers two options. The safer "high road" is an iron or fairway metal down the left, skirting past the marsh and a towering oak. The riskier ploy takes on the carry of 270 yards (247 m) over the mire and goes directly at the green. Success can bring a simple birdie chance, but failure can lead to a severe penalty.

The fairway turns 90 degrees, leading to a burn and then the awkwardly sloping green

HOLE 6 A LONG AND WINDING HOLE
A huge par-5 is unreachable in two for virtually everyone. The secret is not to block yourself out behind any of the oaks dotted along the length of the hole. Nor can you drive it in the rough, or else you will struggle to reach in three—a massive cross bunker means you might have to lay way back from the green after two shots.

Sun City, SOUTH AFRICA

Two hours from Johannesburg, this monumental course in the bushveld, on the edge of the Pilansberg range, is often ranked as the best course on the continent of Africa. The Gary Player Country Club course at Sun City mixes brawn with brains and is a sapping challenge, both mentally and physically. One of the longest in the world, this course is for big hitters, even with the help of the heat and altitude.

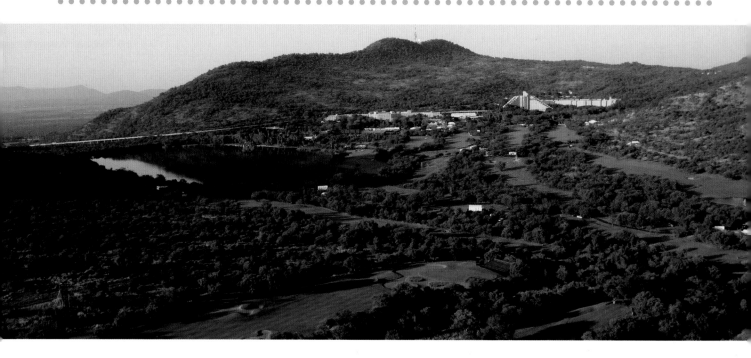

▲ **AN AERIAL VIEW** of the Gary Player Country Club course, with the 1st hole on the right, the red bunkers around the 14th green in the foreground, and the lake on the left.

▼ **THE WATER BESIDE THE 18TH** has a habit of capturing many wayward balls, so they are regularly retrieved.

The Resort at Sun City is a purpose-built land of fun, and revelers from all over the world enjoy its decadence and spirit. The Gary Player Country Club course does not reflect this showy style and is more demure than brash. It has been a playground for golfers since 1979, when Gary Player's team cleared tracts of the harsh native bushveld and laid down its softly surging fairways of kikuyu grass. The course is relatively flat, while all around the hills of the Pilansberg National Park rise and fall, heaved into the air by an ancient volcano. Instead of dramatically swooping holes, it relies on the skill of the route and cleverly placed hazards to keep golfers on their toes. At 7,832 yards (7,162 m) from the championship tees, it is one of the longest courses in the world. Thankfully, Sun City is 3,675 ft (1,120 m) above sea level, so the ball flies like an eagle.

Two years after its opening, it staged the first of its now annual Million Dollar events (now the Nedbank Golf Challenge), where an invitation field of 12 top tour professionals fight it out for vast sums of money. Over the years, they have not only lapped up the hospitality, big baying crowds, and the money, but they have loved the golf course, too. It seems scarcely believable that on a such a long course the best score (but not an official record) is 61 by Pádraig Harrington, and way back in 1993, when technology was not what it is today, Nick Price shot a four-round total of 24-under.

MEAN TRAPS AND TOUGH ROUGH

The course is simply not that easy. Water comes into play on seven holes, most obtrusively on the 9th and 17th, and Player's bunkering is mean and in your face. There is little subtlety to it on the fairways, as most traps appear just at driving distance and pinch already narrow landing zones. By the greens, many traps are dug into the front corners of the putting surface (or ring the front, like at the 14th). These impinging bunkers force approaches to be towering and precise if they are to clear the trouble and hold the

THE COURSE

Ludicrously long and unforgiving, the course takes patience as well as pure striking to play it well, because the clinging rough and sweeps of sand are unrelenting in their full-on challenge. But the heat and altitude help out the power game.

Water waits beside the 9th green at the end of a long par-5

A large bunker guards the 12th green

The 17th fairway has water all the way down the left

A solitary trap on the 9th fairway eats into your driving zone

The 9th green is a wide but shallow island backed by a cascading stream

The picturesque 9th

HOLE 9 A CROWD-PLEASER

The challenge from the tee on the truly crowd-pleasing hole is what you would expect, but up by the green, it gets interesting. Here, a stream cascades around the green's fringes and empties into the lake at the front. This in turn tumbles down a rocky waterfall into another lake below. It takes a brave man to go for it in two. Ernie Els gives his verdict: "The hole is normally set up so as to encourage the second shot at the green, which can be intimidating. I've gone at the green with 2-irons, but if it's 3-wood distance, I back off. Even after laying up short of the lake, if the pin is cut in the back left or right, it is a tough shot; a couple of yards either way and the ball can be in the water."

SUN CITY
PO Box 6, Sun City 0316, South Africa
www.suninternational.com

GARY PLAYER COUNTRY CLUB
FOUNDED 1979
LENGTH 7,832 yards (7,162 m)
DESIGNER Gary Player
COURSE RECORD 63
ERNIE ELS (2002)

SELECTED CHAMPIONS
EDBANK GOLF CHALLENGE (ALSO KNOWN AS THE MILLION DOLLAR CHALLENGE) Nick Price (1997, 1998); Ernie Els (1999, 2000, 2002); Sergio García (2001, 2003); Retief Goosen (2004); Jim Furyk (2005, 2006); Trevor Immelman (2007) **WOMEN'S WORLD CUP OF GOLF** Sweden (2006) (Annika Sorenstam and Liselotte Neumann)

CARD OF THE COURSE

THE FRONT NINE			THE BACK NINE		
HOLE	YARDS	PAR	HOLE	YARDS	PAR
1	403	4	10	500	5
2	520	5	11	419	4
3	411	4	12	200	3
4	195	3	13	406	4
5	449	4	14	550	5
6	388	4	15	431	4
7	206	3	16	193	3
8	450	4	17	437	4
9	545	5	18	459	4
Out	**3,567**	**36**	**In**	**3,595**	**36**

greens. Many of the putting surfaces are tucked away behind these traps, making flags very difficult to get at.

Most holes do have a channel to roll the ball up through, but they are tight and the greens tend to be slightly raised, so a ball can stall on the front. What adds to the difficulty of missing the fairways and greens is the kikuyu grass rough. While a ball can scamper a reasonable distance on the grassy fairways, that same grass is as tough as wire when a few inches taller and flanking the fairways. It is on a par with Bermuda rough, and control from it is virtually nonexistent. Outside of the rough, the bushveld creeps in on every hole and is a no-go area. Steamy heat and chirping insects add to the exotic feel. The last five holes sum up the Country Club's steel. A big par-5 starts the run for home, and a massive cross bunker with islands of rough defends the green. The 15th is two huge smacks to a green with a narrow entrance between traps. Almost half of the green sits behind the bunker front right. It is all carry to the 16th, the shortest par-3 on the course, and the 17th is a monster with water all

the way down the left. Needing to hit a long iron or fairway metal into this green that juts out into the water is a scary proposition.

A HERO'S COURSE

If you have survived the kikuyu, water, thorny bush, and superfast greens, all your hard work can be undone on the 18th, a fantastic par-4 that doglegs left over a lake. The closer you can hit your drive to the water, the better, as it leaves a shorter shot into the gently elevated green. Two gaping bunkers guard the entrance, and the back right pin position is a devil to get at. This is the scene of many rowdy moments in the Million Dollar Challenge, as the crowd is often frenzied in support of their heroes.

It is a hero's course—big and brutal. What it lacks in subtlety and ingenuity, it makes up for in precision, power, immaculate conditioning, and a touch of the wild.

▲ **UNCOMPROMISING BUNKERS** with islands of large, unplayable tufts of kikuyu grass envelop the 14th green.

Mission Hills, CHINA

A mind-boggling resort close to Hong Kong has become China's golfing success story. The largest golf complex in the world, Mission Hills boasts 12 courses of 18 holes, and each has been designed by a renowned figure in golf, mostly touring professionals. The course created by Spanish maestro and double Masters champion José Maria Olazábal is the longest and was chosen to host the Omega Mission Hills World Cup from 2007 to 2009.

China is the fourth-largest country by area on the planet and has around one-quarter of the world's population, yet in golf terms, it is a fledgling. Long ago emperors dabbled, but communism stopped golf from taking any foothold. It was not until 1984 that the People's Republic of China unveiled its first 18-hole course, but since then, it has caught up and made some serious progress. By 2021, more than 500 golf courses have been built in China, with around 300 added in the last decade.

The Mission Hills Resort near Shenzhen, just 35 miles (56 km) from downtown Hong Kong, is leading this remarkable golfing revolution—and on a grand scale. The list of architects who have designed a course here reads like a golfing Who's Who—Jack Nicklaus, Greg Norman, Ernie Els, Annika Sorenstam, Vijay Singh, Nick Faldo, David Duval, Jumbo Ozaki, David Leadbetter, China's own Zhang Lianwei, Pete Dye, and José Maria Olazábal.

To add to the head-scratching size of the resort, Mission Hills is proud to have the largest pro shop in Asia and a monumental clubhouse that occupies a whopping 300,000 sq ft—almost 7 acres (2.8 hectares). Despite the resort being quite close to some major industrial cities, it is perched in a secluded valley surrounded by rolling hills. All the courses enjoy the same cracking backdrops, but the design firm Schmidt-Curley, who collaborated with the pros on the courses, made sure that each course should try as much as possible to have its own identity and reflect the player's thoughts and ideas.

SANDY FEATURES

Olazábal's course pulls no punches but is playable by everyone because of its set of five tees. Yet the best players in the world are always tested, thanks to its sheer length and on-the-edge design that uses creeks and lakes. However, there is something else that dominates play. The Spaniard is regarded as one of the finest short-game players that golf has ever seen, and he is particularly adept from bunkers. It is no surprise then that sand is the major feature on this course.

Despite the five par-3s having only 21 bunkers to contend with between them, finding sand at some time in a round is inevitable, given that there are 68 bunkers on the front nine and a phenomenal 86 on the back. Many are not simply small pots of sand but are large, amoeba-shaped traps with tongues of hairy grass and steep faces. While the fairway bunkers tend to catch bold drives as they

THE PICK OF THE HOLES

Of Mission Hills's 216 holes of joy, the pick are Norman's 4th, a downhill one-shotter to a precarious green with drop-offs to a lake on the left and back; Faldo's 16th, slightly downhill to an island green; and Els' 4th, which falls 44 yards (40 m) and has a rocky stream hugging the left side of the arcing left dogleg.

The 16th on the Faldo Course

▶ **ALTHOUGH IT IS SITUATED** very close to Hong Kong, the Mission Hills Resort enjoys the stunning backdrop of tree-covered hillsides.

tuck into the corners of the gently shaped holes, others are a saving grace and stop your ball from bounding away into yet more trouble.

ELEVATION CHALLENGES

Olazábal has been kind, too, with the shaping of the fairways—most are set in bowl-like channels, which means there is a little more margin for error from the tee. The 1st starts alongside some of the other courses, and gradually the succeeding holes make their way north until the course reaches its farthest point from the clubhouse. Here, the pretty par-3 8th is set on a wooded hillside, with views back down across the resort. The course then intermingles with itself and drops back down the mountain: at two of the par-5s—the 9th and 11th—this descent is particularly spectacular, as they fall some 60 ft (18 m) to the fairways.

Since there are some big elevation changes, the uphill holes such as the 10th have been treated sensitively. They are shorter but much more fiddly than those that have golfers firing down the valleys. At the signature 15th, which is a long, hook-shaped and downhill par-5 (see right), the course rejoins the mix of other courses.

However, the 18th sits in splendid isolation behind a large hill and is overlooked by the gargantuan clubhouse. At 460 yards (420 m), this par-4 is a mighty finish—it is located around a bowing lake with no bunkers waterside to catch a tee shot or approach going left. It is a fitting climax to a powerful but fun course in a resort that catches the imagination and is a golfer's dream.

THE COURSE

The Olazábal Course mixes elevation changes with arcing doglegs and fairways with intrusive bunkers. Rippled green surrounds and fast putting surfaces call for a seriously good short game as well as a powerful and exacting long game.

The 11th fairway is a long, downhill, double dogleg

The 3rd fairway is separated from the green by an open channel

The large 13th green is surrounded by closely mown, sweeping run-offs

A small inlet cuts into the 15th fairway

The 17th green is slightly raised and enveloped by several bunkers

The 18th lies between a lake and the clubhouse

MISSION HILLS

No. 1 Mission Hills Road,
Shenzen 518110, China
www.missionhillschina.com/en

THE OLAZÁBAL COURSE

FOUNDED 2003
LENGTH 7,356 yards (6,726 m)
PAR 72
DESIGNERS José Maria Olazábal

SELECTED CHAMPIONS

OMEGA MISSION HILLS WORLD CUP
Scotland (2007—Colin Montgomerie and Marc Warren)
DYNASTY CUP Asia 16½ Japan 7½ (2003)

CARD OF THE COURSE

THE FRONT NINE			THE BACK NINE		
HOLE	YARDS	PAR	HOLE	YARDS	PAR
1	376	4	10	380	4
2	453	4	11	174	3
3	397	4	12	348	4
4	480	4	13	465	4
5	568	5	14	618	5
6	412	4	15	456	4
7	390	4	16	423	4
8	175	3	17	455	4
9	352	4	18	357	4
OUT	3,616	36	IN	3,740	36

The tee shot fires downhill toward the huge bunkers

HOLE 15 A VICIOUS CURVE

Shaped like a hook, this brilliant hole curves viciously right-to-left around a lake, and the fairway is banked with its right edge finishing high up the hillside. What catches your eye most is the mass of sand. Nine huge bowl bunkers hug the inside of the dogleg and several more are dotted on the outside line. Depending on how far you have struck your drive, you have three choices. Either lay up short of the small inlet that cuts in, splitting the fairway in two; go for the carry to a heavily bunkered second portion of fairway; or have a crack at the green. The big hitters might be able to reach the green as the hole curves back on itself, but it is all carry over water. From the back tees, a drive of around 280 yards (256 m) will leave a shot of about 240 yards (220 m) across the lake to the green—a considerable distance saver, but a very risky policy.

The lake at the 15th

TPC Sawgrass, US

Uncompromising and an assault on your game and spirit, The Stadium Course is a purpose-built tournament venue in the steamy swamplands of Florida. All the holes at Sawgrass have their own particular merit, but the course is most famous for the daunting island green at the 17th. Sawgrass is one of several Tournament Players Clubs (TPCs) where members can experience what it is like to be a touring professional in world golf.

In the late 1970s, the PGA Tour's Commissioner Deane Beman had a brain wave. The headquarters of the PGA Tour were already based in this north Floridian town, so Beman thought it would be a great idea to build on its doorstep a golf course that could permanently host the annual Tournament Players Championship—dubbed the "Fifth Major" due of the strength of its field.

Pete Dye was drafted in to turn this swampy area close to the Atlantic Ocean into a world-beating course. It was a special brief he had to fulfill. Not only was Dye to create a course through the sandy marsh that would test the best, but it had to accommodate hordes of spectators and provide superb vantage points for them. No course had ever before been specifically designed with the galleries in mind. Beman also stipulated that he wanted green complexes with at least four different "shelves" so that they could provide four distinct areas for cutting the hole—one for each day of the tournament.

BUILDING THE COURSE

Dye's team reclaimed massive areas of swampland and brought in truckloads of sand to raise the playing areas off the marsh, and as Dye's nickname "Dye-abolical" suggests, he went on to produce a severe test full of tactical nous and bravery.

The Stadium Course opened in 1980 but was not an instant hit with the players. After the first Tournament Players Championship in 1982, won by Jerry Pate, some respected golfers had some harsh words to say. Ben Crenshaw remarked: "It's Star Wars golf, designed by Darth Vader," and Jack Nicklaus left no one in doubt that it did not suit the way he played: "I've never been good at stopping a 5-iron on the hood of a car." Dye took notice and tweaked his design, making it more friendly, particularly on the greens.

While the routing and the basic course has stayed the same, a huge overhaul was undertaken in 2006.

▶ **THE INFAMOUS AND REMARKABLE 17TH** is the one hole that attracts people to Sawgrass, whether to play it for themselves or to watch from the grandstands as the PGA Tour professionals agonize over its devilish charms.

KEY MOMENTS

◀ **THE FAN'S FAVORITE FRED COUPLES** came of age at the 1984 TPC at Sawgrass when he set the then-course record of 64 in the second round, going on to win the first of his two titles. His course record no longer stands, as it is now 63, shot in 1992 by none other than Couples again! The 17th is one of the holes where Couples entertained the crowd. It is the one hole that people come to Sawgrass for, whether it is to play or simply watch the agony of the Tour pros. Couples made the most incredible comeback on this hole when he found the lake with his first shot but reloaded and holed out with his next for an amazing par-3.

◀ **AT THE AGE OF 48,** the diminutive and popular American Fred Funk won the 2005 TPC to become the oldest man to win this prestigious tournament. Funk is known as the straightest hitter on Tour but not the longest, so his feat of holding the world's best at bay in conditions that made scoring very difficult was remarkable. The whole week was beset by heavy rain and swirling winds, and the average score in round four was a heady 76.5, the highest in the tournament's history. Yet Funk clung on gamely to shoot a 71 and finish at nine-under par, winning by one from Luke Donald, Scott Verplank, and Tom Lehman.

TPC SAWGRASS

110 Championship Way, Ponte Vedra Beach, Florida 32082
www.tpc.com/sawgrass

THE STADIUM COURSE

FOUNDED 1980
LENGTH 7,245 yards (6,625 m)
PAR 72
DESIGNER Pete Dye
COURSE RECORD 63
Fred Couples (1992)

SELECTED CHAMPIONS

THE PLAYERS CHAMPIONSHIP Fred Couples (1996); Steve Elkington (1997); Justin Leonard (1998); David Duval (1999); Hal Sutton (2000); Tiger Woods (2001); Craig Perks (2002); Davis Love III (2003); Adam Scott (2004); Fred Funk (2005); Stephen Ames (2006); Phil Mickelson (2007)

CARD OF THE COURSE

THE FRONT NINE			THE BACK NINE		
HOLE	YARDS	PAR	HOLE	YARDS	PAR
1	423	4	10	424	4
2	532	5	11	558	5
3	177	3	12	358	4
4	384	4	13	181	3
5	471	4	14	481	4
6	393	4	15	470	4
7	451	4	16	523	5
8	237	3	17	137	3
9	583	5	18	462	4
OUT	3,651	36	In	3,594	36

A long bunker awaits on the right of the 4th fairway

Bunkers cause trouble on the right of the 2nd fairway

At the 11th, aim your tee shot up the right, then reassess

N

Bunkers endanger the approach to the 9th green

You will not be the first to find the lake at the 17th

At the 16th, your drive must follow the line of the fairway

A gargantuan strip of sand almost wraps around the green

A huge tree on the left blocks you from going at the green

HOLE 11 RISKS GALORE

This tremendous hole is reachable in two with a couple of exacting shots. Many risks await—a massive bunker, a huge tree, a water hazard that splits the fairway, and a strip of sand beside the green that makes even a wedge approach a tricky deal to clinch.

The carry from the tee to the green is only 120 yards (110 m)

The green is 32 yards (29 m) wide and 25 yards (23 m) deep

HOLE 17 DEVIL ISLAND

The carry to the awesome island green on the 17th is intimidating enough, but the swirling wind makes it worse. Perfectly well-struck shots can stall and plunge short of safety, but a knock-down shot risks bounding over the back.

Trees come into play for a water-avoiding drive right

The green is perilously close to the water on the left

HOLE 18 PLENTY OF PERIL

The 18th is a curving par-4 that arcs around a lake. If you aim to avoid the water on the green's left and bail out right, you find either the grassed humps and hollows or a nasty pot bunker. Chipping and putting from there to a green that slopes toward the water is nerve-racking.

THE COURSE

Designed especially for the world's best to play and for spectators to watch, this modern master trundles over marshland and contains some of the most on-the-edge holes on the planet. The finishing three are worth the entrance fee alone.

THE FRONT NINE ❶ If you dare, drive down the right for the best line into narrow green. **❷** A reachable par-5, but trouble awaits on both sides the entire length. **❸** Short is best as it will leave a chip up the sloping two-tier green. **❹** A snaking bunker protects the right, and the small fiendish green is fronted by water. Accuracy is a premium. **❺** Long four with sand everywhere. The sprawl short of the green is unnerving to the eye. **❻** The drive is over a part of a vast trap that wraps around the left side, and grass bunkers and more sand hem in the green. **❼** Slight S-shape hole with three monstrous strips of sand on the flanks. **❽** Ten bunkers protect this long three. Miss the green, and par is hard. **❾** A plotter's

par-5, with two halves of the hole split by a water channel. Play the third from the right side.

THE BACK NINE ❿ A pull left will end up in the 170-yard (155 m) bunker, but the line in is best from that side. **⓫** Awesome par-5 with a huge risk-and-reward element thanks to offset green sitting next to lake. **⓬** To get a clear view of the green, drive up the right side, flirting with the large bunker. **⓭** Going left on this short hole will surely find water. **⓮** Going into the bunker that runs for 250 yards (229 m) down the right is probably a bogey or worse. **⓯** Slight dogleg right where only the fairway will do. **⓰** Monumental par-5 where eagles and doubles are common. It is all about the second shot, as water awaits right. **⓱** The original island hole that excites and exasperates like no other. A par is one to treasure. **⓲** A sweeping four, edged by water all down the left, but there is little safety out right either.

The brilliant 11th hole

The 15th green

The water hazard beside the 13th

Bunkers were deepened, more waste areas and the lakes were brought closer into play, and 200 palms, oaks, and pines were planted. Most important, all the tees, fairways, and greens were rebuilt with a sand base, with the aim of making the course play firmer and faster. Just when the pros thought they had the course sussed after many years of play, the green slopes were subtly changed, and the lines from the tees and into the greens were altered. One thing that has not changed a huge amount over the years is the length. In 15 years, it has grown by just over 300 yards (274 m), but then the trouble is so severe that length hardly matters.

HEART-STOPPING SHOTS

There is no question that great driving is key to playing this course well. Massively long strips of sand flank many of the fairways, and well-placed trees can block out the direct route to the greens. Water comes into play off the tees on 12 holes, although much is defended by the snaking sand. There is always a preferred line from the tee and most definitely a perfect way to approach the greens to get at any given pin position. All over the course, you face heart-stopping shots. Apart from the ultimate challenge at the infamous 17th, two of the finest examinations of mind and body come at the 11th and 16th. Both are in range in two and eagles are on, but the risks are acute. At the 16th, the drive must go right to left to follow the line of the fairway, or it will run out into clinging rough, from where the only option is to lay up. A huge overhanging oak on the left just short of the green makes the second shot awkward. It tends to push people right, which spells disaster as the green juts out into a lake and water guards all around the right. Where the risk-and-reward 16th comes in the round is significant, as it is followed by two of the toughest holes on the course. For the tournament, this trio always shapes the outcome. In 2002, New Zealander Craig Perks showed how crucial these three are. Behind by one at five-under par with three to play, his gambling second with a 4-iron just cleared the water and stuck in

HOODOO OF THE 17TH

The 17th hole came about by accident. When Dye's team excavated the area, they found a rich seam of quality sand and kept digging until it was all out. They left a craterlike depression, which Dye's wife, Alice, suggested could be an island green. It was the most daring design of a par-3 ever seen and seems to have a hoodoo on it—everybody who tees up there is full of trepidation. An estimated 120,000 balls a year find the surrounding water. At the 2007 TPC, the pros hit 50 balls into the water on Day One, and a tournament total of 94, both records by some margin.

○ Devil Island from above

It's like having a 3 o'clock appointment for a root canal. You're thinking about it all morning and you feel bad all day. You kind of know sooner or later you've got to get to it.

MARK CALCAVECCHIA, TALKING ABOUT THE 17TH HOLE

the rough, from where he chipped in for an eagle to go one ahead. He managed to hit the 17th safely and roll in the birdie to go two in front, but it was not over. Faced with the 18th, the hardest hole on the course, he bailed out right into the trees and had to hack out, leaving him a long iron in. He flew the green into the wiry rough. Remarkably, he chipped in again for his winning par.

The Stadium Course is a devil wrapped up in an immaculate and stunning package. A blood, sweat, and tears experience open to all and the ultimate tournament course, at which the galleries can enjoy the many highs and lows produced by the best players in the world.

○ Reptilian golf fan

○ The sign for the 17th

○ The clubhouse at Sawgrass

THE RECORDS

The Ryder Cup

42 Matches
US 26 Wins; **EUROPE** 14 Wins; **Ties** 2

YEAR	LOCATION	WINNER	
1927	Worcester CC, Worcester, MA, US	**US** 9½	**GB&I** 2½
1929	Moortown GC, Leeds, England	**GB&I** 7	**US** 5
1931	Scioto CC, Columbus, OH, US	**US** 9	**GB&I** 3
1933	Southport & Ainsdale GC, England	**GB&I** 6½	**US** 5½
1935	Ridgewood CC, Ridgewood, NJ, US	**US** 9	**GB&I** 3
1937	Southport & Ainsdale GC, England	**US** 8	**GB&I** 4
1939–45	No Matches played due to World War II		
1947	Portland GC, Portland, OR, US	**US** 11	**GB&I** 1
1949	Ganton GC, Scarborough, England	**US** 7	**GB&I** 5
1951	Pinehurst CC, Pinehurst, NC, US	**US** 9½	**GB&I** 2½
1953	Wentworth GC, Wentworth, England	**US** 6½	**GB&I** 5½
1955	Thunderbird CC, Palm Springs, CA, US	**US** 8	**GB&I** 4
1957	Lindrick GC, Yorkshire, England	**GB&I** 7½	**US** 4½
1959	Eldorado CC, Palm Desert, CA, US	**US** 8½	**GB&I** 3½
1961	Royal Lytham & St. Annes, England	**US** 14½	**GB&I** 9½
1963	East Lake CC, Atlanta, GA, US	**US** 23	**GB&I** 9
1965	Royal Birkdale GC, Southport, England	**US** 19½	**GB&I** 12½
1967	Champions GC, Houston, TX, US	**US** 23½	**GB&I** 18½
1969	Royal Birkdale GC, Southport, England	**US** 16	**GB&I** 16
1971	Old Warson CC, St. Louis, MO, US	**US** 18½	**GB&I** 13½
1973	Muirfield, East Lothian, Scotland	**US** 19	**GB&I** 13
1975	Laurel Valley GC, Ligonier, PA, US	**US** 21	**GB&I** 11
1977	Royal Lytham & St. Annes, England	**US** 12½	**GB&I** 7½
1979	The Greenbrier, WV, US	**US** 17	**EUROPE** 11
1981	Walton Health GC, Surrey, England	**US** 18½	**EUROPE** 9½
1983	PGA National GC, Palm Beach Gardens, FL, US	**US** 14½	**EUROPE** 13½
1985	The Belfry, Sutton Coldfield, England	**EUROPE** 16½	**US** 11½
1987	Muirfield Village GC, Dublin, OH, US	**EUROPE** 15	**US** 13
1989	The Belfry, Sutton Coldfield, England	**EUROPE** 14	**US** 14
1991	The Ocean Course, Kiawah Island, SC, US	**US** 14½	**EUROPE** 13½
1993	The Belfry, Sutton Coldfield, England	**US** 15	**EUROPE** 13
1995	Oak Hill CC, Rochester, NY, US	**EUROPE** 14½	**US** 13½
1997	Valderrama GC, Sotogrande, Spain	**EUROPE** 14½	**US** 13½
1999	The Country Club, Brookline, MA, US	**US** 14½	**EUROPE** 13½
2002	The Belfry, Sutton Coldfield, England	**EUROPE** 15½	**US** 12½
2004	Oakland Hills CC, Bloomfield Hills, MI, US	**EUROPE** 18½	**USA** 9½
2006	The K Club, Straffan, County Kildare, Ireland	**EUROPE** 18½	**US** 9½
2008	Valhalla Golf Club, KY, US	**US** 16½	**EUROPE** 11½
2010	Celtic Manor Resort, Newport, Wales	**EUROPE** 14½	**US** 13½
2012	Medinah CC, IL, US	**EUROPE** 14½	**US** 13½
2014	Gleneagles, Perthshire, Scotland	**EUROPE** 16½	**US** 11½
2016	Hazeltine National GC, MN, US	**US** 17	**EUROPE** 11
2018	Le Golf National, Guyancourt, France	**EUROPE** 17½	**US** 10½

RYDER CUP—MOST APPEARANCES

US

Phil Mickelson	12	1995, 1997, 1999, 2002, 2004, 2006, 2008, 2010, 2012, 2014, 2016, 2018
Jim Furyk	9	1997, 1999, 2002, 2004, 2006, 2008, 2010, 2012, 2014
Tiger Woods	8	1997, 1999, 2002, 2004, 2006, 2010, 2012, 2018
Billy Casper	8	1961, 1963, 1965, 1967, 1969, 1971, 1973, 1975
Raymond Floyd	8	1969, 1975, 1977, 1981, 1983, 1985, 1991, 1993
Lanny Wadkins	8	1977, 1979, 1983, 1985, 1987, 1989, 1991, 1993
Sam Snead	7	1937, 1947, 1949, 1951, 1953, 1955, 1959
Tom Kite	7	1979, 1981, 1983, 1985, 1987, 1989, 1993
Gene Littler	7	1961, 1963, 1965, 1967, 1969, 1971, 1975
Arnold Palmer	6	1961, 1963, 1965, 1967, 1971, 1973
Gene Sarazen	6	1927, 1929, 1931, 1933, 1935, 1937
Jack Nicklaus	6	1969, 1971, 1973, 1975, 1977, 1981
Lee Trevino	6	1969, 1971, 1973, 1975, 1979, 1981

EUROPE

Nick Faldo	11	1977, 1979, 1981, 1983, 1985, 1987, 1989, 1991, 1993, 1995, 1997
Christy O'Connor Sr.	10	1955, 1957, 1959, 1961, 1963, 1965, 1967, 1969, 1971, 1973
Bernhard Langer	10	1981, 1983, 1985, 1987, 1989, 1991, 1993, 1995, 1997, 2002
Lee Westwood	10	1997, 1999, 2002, 2004, 2006, 2008, 2010, 2012, 2014, 2016
Sergio Garcia	9	1999, 2002, 2004, 2006, 2008, 2012, 2014, 2016, 2018
Dai Rees	9	1937, 1947, 1949, 1951, 1953, 1955, 1957, 1959, 1961
Bernard Gallacher	8	1969, 1971, 1973, 1975, 1977, 1979, 1981, 1983
Bernard Hunt	8	1953, 1957, 1959, 1961, 1963, 1965, 1967, 1969
Ian Woosnam	8	1983, 1985, 1987, 1989, 1991, 1993, 1995, 1997
Neil Coles	8	1961, 1963, 1965, 1967, 1969, 1971, 1973, 1977
Peter Alliss	8	1953, 1957, 1959, 1961, 1963, 1965, 1967, 1969
Sam Torrance	8	1981, 1983, 1985, 1987, 1989, 1991, 1993, 1995
Severiano Ballesteros	8	1979, 1983, 1985, 1987, 1989, 1991, 1993, 1995

RYDER CUP—MOST POINTS WON

US		EUROPE	
Billy Casper	23½	Sergio Garcia	25½
Arnold Palmer	23	Nick Faldo	25
Phil Mickelson	21½	Bernhard Langer	24
Lanny Wadkins	21½	Colin Montgomerie	23½
Lee Trevino	20	Lee Westwood	23
Jack Nicklaus	18½	Severiano Ballesteros	22½
Gene Littler	18	José Maria Olazábal	20½
Tom Kite	17	Tony Jacklin	17
Tiger Woods	14½	Ian Woosnam	16½
Hale Irwin	14	Bernard Gallacher	15½
Raymond Floyd	13½	Peter Oosterhuis	15½
Jim Furyk	12	Neil Coles	15½
Davis Love III	11½		
Julius Boros	11		

RYDER CUP—MOST MATCHES PLAYED

US	
Phil Mickelson	47
Billy Casper	37
Tiger Woods	37
Jim Furyk	34
Lanny Wadkins	34
Arnold Palmer	32
Raymond Floyd	31

EUROPE	
Nick Faldo	46
Lee Westwood	44
Bernhard Langer	42
Sergio Garcia	41
Neil Coles	40
Severiano Ballesteros	37

The Tours

US TOUR—CAREER EARNINGS

Tiger Woods	$120,851,706	Ernie Els	$49,339,400
Phil Mickelson	$92,169,822	Jason Day	$48,133,861
Jim Furyk	$71,330,182	Zach Johnson	$46,633,644
Vijay Singh	$71,236,216	Bubba Watson	$46,297,285
Dustin Johnson	$70,865,715	David Love III	$44,944,195
Adam Scott	$55,695,215	Steve Stricker	$44,413,043
Justin Rose	$54,684,092	David Toms	$41,901,709
Rory McIlroy	$54,055,225	Webb Simpson	$41,622,851
Sergio Garcia	$52,012,522	Jordan Spieth	$41,381,522
Matt Kuchar	$51,617,094	Charles Howell III	$40,385,904

EUROPEAN PGA TOUR—CAREER EARNINGS

Lee Westwood	€38,007,976	Francesco Molinari	€22,047,419
Rory McIlroy	€36,630,625	Retief Goosen	€21,978,959
Sergio García	€30,560,076	Martin Kaymer	€21,211,974
Ernie Els	€29,539,154	Thomas Bjørn	€21,138,532
Henrik Stenson	€28,205,995	Darren Clarke	€20,478,393
Justin Rose	€27,492,859	Paul Casey	€19,815,213
Pádraig Harrington	€26,839,462	Tommy Fleetwood	€19,541,723
Ian Poulter	€25,781,147	Graeme McDowell	€19,488,806
Colin Montgomerie	€25,102,089	Louis Oosthuizen	€19,247,350
Miguel Ángel Jiménez	€24,262,812	Ross Fisher	€17,554,314

MOST VICTORIES ON US TOUR

Sam Snead	82	Leo Diegel	28
*Tiger Woods	82	Paul Runyan	28
Jack Nicklaus	73	Henry Picard	26
Ben Hogan	64	Tommy Armour	25
Arnold Palmer	62	Johnny Miller	25
Byron Nelson	52	Macdonald Smith	25
Billy Casper	51	*Dustin Johnson	24
Walter Hagen	45	Gary Player	24
*Phil Mickelson	44	Jim Barnes	22
Cary Middlecoff	39	Johnny Farrell	22
Tom Watson	39	Raymond Floyd	22
Gene Sarazen	38	Davis Love III	21
Lloyd Mangrum	36	Willie Macfarlane	21
*Vijay Singh	34	Lanny Wadkins	21
Jimmy Demaret	31	Craig Wood	21
Horton Smith	30	Hale Irwin	20
Harry Cooper	29	Greg Norman	20
Gene Littler	29	Johnny Revolta	20
Lee Trevino	29	Doug Sanders	20

* currently active on the US Tour

MOST VICTORIES IN A SEASON ON PGA TOUR

Byron Nelson	18	1945
Ben Hogan	13	1946
Sam Snead	11	1950
Ben Hogan	10	1948
Paul Runyan	9	1933
Tiger Woods	9	2000
Vijay Singh	9	2004
Horton Smith	8	1929
Gene Sarazen	8	1930
Arnold Palmer	8	1960, 1962
Johnny Miller	8	1974

The Open

(* won after a playoff)

1860 Prestwick (12-hole course)
Willie Park Sr.	55	59	60	174
Tom Morris Sr.	58	59	59	176

1861 Prestwick
Tom Morris Sr.	54	56	53	163
Willie Park Sr.	54	54	59	167
William Dow	59	58	54	171

1862 Prestwick
Tom Morris Sr.	54	56	53	163
Willie Park Sr.	59	59	58	176
Charlie Hunter	60	60	58	176

1863 Prestwick
Willie Park Sr.	56	54	58	168
Tom Morris Sr.	56	58	56	170
David Park	55	63	54	172

1864 Prestwick
Tom Morris Sr.	54	58	55	167
Andrew Strath	56	57	56	169
Robert Andrew	57	58	60	175

1865 Prestwick
Andrew Strath	55	54	53	162
Willie Park Sr.	56	52	56	164

1866 Prestwick
Willie Park Sr.	54	56	59	169
David Park	58	57	56	171
Robert Andrew	58	59	59	176

1867 Prestwick
Tom Morris Sr.	58	54	58	170
Willie Park Sr.	58	56	58	172
Andrew Strath	61	57	56	174

1868 Prestwick
Tom Morris Jr.	50	55	52	157
Robert Andrew	53	54	52	159
Willie Park Sr.	58	50	54	162

1869 Prestwick
Tom Morris Jr.	51	54	49	154
Tom Morris Sr.	54	50	53	157
S. Mure Fergusson	57	54	54	165

1870 Prestwick
Tom Morris Jr.	47	51	51	149
Bob Kirk	52	52	57	161
Davie Strath	54	49	58	161

1871 No Championship

1872 Prestwick
Tom Morris Jr.	57	56	53	166
Davie Strath	56	52	61	169
William Doleman	63	60	54	177

1873 Royal & Ancient Golf Club, St. Andrews
Tom Kidd	91	88	179
Jamie Anderson	91	89	180
Bob Kirk	91	92	183
Tom Morris Jr.	94	89	183

1874 Musselburgh
Mungo Park	75	84	159
Tom Morris Jr.	83	78	161
George Paxton	80	82	162

1875 Prestwick
Willie Park Sr.	56	59	51	166
Bob Martin	56	58	54	168
Mungo Park	59	57	55	171

1876 Royal & Ancient Golf Club, St. Andrews
Bob Martin won the title after Davie Strath refused to participate in the playoff
Bob Martin	86	90	176
Davie Strath	86	90	176
Willie Park Sr.	94	89	183

1877 Musselburgh
Jamie Anderson	40	42	37	41	160
Bob Pringle	44	38	40	40	162
William Cosgrove	41	39	44	40	164

1878 Prestwick
Jamie Anderson	53	53	51	157
Bob Kirk	53	55	51	159
JOF Morris	50	56	55	161

1879 Royal & Ancient Golf Club, St. Andrews
Jamie Anderson	84	85	169
Jamie Allan	88	84	172
Andrew Kirkaldy	86	86	172

1880 Musselburgh
Bob Ferguson	81	81	162
Peter Paxton	81	86	167
Ned Cosgrove	82	86	168

1881 Prestwick
Bob Ferguson	53	60	57	170
Jamie Anderson	57	60	56	173
Ned Cosgrove	61	59	57	177

1882 Royal & Ancient Golf Club, St. Andrews
Bob Ferguson	83	88	171
Willie Fernie	88	86	174
Jamie Anderson	87	88	175

1883 Musselburgh
*Willie Fernie	75	84	159
Bob Ferguson	78	81	159
William Brown	83	77	160

1884 Prestwick
Jack Simpson	78	82	160
Willie Fernie	80	94	164
Douglas Rolland	81	83	164

1885 Royal & Ancient Golf Club, St. Andrews
Bob Martin	84	87	171
Archie Simpson	83	89	172
David Ayton	89	84	173

1886 Musselburgh
David Brown	79	78	157
Willie Campbell	78	81	159
Ben Campbell	79	81	160

1887 Prestwick
Willie Park Jr.	82	79	161
Bob Martin	81	81	162
Willie Campbell	77	87	164

1888 Royal & Ancient Golf Club, St. Andrews
Jack Burns	86	85	171
David Anderson Jr.	86	86	172
Ben Sayers	85	87	172

1889 Musselburgh
*Willie Park Jr.	39	39	39	38	155
Andrew Kirkaldy	39	38	39	39	155
Ben Sayers	39	40	41	39	159

1890 Prestwick
John Ball Jr.	82	82	164
Willie Fernie	85	82	167
Archie Simpson	85	82	167

1891 Royal & Ancient Golf Club, St. Andrews
Hugh Kirkaldy	83	83	166
Willie Fernie	84	84	168
Andrew Kirkaldy	84	84	168

1892 Musselburgh
First championship to be spread over two days and 72 holes
Harold Hilton	78	81	72	74	305
John Ball	75	80	74	79	308
Sandy Herd	77	78	77	76	308

1893 Prestwick
W. Auchterlonie	78	81	81	82	322
Johnny Laidlay	80	83	80	81	324
Sandy Herd	82	81	78	84	325

1894 St. George's, Sandwich
J. H. Taylor	84	80	80	81	326
Douglas Rolland	86	79	84	82	331
Andrew Kirkaldy	86	79	83	84	332

1895 Royal & Ancient Golf Club, St. Andrews
J. H. Taylor	86	78	80	78	322
Sandy Herd	82	77	82	85	326
Andrew Kirkaldy	81	83	84	84	332

1896 Muirfield
*Harry Vardon	83	78	78	77	316
J. H. Taylor	77	78	81	80	316
Willie Fernie	78	79	82	89	319

1897 Royal Liverpool, Hoylake

Harold Hilton	80	75	84	75	314
James Braid	80	74	82	79	315
George Pulford	80	79	79	79	317

1898 Prestwick

Harry Vardon	79	75	77	76	307
Willie Park Jr.	76	75	78	79	308
Harold Hilton	76	81	77	75	309

1899 St. George's, Sandwich

Harry Vardon	76	76	81	77	310
Jack White	79	79	82	75	315
Andrew Kirkaldy	81	79	82	77	319

1900 Royal & Ancient Golf Club, St. Andrews

J. H. Taylor	79	77	78	75	309
Harry Vardon	79	81	80	77	317
James Braid	82	81	80	79	322

1901 Muirfield

James Braid	79	76	74	80	309
Harry Vardon	77	78	79	78	312
J. H. Taylor	79	83	74	77	313

1902 Royal Liverpool, Hoylake

Sandy Herd	77	76	73	81	307
James Braid	78	76	80	74	308
Harry Vardon	72	77	80	79	308

1903 Prestwick

Harry Vardon	73	77	72	78	300
Tom Vardon	76	81	75	74	306
Jack White	77	78	74	79	308

1904 St. George's, Sandwich

Jack White	80	75	72	69	296
James Braid	77	80	69	71	297
J. H. Taylor	77	78	74	68	297

1905 Royal & Ancient Golf Club, St. Andrews

James Braid	81	78	78	81	318
Rowland Jones	81	77	87	78	323
J. H. Taylor	80	85	78	80	323

1906 Muirfield

James Braid	77	76	74	73	300
J. H. Taylor	77	72	75	80	304
Harry Vardon	77	73	77	78	305

1907 Royal Liverpool, Hoylake

Arnaud Massy	76	81	78	77	312
J. H. Taylor	79	79	76	80	314
George Pulford	81	79	80	75	317

1908 Prestwick

James Braid	70	72	77	72	291
Tom Ball	76	73	76	74	299
Ted Ray	79	71	75	76	301

1909 Royal Cinq Ports, Deal

J. H. Taylor	74	73	74	74	295
Tom Ball	74	75	76	76	301
James Braid	79	75	73	74	301

1910 Royal & Ancient Golf Club, St. Andrews

James Braid	76	73	74	76	299
Sandy Herd	78	74	75	76	303
George Duncan	73	77	71	83	304

1911 St. George's, Sandwich

*Harry Vardon	74	74	75	80	303
Arnaud Massy	75	78	74	76	303
Sandy Herd	77	73	76	78	304

1912 Muirfield

Ted Ray	71	73	76	75	295
Harry Vardon	75	72	81	71	299
James Braid	77	71	77	78	303

1913 Royal Liverpool, Hoylake

J. H. Taylor	73	75	77	79	304
Ted Ray	73	74	81	84	312
Michael Moran	76	74	89	74	313

1914 Prestwick

Harry Vardon	73	77	78	78	306
J. H. Taylor	74	78	74	73	309
Harry Simpson	77	80	78	75	310

1915–1919 No Championship—World War I

1920 Royal Cinq Ports, Deal

George Duncan	80	80	71	72	303
Sandy Herd	72	81	77	75	305
Ted Ray	72	83	78	73	306

1921 Royal & Ancient Golf Club, St. Andrews

*Jock Hutchinson	72	75	79	70	296
Roger Wethered	78	75	72	71	296
Tom Kerrigan	74	80	72	72	298

1922 Royal St. George's, Sandwich

Walter Hagen	76	73	79	72	300
Jim Barnes	75	76	77	73	301
George Duncan	76	75	81	69	302

1923 Troon

Arthur Havers	73	73	73	76	295
Walter Hagen	76	71	74	75	296
Macdonald Smith	80	73	69	75	297

1924 Royal Liverpool, Hoylake

Walter Hagen	77	73	74	77	301
Ernest R. Whitcombe	77	70	77	78	302
Frank Ball	78	75	74	77	304

1925 Prestwick

Jim Barnes	70	77	79	74	300
Archie Compston	76	75	75	75	301
Ted Ray	77	76	75	73	301

1926 Royal Lytham & St. Annes

Bobby Jones	72	72	73	74	291
Al Waltrous	71	75	69	78	293
Walter Hagen	68	77	74	76	295

1927 Royal & Ancient Golf Club, St. Andrews

Bobby Jones	68	72	73	72	285
Aubrey Boomer	76	70	73	72	291
Fred Robson	76	72	69	74	291

1928 Royal St. George's, Sandwich

Walter Hagen	75	73	72	72	292
Gene Sarazen	72	76	73	73	294
Archie Compston	75	74	73	73	295

1929 Muirfield

Walter Hagen	75	67	75	75	292
Johnny Farrell	72	75	76	75	298
Leo Diegel	71	69	82	77	299

1930 Royal Liverpool, Hoylake

Bobby Jones	70	72	74	75	291
Leo Diegel	74	73	71	75	293
Macdonald Smith	70	77	75	71	293

1931 Carnoustie

Tommy Armour	73	75	77	71	296
Jose Jurado	76	71	73	77	297
Percy Alliss	74	78	73	73	298

1932 Prince's, Sandwich

Gene Sarazen	70	69	70	74	283
Macdonald Smith	71	76	71	70	288
Arthur Havers	74	71	68	76	289

1933 Royal & Ancient Golf Club, St. Andrews

*Denny Shute	73	73	73	73	292
Craig Wood	77	72	68	75	292
Leo Diegel	75	70	71	77	293
Syd Easterbrook	73	72	71	77	293
Gene Sarazen	72	73	73	75	293

1934 Royal St. George's, Sandwich

Henry Cotton	67	65	72	79	283
Sid Brews	76	71	70	71	288
Alf Padgham	71	70	75	74	290

1935 Muirfield

Alf Perry	69	75	67	72	283
Alf Padgham	70	72	74	71	287
Charles Whitcombe	71	68	73	76	288

1936 Royal Liverpool, Hoylake

Alf Padgham	73	72	71	71	287
Jimmy Adams	71	73	71	73	288
Henry Cotton	73	72	70	74	289

1937 Carnoustie

Henry Cotton	74	73	72	71	290
Reg Whitcombe	72	70	74	76	292
Charles Lacey	76	75	70	72	293

1938 Royal St. George's, Sandwich

Reg Whitcombe	71	71	75	78	295
Jimmy Adams	70	71	78	78	297
Henry Cotton	74	73	77	74	298

1939 Royal & Ancient Golf Club, St. Andrews

Dick Burton	70	72	77	71	290
Johnny Bulla	77	71	71	73	292
Johnny Fallon	71	73	71	79	294

1946 Royal & Ancient Golf Club, St. Andrews

Sam Snead	71	70	74	75	290
Johnny Bulla	71	72	72	79	294
Bobby Locke	69	74	75	76	294

1947 Royal Liverpool, Hoylake

Fred Daly	73	70	78	72	293
Reg Horne	77	74	72	71	294
Frank Stranahan	71	74	72	71	294

1948 Muirfield

Henry Cotton	71	66	75	72	284
Fred Daly	72	71	73	73	289
Roberto de Vicenzo	70	73	72	75	290

1949 Royal St. George's, Sandwich

*Bobby Locke	69	76	68	70	283
Harry Bradshaw	68	77	68	70	283
Roberto de Vicenzo	68	75	73	69	285

1950 Troon

Bobby Locke	69	72	70	68	279
Roberto de Vicenzo	72	71	68	70	281
Fred Daly	75	72	69	66	282

1951 Royal Portrush, Co Antrim

Max Faulkner	71	70	70	74	285
Antonio Cerda	74	72	71	70	287
Charlie Ward	75	73	74	68	290

1952 Royal Lytham & St. Annes

Bobby Locke	69	71	74	73	287
Peter Thomson	68	73	77	70	288
Fred Daly	67	69	77	76	289

1953 Carnoustie

Ben Hogan	73	71	70	68	282
Antonio Cerda	75	71	69	71	286
Dai Rees	72	70	73	71	286

1954 Birkdale

Peter Thomson	72	71	69	71	283
Bobby Locke	74	71	69	70	284
Dai Rees	72	71	69	70	284

1955 Royal & Ancient Golf Club, St. Andrews

Peter Thomson	71	68	70	72	281
Johnny Fallon	73	67	73	70	283
Frank Jowle	70	71	69	74	284

1956 Royal Liverpool, Hoylake

Peter Thomson	70	70	72	74	286
Flory van Donck	71	74	70	74	289
Roberto de Vicenzo	71	70	79	70	290

1957 Royal & Ancient Golf Club, St. Andrews

Bobby Locke	69	72	68	70	279
Peter Thomson	73	69	70	70	282
Eric Brown	67	72	73	71	283

1958 Royal Lytham & St. Annes

*Peter Thomson	66	72	67	73	278
Dave Thomas	70	68	69	71	278
Eric Brown	73	70	65	71	279

1959 Muirfield

Gary Player	75	71	70	68	284
Fred Bullock	68	70	74	74	286
Flory van Donck	70	70	73	73	286

1960 Royal & Ancient Golf Club, St. Andrews

Kel Nagle	69	67	71	71	278
Arnold Palmer	70	71	70	68	279
Roberto de Vicenzo	67	67	75	73	282

1961 Birkdale

Arnold Palmer	70	73	69	72	284
Dai Rees	68	74	71	72	285
Neil Coles	70	77	69	72	288

1962 Troon

Arnold Palmer	71	69	67	69	276
Kel Nagle	71	71	70	70	282
Brian Huggett	75	71	74	69	289
Phil Rodgers	75	70	72	72	289

1963 Royal Lytham & St. Annes

Bob Charles	68	72	66	71	277
Phil Rodgers	67	68	73	69	277
Jack Nicklaus	71	67	70	70	278

1964 Royal & Ancient Golf Club, St. Andrews

Tony Lema	73	68	68	70	279
Jack Nicklaus	76	74	66	68	284
Roberto de Vicenzo	76	72	70	67	285

1965 Royal Birkdale

Peter Thomson	74	68	72	71	285
Brian Huggett	73	68	76	70	287
Christy O'Connor Sr.	69	73	74	71	287

1966 Muirfield

Jack Nicklaus	70	67	75	70	282
Doug Sanders	71	70	72	70	283
Dave Thomas	72	73	69	69	283

1967 Royal Liverpool, Hoylake

Roberto de Vicenzo	70	71	67	70	278
Jack Nicklaus	71	69	71	69	280
Clive Clark	70	73	69	72	284
Gary Player	72	71	67	74	284

1968 Carnoustie

Gary Player	74	71	71	73	289
Bob Charles	72	72	71	76	291
Jack Nicklaus	76	69	73	73	291

1969 Royal Lytham & St. Annes

Tony Jacklin	68	70	70	72	280
Bob Charles	66	69	75	72	282
Roberto de Vicenzo	72	73	66	72	283
Peter Thomson	71	70	70	72	283

1970 St. Andrews

*Jack Nicklaus	68	69	73	73	283
Doug Sanders	68	71	71	73	283
Harold Henning	67	72	73	73	285
Lee Trevino	68	68	72	77	285

1971 Royal Birkdale

Lee Trevino	69	70	69	70	278
Lu Liang-Huan	70	70	69	70	279
Tony Jacklin	69	70	70	71	280

1972 Muirfield

Lee Trevino	71	70	66	71	278
Jack Nicklaus	70	72	71	66	279
Tony Jacklin	69	72	67	72	280

1973 Royal Troon

Tom Weiskopf	68	67	71	70	276
Neil Coles	71	72	70	66	279
Johnny Miller	70	68	69	72	279

1974 Royal Lytham & St. Annes

Gary Player	69	68	75	70	282
Peter Oosterhuis	71	71	73	71	286
Jack Nicklaus	74	72	70	71	287

1975 Carnoustie

*Tom Watson	71	67	69	72	279
Jack Newton	69	71	65	74	279
Bobby Cole	72	66	66	76	280
Johnny Miller	71	69	66	74	280
Jack Nicklaus	69	71	68	72	280

1976 Royal Birkdale

Johnny Miller	72	68	73	66	279
Jack Nicklaus	74	70	72	69	285
Severiano Ballesteros	69	69	73	74	285

1977 Turnberry

Tom Watson	68	70	65	65	268
Jack Nicklaus	68	70	65	66	269
Hubert Green	72	66	74	67	279

1978 St. Andrews

Jack Nicklaus	71	72	69	69	281
Tom Kite	72	69	72	70	283
Simon Owen	70	75	67	71	283
Ben Crenshaw	70	69	73	71	283
Raymond Floyd	69	75	71	68	283

1979 Royal Lytham & St. Annes

Severiano Ballesteros	73	65	75	70	283
Jack Nicklaus	72	69	73	72	286
Ben Crenshaw	72	71	72	71	286

1980 Muirfield

Tom Watson	68	70	64	69	271
Lee Trevino	68	67	71	69	275
Ben Crenshaw	70	70	68	69	277

1981 Royal St. George's

Bill Rogers	72	66	67	71	276
Bernhard Langer	73	67	70	70	280
Mark James	72	70	68	73	283
Raymond Floyd	74	70	69	70	283

1982 Royal Troon

Tom Watson	69	71	74	70	284
Peter Oosterhuis	74	67	74	70	285
Nick Price	69	69	74	73	285

1983 Royal Birkdale

Tom Watson	67	68	70	70	275
Andy Bean	70	69	70	67	276
Hale Irwin	69	68	72	67	276

1984 St. Andrews

Severiano Ballesteros	69	68	70	69	276
Bernhard Langer	71	68	68	71	278
Tom Watson	71	68	66	73	278

1985 Royal St. George's

Sandy Lyle	68	71	73	70	282
Payne Stewart	70	75	70	68	283
Mark O'Meara	70	72	70	72	284

1986 Turnberry

Greg Norman	74	63	74	69	280
Gordon J Brand	71	68	75	71	285
Bernhard Langer	72	70	76	68	286
Ian Woosnam	70	74	70	72	286

1987 Muirfield

Nick Faldo	68	69	71	71	279
Rodger Davis	64	73	74	69	280
Paul Azinger	68	68	71	73	280

1988 Royal Lytham & St. Annes

Severiano Ballesteros	67	71	70	65	273
Nick Price	70	67	69	69	275
Nick Faldo	71	69	68	71	279

1989 Royal Troon

*Mark Calcavecchia	71	68	68	68	275
Wayne Grady	68	67	69	71	275
Greg Norman	69	70	72	64	275

1990 St. Andrews

Nick Faldo	67	65	67	71	270
Mark McNulty	74	68	68	65	275
Payne Stewart	68	68	68	71	275

1991 Royal Birkdale

Ian Baker-Finch	71	71	64	66	272
Mike Harwood	68	70	69	67	274
Mark O'Meara	71	68	67	69	275

1992 Muirfield

Nick Faldo	66	64	69	73	272
John Cook	66	67	70	70	273
José-Maria Olazábal	70	67	69	68	274

1993 Royal St. George's

Greg Norman	66	68	69	64	267
Nick Faldo	69	63	70	67	269
Bernhard Langer	67	66	70	67	270

1994 Turnberry

Nick Price	69	66	67	66	268
Jesper Parnevik	68	66	68	67	269
Fuzzy Zoeller	71	66	64	70	271

1995 St. Andrews

*John Daly	67	71	73	71	282
Costantino Rocca	69	70	70	73	282
Steven Bottomley	70	72	72	69	283

1996 Royal Lytham & St. Annes

Tom Lehman	67	67	64	73	271
Mark McCumber	67	69	71	66	273
Ernie Els	68	67	71	67	273

1997 Royal Troon

Justin Leonard	69	66	72	65	272
Jesper Parnevik	70	66	66	73	275
Darren Clarke	67	66	71	71	275

1998 Royal Birkdale

*Mark O'Meara	72	68	72	68	280
Brian Watts	68	69	73	70	280
Tiger Woods	65	73	77	66	281

1999 Carnoustie

*Paul Lawrie	73	74	76	67	290
Justin Leonard	73	74	71	72	290
Jean Van de Velde	75	68	70	77	290

2000 St. Andrews

Tiger Woods	67	66	67	69	269
Ernie Els	66	72	70	69	277
Thomas Bjorn	69	69	68	71	277

2001 Royal Lytham & St. Annes

David Duval	69	73	65	67	274
Niclas Fasth	69	69	72	67	277
Billy Mayfair	69	72	67	70	278

2002 Muirfield

*Ernie Els	70	66	72	70	278
Steve Elkington	71	73	68	66	278
Stuart Appleby	73	70	70	65	278
Thomas Levet	72	66	74	66	278

2003 Royal St. George's, Sandwich

Ben Curtis	72	72	70	69	283
Vijay Singh	75	70	69	70	284
Thomas Bjorn	73	70	69	72	284

2004 Royal Troon

*Todd Hamilton	71	67	67	69	274
Ernie Els	69	69	68	68	274
Phil Mickelson	73	66	68	68	275

2005 St. Andrews

Tiger Woods	66	67	71	70	274
Colin Montgomerie	71	66	70	72	279
Fred Couples	68	71	73	68	280

2006 Royal Liverpool, Hoylake

Tiger Woods	67	65	71	67	270
Chris DiMarco	70	65	69	68	272
Ernie Els	68	65	71	71	275

2007 Carnoustie

*Pádraig Harrington	69	73	68	67	277
Sergio Garcia	65	71	68	73	277
Andres Romero	71	70	70	67	278

2008 Royal Birkdale

Pádraig Harrington	74	68	72	69	283
Ian Poulter	72	71	75	69	287
Greg Norman	70	70	72	77	289
Henrik Stenson	76	72	70	71	289

2009 Turnberry

*Stewart Cink	66	72	71	69	278
Tom Watson	65	70	71	72	278
Lee Westwood	68	70	70	71	279
Chris Wood	70	70	72	67	279

2010 St. Andrews

Louis Oosthuizen	65	67	69	71	272
Lee Westwood	67	71	71	70	279
Rory McIlroy	63	80	69	68	280
Henrik Stenson	68	74	67	71	280
Paul Casey	69	69	67	75	280

2011 Royal St. George's, Sandwich

Darren Clarke	68	68	69	70	275
Phil Mickelson	70	69	71	68	278
Dustin Johnson	70	68	68	72	278

2012 Royal Lytham & St. Annes

Ernie Els	67	70	68	68	273
Adam Scott	64	67	68	75	274
Brandt Snedeker	66	64	73	74	277
Tiger Woods	67	67	70	73	277

2013 Muirfield

Phil Mickelson	69	74	72	66	281
Henrik Stenson	70	70	74	70	284
Ian Poulter	72	71	75	67	285
Adam Scott	71	72	70	72	285
Lee Westwood	72	68	70	75	285

2014 Royal Liverpool, Hoylake

Rory McIlroy	66	66	68	71	271
Rickie Fowler	69	69	68	67	273
Sergio Garcia	68	70	69	66	273

2015 St. Andrews

*Zach Johnson	66	71	70	66	273
Marc Leishman	70	73	64	66	273
Louis Oosthuizen	67	70	67	69	273
Jason Day	66	71	67	70	274
Jordan Speith	67	72	66	69	274

2016 Royal Troon

Henrik Stenson	68	65	68	63	264
Phil Mickelson	63	69	70	65	267
J.B. Holmes	70	70	69	69	278

2017 Royal Birkdale

Jordan Speith	65	69	65	69	268
Matt Kuchar	65	71	66	69	271
Li Haotong	69	73	69	63	274

2018 Carnoustie

Francesco Molinari	70	72	65	69	276
Kevin Kisner	66	70	68	74	278
Rory McIlroy	69	69	70	70	278
Justin Rose	72	73	64	69	278
Xander Schauffele	71	66	67	74	278

2019 Royal Portrush

Shane Lowry	67	67	63	72	269
Tommy Fleetwood	68	67	66	74	275
Tony Finau	68	70	68	71	278

The Masters

Augusta National, Augusta, GA, US
(* won after a playoff)

1934
Horton Smith	70	72	70	72	284
Craig Wood	71	74	69	71	285
Billy Burke	72	71	70	73	286
Paul Runyan	74	71	70	71	286

1935
Gene Sarazen	68	71	73	70	282
Craig Wood	69	72	68	73	282
Olin Dutra	70	70	70	74	284

1936
Horton Smith	74	71	68	72	285
Harry Cooper	70	69	71	76	286
Gene Sarazen	78	67	72	70	287

1937
Byron Nelson	66	72	75	70	283
Ralph Guldahl	69	72	68	76	285
Ed Dudley	70	71	71	74	286

1938
Henry Picard	71	72	72	70	285
Harry Cooper	68	77	71	71	287
Ralph Guldahl	73	70	73	71	287

1939
Ralph Guldahl	72	68	70	69	279
Sam Snead	70	70	72	68	280
Billy Burke	69	72	71	70	282
Lawson Little Jr.	72	72	68	70	282

1940
Jimmy Demaret	67	72	70	71	280
Lloyd Mangrum	64	75	71	74	284
Byron Nelson	69	72	74	70	285

1941
Craig Wood	66	71	71	72	280
Byron Nelson	71	69	73	70	283
Sam Byrd	73	70	68	74	285

1942
*Byron Nelson	68	67	72	73	280
Ben Hogan	73	70	67	70	280
Paul Runyan	67	73	72	71	283

1946
Herman Keiser	69	68	71	74	282
Ben Hogan	74	70	69	70	283
Bob Hamilton	75	69	71	72	287

1947
Jimmy Demaret	69	71	70	71	281
Byron Nelson	69	72	72	70	283
Frank Stranahan	73	72	70	68	283

1948
Claude Harmon	70	70	69	70	279
Cary Middlecoff	74	71	69	70	284
Chick Harbert	71	70	70	76	287

1949
Sam Snead	73	75	67	67	282
Johnny Bulla	74	73	69	69	285
Lloyd Mangrum	69	74	72	70	285

1950
Jimmy Demaret	70	72	72	69	283
Jim Ferrier	70	67	73	75	285
Sam Snead	71	74	70	72	287

1951
Ben Hogan	70	72	70	68	280
Skee Riegel	73	68	70	71	282
Lloyd Mangrum	69	74	70	73	286
Lew Worsham	71	71	72	72	286

1952
Sam Snead	70	67	77	72	286
Jack Burke Jr.	76	67	78	69	290
Al Besselink	70	76	71	74	291
Tommy Bolt	71	71	75	74	291
Jim Ferrier	72	70	77	72	291

1953
Ben Hogan	70	69	66	69	274
Ed Oliver	69	73	67	70	279
Lloyd Mangrum	74	68	71	69	282

1954
*Sam Snead	74	73	70	72	289
Ben Hogan	72	73	69	75	289
William Patton	70	74	75	71	290

1955
Cary Middlecoff	72	65	72	70	279
Ben Hogan	73	68	72	73	286
Sam Snead	72	71	74	70	287

1956
Jack Burke Jr.	72	71	75	71	289
Ken Venturi	66	69	75	80	290
Cary Middlecoff	67	72	75	77	291

1957
Doug Ford	72	73	72	66	283
Sam Snead	72	68	74	72	286
Jimmy Demaret	72	70	75	70	287

1958
Arnold Palmer	70	73	68	73	284
Doug Ford	74	71	70	70	285
Fred Hawkins	71	75	68	71	285

1959
Art Wall Jr.	73	74	71	66	284
Cary Middlecoff	74	71	68	72	285
Arnold Palmer	71	70	71	74	286

1960
Arnold Palmer	67	73	72	70	282
Ken Venturi	73	69	71	70	283
Dow Finsterwald	71	70	72	71	284

1961
Gary Player	69	68	69	74	280
Charles Coe	72	71	69	69	281
Arnold Palmer	68	69	73	71	281

1962
Arnold Palmer	70	66	69	75	280
Gary Player	67	71	71	71	280
Dow Finsterwald	74	68	65	73	280

1963
Jack Nicklaus	74	66	74	72	286
Tony Lema	74	69	74	70	287
Julius Boros	76	69	71	72	288
Sam Snead	70	73	74	71	288

1964
Arnold Palmer	69	68	69	70	276
Dave Marr	70	73	69	70	282
Jack Nicklaus	71	73	71	67	282

1965
Jack Nicklaus	67	71	64	69	271
Arnold Palmer	70	68	72	70	280
Gary Player	65	73	69	73	280

1966
*Jack Nicklaus	68	76	72	72	288
Tommy Jacobs	75	71	70	72	288
Gay Brewer Jr.	74	72	72	70	288

1967
Gay Brewer Jr.	73	68	72	67	280
Bobby Nichols	72	69	70	70	281
Bert Yancey	67	73	71	73	284

1968
Bob Goalby	70	70	71	66	277
Roberto De Vicenzo	69	73	70	66	278
Bert Yancey	71	71	72	65	279

1969
George Archer	67	73	69	72	281
Billy Casper Jr.	66	71	71	74	282
George Knudson	70	73	69	70	282
Tom Weiskopf	71	71	69	71	282

1970
*Billy Casper Jr.	72	68	68	71	279
Gene Littler	69	70	70	70	279
Gary Player	74	68	68	70	280

1971
Charles Coody	66	73	70	70	279
Johnny Miller	72	73	68	68	281
Jack Nicklaus	70	71	68	72	281

1972

Jack Nicklaus	68	71	73	74	286
Bruce Crampton	72	75	69	73	289
Bobby Mitchell	73	72	71	73	289
Tom Weiskopf	74	71	70	74	289

1973

Tommy Aaron	68	73	74	68	283
Jesse Snead	70	71	73	70	284
Jim Jamieson	73	71	70	71	285
Jack Nicklaus	69	77	73	66	285
Peter Oosterhuis	73	70	68	74	285

1974

Gary Player	71	71	66	70	278
Dave Stockton	71	66	70	73	280
Tom Weiskopf	71	69	70	70	280

1975

Jack Nicklaus	68	67	73	68	276
Johnny Miller	75	71	65	66	277
Tom Weiskopf	69	72	66	70	277

1976

Raymond Floyd	65	66	70	70	271
Ben Crenshaw	70	70	72	67	279
Jack Nicklaus	67	69	73	73	282
Larry Ziegler	67	71	72	72	282

1977

Tom Watson	70	69	70	67	276
Jack Nicklaus	72	70	70	66	278
Tom Kite	70	73	70	67	280
Rik Massengale	70	73	67	70	280

1978

Gary Player	72	72	69	64	277
Rod Funseth	73	66	70	69	278
Hubert Green	72	69	65	72	278
Tom Watson	73	68	68	69	278

1979

Fuzzy Zoeller	70	71	69	70	280
Ed Sneed	68	67	69	76	280
Tom Watson	68	71	70	71	280

1980

Severiano Ballesteros	66	69	68	72	275
Gibby Gilbert	70	74	68	67	279
Jack Newton	68	74	69	68	279

1981

Tom Watson	71	68	70	71	280
Johnny Miller	69	72	73	68	282
Jack Nicklaus	70	65	75	72	282

1982

*Craig Stadler	75	69	67	73	284
Dan Pohl	75	75	67	67	284
Severiano Ballesteros	73	73	68	71	285
Jerry Pate	74	73	67	71	285

1983

Severiano Ballesteros	68	70	73	69	280
Ben Crenshaw	76	70	70	68	284
Tom Kite	70	72	73	69	284

1984

Ben Crenshaw	67	72	70	68	277
Tom Watson	74	67	69	69	279
David Edwards	71	70	72	67	280
Gil Morgan	73	71	69	67	280

1985

Bernhard Langer	72	74	68	68	282
Severiano Ballesteros	72	71	71	70	284
Raymond Floyd	70	73	69	72	284
Curtis Strange	80	65	68	71	284

1986

Jack Nicklaus	74	71	69	65	279
Tom Kite	70	74	68	68	280
Greg Norman	70	72	68	70	280

1987

*Larry Mize	70	72	72	71	285
Severiano Ballesteros	73	71	70	71	285
Greg Norman	73	74	66	72	285

1988

Sandy Lyle	71	67	72	71	281
Mark Calcavecchia	71	69	72	70	282
Craig Stadler	76	69	70	68	283

1989

*Nick Faldo	68	73	77	65	283
Scott Hoch	69	74	71	69	283
Ben Crenshaw	71	72	70	71	284
Greg Norman	74	75	68	67	284

1990

*Nick Faldo	71	72	66	69	278
Raymond Floyd	70	68	68	72	278
John Huston	66	74	68	75	283
Lanny Wadkins	72	73	70	68	283

1991

Ian Woosnam	72	66	67	72	277
José Maria Olazábal	68	71	69	70	278
Ben Crenshaw	70	73	68	68	279
Steve Pate	72	73	69	65	279
Lanny Wadkins	67	71	70	71	279
Tom Watson	68	68	70	73	279

1992

Fred Couples	69	67	69	70	275
Raymond Floyd	69	68	69	71	277
Cory Pavin	72	71	68	67	278

1993

Bernhard Langer	68	70	69	70	277
Chip Beck	72	67	72	70	281
John Daly	70	71	73	69	283
Steve Elkington	71	70	71	71	283
Tom Lehman	67	75	73	68	283

1994

José Maria Olazábal	74	67	69	69	279
Tom Lehman	70	70	69	72	281
Larry Mize	68	71	72	71	282

1995

Ben Crenshaw	70	67	69	68	274
Davis Love III	69	69	71	66	275
Jay Haas	71	64	72	70	277
Greg Norman	73	68	68	68	277

1996

Nick Faldo	69	67	73	67	276
Greg Norman	63	69	71	78	281
Phil Mickelson	65	73	72	72	282

1997

Tiger Woods	70	66	65	69	270
Tom Kite	77	69	66	70	282
Tommy Tolles	72	72	72	67	283

1998

Mark O'Meara	74	70	68	67	279
Fred Couples	69	70	71	70	280
David Duval	71	68	74	67	280

1999

José Maria Olazábal	70	66	73	71	280
Davis Love III	69	72	70	71	282
Greg Norman	71	68	71	73	283

2000

Vijay Singh	72	67	70	69	278
Ernie Els	72	67	74	68	281
Loren Roberts	73	69	71	69	282
David Duval	73	65	74	70	282

2001

Tiger Woods	70	66	68	68	272
David Duval	71	66	70	67	274
Phil Mickelson	67	69	69	70	275

2002

Tiger Woods	70	69	66	71	276
Retief Goosen	69	67	69	74	279
Phil Mickelson	69	72	68	71	280

2003

Mike Weir	70	68	75	68	281
Len Mattiace	73	74	69	65	281
Phil Mickelson	73	70	72	68	283

2004

Phil Mickelson	72	69	69	69	279
Ernie Els	70	72	71	67	280
KJ Choi	71	70	72	69	282

2005

Tiger Woods	74	66	65	71	276
Chris DiMarco	67	67	74	68	276
Luke Donald	68	77	69	69	283
Retief Goosen	71	75	70	67	283

2006

Phil Mickelson	70	72	70	69	281
Tim Clark	70	72	72	69	283

2007

Zach Johnson	71	73	76	69	289
Rory Sabbatini	73	76	73	69	290
Retief Goosen	76	76	70	69	290
Tiger Woods	73	74	72	72	290

2008

Trevor Immelman	68	68	69	75	280
Tiger Woods	72	71	68	72	283
Stewart Cink	72	69	71	72	284
Brandt Snedeker	69	68	70	77	284

2009

*Angel Cabrera	68	68	69	71	276
Chad Campbell	65	70	72	69	276
Kenny Perry	68	67	70	71	276
Shingo Katayama	67	73	70	68	278

2010

Phil Mickelson	67	71	67	67	272
Lee Westwood	67	69	68	71	275
Anthony Kim	68	70	73	65	276

2011

Charl Schwartzel	69	71	68	66	274
Jason Day	72	64	72	68	276
Adam Scott	72	70	67	67	276

2012

*Bubba Watson	69	71	70	68	278
Louis Oosthuizen	68	72	69	69	278
Peter Hanson	68	74	65	73	280
Matt Kuchar	71	70	70	69	280
Phil Mickelson	74	68	88	72	280
Lee Westwood	67	73	72	68	280

2013

*Adam Scott	69	72	69	69	279
Angel Cabrera	71	69	69	70	279
Jason Day	70	68	73	70	281

2014

Bubba Watson	69	68	74	69	280
Jonas Blixt	70	71	71	71	283
Jordan Speith	71	70	70	72	283

2015

Jordan Speith	64	66	70	70	270
Phil Mickelson	70	68	67	69	274
Justin Rose	67	70	67	70	274
Rory McIlroy	71	71	68	66	276

2016

Danny Willett	70	74	72	67	283
Jordan Speith	66	74	73	73	286
Lee Westwood	71	75	71	69	286

2017

*Sergio Garcia	71	69	70	69	279
Justin Rose	71	72	67	69	279
Charl Schwartzel	74	72	68	68	282

2018

Patrick Reed	69	66	67	71	273
Rickie Fowler	70	72	65	67	274
Jordan Speith	66	74	71	64	275

2019

Tiger Woods	70	68	67	70	275
Dustin Johnson	68	70	70	68	276
Brooks Koepka	66	71	69	70	276
Xander Schauffele	73	65	70	68	276

2020

Dustin Johnson	65	70	65	68	268
Im Sung-jae	66	70	68	69	273
Cameron Smith	67	68	69	69	273

The US Open

1895 Newport GC, Newport, RI

Horace Rawlins	45	46	41	41	173
Willie Dunn Jr.	43	46	44	42	175
James Foulis	46	43	44	43	176
AW Smith	47	43	44	42	176

1896 Shinnecock Hills, GC Southampton, NY

James Foulis	78	74	152
Horace Rawlins	79	76	155
Joe Lloyd	76	81	157

1897 Chicago GC, Wheaton, IL

Joe Lloyd	83	79	162
Willie Anderson	79	84	163
Willie Dunn Jr.	87	81	168
James Foulis	80	89	168

1898 Myopia Hunt Club, S. Hamilton, MA

Fred Herd	84	85	75	84	328
Alex Smith	78	86	86	85	335
Willie Anderson	81	82	87	86	336

1899 Baltimore CC, Baltimore, MD

Willie Smith	77	82	79	77	315
Val Fitzjohn	85	80	79	82	326
George Low	82	79	89	76	326
W. H. Way	80	85	80	81	326

1900 Chicago GC, Wheaton, IL

Harry Vardon	79	78	76	80	313
J. H. Taylor	76	82	79	78	315
David Bell	78	83	83	78	322

1901 Myopia Hunt Club, S. Hamilton, MA

*Willie Anderson	84	83	83	81	331
Alex Smith	82	82	87	80	331
Willie Smith	84	86	82	81	333

1902 Garden City GC, Garden City, NY

Laurence Auchterlonie	78	78	74	77	307
Stewart Gardner	82	76	77	78	313
Walter Travis	82	82	75	74	313

1903 Baltusrol GC, Springfield, NJ

*Willie Anderson	73	76	76	82	307
David Brown	79	77	75	76	307
Steward Gardner	77	77	82	79	315

1904 Glen View GC, Club, IL

Willie Anderson	75	78	78	72	303
Gilbert Nicholls	80	76	79	73	308
Fred MacKenzie	76	79	74	80	309

1905 Myopia Hunt Club, S. Hamilton, MA

Willie Anderson	81	80	76	77	314
Alex Smith	76	80	80	80	316
Percy Barrett	81	80	77	79	317
Peter Robertson	97	80	81	77	317

1906 Onwentsia Club, Lake Forest, IL

Alex Smith	73	74	73	75	295
Willie Smith	73	81	74	74	302
Laurie Auchterionie	76	78	75	76	305
James Maiden	80	73	77	75	305

1907 Philadelphia CC, Philadelphia, PA

Alex Ross	76	74	76	76	302
Gilbert Nicholls	80	73	72	79	304
Alex Campbell	78	74	78	75	305

1908 Myopia Hunt Club, S. Hamilton, MA

*Fred McLeod	82	82	81	77	322
Willie Smith	77	82	85	78	322
Alex Smith	80	83	83	81	327

1909 Englewood GC, Englewood, NJ

George Sargent	75	72	72	71	290
Tom McNamara	73	69	75	77	294
Alex Smith	76	73	74	72	295

1910 Philadelphia CC, Philadelphia, PA

*Alex Smith	73	73	79	73	298
John McDermott	74	74	75	75	298
Macdonald Smith	74	78	75	71	298

1911 Chicago GC, Wheaton, IL

*John J McDermott	81	72	75	79	307
Mike Brady	76	77	79	75	307
George Simpson	76	77	79	75	307

1912 Cricket Club of Buffalo, Buffalo, NY

John J. McDermott	74	75	74	71	294
Tom McNamara	74	80	73	69	296
Mike Brady	72	75	73	79	299
Alex Smith	77	70	77	75	299

1913 The Country Club, Brookline, MA

*Francis Ouimet	77	74	74	79	304
Harry Vardon	75	72	78	79	304
Ted Ray	79	70	76	79	304

1914 Midlothian CC, Blue Island, IL

Walter Hagen	68	74	75	73	290
Charles Evans Jr.	76	74	71	70	291
Fred McLeod	78	73	75	71	297
George Sargent	74	77	74	72	297

1915 Baltusrol GC, Springfield, NJ

Jerome D. Travers	76	72	73	76	297
Tom McNamara	78	71	74	75	298
Bob MacDonald	72	77	73	78	300

1916 Minikahda Club, Minneapolis, MN

Charles Evans Jr.	70	69	74	73	286
Jock Hutchison	73	75	72	68	288
Jim Barnes	71	74	71	74	290

1917–18 No Championships played due to World War I

1919 Brae Burn CC, West Newton, MA

*Walter Hagen	78	73	75	75	301
Mike Brady	74	74	73	80	301
Jock Hutchison	78	76	76	76	306
Tom McNamara	80	73	79	74	306

1920 Inverness Club, Toledo, OH

Edward Ray	74	73	73	75	295
Jack Burke Sr.	75	77	72	72	296
Leo Diegel	71	74	73	77	296
Jock Hutchison	69	76	74	77	296
Harry Vardon	74	73	71	78	296

1921 Columbia CC, Chevy Chase, MD

James M. Barnes	69	75	73	72	289
Walter Hagen	79	73	72	74	289
Fred McLeod	74	74	76	74	298

1922 Skokie CC, Glencoe, IL

Gene Sarazen	72	73	75	68	288
John Black	71	71	75	72	289
Bobby Jones	74	72	70	73	289

1923 Inwood CC, Inwood, NY

*Bobby Jones	71	73	76	76	296
Bobby Cruikshank	73	72	78	73	296
Jock Hutchison	70	72	82	78	302

1924 Oakland Hills CC, Bloomfield Hills, MI

Cyril Walker	74	74	74	75	297
Bobby Jones	74	73	75	78	300
Bill Mehlhorn	72	75	76	78	301

1925 Worcester CC, Worcester, MA

*William Macfarlane	74	67	72	78	291
Bobby Jones	77	70	70	74	291
Johnny Farrell	71	74	69	78	292
Francis Quimet	70	73	73	76	292

1926 Scioto CC, Columbus, OH

Bobby Jones	70	79	71	73	293
Joe Turnesa	71	74	72	77	294
Leo Diegel	72	76	75	74	297
Johnny Farrell	76	79	69	73	297
Bill Mehlhorn	68	75	76	78	297
Gene Sarazen	78	77	72	70	297

1927 Oakmont CC, Oakmont, PA

*Tommy Armour	78	71	76	76	301
Harry Cooper	74	76	74	77	301
Gene Sarazen	74	74	80	74	302

1928 Olympia Fields CC, Matteson, IL

*Johnny Farrell	77	74	71	72	294
Bobby Jones	73	71	73	77	294
Roland Hancock	74	77	72	72	295

1929 Winged Foot GC, Mamaroneck, NY

*Robert T. Jones Jr.	69	75	71	79	294
Al Espinosa	70	72	77	75	294
Gene Sarazen	71	71	76	78	296
Denny Shute	73	71	76	76	296

1930 Interlachen CC, Minneapolis, MN

Robert T. Jones Jr.	71	73	68	75	287
Macdonald Smith	70	75	74	70	289
Horton Smith	72	70	76	74	292

1931 Inverness Club, Toledo, OH

*Billy Burke	73	72	74	73	292
George von Elm	75	69	73	75	292
Leo Diegel	75	73	74	72	294

1932 Fresh Meadow CC, Flushing, NY

Gene Sarazen	74	76	70	66	286
Bobby Cruikshank	78	74	69	68	289
Phil Perkins	76	69	74	70	289

1933 North Shore GC, Glenview, IL

John Goodman	75	66	70	76	287
Ralph Guldahl	76	71	70	71	288
Craig Wood	73	74	71	72	290

1934 Merion CC, Ardmore, PA

Olin Dutra	76	74	71	72	293
Gene Sarazen	73	72	73	76	294
Harry Cooper	76	74	74	71	295
Wiffy Cox	71	75	74	75	295
Bobby Cruikshank	71	71	77	76	295

1935 Oakmont CC, Oakmont PA

Sam Parks Jr.	77	73	73	76	299
Jimmy Thomson	73	73	77	78	301
Walter Hagen	77	76	73	76	302

1936 Baltusrol GC, Springfield, NJ

Tony Manero	73	69	73	67	282
Harry Cooper	71	70	70	73	284
Clarence Clark	69	75	71	72	287

1937 Oakland Hills CC, Bloomfield Hills, MI

Ralph Guldahl	71	69	72	69	281
Sam Snead	69	73	70	71	283
Bobby Cruikshank	73	73	67	72	285

1938 Cherry Hills CC, Englewood, CO

Ralph Guldahl	74	70	71	69	284
Dick Metz	73	68	70	79	290
Harry Cooper	76	69	76	71	292
Tony Penna	78	72	74	68	292

1939 Philadelphia CC, West Conshohocken, PA

*Byron Nelson	72	73	71	68	284
Craig Wood	70	71	71	72	284
Denny Shute	70	72	70	72	284

1940 Canterbury GC, Cleveland, OH

*Lawson Little	72	69	73	73	287
Gene Sarazen	71	74	70	72	287
Horton Smith	69	72	78	69	288

1941 Colonial CC, Fort Worth, TX

Craig Wood	73	71	70	70	284
Denny Shute	69	75	72	71	287
Johnny Bulla	75	71	72	71	289
Ben Hogan	74	77	68	70	289

1942–45 No Championships played due to World War II

1946 Canterbury GC, Cleveland, OH

*Lloyd Mangrum	74	70	68	72	284
Vic Ghezzi	71	69	72	72	284
Byron Nelson	71	71	69	73	284

1947 St Louis CC, Clayton, MO

*Lew Worsham	70	70	71	71	282
Sam Snead	72	70	70	70	282
Bobby Locke	68	74	70	73	285
Ed Oliver	73	70	71	71	285

1948 Riviera CC, Los Angeles, CA

Ben Hogan	67	72	68	69	276
Jimmy Demaret	71	70	68	69	278
Jim Turnesa	71	69	70	70	280

1949 Medinah CC, Medinah, IL

Cary Middlecoff	75	67	69	75	286
Clayton Heafner	72	71	71	73	287
Sam Snead	73	73	71	70	287

1950 Merion GC, Ardmore, PA

*Ben Hogan	72	69	72	74	287
Lloyd Mangrum	72	70	69	76	287
George Fazio	73	72	72	70	287

1951 Oakland Hills CC, Bloomfield Hills, MI

Ben Hogan	76	73	71	67	287
Clayton Heafner	72	75	73	69	289
Bobby Locke	73	71	74	73	291

1952 Northwood Club, Dallas, TX

Julius Boros	71	71	68	71	281
Ed Oliver	71	72	70	72	285
Ben Hogan	69	69	74	74	286

1953 Oakmont CC, Oakmont, PA

Ben Hogan	67	72	73	71	283
Sam Snead	72	69	72	76	289
Lloyd Mangrum	73	70	74	75	292

1954 Baltusrol GC, Springfield, NJ

Ed Furgol	71	70	71	72	284
Gene Littler	70	69	76	70	285
Lloyd Mangrum	72	71	72	71	286
Dick Mayer	72	71	70	73	286

1955 The Olympic Club, San Francisco, CA

*Jack Fleck	76	69	75	67	287
Ben Hogan	72	73	72	70	287
Tommy Bolt	67	77	75	73	292
Sam Snead	79	69	70	74	292

1956 Oak Hill CC, Rochester, NY

Cary Middlecoff	71	70	70	70	281
Julius Boros	71	71	71	69	282
Ben Hogan	72	68	72	70	282

1957 Inverness Club, Toledo, OH

*Dick Mayer	70	68	74	70	282
Cary Middlecoff	71	75	68	68	282
Jimmy Demaret	68	73	70	72	293

1958 Southern Hills CC, Tulsa, OK

Tommy Bolt	71	71	69	72	283
Gary Player	75	68	73	71	287
Julius Boros	71	75	72	71	289

1959 Winged Foot GC, Mamaroneck, NY

Bill Casper Jr.	70	68	69	74	282
Bob Rosburg	75	70	67	71	283
Claude Harmon	72	70	70	71	284
Mike Souchak	71	70	72	71	284

1960 Cherry Hills CC, Englewood, CO

Arnold Palmer	72	71	72	65	280
Jack Nicklaus	71	71	69	71	282
Julius Boros	73	69	68	73	283
Dow Finsterwald	71	69	70	73	283
Jack Fleck	70	70	72	71	283
Dutch Harrison	74	70	70	69	283
Ted Kroll	72	69	75	67	283
Mike Souchak	68	67	73	75	283

1961 Oakland Hills CC, Bloomfield Hills, MI

Gene Littler	73	68	72	68	281
Bob Goalby	70	72	69	71	282
Doug Sanders	72	67	71	72	282

1962 Oakmont CC, Oakmont, PA

*Jack Nicklaus	72	70	72	69	283
Arnold Palmer	71	68	73	71	283
Bobby Nichols	70	72	70	73	285
Phil Rodgers	74	70	69	72	285

1963 The Country Club, Brookline, MA

*Julius Boros	71	74	76	72	293
Jacky Cupit	70	72	76	75	293
Arnold Palmer	73	69	77	74	293

1964 Congressional CC, Washington, DC

Ken Venturi	72	70	66	70	278
Tommy Jacobs	72	64	70	76	282
Bob Charles	72	72	71	68	283

1965 Bellerive CC, St. Louis, MO

*Gary Player	70	70	71	71	282
Kel Nagle	68	73	72	69	282
Frank Beard	74	69	70	71	284

1966 The Olympic Club, San Francisco, CA

*Bill Casper Jr.	69	68	73	68	278
Arnold Palmer	71	66	70	71	278
Jack Nicklaus	71	71	69	74	285

1967 Baltusrol GC, Springfield, NJ

Jack Nicklaus	71	67	72	65	275
Arnold Palmer	69	68	73	69	279
Don January	69	72	70	70	281

1968 Oak Hill CC, Rochester, NY

Lee Trevino	69	68	69	69	275
Jack Nicklaus	72	70	70	67	279
Bert Yancey	67	68	70	76	281

1969 Champions GC, Houston, TX

Orville Moody	71	70	68	70	281
Deane Beman	68	69	73	72	282
Al Geiberger	68	72	72	70	282
Bob Rosburg	70	69	72	71	282

1970 Hazeltine National GC, Chaska, MN

Tony Jacklin	71	70	70	70	281
Dave Hill	75	68	71	73	288
Bob Charles	76	71	75	67	289
Bob Lunn	77	72	70	70	289

1971 Merion GC, Ardmore, PA

*Lee Trevino	70	72	69	69	280
Jack Nicklaus	69	72	68	71	280
Jim Colbert	69	69	73	71	282
Bob Rosburg	71	72	70	69	282

1972 Pebble Beach GL, Pebble Beach, CA

Jack Nicklaus	71	73	72	74	290
Bruce Crampton	74	70	72	74	293
Arnold Palmer	77	68	73	76	294

1973 Oakmont CC, Oakmont, PA

John Miller	71	69	76	63	279
John Schlee	73	70	67	70	279
Tom Weiskopf	73	69	69	70	281

1974 Winged Foot GC, Mamaroneck, NY

Hale Irwin	73	70	71	73	287
Forrest Fezler	75	70	74	70	287
Lou Graham	71	75	74	70	290
Bert Yancey	76	69	73	72	290

1975 Medinah CC, Medinah, IL

*Lou Graham	74	72	68	73	287
John Mahaffey	73	71	72	71	287
Frank Beard	74	69	67	78	288
Ben Crenshaw	70	68	76	74	288
Hale Irwin	74	71	73	70	288
Bob Murphy	74	73	72	69	288

1976 Atlanta Athletic Club, Duluth, GA

Jerry Pate	71	69	69	68	277
Al Geiberger	70	69	71	69	279
Tom Weiskopf	73	70	68	68	279

1977 Southern Hills CC, Tulsa, OK

Hubert Green	69	67	72	70	278
Lou Graham	72	71	68	68	279
Tom Weiskopf	71	71	68	71	281

1978 Cherry Hills CC, Englewood, CO

Andy North	70	70	71	74	285
J. C. Snead	70	72	72	72	286
Dave Stockton	71	73	70	72	286

1979 Inverness Club, Toledo, OH

Hale Irwin	74	68	67	75	284
Jerry Pate	71	74	69	72	286
Gary Player	73	73	72	68	286

1980 Baltusrol GC, Springfield, NJ

Jack Nicklaus	63	71	70	68	272
Isao Aoki	68	68	68	70	274
Keith Fergus	66	70	70	70	276
Lon Hinkle	66	70	69	71	276
Tom Watson	71	68	67	70	276

1981 Merion GC, Ardmore, PA

David Graham	68	68	70	67	273
George Burns	69	66	68	73	276
Bill Rogers	70	68	69	69	276

1982 Pebble Beach GL, Pebble Beach, CA

Tom Watson	72	72	68	70	282
Jack Nicklaus	74	70	71	69	284
Bobby Clampett	71	73	72	70	286
Dan Pohl	72	74	70	70	286
Bill Rogers	70	73	69	74	286

1983 Oakmont CC, Oakmont, PA

Larry Nelson	75	73	65	67	280
Tom Watson	72	70	70	69	281
Gil Norman	73	72	70	68	283

1984 Winged Foot GC, Mamaroneck, NY

*Fuzzy Zoeller	71	66	69	70	276
Greg Norman	70	68	69	69	276
Curtis Strange	69	70	74	68	281

1985 Oakland Hills CC, Bloomfield Hills, MI

Andy North	70	65	70	74	279
Dave Barr	70	68	70	72	280
Chen Tze-chung	65	69	69	77	280
Dennis Watson	72	65	73	70	280

1986 Shinnecock Hills GC, Southampton, NY

Raymond Floyd	75	68	70	66	279
Chip Beck	75	73	68	65	281
Lanny Watkins	74	70	72	65	281

1987 The Olympic Club, San Francisco, CA

Scott Simpson	71	68	70	68	277
Tom Watson	72	65	71	70	278
Seve Ballesteros	68	75	68	71	282

1988 The Country Club, Brookline, MA

*Curtis Strange	70	67	69	72	278
Nick Faldo	72	67	68	71	278
Mark O'Meara	71	72	66	71	280
Steve Pate	72	69	72	67	280

1989 Oak Hill CC, Rochester, NY

Curtis Strange	71	64	73	70	278
Chip Beck	71	69	71	68	279
Mark McCumber	70	68	72	69	279
Ian Woosnam	70	68	73	68	279

1990 Medinah CC, Medinah, IL

*Hale Irwin	69	70	74	67	280
Mike Donald	67	70	72	71	280
Billy Ray Brown	69	71	69	72	281
Nick Faldo	72	72	68	68	281

1991 Hazeltine National GC, Chaska, MN

*Payne Stewart	67	70	73	72	282
Scott Simpson	70	68	72	72	282
Fred Couples	70	70	75	70	285
Larry Nelson	73	72	72	68	285

1992 Pebble Beach GL, Pebble Beach, CA

Tom Kite	71	72	70	72	285
Jeff Sluman	73	74	69	71	287
Colin Montgomerie	70	71	77	70	288

1993 Baltusrol GC, Springfield, NJ

Lee Janzen	67	67	69	69	272
Payne Stewart	70	66	68	70	274
Paul Azinger	71	68	69	69	277

1994 Oakmont CC, Oakmont, PA

*Ernie Els	69	71	66	73	279
Loren Roberts	76	69	74	70	279
Colin Montgomerie	71	65	73	70	279

1995 Shinnecock Hills GC, Southampton, NY

Corey Pavin	72	69	71	68	280
Greg Norman	68	67	74	73	282
Tom Lehman	70	72	67	74	283

1996 Oakland Hills CC, Bloomfield Hills, MI

Steve Jones	74	66	69	69	278
Tom Lehman	71	72	65	71	279
Davis Love III	71	69	70	69	279

1997 Congressional CC, Bethesda, MD

Ernie Els	71	67	69	69	276
Colin Montgomerie	65	76	67	69	277
Tom Lehman	67	70	68	73	278

1998 The Olympic Club, San Francisco, CA

Lee Janzen	73	66	73	68	280
Payne Stewart	66	71	70	74	281
Bob Tway	68	70	73	73	284

1999 No. 2 Course at Pinehurst R & CC, Village of Pinehurst, NC

Payne Stewart	68	69	72	70	279
Phil Mickelson	67	70	73	70	280
Vijay Singh	69	70	73	69	281
Tiger Woods	68	71	72	70	281

2000 Pebble Beach GL, Pebble Beach, CA

Tiger Woods	65	69	71	67	272
Miguel Ángel Jiménez	66	74	76	71	287
Ernie Els	74	73	68	72	287
John Huston	67	75	76	70	288

2001 Southern Hills CC, Tulsa, OK

Retief Goosen	66	70	69	71	276
Mark Brooks	72	64	70	70	276
Stewart Cink	69	69	67	72	277

2002 Bethpage State Park (Black Course), Farmingdale, NY

Tiger Woods	67	68	70	72	277
Phil Mickelson	70	73	67	70	280
Jeff Maggert	69	73	68	72	282

2003 Olympia Fields CC, Olympia Fields, IL

Jim Furyk	67	66	67	72	272
Stephen Leaney	67	68	68	72	275
Kenny Perry	72	71	69	67	279
Mike Weir	73	67	68	71	279

2004 Shinnecock Hills GC, Southampton, NY

Retief Goosen	70	66	69	71	276
Phil Mickelson	68	66	73	71	278
Jeff Maggert	68	67	74	72	281

2005 No. 2 Course at Pinehurst Resort, Village of Pinehurst, NC

Michael Campbell	71	69	71	69	280
Tiger Woods	70	71	72	69	282
Sergio Garcia	71	69	75	70	285
Tim Clark	76	69	70	70	285
Mark Hensby	71	68	72	74	285

2006 Winged Foot GC, Mamaroneck, NY

Geoff Ogilvy	71	70	72	72	285
Jim Furyk	70	72	74	70	286
Colin Montgomerie	69	71	75	71	286
Phil Mickelson	70	73	69	74	286

2007 Oakmont CC, Oakmont, PA

Angel Cabrera	69	71	76	69	285
Jim Furyk	71	75	70	70	286
Tiger Woods	71	74	69	72	286

2008 Torrey Pines GC, San Diego, CA

*Tiger Woods	72	68	70	73	283
Rocco Mediate	69	71	72	71	283
Lee Westwood	70	71	70	73	284

2009 Bethpage State Park (Black Course), Farmingdale, NY

Lucas Glover	69	64	70	73	276
Ricky Barnes	67	65	70	76	278
David Duval	67	70	70	71	278
Phil Mickelson	69	70	69	70	278

2010 Pebble Beach GL, Pebble Beach, CA

Graeme McDowell	71	68	71	74	284
Gregory Havret	73	71	69	72	285
Ernie Els	73	68	72	73	286

2011 Congressional CC, Bethesda, MD

Rory McIlroy	65	66	68	69	268
Jason Day	71	72	65	68	276
Kevin Chappell	76	67	69	66	278
Robert Garrigus	70	70	68	70	278
Lee Westwood	75	68	65	70	278
Y. E. Yang	68	69	70	71	278

2012 The Olympic Club, San Francisco, CA

Webb Simpson	72	73	68	68	281
Graeme McDowell	69	72	68	73	282
Michael Thompson	66	75	74	67	282

2013 Merion CC, Ardmore, PA

Justin Rose	71	69	71	70	281
Jason Day	70	74	68	71	283
Phil Mickelson	67	72	70	74	283

2014 No. 2 Course at Pinehurst R & CC, Village of Pinehurst, NC

Martin Kaymer	65	65	72	69	271
Erik Compton	72	68	67	72	279
Rickie Fowler	70	70	67	72	279

2015 Chambers Bay, Washington, WA

Jordan Speith	68	67	71	69	275
Dustin Johnson	65	71	70	70	276
Louis Oosthuizen	77	66	66	67	276

2016 Oakmont CC, Oakmont, PA

Dustin Johnson	67	69	71	69	276
Jim Furyk	71	68	74	66	279
Shane Lowry	68	70	65	76	279
Scott Piercy	68	70	72	69	279

2017 Erin Hills, Wisconsin, WI

Brooks Koepka	67	70	68	67	272
Brian Harman	67	70	67	72	276
Hideki Matsuyama	74	65	71	66	276

2018 Shinnecock Hills GC, Southampton, NY

Brooks Koepka	75	66	72	68	281
Tommy Fleetwood	75	66	78	63	282
Dustin Johnson	69	67	77	70	283

2019 Pebble Beach GL, Pebble Beach, CA

Gary Woodland	68	65	69	69	271
Brooks Koepka	69	69	68	68	274
Jon Rahm	69	70	70	68	277
Chez Reavie	68	70	68	71	277
Justin Rose	65	70	68	74	277
Xander Schauffele	66	73	71	67	277

2020 Winged Foot GC, Mamaroneck, NY

Bryson DeChambeau	69	68	70	67	274
Matthew Wolff	66	74	65	75	280
Louis Oosthuizen	67	74	68	73	282

The USPGA

(* won after a playoff)

1916 Siwanoy CC, Bronxville, NY
Jim Barnes bt. Willie MacFarlane 1 up

1919 Engineers CC, Long Island, NY
Jim Barnes bt. Fred McLeod 6&5

1920 Flossmore, Chicago, IL
Jock Hutchinson bt. Douglas Edgar 1 up

1921 Inwood CC, Rockaway, NY
Walter Hagen bt. Jim Barnes 3&2

1922 Oakmont CC, Oakmont, PA
Gene Sarazen bt. Emmett French 1 up

1923 Pelham GC, NY
Gene Sarazen bt. Walter Hagen 1 up (after 38)

1924 French Springs, IN
Walter Hagen bt. Jim Barnes 2 up

1925 Olympia Fields CC, Olympia Fields, IL
Walter Hagen bt Bill Mehlorn 6&5

1926 Salisbury GC, Long Island, NY
Walter Hagen bt. Leo Diegel 5&3

1927 Cedar Crest GC, Dallas, TX
Walter Hagen bt. Joe Turnesa 1 up

1928 Five Farms CC, Baltimore, MD
Leo Diegel bt. Al Espinosa 6&5

1929 Hillcrest GC, Los Angles, CA
Leo Diegel bt. Johnny Farrell 6&4

1930 Fresh Meadows CC, Flushing Meadows, NY
Tommy Armour bt. Gene Sarazen 1 up

1931 Wannamoisett CC, Romford, RI
Tom Creavy bt. Denny Shute 2&1

1932 Keller GC, St Paul, MN
Olin Dutra bt. Frank Walsh 4&3

1933 Blue Mound CC, Milwaukee, WI
Gene Sarazen bt. Willie Goggin 5&4

1934 Park Club of Buffalo, Williamsville, NY
Paul Runyan bt. Craig Wood 1 up (after 38)

1935 Twin Hills CC, Oklahoma City, OK
Johnny Revolta bt. Tommy Armour 5&4

1936 Pinehurst CC, NC
Denny Shute bt. Jimmy Thomson 3&2

1937 Pittsburgh Field Club, Aspinwall, PA
Denny Shute bt. Harold McSpaden 1 up

1938 Shawnee CC, Shawnee-on-Delaware, PA
Paul Runyon bt. Sam Snead 8&7

1939 Pomonock CC, Flushing, NY
Henry Picard bt. Byron Nelson 1 up (after 37)

1940 Hershey CC, Hershey, PA
Byron Nelson bt. Sam Snead 1 up

1941 Cherry Hill CC, Denver, CO
Vic Ghezzi bt. Byron Nelson 1 up (after 38)

1942 Seaview CC, Atlantic City, NJ
Sam Snead bt. Jim Turnesa 2&1

1943 – No Championship played due to World War II

1944 Manito CC, Spokane, WA
Bob Hamilton bt. Byron Nelson 1 up

1945 Moraine CC, Dayton, OH
Byron Nelson bt. Sam Byrd 4&3

1946 Portland GC, Portland, OR
Ben Hogan bt. Ed Oliver 6&4

1947 Plum Hollow CC, Detroit, MI
Jim Ferrier bt. Chick Harbert 5&4

1948 Northwood Hills CC, St Louis, MO
Ben Hogan bt. Mike Turnesa 7&6

1949 Hermitage CC, Richmond, VA
Sam Snead bt. Johnny Palmer 3&2

1950 Scioto CC, Columbus, OH
Chandler Harper bt Henry Williams Jr 4&3

1951 Oakmont CC, Oakmont, PA
Sam Snead bt. Walter Burkemo 7&6

1952 Big Spring CC, Louisville, KY
Jim Turnesa bt. Chick Harbert 1 up

1953 Birmingham CC, Birmingham, MI
Walter Burkemo bt. Felice Torza 2&1

1954 Keller GC, St Paul, MN
Chick Harbert bt. Walter Burkemo 4&3

1955 Meadowbrook CC, Northville, MI
Doug Ford bt. Cary Middlecoff 4&3

1956 Blue Hill G&CC, Canton, MA
Jack Burke bt. Ted Kroll 3&2

1957 Miami Valley GC, Dayton, OH
Lionel Heart bt. Dow Finterwald 3&1

1958 Llanerch CC, Havertown, PA

Dow Finsterwald	67	72	70	67	276
Billy Casper	73	67	68	70	278
Sam Snead	73	67	67	73	280

1959 Minneapolis GC, St. Louis Park, MN

Bob Rosburg	71	72	68	66	277
Jerry Barber	69	65	71	73	278
Doug Sanders	72	66	68	72	278

1960 Firestone CC, Akron, OH

Jay Herbert	72	67	72	70	281
Jim Ferrier	71	74	66	71	282
Doug Sanders	70	71	69	73	283
Sam Snead	68	73	70	72	283

1961 Olympia Fields CC, Olympia Fields, IL

Jerry Barber	69	67	71	70	277
Don January	72	66	67	72	277
Doug Sanders	70	68	74	68	280

1962 Aronimink GC, Newton Square, PA

Gary Player	72	67	69	70	278
Bob Goalby	69	72	71	67	279
George Bayer	69	70	71	71	281
Jack Nicklaus	71	75	69	67	281

1963 Dallas Athletic Club, TX

Jack Nicklaus	69	73	69	68	279
Dave Ragan	75	70	67	69	281
Bruce Crampton	70	73	65	74	282

1964 Columbus CC, Columbus, OH

Bobby Nichols	64	71	69	67	271
Jack Nicklaus	67	73	70	64	274
Arnold Palmer	68	68	69	69	274

1965 Laurel Valley GC, Ligonier, PA

Dave Marr	70	69	70	71	280
Billy Casper	70	70	71	71	282
Jack Nicklaus	69	70	72	71	282

1966 Firestone CC, Akron, OH

Al Geiberger	68	72	68	72	280
Dudley Wysong	74	72	66	72	284
Billy Casper	73	73	70	70	286

1967 Columbine CC, Denver, CO

*Don January	71	71	70	68	281
Don Massingale	70	75	70	66	281
Jack Nicklaus	67	75	69	71	282

1968 Pecan Valley CC, San Antonio, TX

Julius Boros	71	71	70	69	281
Bob Charles	72	70	70	70	282
Arnold Palmer	71	69	72	70	282

1969 NCR CC, Dayton, OH

Ray Floyd	69	66	67	74	276
Gary Player	71	65	71	70	277
Bert Greene	71	68	68	71	279

1970 Southern Hills CC, Tulsa, OK

Dave Stockton	70	70	66	73	279
Bob Murphy	71	73	71	66	281
Arnold Palmer	70	72	69	70	281

1971 PGA National, Palm Beach, FL

Jack Nicklaus	69	69	70	73	281
Billy Casper	71	73	71	68	283
Tommy Bolt	72	74	69	69	284

1972 Oakland Hills CC, Bloomfield Hills, MI

Gary Player	71	71	67	72	281
Tommy Aaron	71	71	70	71	283
Jim Jamieson	69	72	72	70	283

1973 Canterbury GC, Cleveland, OH

Jack Nicklaus	72	68	68	69	277
Bruce Crampton	71	73	67	70	281
Manson Rudolph	69	70	70	73	282
J. C. Snead	71	74	68	69	282
Lanny Wadkins	73	69	71	69	282

1974 Tanglewood GC, Clemmons, NC

Lee Trevino	73	66	68	69	276
Jack Nicklaus	69	69	70	69	277
Bobby Cole	69	68	71	71	279

1975 Firestone CC, Akron, OH

Jack Nicklaus	70	68	67	71	276
Bruce Crampton	71	63	75	69	278
Tom Weiskopf	70	71	70	68	279

1976 Congressional CC, Bethesda, MD

Dave Stockton	70	72	69	70	281
Ray Floyd	72	68	71	71	282
Don January	70	69	71	72	282

1977 Pebble Beach GL, Pebble Beach, CA

*Lanny Wadkins	69	71	72	70	282
Gene Littler	67	69	70	76	282
Jack Nicklaus	69	71	70	73	283

1978 Oakmont CC, Oakmont, PA

*John Mahaffey	75	67	68	66	276
Jerry Pate	72	70	66	68	276
Tom Watson	67	69	67	73	276

1979 Oakland Hills CC, Bloomfield Hills, MI

*David Graham	69	68	70	65	272
Ben Crenshaw	69	67	69	67	272
Red Caldwell	67	70	66	71	274

1980 Oak Hill CC, Rochester, NY

Jack Nicklaus	70	69	66	69	274
Andy Bean	72	71	68	70	281
Lon Hickle	70	69	69	75	283

1981 Atlanta Athletic Club, Duluth, GA

Larry Nelson	70	66	66	71	273
Fuzzy Zoeller	70	68	68	71	277
Dan Pohl	69	67	73	69	278

1982 Southern Hills CC, Tulsa, OK

Ray Floyd	63	69	68	72	272
Lanny Wadkins	71	68	69	67	275
Fred Couples	67	71	72	66	276
Calvin Peete	69	70	68	69	276

1983 Riviera CC, Pacific Palisades, CA

Hal Sutton	65	66	72	71	274
Jack Nicklaus	73	65	71	66	275
Peter Jacobsen	73	70	68	65	276

1984 Shoal Creek CC, Birmingham, AL

Lee Trevino	69	68	67	69	273
Gary Player	74	63	69	71	277
Lanny Wadkins	68	69	68	72	277

1985 Cherry Hills CC, Englewood, CO

Hubert Green	67	69	70	72	278
Lee Trevino	66	68	75	71	280
Andy Bean	71	70	72	68	281

1986 Inverness Club, Toledo, OH

Bob Tway	72	70	64	70	276
Greg Norman	65	68	69	76	278
Peter Jacobson	68	70	70	71	279

1987 PGA National, Palm Beach, FL

*Larry Nelson	70	72	73	72	287
Lanny Wadkins	70	70	74	73	287
Scott Hoch	74	74	71	69	288

1988 Oak Tree GC, Edmond, OK

Jeff Sluman	69	70	68	65	272
Paul Azinger	67	66	71	71	275
Tommy Nakajima	69	68	74	67	278

1989 Kemper Lakes GC, Hawthorn Woods, IL

Payne Stewart	74	66	69	67	276
Andy Bean	70	67	74	66	277
Mike Reid	66	67	70	74	277
Curtis Strange	70	68	70	69	277

1990 Shoal Creek CC, Birmingham, AL

Wayne Grady	72	67	72	71	282
Fred Couples	69	71	73	72	285
Gil Morgan	77	72	65	72	286

1991 Crooked Stick GC, Carmel, IN

John Daly	69	67	69	71	276
Bruce Lietzke	68	69	72	70	279
Jim Gallagher Jr	70	72	72	67	281

1992 Bellerive CC, St Louis, MO

Nick Price	70	70	68	70	278
John Cook	71	72	67	71	281
Nick Faldo	68	70	76	67	281
Jim Gallagher Jr.	72	66	76	67	281
Gene Sauers	67	69	70	75	281

1993 Inverness Club, Toledo, OH

*Paul Azinger	69	66	69	68	272
Greg Norman	68	68	67	69	272
Nick Faldo	68	68	69	68	274

1994 Southern Hills CC, Tulsa, OK

Nick Price	67	65	70	67	269
Corey Pavin	70	67	69	69	275
Phil Mickelson	68	71	67	70	276

1995 Riviera CC, Pacific Palisades, CA

*Steve Elkington	68	67	68	64	267
Colin Montgomerie	68	67	67	65	267
Ernie Els	66	65	66	72	269
Jeff Maggert	66	69	65	69	269

1996 Valhalla GC, Louisville, KY

*Mark Brooks	68	70	69	70	277
Kenny Perry	66	72	71	68	277
Steve Elkington	67	74	67	70	278
Tommy Tolles	69	71	71	67	278

1997 Winged Foot GC, Mamaroneck, NY

Davis Love	66	71	66	66	269
Justin Leonard	68	70	65	71	274
Jeff Maggert	69	69	73	65	276

1998 Sahalee CC, Redmond, WA

Vijay Singh	70	66	67	68	271
Steve Stricker	69	68	66	70	273
Steve Elkington	69	69	69	67	274

1999 Medinah CC, Medinah, IL

Tiger Woods	70	67	68	72	277
Sergio Garcia	66	73	68	71	278
Stewart Cink	69	70	68	73	280

2000 Valhalla GC, Louisville, KY

*Tiger Woods	66	67	70	67	270
Bob May	72	66	66	66	270
Thomas Bjørn	72	68	67	68	275

2001 Atlanta Athletic Club, Duluth, GA

David Toms	66	65	65	69	265
Phil Mickelson	66	66	66	68	266
Steve Lowery	67	67	66	68	268

2002 Hazeltine National GC, Chaska, MN

Rich Beem	72	66	72	68	278
Tiger Woods	71	69	72	67	279
Chris Riley	71	70	72	70	283

2003 Oak Hill CC, Rochester, NY

Shaun Micheel	69	68	69	70	276
Chad Campbell	69	72	65	72	278
Timothy Clark	72	70	68	69	279

2004 Whistling Straits, Kohler, WI

*Vijay Singh	67	68	69	76	280
Chris DiMarco	68	70	71	71	280
Justin Leonard	66	69	70	75	280

2005 Baltusrol GC, Springfield, NJ

Phil Mickelson	67	65	72	72	276
Thomas Bjørn	71	71	63	72	277
Steve Elkington	68	70	68	71	277

2006 Medinah CC, Medinah, IL

Tiger Woods	69	68	65	68	270
Shaun Micheel	69	70	67	69	275
Luke Donald	68	68	66	74	276
Sergio Garcia	69	70	67	70	276
Adam Scott	71	69	69	67	276

2007 Southern Hills CC, Tulsa, OK

Tiger Woods	71	63	69	69	272
Woody Austin	68	70	69	67	274
Ernie Els	72	68	69	66	275

2008 Oakland Hills CC, Bloomfield Hills, MI

Pádraig Harrington	71	74	66	66	277
Ben Curtis	73	67	68	71	279
Sergio Garcia	69	73	69	68	279

2009 Hazeltine National GC, Chaska, MN

Y. E. Yang	73	70	67	70	280
Tiger Woods	67	70	71	75	283
Rory McIlroy	71	73	71	70	285
Lee Westwood	70	72	73	70	285

2010 Whistling Straits, Kohler, WI

*Martin Kaymer	72	68	67	70	277
Bubba Watson	68	71	70	68	277
Zach Johnson	69	70	69	70	278
Rory McIlroy	71	68	67	72	278

2011 Atlanta Athletic Club, Duluth, GA

*Keegan Bradley	71	64	69	68	272
Jason Dufner	70	65	68	69	272
Anders Hansen	68	69	70	66	273

2012 The Ocean Course, Kiawah Island, SC

Rory McIlroy	67	75	67	66	275
David Lynn	73	74	68	68	283
Keegan Bradley	68	77	71	68	284
Carl Patterson	66	74	72	72	284
Ian Poulter	70	71	74	69	284
Justin Rose	69	79	70	66	284

2013 Oak Hill CC, Rochester, NY

Jason Dufner	68	63	71	68	270
Jim Furyk	65	68	68	71	272
Henrik Stenson	68	66	69	70	273

2014 Valhalla GC, Louisville, KY

Rory McIlroy	66	67	67	68	268
Phil Mickelson	69	67	67	66	269
Rickie Fowler	69	66	67	68	270
Henrik Stenson	66	71	67	66	270

2015 Whistling Straits, Kohler, WI

Jason Day	68	67	66	67	268
Jordan Speith	71	67	65	68	271
Branden Grace	71	69	64	69	273

2016 Baltusrol GC, Springfield, NJ

Jimmy Walker	65	66	68	67	266
Jason Day	68	65	67	67	267
Daniel Summerhays	70	67	67	66	270

2017 Quail Hollow Club, Charlotte, NC

Justin Thomas	73	66	69	68	276
Francesco Molinari	73	64	74	67	278
Louis Oosthuizen	70	67	71	70	278
Patrick Reed	69	73	69	67	278

2018 Bellerive CC, St. Louis, MO

Brooks Koepka	69	63	66	66	264
Tiger Woods	70	66	66	64	266
Adam Scott	70	65	65	67	267

2019 Bethpage State Park (Black Course), Farmingdale, NY

Brooks Koepka	63	65	70	74	272
Dustin Johnson	69	67	69	69	274
Patrick Cantlay	69	70	68	71	278
Jordan Speith	69	66	72	71	278
Matt Wallace	69	67	70	72	278

2020 TPC Harding Park, San Francisco, CA

Collin Morikawa	69	69	65	64	267
Paul Casey	68	67	68	66	269
Dustin Johnson	69	67	65	68	269

ANA Inspiration

Formerly Kraft Nabisco Championship and Colgate Dinah Shore

1972

Jane Blalock	213	(−3)
Carol Mann	216	
Judy Rankin	216	

1973

Mickey Wright	284	(−4)
Joyce Kazmierski	286	

1974

*JoAnn Prentice	289	(+1)
Jane Blalock	289	
Sandra Haynie	289	

1975

Sandra Palmer	283	(−5)
Kathy McMullen	284	

1976

Judy Rankin	285	(−3)
Betty Burfeindt	288	

1977

Kathy Whitworth	289	(+1)
JoAnne Carner	290	
Sally Little	290	

1978

*Sandra Post	283	(−5)
Penny Pulz	283	

1979

*Sandra Post	276	(−12)
Nancy Lopez	277	

1980

Donna Caponi	275	(−13)
Amy Alcott	277	

1981

Nancy Lopez	277	(−11)
Carolyn Hill	279	

1982

Sally Little	278	(−10)
Hollis Stacy	281	
Sandra Haynie	281	

1983

Amy Alcott	282	(−6)
Beth Daniel	284	
Kathy Whitworth	284	

1984

*Juli Inkster	280	(−8)
Pat Bradley	280	

1985

Alice Miller	275	(−13)
Jan Stephenson	278	

1986

Pat Bradley	280	(−8)
Val Skinner	282	

1987

*Betsy King	283	(−5)
Patty Sheehan	283	

1988

Amy Alcott	274	(−14)
Colleen Walker	276	

1989

Juli Inkster	279	(−9)
Tammie Green	284	
JoAnne Carner	284	

1990

Betsy King	283	(−5)
Kathy Postlewait	285	
Shirley Furlong	285	

1991

Amy Alcott	273	(−15)
Dottie (Pepper) Mochrie	281	

1992

*Dottie (Pepper) Mochrie	279	(−9)
Juli Inkster	279	

1993

Helen Alfredsson	284	(−4)
Amy Benz	286	
Tina Barrett	286	

1994

Donna Andrews	276	(−12)
Laura Davies	277	

1995

Nanci Bowen	285	(−3)
Susie Redman	286	

1996

Patty Sheehan	281	(−7)
Kelly Robbins	282	
Meg Mallon	282	
Annika Sorenstam	282	

1997

Betsy King	276	(−12)
Kris Tschetter	278	

1998

Pat Hurst	281	(−7)
Helen Dobson	282	

1999

Dottie Pepper	269	(−19)
Meg Mallon	275	

2000

Karrie Webb	274	(−14)
Dottie Pepper	284	

2001

Annika Sorenstam	281	(−7)
Karrie Webb	284	
Janice Moodie	284	
Dottie Pepper	284	
Akiko Fukushima	284	
Rachel (Hetherington) Teske	284	

2002

Annika Sorenstam	280	(−8)
Liselotte Neumann	281	

2003

Patricia Meunier-Lebouc	281	(−7)
Annika Sorenstam	282	

2004

Grace Park	277	(−11)
Aree Song	278	

2005

Annika Sorenstam	273	(−15)
Rosie Jones	281	

2006

*Karrie Webb	279	(−9)
Lorena Ochoa	279	

Women's PGA Championship

2007
Morgan Pressel   285 (-3)
Catriona Matthew   286
Brittany Lincicome   286

2008
Lorena Ochoa   277 (-11)
Suzann Petterson   282
Annika Sorenstam   282

2009
Brittany Lincicome   279 (-9)
Cristie Kerr   280
Kristy McPherson   280

2010
Yani Tseng   275 (-13)
Suzann Pettersen   276

2011
Stacy Lewis   275 (-13)
Yani Tseng   278

2012
*Yoo Sun-young   279 (-9)
I.K. Kim   279
Yani Tseng   280

2013
Inbee Park   273 (-15)
Ryu So-yeon   277

2014
Lexi Thompson   274 (-14)
Michelle Wie   277

2015
*Brittany Linicombe   279 (-9)
Stacy Lewis   279
Morgan Pressel   280

2016
Lydia Ko   276 (-12)
Chun In-gee   277
Charley Hull   277

2017
*Ryu So-yeon   274 (-14)
Lexi Thompson   274

2018
*Pernilla Lindberg   273 (-15)
Inbee Park   273
Jennifer Song   273

2019
Ko Jin-young   278 (-10)
Lee Mi-hyang   281

2020
*Mirim Lee   273 (-15)
Nelly Korda   273
Brooke Henderson   273

1955
Orchard Ridge, CC, Ft Wayne, IN
††Beverly Hanson   220   4&3
Louise Suggs   223

1956
Forest Lake CC, Detroit, MI
*Marlene Hagge   291
Patty Berg   291

1957
Churchill Valley CC, Pittsburgh, PA
Louise Suggs   285
Wiffi Smith   288

1958
Churchill CC, Pittsburgh, PA
Mickey Wright   288
Fay Crocker   294

1959
Sheraton Hotel CC, French Lick, IN
Betsy Rawls   288
Patty Berg   289

1960
Sheraton Hotel CC, French Lick, IN
Mickey Wright   292
Louise Suggs   295

1961
Stardust CC, Las Vegas, NE
Mickey Wright   287
Louise Suggs   296

1962
Stardust CC, Las Vegas, NE
Judy Kimball   282
Shirley Spork   286

1963
Stardust CC, Las Vegas, NE
Mickey Wright   294   (+10)
Mary Lena Faulk   296
Mary Mills   296
Louise Suggs   296

1964
Stardust CC, Las Vegas, NE
Mary Mills   278   (-6)
Mickey Wright   280

1965
Stardust CC, Las Vegas, NE
Sandra Haynie   279   (-5)
Clifford A. Creed   280

1966
Stardust CC, Las Vegas, NE
Gloria Ehret   282   (-2)
Mickey Wright   285

1967
Pleasant Valley CC, Sutton, MA
Kathy Whitworth   284   (-8)
Shirley Englehorn   285

1968
Pleasant Valley CC, Sutton, MA
†Sandra Post   294   (+2)   68
Kathy Whitworth   294   75

1969
Concord GC, Kiameshia Lake, NY
Betsy Rawls   293   (+1)
Susie Berning   297
Carol Mann   297

1970
Pleasant Valley CC, Sutton, MA
*Shirley Englehorn   285   (-7)
Kathy Whitworth   285

1971
Pleasant Valley CC, Sutton, MA
Kathy Whitworth   288   (-4)
Kathy Ahern   292

1972
Pleasant Valley CC, MA
Kathy Ahern   293   (+1)
Jane Blalock   299

1973
Pleasant Valley CC, Sutton, MA
Mary Mills   288   (-4)
Betty Burfeindt   289

1974
Pleasant Valley CC, Sutton, MA
Sandra Haynie   288   (-4)
JoAnne Carner   290

1975
Pine Ridge GC, Baltimore, MD
Kathy Whitworth   288   (-4)
Sandra Haynie   289

1976
Pine Ridge GC, Baltimore, MD
Betty Burfeindt   287   (-5)
Judy Rankin   288

1977
Bay Tree Golf Plantation,
N. Myrtle Beach, SC
Chako Higuchi   279   (-9)
Pat Bradley   282
Sandra Post   282
Judy Rankin   282

1978
Jack Nicklaus Golf Center,
Kings Island, OH
Nancy Lopez   275   (-13)
Amy Alcott   281

1979
Jack Nicklaus Golf Center,
Kings Island, OH
Donna Caponi   279   (-9)
Jerilyn Britz   282

1980
Jack Nicklaus Golf Center,
Kings Island, OH
Sally Little   285   (-3)
Jane Blalock   288

1981
Jack Nicklaus Golf Center,
King's Island, OH
Donna Caponi   280   (-8)
Jerilyn Britz   281
Pat Meyers   281

1982
Jack Nicklaus Sports Center,
Kings Island, OH
Jan Stephenson   279   (-9)
JoAnne Carner   281

1983
Jack Nicklaus Sports Center,
Kings Island, OH
Patty Sheehan   279   (-9)
Sandra Haynie   281

1984
Jack Nicklaus Sports Center,
Kings Island, OH
Patty Sheehan   272   (-16)
Beth Daniel   282
Pat Bradley   282

1985
Jack Nicklaus Sports Center,
Kings Island, OH
Nancy Lopez   273   (-15)
Alice Miller   281

1986
Jack Nicklaus Sports Center,
Kings Island, OH
Pat Bradley 277 (–11)
Patty Sheehan 278

1987
Jack Nicklaus Sports Center,
Kings Island, OH
Jane Geddes 275 (–13)
Betsy King 276

1988
Jack Nicklaus Sports Center,
Kings Island, OH
Sherri Turner 281 (–7)
Amy Alcott 282

1989
Jack Nicklaus Sports Center,
Kings Island, OH
Nancy Lopez 274 (–14)
Ayako Okamoto 277

1990
Bethesda CC, Bethesda, MD
Beth Daniel 280 (–4)
Rosie Jones 281

1991
Bethesda CC, Bethesda, MD
Meg Mallon 274 (–10)
Pat Bradley 275
Ayako Okamoto 275

1992
Bethesda CC, Bethesda, MD
Betsy King 267 (–17)
JoAnne Carner 278
Karen Noble 278
Liselotte Neumann 278

1993
Bethesda CC, Bethesda, MD
Patty Sheehan 275 (–9)
Lauri Merten 276

1994
DuPont CC, Wilmington, DE
Laura Davies 279 (–5)
Alice Ritzman 280

1995
DuPont CC, Wilmington, DE
Kelly Robbins 274 (–10)
Laura Davies 275

1996
DuPont CC, Wilmington, DE
Laura Davies 213 (E)
Julie Piers 214

1997
DuPont CC, Wilmington, DE
*Chris Johnson 281 (–3)
Leta Lindley 281

1998
DuPont CC, Wilmington, DE
Se Ri Pak 273 (–11)
Donna Andrews 276
Lisa Hackney 276

1999
DuPont CC, Wilmington, DE
Juli Inkster 268 (–16)
Liselotte Neumann 272

2000
DuPont CC, Wilmington, DE
*Juli Inkster 281 (–3)
Stefania Croce 281

2001
DuPont CC, Wilmington, DE
Karrie Webb 270 (–14)
Laura Diaz 272

2002
DuPont CC, Wilmington, DE
Se Ri Pak 279 (–5)
Beth Daniel 282

2003
DuPont CC, Wilmington, DE
*Annika Sorenstam 278 (–6)
Grace Park 278

2004
DuPont CC, Wilmington, DE
Annika Sorenstam 271 (–13)
Shi Hyun Ahn 274

2005
Bulle Rock GC, Havre de Grace, MD
Annika Sorenstam 277 (–11)
(a) Michelle Wie 280

2006
Bulle Rock GC, Havre de Grace, MD
*Se Ri Pak 280 (–8)
Karrie Webb 280

2007
Bulle Rock GC, Havre de Grace, MD
Suzann Pettersen 274 (–14)
Karrie Webb 275

2008
Bulle Rock GC, Havre de Grace, MD
*Yani Tseng 276 (–12)
Maria Hjorth 276

2009
Bulle Rock GC, Havre de Grace, MD
Anna Nordqvist 273 (–15)
Lindsey Wright 277

2010
Locust Hill CC, Pittsford, NY
Cristie Kerr 269 (–19)
Song-Hee Kim 281

2011
Locust Hill CC, Pittsford, NY
Yani Tseng 269 (–19)
Morgan Pressel 279

2012
Locust Hill CC, Pittsford, NY
Shanshan Feng 282 (–6)
Eun-Hee Ji 284
Stacy Lewis 284
Mike Miyazato 284
Suzann Pettersen 284

2013
Locust Hill CC, Pittsford, NY
*Inbee Park 283 (–5)
Catriona Matthew 283

2014
Monroe GC, Pittsford, NY
*Inbee Park 277 (–11)
Brittany Linicicome 277

2015
Westchester CC, Harrison, NY
Inbee Park 273 (–19)
Kim Sei-young 278

2016
Sahalee CC, Sammamish, WA
*Brooke Henderson 278 (–6)
Lydia Ko 278

2017
Olympia Fields CC, Olympia Fields, IL
Danielle Kang 271 (–13)
Brooke Henderson 272

2018
Kemper Lakes GC, Long Grove, IL
*Park Sung-hyun 278 (–10)
Nasa Hataoka 278
Ryu So-yeon 278

2019
Hazeltine GC, Minneapolis, MI
Hannah Green 279 (–9)
Park Sung-hyun 280

2020
Aronimink GC, Newton Square, PA
Sei Young Kim 266 (–14)
Inbee Park 271 (–9)

Women's US Open

1946
Spokane CC, Spokane, WA
††Patty Berg 145 5&4
Betty Jameson 158

1947
Starmount Forest CC, Greensboro, NC
Betty Jameson 295
(a) Sally Sessions 301
(a) Polly Riley 301

1948
Atlantic City CC, Northfield, NJ
Babe Zaharias 300
Betty Hicks 308

1949
Prince Georges CC, Landover, MD
Louise Suggs 291
Babe Zaharias 305

1950
Rolling Hills CC, Wichita, KA
Babe Zaharias 291
(a) Betsy Rawls 300

1951
Druid Hills Golf Club/Course,
Atlanta, GA
Betsy Rawls 293
Louise Suggs 298

1952
Bala Golf Club/Course, Philadelphia, PA
Louise Suggs 284
Marlene Hagge 291
Betty Jameson 291

1953
Country Club of Rochester,
Rochester, NY
†Betsy Rawls 302 70
Jackie Pung 302 77

1954
Salem CC, Peabody, MA
Babe Zaharias 291
Betty Hicks 303

1955
Wichita CC, Wichita, KA
Fay Crocker 299
Mary Lena Faulk 303
Louise Suggs 303

1956
Northland CC, Duluth, MN
| †Kathy Cornelius | 302 | 75 |
| Barbara McIntire | 302 | 82 |

1957
Winged Foot CC, Mamaroneck, NY
| Betsy Rawls | 299 |
| Patty Berg | 305 |

1958
Forest Lake CC, Detroit, MI
| Mickey Wright | 290 |
| Louise Suggs | 295 |

1959
Churchill Valley CC, Pittsburgh, PA
| Mickey Wright | 287 |
| Louise Suggs | 289 |

1960
Worcester CC, Worcester, MA
| Betsy Rawls | 292 |
| Joyce Ziske | 293 |

1961
Baltusrol GC, Springfield, NJ
| Mickey Wright | 293 |
| Betsy Rawls | 299 |

1962
Dunes Golf Club, Myrtle Beach, SC
Murle Breer	301
Jo Anne Prentice	303
Ruth Jessen	303

1963
Kenwood CC, Cincinnati, OH
Mary Mills	289	(−3)
Sandra Haynie	292
Louise Suggs	292

1964
San Diego CC, Chula Vista, CA
| †Mickey Wright | 290 | (−2) | 70 |
| Ruth Jessen | 290 | | 72 |

1965
Atlantic City CC, Northfield, NJ
| Carol Mann | 290 | (+2) |
| Kathy Cornelius | 292 |

1966
Hazeltine GC, Minneapolis, MI
| Sandra Spuzich | 297 | (+9) |
| Carol Mann | 298 |

1967
Hot Springs Golf & Tennis Club, Hot Springs, VA
(a) Catherine LaCoste	294	(+10)
Susie Berning	296
Beth Stone	296

1968
Moselem Springs GC, Fleetwood, PA
| Susie Berning | 289 | (+5) |
| Mickey Wright | 292 |

1969
Scenic Hills CC, Pensacola, FL
| Donna Caponi | 294 | (+2) |
| Peggy Wilson | 295 |

1970
Muskogee CC, Muskogee, OK
Donna Caponi	287	(+3)
Sandra Haynie	288
Sandra Spuzich	288

1971
Kahkwa CC, Erie, PA
| JoAnne Carner | 288 | (even) |
| Kathy Whitworth | 295 |

1972
Winged Foot CC, Mamaroneck, NY
Susie Berning	299	(+11)
Kathy Ahern	300
Pam Barnett	300
Judy Rankin	300

1973
Country Club of Rochester, Rochester, NY
| Susie Berning | 290 | (+2) |
| Gloria Ehret | 295 |

1974
La Grange CC, La Grange, IL
Sandra Haynie	295	(+7)
Carol Mann	296
Beth Stone	296

1975
Atlantic City CC, Northfield, NJ
Sandra Palmer	295	(+7)
Jo Anne Carner	299
Sandra Post	299
(a) Nancy Lopez	299

1976
Rolling Green CC, Springfield, PA
| †Jo Anne Carner | 292 | (+8) | 76 |
| Sandra Palmer | 292 | | 78 |

1977
Hazeltine GC, Chaska, MI
| Hollis Stacy | 292 | (+4) |
| Nancy Lopez | 294 |

1978
Country Club of Indianapolis, Indianapolis, IN
Hollis Stacy	289	(+5)
Jo Anne Carner	290
Sally Little	290

1979
Brooklawn CC, Fairfield, CT
Jerilyn Britz	284	(even)
Debbie Massey	286
Sandra Palmer	286

1980
Richland CC Nashville, TN
| Amy Alcott | 280 | (−4) |
| Hollis Stacy | 289 |

1981
La Grange CC, La Grange, IL
| Pat Bradley | 279 | (−9) |
| Beth Daniel | 280 |

1982
Del Paso CC, Sacramento, CA
Janet Anderson	283	(−5)
Beth Daniel	289
Sandra Haynie	289
Donna White	289
Jo Anne Carner	289

1983
Cedar Ridge CC, Tulsa, OK
Jan Stephenson	290	(+6)
JoAnne Carner	291
Patty Sheehan	291

1984
Salem CC, Peabody, MA
| Hollis Stacy | 290 | (+2) |
| Rosie Jones | 291 |

1985
Baltusrol GC, Springfield, NJ
| Kathy Baker (Guadagnino) | 280 | (−8) |
| Judy Dickinson | 283 |

1986
NCR Golf Club, Dayton, OH
| †Jane Geddes | 287 | (−1) | 71 |
| Sally Little | 287 | | 73 |

1987
Plainfield CC, Plainfield, NJ
†Laura Davies	285	(−3)	71
Ayako Okamoto	285		73
Jo Anne Carner	285		74

1988
Baltimore CC, Baltimore, MD
| Liselotte Neumann | 277 | (−7) |
| Patty Sheehan | 280 |

1989
Indianwood Golf & Country Club, Lake Orion, MI
| Betsy King | 278 | (−4) |
| Nancy Lopez | 282 |

1990
Atlanta Athletic Club, Duluth, GA
| Betsy King | 284 | (−4) |
| Patty Sheehan | 285 |

1991
Colonial CC, Ft Worth, TX
| Meg Mallon | 283 | (−1) |
| Pat Bradley | 285 |

1992
Oakmont CC, Oakmont, PA
| †Patty Sheehan | 280 | (−4) | 72 |
| Juli Inkster | 280 | | 74 |

1993
Crooked Stick GC, Carmel, IN
Lauri Merten	280	(−8)
Donna Andrews	281
Helen Alfredsson	281

1994
Indianwood CC, Lake Orion, MI
| Patty Sheehan | 277 | (−7) |
| Tammie Green | 278 |

1995
The Broadmoor Colorado Springs, CO
| Annika Sorenstam | 278 | (−2) |
| Meg Mallon | 279 |

1996
Pine Needles Lodge & Golf Club, Southern Pines, NC
| Annika Sorenstam | 272 | (−8) |
| Kris Tschetter | 278 |

1997
Pumpkin Ridge GC, Cornelius, OR
| Alison Nicholas | 274 | (−10) |
| Nancy Lopez | 275 |

1998
Blackwolf Run Golf Resort, Kohler, WI
| †*Se Ri Pak | 290 | (+6) | 73 |
| (a) Jenny Chuasiriporn | 290 | | 73 |

1999
Old Waverly GC, West Point, MS
| Juli Inkster | 272 | (−16) |
| Sherri Turner | 277 |

2000
Merit Club, Libertyville, IL
Karrie Webb	282	(−6)
Meg Mallon	287
Cristie Kerr	287

2001
Pine Needles Lodge & GC, Southern Pines, NC
| Karrie Webb | 273 | (−7) |
| Se Ri Pak | 281 |

2002
Prairie Dunes CC, Hutchinson, KA
Juli Inkster   276   (−4)
Annika Sorenstam   278

2003
Pumpkin Ridge GC, North Plains, OR
†Hilary Lunke   283   (−1)   70
Angela Stanford   283   71
Kelly Robbins   283   73

2004
Orchards GC, South Hadley, MA
Meg Mallon   274   (−10)
Annika Sorenstam   276

2005
Cherry Hills GC,
Cherry Hills Village, CO
Birdie Kim   287   (+3)
(a) Brittany Lang   289
(a) Morgan Pressel   289

2006
Newport CC, Newport, RI
†Annika Sorenstam   284   (E)   70
Pat Hurst   284   74

2007
Pine Needles Lodge & Golf Club,
Southern Pines, NC
Cristie Kerr   279   (−5)
Angela Park   281
Lorena Ochoa   281

2008
Interlachen CC, Edina, MN
Inbee Park   283   (−9)
Helen Alfredsson   287

2009
Saucon Valley CC, Bethlehem, PA
Eun-Hee Ji   284   (E)
Candie Kung   285

2010
Oakmont CC, Oakmont, PA
Paula Creamer   281   (−3)
Na Yeon Choi   285
Suzann Pettersen   285

2011
The Broadmoor East Course,
Colorado Springs, CO
*Ryu So-yeon   281   (−3)
Seo Hee-kyung   281

2012
Blackwolf Run, Kohler, WI
Na Yeon Choi   281   (−7)
Amy Yang   285

2013
Sebonack GC, Southampton, NY
Inbee Park   280   (−8)

2014
Pinehurst Resort Course No. 2,
Pinehurst, NC
Michelle Wie   278   (−2)
Stacy Lewis   280

2015
Lancaster CC, Lancaster, PA
Chun In-gee   272   (−8)
Amy Yang   273

2016
CordeValle GC, San Martin, CA
*Brittany Lang   282   (−6)
Anna Nordqvist   282

2017
Trump National GC, Bedminster, NJ
Park Sung-hyun   277   (−11)
Choi Hye-jin   279

2018
Shoal Creek Club, Shoal Creek, AL
*Ariya Jutanugarn   277   (−11)
Kim Hyo-joo   277

2019
Country Club of Charleston,
Charleston, SC
Lee Jeong-eun   278   (−6)
Ryu So-yeon   280
Lexi Thompson   280
Angel Yin   280

2019
Champions Golf Club, Houston, TX
Kim A-lim   281   (−3)
Ko Jin-young   282   (−2)
Amy Olson   282   (−2)

Women's British Open

1994
Woburn G&CC, Milton Keynes, England
Liselotte Neumann   280   (−12)

1995
Woburn G&CC, Milton Keynes,
England
Karrie Webb   278   (−14)

1996
Woburn G&CC, Milton Keynes, England
Emilee Klein   277   (−15)

1997
Sunningdale GC, Berkshire, England
Karrie Webb   269   (−19)

1998
Royal Lytham & St. Annes,
Lancashire, England
Sherri Steinhauer   292   (+4)

1999
Woburn G&CC, Milton Keynes, England
Sherri Steinhauer   283   (−9)

2000
Royal Birkdale Golf Club,
Southport, England
Sophie Gustafson   282   (−10)

2001
Sunningdale Golf Club, Berkshire,
England
Se Ri Pak   277   (−11)
Mi-Hyun Kim   279

2002
Turnberry GC, Ailsa Course,
Ayrshire, Scotland
Karrie Webb   273   (−15)
Michelle Ellis   275
Paula Marti   275

2003
Royal Lytham & St. Annes
Lancashire, England
Annika Sorenstam   278   (−10)
Se Ri Pak   279   (−9)

2004
Sunningdale GC, Berkshire, England
Karen Stupples   269   (−19)
Rachel (Hetherington)
Teske   274   (−14)

2005
Royal Birkdale GC, Merseyside, England
Jeong Jang   272   (−16)
Sophie Gustafson   276

2006
Royal Lytham & St. Annes
Lancashire, England
Sherri Steinhauer   281   (−7)
Sophie Gustafson   284
Cristie Kerr   284

2007
St. Andrews, Scotland
Lorena Ochoa   287   (−5)
Maria Hjorth   291
Jee-Young Lee   291

2008
Sunningdale GC, Berkshire, England
Jiyai Shin   270   (−18)
Yani Tseng   273

2009
Royal Lytham & St. Annes,
Lancashire, England
Catriona Matthew   285   (−3)
Karrie Webb   288

2010
Royal Birkdale GC, Merseyside, England
Yani Tseng   277   (−11)
Katherine Hull   278

2011
Carnoustie Golf Links, Angus, Scotland
Yani Tseng   272   (−16)
Brittany Lang   276

2012
Royal Liverpool, Merseyside, England
Jiyai Shin   135 (−9)
Inbee Park   140

2013
St. Andrews, Scotland
Stacy Lewis   280 (−8)
Na Yeon Choi   282
Park Hee-Young   282

2014
Royal Birkdale GC, Southport, England
Mo Martin   287   (−1)
Shanshan Feng   288
Suzann Pettersen   288

2015
Trump Turnberry, South Ayrshire,
Scotland
Inbee Park 276 (−12)
Ko Jin-young 279

2016
Woburn GC, Buckinghamshire, England
Ariya Jutanugarn 272 (−16)
Mirim Lee 275
Mo Martin 275

2017
Kingsbarns Golf Links, Fife, Scotland
In-Kyung Kim 270 (−18)
Jodi Ewart Shadoff 272

2018
Royal Lytham & St. Annes,
Lancashire, England
Georgia Hall 271 (−17)
Pornanong Phatium 273

2019
Woburn GC, Buckinghamshire, England
Hinako Shibuno 270 (−18)
Lizette Salas 271

2020
Royal Troon, South Ayrshire, Scotland
Sophia Popov 277 (−7)
Thidapa Suwannapura 279 (−5)
Minjee Lee 281 (−3)

The Solheim Cup

YEAR	LOCATION	EUROPE	US
1990	Lake Nona, FL, US	4.5	11.5
1992	Dalmahoy, Edinburgh, Scotland	11.5	6.5
1994	Greenbrier, WV, US	7.0	13.0
1996	Marriott St Pierre Hotel, Wales	11.0	17.0
1998	Muirfield Village GC, OH, US	12.0	16.0
2000	Loch Lomond Golf Club, Scotland	14.5	11.5
2002	Interlachen Country Club, MN, US	12.5	15.5
2003	Bärseback Golf & CC, Sweden	17.5	10.5
2005	Crooked Stick Golf Club, IN, US	12.5	15.5
2007	Halmstad Golfklubb, Sweden	12	16
2009	Rich Harvest Farms, IL, US	12	16
2011	Killeen Castle, Ireland	15	13
2013	Colorado Golf Club, CO, US	18	10
2015	Golf Club St Leon-Rot, Germany	13.5	14.5
2017	Des Moines GC, IA, US	11.5	16.5
2019	Gleneagles, Perth and Kinross, Scotland	14.5	13.5
TOTAL		6	10

KEY
* Won sudden-death playoff
† Won 18-hole playoff
†† Won matchplay final

Index

Page numbers in **bold** refer to main articles on players and courses. Page numbers in *italics* refer to illustrations and information in captions.

Acknowledgments

Second Edition

Consultant Kevin Pettman

DYNAMO LIMITED
Managing Editor Claire Lister
Project Art Editor Andrew Fishleigh

DK DELHI
Project Editor Tina Jindal
Project Art Editor Anjali Sachar
Picture Research Coordinator Sumita Khatwani
DTP Designers Anita Yadav, Nand Kishor Acharya

DK LONDON
Editor Lucy Sienkowska
Senior Editor Victoria Heyworth-Dunne
Senior Designer Nicola Rodway
Production Editor Gillian Reid
Managing Editor Gareth Jones
Senior Managing Art Editor Lee Griffiths

US Editor Jennette ElNaggar

Dorling Kindersley would like to thank: Gill Sheldon at the Phil Sheldon Golf Picture Library, Jenny Baskaya, and Liz Moore for picture research; Angus Murray for photography; Julian Small, Annie Nicholson, and all the greens staff at Wentworth Golf Club; Stuart Collier, Jason Brant, Kelly Ford, and Ajay Patel for modeling the instruction photographs; Julian Sandys at Mizuno, Gary McQuaid at TaylorMade, and Jon Parsons at Srixon for the loan of golf equipment.

Picture credits

The publisher would like to thank the following for their kind permission to reproduce their photographs:

Key:
a-above; b-below/bottom; c-center; f-far; l-left; r-right; t-top
Alamy Images: DPA picture-alliance / Axel Heimken 200tc; Newscom / BJ Warnick 193br; PA Images / Richard Sellers 196cr; REUTERS / Lucy Nicholson 201tr; **Helene Rogers:** 346b
Angus Murray Photography: 2l (scoreboard), 34-35, 35br, 36-37, 39br, 39crb, 39tr, 55b, 67bl, 102-103
Tony Arruza: 335b
Bob Atkins: 248-249, 250tr, 251t, 260-261, 276-277, 280-281, 282-283t, 286cl, 286-287, 287cr, 323tl, 324-325, 343tl, 358tr, 359tl
Tom Breazeale: 363cr
Callaway Golf: 49tr, 67br, 92br, 93bl
Steve Carr: 281tl, 296-297
Corbis: 180t, 192bl; Lewis Alan/Corbis Sygma 255br; Yann Arthus-Bertrand 345b; Denis Balibouse/Reuters 171t; Bettmann 2r (lee trevino), 3cr (jess sweetser), 8-9, 20-21, 23c, 24, 24-25, 64bl, 109r, 111bl, 111cr, 112bl, 112br, 112fbr, 112tl, 113bc, 113bl, 113br, 113fbl, 113fbl (trophy), 113fbr, 116t, 117b, 117tc, 117tr, 118t, 119br, 120-121, 121l, 122bl, 122r, 122t, 126c, 126t, 127bl, 127br, 127t, 128r, 130bc (1961), 130bl, 130br, 130fbl, 130fbr, 130-131t, 131bl, 132l, 132tr, 135cr, 137l, 137r, 138bc, 138br, 138-139tc, 140t, 142bl, 144br, 146t, 148r, 149t, 150tl, 160tr, 212-213, 219tr, 220tl, 220-221, 222-223, 262bl, 293b, 301tl, 319tl, 329b, 332cla; Mike Blake/Reuters 131crb; Will Burgess/Reuters 171c; Matt Campbell/epa 297tl; Sebastian Derungs/Reuters 180br; Richard Dole 192bl (1994); Duomo 185r, 192fbl; Don Feria 332tr; Robert Galbraith/Reuters 193tr, 317br; Raymond Gehman 341tl; Sam Greenwood/NewSport 73b; Gunter Marx Photography 339b; Hulton-Deutsch Collection 30-31 (background), 112bc, 114crb, 123t, 159cra; Dimitri Iundt 161t; Dimitri Iundt/TempSport 131br; Mark A. Johnson 338; Keystone 19br; Justin Lane/epa 301tc; Peter Macdiarmid/Reuters 308cr; Paul McErlane/Reuters 29r; Yuriko Nakao/Reuters 184t; Juda Ngwenya/Reuters 275br; Reuters 3fcl, 32-33, 90r, 168bl, 169t, 178br, 331tr; Jim Richardson 325cra; Tony Roberts 109bl, 147bl, 156t, 166t, 170l, 257, 259crb, 294b, 320tc, 321tl, 332bc, 343tr, 344l, 344-345, 349b, 351tl; Galen Rowell 355tr; Christina Salvador/Sygma 192tl; Scott T. Smith 307bl; John Sommers II/Reuters 148l; Jim Sugar 323tr, 324br; Swim Ink 2, LLC 340cr; Tim Thompson 336-337; Underwood & Underwood 31br, 108tl; Nik Wheeler 355cla; Rick Wilking/Reuters 176bl; Julia Xanthos/EPA 185b; Michael S. Yamashita 14-15
Dreamstime.com: Pincarel 1
Ernie Els Wines: 27br
Flickr.com: Carl Doose 353br; Farrel Lifson 353bc; ludwig428 351cb
Getty Images: AFP 28-29t, 72r, 131fbr, 139br, 193fbl, 215tr, 313tl; AFP / Brenton Edwards 30-31, 197bl; AFP / Andy Buchanan 196bl, 197tl; Augusta National 238-239; Aurora 165br; Michael Cohen 204cra; Mike Comer 206bc; Kevin C. Cox 239tr; David Cannon Collection 196tl, 197crb, 200-201tc; Steve Dykes 206t; Mike Ehrmann 204bl, 206br, 207r; Focus On Sport 128tr; Stuart Franklin 357tr; Gerald French 328b; Hulton Archive 16-17, 46ca, 111tl, 114t, 120tl, 210-211, 218-219; Icon Sports Wire 27l; Icon Sportswire 203br; Chung Sung-Jun 205; Jonathan Kantor 1; Kyodo News 198cl, 200bc; Andy Lyons 207tl; Masterpress 203tc; MediaNews Group / The Mercury News 199; Brian Morgan 131bc; Don Morley 130-131b; National Geographic 321crb; Panoramic Images 353bl; Octavio Passos 202-203tc; PGA of America 23bl; PGA 2r, 334br, 364-365, 366bl, 366br, 367bl, 367br, 367t; Andrew Redington 193bc (woods); Ezra Shaw 201l; Patrick

Smith 201crb, 202crb, 203bl; Jamie Squire 207cl; Time & Life Pictures 20bl, 23t, 45bl, 118-119, 121r, 128l, 130bc, 134bl, 138bl, 142cl, 216tl, 232tl, 285tl; 4b, 4t, 5b, 5t, 29bl, 29br, 32bl, 40bc, 54l, 55t, 62r, 63b, 63t, 72l, 73t, 82l, 82r, 83b, 86, 87bl, 87t, 91b, 93, 98b, 98r, 99b, 99t, 104ftr, 105ftr, 105l, 105tr, 106ftr, 106tc, 108bl, 112-113t, 113tc, 115b, 124l, 125b, 125cra, 129, 131fbl, 134fbr, 136cr, 138bc (1969), 138fbr, 139bc, 139bl, 139fbl, 142t, 147br, 147t, 148t, 153b, 153t, 155fbr (trophy), 160l, 162cr, 162tr, 167b, 167t, 168t, 170b, 170t, 172t, 173t, 174t, 175b, 175t, 176t, 179t, 181t, 182t, 185t, 186tl, 187t, 189t, 191t, 192br, 208-209, 225tr, 228-229, 232-233, 238-239, 240-241, 241tr, 243tr, 245tr, 250bl, 252r, 256br, 258bl, 259bl, 264-265, 265tc, 267tr, 269tl, 269tr, 270br, 271br, 274c, 275c, 276cla, 277crb, 277tl, 278b, 284b, 284r, 289tl, 297tr, 301tr, 302bc, 303bl, 303br, 309b, 310b, 311bc, 311tl, 312-313, 314bl, 314cla, 315br, 316c, 318-319, 319tr, 325b, 326c, 327cb, 327tl, 334cl, 341cb, 349c, 349cra, 356-357, 357tl, 358tl, 360c, 362-363, 365tc, 365tl, 367bc, 367c, 368-369; WireImage 135fbr, 300-301

Google Earth: 2007 Digital Earth Technology 292tl; 2007 DigitalGlobe 252tl, 264tl, 274tl, 312tl, 316tl, 328tl, 346tl, 350tl, 356tl; 2007 DigitalGlobe/Europa Technologies 362tl; 2007 DigitalGlobe/Image AMBAG 330tl; 2007 DigitalGlobe/NASA 276tl; 2007 DigitalGlobe/ TerraMetrics 254tl, 326tl; 2007 DigitalGlobe/TerraMetrics/ Tele Atlas 256tl; 2007 New York GIS 278tl; 2007 State of New Jersey 318tl; 2007 TerraMetrics 258tl, 268tl, 340tl; 260tl, 262tl, 284tl, 294tl, 296tl, 300tl, 306tl, 308tl, 334tl, 348tl; Cnes/Spot Image 286tl, 288tl; Infoterra Ltd & Bluesky 272tl, 310tl; NASA 364tl

Eric Hepworth: 250c, 305bl, 305br, 307crb, 310cr

Historic Golf Photos: 112fbl, 119tr, 138fbl, 140crb, 150b, 157bl

iStockphoto.com: Dan Cooper 337bl; Chris Neale 337br; Jess Wiberg 339t

Bryan Izatt: 335ca

Barry Jennings (ViewCalgary.com): 340b

Craig Jones: 330-331

Kingsbarns Golf Links: Iain Lowe 260cr

Russell Kirk / golflinksphotography.com: 246-247, 251br, 279b, 281tc, 281tr, 282b, 283b, 288-289, 304-305, 306-307, 307tr, 322-323, 342-343, 343tc, 350c, 352-353, 354-355, 366bc

Lambrecht Photography: 249br

Mirrorpix: 125t

Picture by Brian D Morgan: 358crb

Old Golf Images: 16l, 44bl, 104cra, 104tr, 106bl, 106br, 107l, 107r, 108r, 110b, 110t, 113cr, 115cr, 116br, 120bl, 123b, 298crb, 313tr

PA Photos: PA Archive 134fbl, 138cl, 142cr, 145tl, 158-159; Elise Amendola/AP 188l; AP 112crb, 114bl, 116bl, 134bc (trophy), 161bl; AP Photo 162l, 212tl, 214-215, 216-217, 224-225, 238tl; Matthew Ashton/ Empics Sport 347br; Chris Bacon/PA Archive 252cl; Barry Batchelor/ PA Archive 172l; Michael Boyd/PA Wire 165fbr; Michael Conroy/AP 91t; Olivier Douliery/ABACA 139fbr; Damien Eagers/PA Wire 155tr; Phelan M. Ebenhack/AP 160cr; EMPICS Sport 105br; HC/AP 140bl; Chris O'Meara/AP 26-27; PA Photos 211tr; David J.Phillip/AP 178t; S&G 87bc, 106tr, 124br, 141bl, 141br, 150tc; Scanpix 177l

Pine Valley Golf Club, NJ: 321br

popperfoto.com: 115t, 124t, 136tr, 141t, 144t, 151t, 157t, 158t

PunchStock: Comstock 42-43

Reuters: 185t; John Sommers II 151r

Phil Sheldon: 2l (annika sorenstam), 22, 38-39, 39cra, 40tr, 40-41, 41t, 62bl, 90l, 104bl, 118b, 131cra, 131tc, 133l, 133r, 134br, 134tl, 134-135, 135bc, 135bl, 135br, 135fbl, 136crb, 136l, 139tr, 143l, 143r, 144l, 145r, 146bl, 146br, 149l, 149r, 151b, 152br, 152cr, 152l, 154bc, 154bl, 154br, 154fbl, 154fbr, 154tc, 154-155c, 155bl, 155br, 155fbl, 155fbr, 156l, 156r, 157r, 158b, 159br, 161br, 163l, 163r, 164bc, 164bl, 164br, 164fbl, 164fbl (1978), 164fbr, 164l, 164r, 164-165b, 165bc, 165bl, 165br (MBE), 165fbl (trophy), 165t, 166l, 166r, 167cl, 167cla, 167r, 168br, 168r, 169l, 169r, 171b, 172r, 173bl, 173br, 174b, 175r, 177r, 180l, 179r, 180bl, 181b, 181c, 182b, 182l, 183b, 183c, 184b, 186b, 186c, 187bl, 187r, 188br, 188tr, 189b, 189r, 190, 191b, 192fbr, 192-193, 193bc, 193bl, 193br, 222tl, 226tl, 226-227, 228tl, 230-231, 231tr, 234tl, 234-235, 236-237, 237tr, 239r, 242-243, 244-245, 254c, 255c, 256bc, 261tc, 262c, 263bl, 263br, 263tl, 265tl, 266tc, 266tl, 266tr, 267b, 267tl, 268-269, 270bc, 270bl, 270crb, 270t, 271bl, 272b, 273b, 273t, 274br, 276clb, 278c, 279cla, 285c, 289tr, 290bc, 290bl, 290br, 291bl, 291br, 291cra, 291tl, 295br, 295cr, 298br, 298cl, 298tc, 298tl, 298tr, 299tc, 299tl, 299tr, 302bl, 302br, 303bc, 303t, 308bl, 309cl, 314br, 314tr, 315bl, 317cla, 320tl, 320tr, 321tc, 321tr, 329cla, 329crb, 331tl, 332bl, 332br, 332cb, 333bc, 333bl, 333br, 346cl, 358cra, 359tr, 360bl, 361b, 361tc, 362cr

Shutterstock.com: AP / Darron Cummings 201bl; Matt York / AP 198cra

TaylorMade: 47bl

TopFoto.co.uk: 109tl

Tufts Archives: 317clb

Visions in Golf: 293t; Hobbs Golf Collection 54br; Michael Hobbs/Mark Newcombe 104br, 134bc; Christer Hoglund 176br; Mark Newcombe 18-19, 83t

Waterville Golf Links: 3cr (Waterville), 249bl, 253b, 253ca

All other images © Dorling Kindersley.
For further information see: www.dkimages.com